The Khrushchev Years
1953–1964

The four volumes in this series are edited as an integral set. Each contains a subject index in which Russian abbreviations and acronymic names are translated. Tables summarizing the personnel of the main party executive bodies since 1917 are also provided. At the same time each of the volumes is built around a coherent period in the development of Russian Communism, and each reflects the special features of its time.

Volume 4 covers the rise and fall of Khrushchev. Once again factional activity surfaced in the party, as is manifest in the materials translated here. Khrushchev's diverse campaigns emerge not only in party congress documents, but also in a variety of major decisions that have not been translated into English previously and are too little known. The muted nature of the anti-Stalin campaign, as it appeared in party resolutions, is particularly important to study in view of its contrast with the Khrushchev speeches which have been given much fuller dissemination.

GREY HODNETT is Associate Professor of Political Science at York University in Toronto. He is co-author of *The Ukraine and the Czechoslovak Crisis* and of *Leaders of the Soviet Republics 1955–1972: A guide to posts and occupants.*

**Resolutions and decisions of the
Communist Party of the Soviet Union**

Volume 4
The Khrushchev Years
1953–1964
Editor: Grey Hodnett

University of Toronto Press

© University of Toronto Press 1974
Toronto and Buffalo
Reprinted in paperback 2017

ISBN 978-0-8020-2157-1 (cloth)
ISBN 978-1-4875-9172-4 (paper)
LC 74-81931

Editor's Preface

Russian terms are translated if a generally accepted English form exists, but are transliterated otherwise. In the latter case the term (e.g., oblast) is treated as an anglicized expression, without hard and soft signs (except in titles), to simplify the appearance of the text. The index of the volume provides parenthetical translations of transliterated terms and Russian transliteration of translated terms. Translations of periodical titles appear with the first occurrence of a given title.

Document numbers (e.g., 4.37) are supplied by the editor of the volume; the prefix '4.' indicates the volume number in the present series. Whenever cited such a decimal number implies reference to a document number.

Square brackets [ ] enclose material added by the editor of this volume, while parentheses appearing in documents are in the original Russian text. To assist the reader in identifying changes in successive versions of the party Rules, bracketed notes are inserted with each article, indicating whether it is a new, revised, or unchanged article, with respect to the previous version of the Rules. Ellipses (...) indicate an excision in the interest of economy made by the editor.

At the end of each document or group of documents from a congress or Central Committee plenum source attributions are provided. On the left the earliest published source that was accessible to the editor is cited. On the right the location of the material in the standard Soviet reference work is cited: *Kommunisticheskaia Partiia Sovetskogo Soiuza v rezoliutsiiakh i resheniiakh s"ezdov, konferentsii i plenumov TsK* (Communist Party of the Soviet Union in Resolutions and Decisions of Congresses, Conferences and Plenums of the Central Committee), 8th edition, Moscow, 1970–72 (hereafter abbreviated *KPSS v rezoliutsiiakh*). Not all documents published in the present work appear in *KPSS v rezoliutsiiakh*, so citations of this source do not appear in every case.

The end of each set of documents emerging from a congress or Central Committee plenum is indicated by the following symbol: ✺

Contents

	Editor's Preface	v
	Introduction	3
	1953	
4.1	To All Party Members, To All Toilers of the Soviet Union: From the Central Committee of the CPSU, the Council of Ministers of the USSR, and the Presidium of the Supreme Soviet of the USSR [On the death of Stalin]	21
	Plenum of the Central Committee (September)	24
4.2	On Measures Promoting the Further Development of the Agriculture of the USSR	25
	1954	
	Plenum of the Central Committee (February–March)	30
4.3	On the Further Increase of Grain Production in the Country and the Development of the Virgin and Unused Lands	30
4.4	On Errors in the Conduct of Scientific and Atheistic Propaganda among the Populace	33
	1956	
	XX Party Congress (February)	36
4.5	On the Report of the Central Committee	37
4.6	On the Sixth Five-Year Plan of Development of the National Economy of the USSR from 1956 to 1960	46
4.7	On Partial Changes in the Rules of the CPSU	51
4.8	On the Cult of Personality and its Consequences	52
4.9	On Preparing a New Programme for the CPSU	52
4.10	On the Formation of the RSFSR Bureau of the Central Committee of the CPSU	53

4.11 On Measures for Further Improving the Training of Leading Party and Soviet Cadres … 54

4.12 On Overcoming the Cult of Personality and its Consequences … 58

4.13 On the Party Organizers of the Central Committee of the CPSU … 72

4.14 On Improving the Work of the Soviets of Workers' Deputies and Strengthening their Ties with the Masses (1957) … 73

4.15 On the Organization of the Publication of Works about V. I. Lenin … 81

1957
Plenum of the Central Committee (February) … 82

4.16 On Further Improving the Organization of the Management of Industry and Construction … 82

4.17 On the Journal *Voprosy Istorii* … 88

4.18 On Released Secretaries of Primary Party Organizations … 90

Plenum of the Central Committee (June) … 92

4.19 On the Anti-Party Group of Malenkov, G.M., Kaganovich, L.M., and Molotov, V.M. … 93

4.20 On Granting to the Central Committees of the Union Republic Parties the Right to Resolve Certain Party-Organizational and Budgetary-Financial Questions … 98

Plenum of the Central Committee (October) … 100

4.21 On Improving Party Political Work in the Soviet Army and Navy … 100

Plenum of the Central Committee (December) … 103

4.22 On the Work of the Trade Unions of the USSR … 103

1958
Plenum of the Central Committee (February) … 110

4.23 On the Further Development of the Kolkhoz System and the Reorganization of MTSs … 111

CONTENTS ix

4.24 On Correcting Errors in the Evaluation of the Operas 'The Great Friendship,' 'Bogdan Khmelnitsky,' and 'With The Whole Heart'   115

4.25 On the Further Expansion of the Rights of the Central Committees of the Union Republic Parties, of Krai, Oblast, City and Raion Party Committees and of Primary Party Organizations in Resolving Party-Organizational and Financial-Budgetary Questions   117

4.26 On Work with Cadres in the Party Organization of Kirgiziia   118

1959
XXI Extraordinary Party Congress (January–February)   124

4.27 On the Report by Comrade N.S. Khrushchev 'Control Figures for the Development of the Economy of the USSR in the Years 1959–65'   124

4.28 On the State of Mass Political Work among the Toilers of Stalino Oblast and Measures for Improving It   133

4.29 On the Formation in Primary Party Organizations of Industrial and Commercial Enterprises of Commissions to Implement the Right of Party Organizations to Supervise the Administrative Activities of these Enterprises   138

1960
4.30 On the Tasks of Party Propaganda under Present Conditions   140

4.31 On the Experimental Creation of Party Commissions in the City and Raion Party Committees of Moscow, Leningrad, and Moscow Oblast   153

1961
XXII Party Congress (October)   154

4.32 On the Report of the Central Committee   155
4.33 Programme of the CPSU   167
4.34 Rules of the CPSU   264
4.35 On the Mausoleum of Vladimir Ilyich Lenin   281

1962

4.36 On the Creation in City and Raion Party Committees of Non-Staff Party Commissions for the Preliminary Examination of Questions of Admission to the Party and the Personal Affairs of Communists ... 282

Plenum of the Central Committee (March) ... 283

4.37 The Present Stage of Communist Construction and the Party's Tasks with Respect to the Improvement of Agricultural Leadership ... 283

4.38 Instruction on the Conduct of Elections of Leading Party Organs ... 285

Plenum of the Central Committee (November) ... 291

4.39 On the Development of the National Economy of the USSR and the Reorganization of Party Leadership of the Economy ... 292

1963

4.40 Regulation Establishing the Committee of Party-State Control of the Central Committee of the CPSU and the Council of Ministers of the USSR ... 298

4.41 On Reorganizing the Work of the Higher Party Schools in Accordance with the Resolution of the November Plenum [4.39] of the Central Committee ... 303

4.42 On the Implementation of the Decisions of the XXII Congress of the CPSU, and of the November Plenum of the Central Committee, with Respect to the Selection, Assignment, and Training of Leading Cadres in the Industrial Party Organization of Donets Oblast ... 304

Plenum of the Central Committee (June) ... 308

4.43 On the Current Tasks of Ideological Work of the Party ... 308

1964

Plenum of the Central Committee (October) ... 316

4.44 Communiqué [On the retirement of Khrushchev] ... 317

Appendix ... 319

Index ... 325

**The Khrushchev Years
1953–1964**

Introduction

The political history of the Soviet Union in the post-Stalin era may conveniently be divided into three periods. In the first, a struggle among Stalin's successors over policies and personal power culminated in the unsuccessful bid by the 'anti-party group' (a majority of the party Presidium) to oust Khrushchev from office in June 1957. Having consolidated his own position as principal Soviet leader, Khrushchev seized the initiative during the second period to promote further changes in the Soviet Union's external relations, military posture, agriculture, industrial priorities, educational system, and social structure. This period was abruptly terminated in October 1964 when broad discontent within officialdom over Khrushchev's management of the country's affairs came to a head in a successful conspiracy to remove him from power. The third period witnessed the retention of the two highest posts in the land, General Secretary of the party and Chairman of the Council of Ministers, by Brezhnev and Kosygin.

DECISION-MAKING STRUCTURE
Changes in the distribution of power among the leaders since Stalin's death were accompanied by changes in the party's role in the Soviet political system. In the most general sense, the party gained stature in comparison with the position it had occupied in the latter days of Stalin's rule. As Khrushchev's power increased between 1953 and 1957, so did the authority of the party. It began once again to perform a strategic role in bringing about economic and social change. Plenary meetings of the Central Committee took place regularly, and party congresses were held more or less within the statutorily prescribed intervals. There were also indications that the Central Committee – although not the party congress – was consulted on important policy questions and may have played more than a rubber-stamp role in the leadership crises of June 1957 and October 1964. In speaking of the enhanced status of the party, however, misconceptions may arise from a failure to distinguish between the party bureaucracy (supervised at the top by the Secretariat) and the highest 'party' policy-making bodies – the Presidium and the Central Committee.

Throughout the Khrushchev era the Central Committee Secretariat and the departments under its supervision (the Central Committee 'apparatus'), together with their equivalent organs at lower administrative levels, played an important role in co-ordinating the activities of the other bureaucratic hierarchies – governmental, military, police, economic, and 'social' (youth, trade union, cultural, etc.) – which collectively constitute the Soviet power structure. However, the precise degree of influence wielded by the party apparatus in this period waxed and waned depending upon the degree to which leaders relied upon it as their main administrative arm, the opportunity for party apparatus influence afforded by the organizational structure of the state and economic bureaucracies, and the weight of Secretariat representation in the Presidium. It must be emphasized that in terms of its occupational composition (as opposed to its merely nominal identity), the Presidium has always been an organ of mixed membership. It has included individuals such as the Chairman of the USSR Council of Ministers, the Chairman of the Presidium of the Supreme Soviet, and the Chairman of the RSFSR Council of Ministers who are top leaders outside the party apparatus. The representation of non-'party' organizations is, of course, reflected to an even greater extent in the composition of the Central Committee. Thus, one practical effect of increasing the authority of the Presidium (Politburo) and the Central Committee as collective deliberative and/or decision-making bodies (i.e., of the 'restoration of leninist norms of party life') is to institutionalize participation by organizations *other* than the party apparatus in policy-making. The reaction that occurred following Khrushchev's overthrow was a response to his attempts (after 1957) to bypass or manipulate the party Presidium and to undermine the conditions required for effective Central Committee influence. It should therefore be understood not so much as a reassertion by the party apparatus of its 'party' prerogatives, as a demand for the maintenance of regularized and effective participation in policy-making by all the important sectors of the Soviet political elite.

An essential condition necessary to assure 'collectivity' in decision making at the Central Committee and Presidium levels is confidentiality of deliberation in these forums and public adherence by leaders to decisions adopted at meetings of both bodies. This norm was violated with increasing frequency by Khrushchev. The publication of eleven stenographic reports of Central Committee plenums held between December 1958 and March 1965 constituted a fundamental infringement of confidentiality. Confidentiality was further undermined by the practice followed by Khrushchev from the June 1959 through the February 1964 plenums (July 1960 excepted) of inviting large numbers of non-members to Central Committee meetings. This procedure, which had occurred earlier at the March 1954 Plenum of the Central Committee, was initially put forward by Khrushchev as a matter that Central Committee members might conceivably wish to object to; however, he soon began simply to tell

INTRODUCTION 5

the members which categories of non-member officials were in attendance. Members of the Presidium were probably even more offended by Khrushchev's preemptive tactics of commenting publicly on controversial measures currently being considered by the Presidium, suggesting to lower-level officials that certain decisions were imminent which had not yet been approved by the Presidium, and revealing – as is apparent in the eight-volume collection of his speeches on agricultural questions – the nature of specific proposals he had made to his Presidium colleagues. Khrushchev's opponents in the Presidium no doubt perceived these deviations from 'collectiveness' as an attempt by him to increase his own personal power; he himself may well have looked upon them as a way of pushing correct policies through in the face of wrong-headed opposition.

Just as the history of the Soviet Union in the post-Stalin period may be divided into three periods, so may the history of the CPSU: destalinization, khrushchevism, and post-Khrushchev conservative reaction. The essential features of the first two of these phases are reflected in the decisions approved by the respective party congresses of the period – the XX (February 1956), XXI (February 1959), and XXII (October 1961). These congresses, which took place under conditions of less inhibited political conflict in the inner recesses of the party, tell us somewhat more about the real objectives of the Soviet leadership, perhaps, than do the two last congresses under Stalin.

DESTALINIZATION

The XX Congress of the CPSU (February 1956) was a watershed in the history of the party in the post-war period. The congress gave formal recognition to destalinizing policy trends in both the foreign and domestic spheres – trends which had become evident in various decisions taken after March 1953. In the post-war world, interconnections between developments outside and within the Soviet Union became more ramified and had a more immediate bearing upon larger numbers of ordinary Soviet citizens than before the war. Thus, official attitudes toward the outside world cannot be ignored in a discussion of party history during this period. Destalinization in foreign affairs included a relaxation of tensions with the West (as manifested in the Geneva summit meeting in the summer of 1955 and the treaty with Austria), a reappraisal of Soviet tactics in Eastern Europe (as displayed by Soviet approval in 1953 of the premiership of Imre Nagy in Hungary, and by the attempt in 1955 to achieve a rapprochement with Yugoslavia), and a far more flexible approach to non-communist governments in Asia and Africa (as revealed by the trip of Bulganin and Khrushchev to India, Burma, and Afghanistan in 1955). The major domestic sign of destalinization in the period 1953–56 was, of course, the cessation of terror and imposition of restraints upon the security police.

The resolution on the Central Committee Report adopted by the XX

Congress (4.5) suggests how far the Soviet leaders were collectively willing to go in approving destalinization. The image of the world situation presented in the resolution was one which stressed the growing might of the Soviet Union and its rapidly declining vulnerability to attack by imperialist powers. The emergence of the 'socialist camp' and the appearance of developing nations on the international scene had brought into existence a 'zone of peace,' the efforts of which could frustrate attempts by imperialist circles to unleash war. This shift in the world balance of power created conditions under which 'peaceful coexistence of states with different social systems' could be the guiding principle of Soviet foreign policy. War was no longer 'fatalistically inevitable,' if Communists created broad alliances with non-communist 'peace-loving' forces, worked for disarmament, and struggled against those who sought to perpetuate the Cold War. However, the resolution conceded to the opponents of this image of the external world that 'Naturally, the leninist concept remains in force that as long as imperialism exists, the economic foundation for the outbreak of wars will still be preserved. This is why we must observe the greatest vigilance.'

The outstanding event of the XX Congress was Khrushchev's 'secret speech' denouncing Stalin as a tyrant who had killed thousands of fellow Communists, violated 'leninist norms of party life,' and committed grievous mistakes as a military leader during the Second World War. This speech found only the palest reflection in the resolution, which did not mention Stalin by name but spoke vaguely of the 'cult of personality' and 'violations of socialist legality.' Nor did the special resolution of the Congress 'On the Cult of Personality and its Consequences' (4.8) offer much evidence that the image of the Stalin era presented by Khrushchev was one approved for public view. After the defeat of the 'anti-party group' in June 1957 (see 4.19) it was revealed that Molotov, Malenkov, and Kaganovich had strongly opposed Khrushchev's revelations in 1956 – fragmentary though they were. This opposition to destalinization was reflected not only in the resolutions of the XX Congress, but in the length of time it took the leadership to reach agreement on a public denunciation of the 'cult' (the 'secret speech' was read to party members but has still not been published in the Soviet Union) and in the watered-down official explanation that was finally offered (4.12).

KHRUSHCHEVISM

Khrushchevism, as an image of foreign and domestic 'realities,' was elaborated at the XXI and XXII congresses. It received its most thorough expression in the new party Programme (the writing of which was authorized by the XX Congress [4.9]) that was approved at the XXII Congress (4.33). Whereas destalinization had focused strongly upon the benign international environment and upon past 'distortions' in the internal development of the Soviet system, khrushchevism painted a more complicated picture of the foreign situation, and was future- rather than past-oriented in its perspective on the course of events within the Soviet Union itself.

The world situation, to be sure, had changed since 1956. Soviet successes in military technology provided continued grounds for an optimistic view of the USSR's international position, although not all Soviet leaders, particularly military leaders, took this view. Likewise, Soviet efforts to cultivate relationships with countries in Asia, Africa, and the Middle East seemed to be bearing fruit. At the same time, however, disturbing signs had begun to appear in relations between the Soviet Union and other countries of the socialist camp. The optimistic estimate of the political stability and loyalty of Eastern Europe implicit in Khrushchev's speeches at the XX Congress had been contradicted by the Hungarian Revolution and 'Polish October' of 1956. The example of the Yugoslav party, which (through its Programme of 1958) continued to challenge Soviet doctrine, exerted a strong pull in Eastern Europe. And the steady seepage of skilled personnel from East to West Germany revealed the shaky underpinnings of the Pankow regime. More important still, differences with China became increasingly contentious, threatening to come into the open – as they finally did when Chou En-lai, provoked by Khrushchev's attacks upon China's ally, Albania, walked out of the XXII Party Congress. Hence it was not surprising that the resolution of the XXI Congress called attention to the dangers of both 'revisionism' and 'dogmatism and sectarianism' – a theme repeated at the XXII Congress.

Khrushchevism, however, was more than a response to 'objective' realities. The central feature of the khrushchevist image of the domestic scene was that the Soviet Union had entered a qualitatively new phase of development – the period of 'intensified construction of communism.' This view, which was broached at least as early as Khrushchev's report to the Jubilee Session of the Supreme Soviet on 6 November 1957, was asserted as doctrine in the resolution on Khrushchev's report to the XXI Congress (4.27) and elaborated in the party Programme and resolutions approved by the XXII Congress. It was precisely this view of Soviet realities that Molotov had rejected in 1955, when he stated that the Soviet Union was *still* building 'socialism' – a proposition that he was later forced to recant. A corollary of the 'new phase' notion was the important concept in the Programme that the 'dictatorship of the proletariat' in the Soviet Union had exhausted its role (at least 'domestically') and was being replaced by a 'state of all the people.' The obvious implication of this argument was that the political loyalty of all strata of the Soviet population was now beyond question, that the need for internal police and other forms of 'state' control had drastically declined, and that criteria other than political reliability should be central in decisions affecting party recruitment and personnel policy. But the deeper implications of the 'state of all the people' were even more significant.

The essence of khrushchevism was not its liberalism, as some have thought, but its radicalism. What the new doctrine said, in effect, was that the basic social and political problems of the Soviet Union (i.e., those associated with the divergent interests of white-collar and blue-collar workers, city dwellers and farmers, young and old, and Russians and non-Russians) had already been almost eliminated. In other words, the claim in the Programme that 'communism' (or at least important elements of it) could be attained in the space of twenty years implied that technical rather than socio-political obstacles were the main hindrance to progress toward the glorious future. This proposition encouraged a redirection of attention to economic problems. Indeed, the most characteristic feature of domestic khrushchevism was its insistence that all party activities be evaluated in terms of their contribution to economic production. The 'production' emphasis, in combination with the optimistic diagnosis of the socio-political difficulties confronting the party, led to a dismantling of traditional 'negative' bureaucratic controls over the Soviet population and the substitution for them of new structures and devices intended to mobilize people's efforts to achieve the extremely ambitious economic targets set by the Seven-Year Plan (1959–65).

STRUCTURE AND FUNCTIONING OF THE PARTY

Destalinization of the internal structure and functioning of the party involved a number of interrelated processes. At the time of Stalin's death, the party was exceedingly 'bureaucratized' in the pejorative sense of the word. Communications from the top reached the bottom of the party with considerable delay, and it appears that lower levels were not systematically informed of points of view held by higher officials. Upward communication channels were clogged with obligatory formal reports which lower officials spent much of their working time preparing. Despite the mass of reports that flowed into Moscow, the party leadership was not really well informed about local problems. Hence, destalinization in the first place meant improving communications. A parallel process was a limited devolution of authority within the party, especially with respect to purely administrative matters. An attempt was also made to regularize decision-making processes. Under stalinism there had been a marked tendency for decision-making at lower levels to emulate decision-making at the top. Destalinization meant compelling the thousands of 'little Stalins' in the party to pay heed to the views of fellow members of bureaus, presidiums, committees, and other 'collective' decision-making organs. Finally, destalinization meant creating conditions under which rank-and-file party members would be able to participate more actively and effectively in the affairs of their own primary party organization. In brief, destalinization implied an attempt to make the party function somewhat more in practice as it was claimed to function in theory.

Most of the published party decisions in this area which could be classified as 'destalinizing' appeared in 1956 and 1957. The XX Party Congress provided the main impetus here, as it did in other policy areas. The Congress' general injunction to restore 'leninist norms of party life,' 'intra-party democracy,' and 'collective leadership' was supported by changes in the party Rules approved by the Congress (4.7). Thus, among other measures, the independent organs of the Party Control Committee at the republic and oblast levels, which had been established by the XIX Congress in 1952 (presumably as an instrument for purging the party), were eliminated; lower party organs were given greater authority to create subdivisions within primary party organizations; and the centralized party structure in the field of transportation was liquidated. Later in 1956 the *appointive* position of party organizer of the Central Committee of the CPSU was eliminated (4.13). This decision restored jurisdiction over the primary party organizations in important workplaces to the local party apparatus, and made it possible for 'intra-party democracy' to acquire some meaning within these organizations themselves. Further rights were granted to the local party organs by the resolutions of 2 August 1957 (4.20) and 30 September 1958 (4.25). Basically, however, these structural changes were less significant than the destalinization of the functioning of the party – as far as this took place.

Khrushchevism in the party organizational sphere may be said to have begun almost simultaneously with destalinization. Its main features were: a tailoring of structures to economic tasks; disregard for the boundary between 'party' and 'state' spheres; a willingness to sacrifice organizational stability for the sake of presumed efficiency; a stress on constant supervision and control of everything by party organs; and a blurring of the boundary between the paid, full-time party apparatus and volunteer party workers. As early as the fall of 1953, so-called party instructor groups for MTS zones were set up (see 4.2). This typically khrushchevist measure placed a raikom secretary and several instructors out in the countryside and made them, rather than the local organs of the state Ministry of Agriculture, responsible for on-the-spot management of the collective farms.

Khrushchev's war against 'bureaucratism' in the party apparatus was brought home to local party officials in the Central Committee resolution of 21 May 1957 that attempted to reduce the number of paid, full-time secretaries of primary party organizations (4.18). The principle of 'non-staff' (volunteer) participation in the implementation of tasks of the party apparatus, which was operative in most of the major fields of party work in the late 1950s and early 1960s, was approved by the XXII Congress (4.32) and even extended to the sphere of party disciplinary proceedings (see 4.31 and 4.36). At the XXII Congress Khrushchev succeeded in having the principle of 'systematic renewal of elective organs' written into the party Rules (see 4.34), but did not succeed – if he really wanted to – in making it more difficult for higher party organs to control who would be chosen as secretaries of primary party organizations. Despite impressions to the contrary, the Instruction on Holding Elections to Leading Party Organs issued on 29 March 1962 (probably under the aegis of Frol Kozlov) made it easier rather than more difficult for party organs to assure the election of unpopular leaders in primary organizations (4.38).

The most radical stage in organizational khrushchevism began in March 1962. In this month a plenum of the Central Committee, on Khrushchev's initiative, approved the formation of 'kolkhoz-sovkhoz territorial production administrations' in rural areas. These joint party/state organizations were placed in complete charge of agriculture at the local level, thus rendering the party rural raikoms virtually superfluous. Although a 'democratic' element was to be built into the administrations, the key to their success was obviously felt to lie in the fact that they were headed by party organizers *appointed* by party oblast or republic committees. The administrations, in turn, were placed under the supervision of an oblast or republic committee for agriculture, headed by the obkom first secretary or – in republics without oblast divisions – the first secretary of the republic central committee of the party (4.37).

The reasoning behind the kolkhoz-sovkhoz production administrations was carried to its logical conclusion at the November (1962) Plenum of the Central Committee (4.39). The plenum approved the reconstruction of the raion, city, and oblast levels of the party according to the 'production principle.' Rural raikoms were eliminated. Their agricultural functions were transferred to kolkhoz-sovkhoz production administrations (whose boundaries were larger than the former raions), while their functions related to industry and construction were shifted to newly created 'zone industrial-production party committees.' In most but not all oblasts completely separate oblast party organizations for agricultural and industry were created, and these were placed under the supervision of agricultural and industrial bureaus organized under republic party central committees. The bureaus in a republic, in turn, were supervised both by the remaining unified republic party organ, the presidium of the republic central committee, and by the new Bureau for Agriculture or Bureau for Industry and Construction of the Central Committee of the CPSU, together with the various Central Committee departments. The reorganization of the party necessitated a parallel reorganization of the soviets, trade unions, and Komsomol.

At the November Plenum several other important organizational decisions were approved. The most significant of these involved the abolition of the State Control Commission and the formation of a high-powered joint Party-State Control Committee. It was vested with broad investigative and punitive powers (4.40). Changes were also introduced in the structure of scientific research, design, construction, and planning organs. Finally, the creation in early 1963 of separate bureaus under the Central Committee, one for Central Asia and another for Transcaucasia, was a product of the November Plenum. These bodies, designed to 'co-ordinate' the activities of the respective republic party organizations, were mentioned in Khrushchev's report to the plenum but not in the resolution; it is likely that their formation was opposed by the republics involved. The reorganizations of March and November 1962, which generated a wealth of bitterness toward Khrushchev within the party apparatus, should be understood essentially as a response by him to the increasingly serious economic dilemmas which had arisen from 1959 on. The aim common to these measures was to pinpoint responsibility and *concentrate* and *centralize* power, in order to carry out policies aimed at meeting the economic crisis.

PERSONNEL MATTERS

The area of party personnel affairs, strictly defined, encompasses appointment criteria, party in-service training, admissions to the party, and party disciplinary procedures. The most important destalinizing measure affecting appointments was undoubtedly a diminution of the role of the security police in personnel decisions, although our knowledge of this is based largely on inference. The 'special departments' at workplaces, so ubiquitous under Stalin, declined in prominence. While KGB security clearances are undoubtedly still required for many (perhaps all) appointments to top positions falling within the jurisdiction of various party and other organs, it is probable that the informal power of the police to make or break careers on a large scale was quickly curtailed after the liquidation of Lavrenti Beria in the summer of 1953.

The policy of admissions to the party in effect when Stalin died was restrictive and discriminated in favour of white-collar workers and officials. This policy was reversed in both respects by 1955, when recruitment was stepped up and efforts made to draw more factory workers and collective farmers into the party. The thrust of destalinization in disciplinary affairs was to restrict the arbitrariness and petty vengeance which had all too frequently characterized party discipline under Stalin. In effect, the regularization of discipline sought to combat the transference to party affairs of occupational power relationships, to introduce a single standard of justice for all party members, and to reduce collusion between party leaders and economic managers.

Appointments policy assumed a central role in khrushchevism. Its nature was determined by the 'production' criterion of personnel evaluation and by the frequent absence of economic solutions to the economic dilemmas with which party and other cadres were confronted. The criteria of proper personnel selection expressed at the XX, XXI and XXII Party congresses and in Central Committee decisions (see 4.42) stressed formal educational qualifications, technical knowledge and experience in general, youthfulness, and vigour. In practice what frequently happened was that party organs strove, come what might, to recruit as many diploma-holders as possible for party jobs. One of the original motives behind Khrushchev's appointment policy had undoubtedly been to weed out incompetent leaders who had been appointed to their jobs on the basis of purely 'political' or personal considerations. As difficulties began to mount after 1958 in the implementation of the Seven-Year Plan, appointment policy to some extent became simply a pretext for getting rid of leaders who were unable to fulfil their plan or unwilling to put Khrushchev's latest nostrum into practice. The Seven-Year Plan period was marked by high rates of turnover in many types of jobs (especially those related to agriculture). The introduction into the party Rules at the XXII Congress of specific provisions governing turnover in occupancy of elective party posts exemplified the job instability that Khrushchev had deliberately fostered.

In-service training in the party schools was also strongly affected by the production orientation of khrushchevism. A resolution of 26 June 1956 placed 'concrete economics and the organization of industry and agriculture' in the centre of the curriculum (4.11). Following the November 1962 reorganization of the party, the 'production principle' was incorporated into the structure of the party schools by the creation of separate divisions for training industrial and agricultural leaders (4.41).

Admissions to the party continued to expand rapidly between 1955 and 1964. By 1965 there were over twelve million members, as against somewhat under seven million in 1953. There was no peculiarly 'khrushchevist' phase of admission policy. However, the injunction issued in 1961 to recruit people engaged in 'production' represented a shift away from the post-Stalin working-class emphasis and led to a relative decline in admissions of collective farmers. In disciplinary proceedings, as already indicated, some attempt was made to reduce exclusive control by the party apparatus over discipline, through involving rank-and-file participants in the process on an unpaid basis. The 'production' criterion, applied to party discipline, tended to mean that members were held accountable to the party only for occupational misdemeanours.

THE PARTY PROPAGANDA AND AGITATION SYSTEM

Destalinization of propaganda may be defined simply as getting rid of the pervasive falsehood and obscurantism introduced under Stalin. It should be distinguished in principle from Khrushchev's manipulation of antistalinism as a weapon to promote his own political ends. Retrospectively, the high point of the destalinization of propaganda was 1956. The XX Party Congress was preceded by certain attempts in literature and historiography to break out of the stalinist mould, to question the official interpretation of Soviet history (including party history), and to deal critically with some ideological issues. All of these attempts, however, were constrained by the persistence of certain stalinist doctrines, which had to be destroyed before serious progress was possible. At the XX Congress, initiative in attacking the stalinist ideological heritage was seized by Mikoyan, who stated in almost as many words that the bible of stalinism, the *History of the All-Union Communist Party (Bolsheviks). Short Course*, was both irrelevant and full of lies. Mikoyan also asserted that the entire propaganda system needed overhauling. After Khrushchev's 'secret speech' at the Congress, the ideological clock could never again be turned *all* the way back to stalinism. In the shorter run, the publication following the Congress of Lenin's famous 'Testament,' with its highly critical comments about Stalin, was a crucial step that made it extremely difficult thereafter to argue that stalinism was nothing more than applied leninism. With Stalin dethroned, and stalinism discredited as doctrine, the party found it necessary to encourage the growth of a new Lenin cult and to couch justifications of policy in terms of 'leninism.' A massive fifth edition of Lenin's collected works was published, and from time to time hitherto overlooked documents written by Lenin opportunely appeared in print. While the tabooing of overt references to stalinist doctrines complicated the expression of conservative points of view, it certainly did not altogether suppress their articulation. Henceforth policy battles simply took the form of arguments over the correct interpretation of 'leninism,' supported by appropriate quotations from Lenin rather than Stalin. Destalinizing trends in party propaganda unleashed by the Congress and the July 1956 resolution on the Cult of Personality (4.12) were seriously retarded as a result of the upheavals in Hungary and Poland later in 1956. The change in atmosphere was signaled by the resolution of 9 March 1957, 'On the Journal *Voprosy Istorii* (Problems of History)' (4.17). This resolution, said to have been drawn up under the supervision of Suslov, warned historians against uninhibited reinterpretation of the party's pre-revolutionary past.

The resolution on the Central Committee Report to the XX Congress had spoken in passing of 'overcoming the divorce of propaganda from the practice of communist construction.' This idea became the keystone of the khrushchevist reform of the party's own study system. The main elements of the reform were spelled out in the Central Committee resolution on propaganda of 9 January 1960 (4.30). In line with the production orientation of party work, it was stated that the criterion of success in propaganda would be high economic achievement by the enterprise in which party members worked. 'Abstractness,' lack of contact between enterprise tasks and the system of party indoctrination would no longer be countenanced. Hence, the curriculum had to centre on concrete economic problems. Moreover – and this was an integral part of khrushchevism in propaganda – the party instruction network should be extended to bring within its compass as many non-party members as possible. Both of these objectives necessitated a thorough restaffing of the corps of teachers ('propagandists') in the system. Technically literate people who understood the production process in a given workplace had to replace propagandists whose main virtue was their knowledge by heart of the *Short Course*. Similarly, one of the main directives of the Khrushchev period on political *agitation* (the resolution on Stalino Oblast – 4.28), enjoined party officials to focus the attention of the masses upon the economic tasks set by the Seven-Year Plan.

THE PARTY AND THE ECONOMY
Destalinization of the Soviet economy took place between 1953 and 1958. Its main elements included a moderate decentralization of economic administrative authority (which also represented a concession to national feelings in the non-Russian republics); recognition that agriculture required serious attention (4.2); acceptance of the idea that technical innovation and increased labour productivity were now important keys to industrial progress; and a relaxation of coercive controls over labour in favour of greater material incentives. These particular measures did not greatly affect the role of the party in relation to the economy, except in the sense that any change in the system of tight ministerial control from Moscow was likely to give more scope to the local party organs.

Economic khrushchevism was in a sense a new version of the stalinist idea of 'leading links'; once the 'key' solution to an economic problem had been defined, a campaign was mounted to mobilize all resources to put this solution into practice. Economic khrushchevism was also highly innovative. In organizational terms it was not tolerant of the traditional dividing line between 'state' and 'party' jurisdictions. Its drift was to concentrate the powers required to 'solve' a particular problem at some single point. Frequently, but not always, this point happened to be 'party'-dominated.

Despite repeated approving references by Khrushchev to the principle of material interest, khrushchevist schemes in practice – especially after 1958 – revealed what could charitably be described as indifference to the question of individual incentives.

It is not surprising that khrushchevism first intruded in that sphere of the economy for which Khrushchev himself was responsible – agriculture. And here its effects continued to be most keenly felt. The creation of raikom instructor groups for MTS zones in September 1953 has already been mentioned. (These lasted until December 1957.) This step was soon followed, in 1954, by the risky decision – taken at Khrushchev's insistence – to solve the grain crisis by plowing up millions of acres in the so-called Virgin Lands (4.3). The Virgin Lands scheme involved a massive party-led mobilization of men and machinery to build farms on the bare steppes east of the Volga, in Kazakhstan, and in western Siberia. A by-product was the purging of Kazakh leaders who rightly feared that the campaign would bring hundreds of thousands of Russian and Ukrainian settlers into traditionally Kazakh lands. The next notable step was the abolition of the MTS in February 1958 (4.23). This historic decision, which destroyed one of the holiest of all stalinist economic institutions, was justified on the grounds that it created a 'single master' on the farm.

The good results which had been achieved in agriculture between 1953 and 1958 led to the projection of quite unrealistic agricultural targets in the Seven-Year Plan (1959–65). At the same time (it was later revealed), investment in agriculture was sharply cut back – perhaps in response to demands for more investment in the armaments industry. These decisions taken in 1958 conditioned the role of the party in agriculture throughout the remaining years of Khrushchev's rule. Inevitably, performance in agriculture began to lag further and further behind the plan. Khrushchev's response was to 'suggest' various solutions – square-cluster corn growing, ploughing up grasslands, alterations in crop structure, etc. – which then became virtually mandatory across the entire Soviet Union. Simultaneously, Khrushchev struck out at existing incentives by insisting that peasants' private plots be cut back, that private cattle herds be reduced, and that farms increase their level of self-investment by reducing the percentage of income paid out in wages to farm members. Responsibility for solving the crisis which arose was adroitly shifted to the shoulders of local leaders at a series of agricultural plenums of the Central Committee from 1959 to 1964. Large numbers of leaders at both the lowest and intermediate levels who failed to meet their plans were sacked, which understandably generated great anxiety. As the situation deteriorated, Khrushchev withdrew power from the State Ministry of Agriculture and concentrated it in party organs – notably those created in 1962 (see above).

In industry the main monument to khrushchevism was the sovnarkhoz system created in May 1957 (4.16). This reorganization, which dismantled the stalinist pattern of control over branches of the economy by vertically structured ministries, concentrated power over factories and other economic units within oblasts and republics in the hands of a single supervisory body – the Council of National Economy (sovnarkhoz). These councils, not accidentally, were more amenable to control by the local party organs than were the plants formerly controlled from Moscow. At the plant level a characteristically khrushchevist step was the introduction of primary party organization 'control commissions' in 1959 (4.29). These were followed by the Party-State Control Committee 'assistance groups' created in 1963 (4.40). Both innovations permitted party officials to intrude more upon the functions of management if they wished – although basically they did not.

THE PARTY AND SOCIAL CONTROL

The party's approach to the question of social control in the post-Stalin period was related both to its estimation of the political loyalty of the population, and to the immediate economic, political, and social problems which confronted it. Destalinization of social control involved restoration of some civil rights (which is what 'socialist legality' meant in the context of 1954–56); less heavy-handedness in combating religion (4.4); a grant of somewhat greater power to trade unions to defend the minimum interests of workers (4.22); greater cultural freedom and scope for discussion among the intelligentsia; less bureaucratic regimentation of youth by the Komsomol; and greater toleration of national self-expression by non-Russians (see 4.24). The fundamental assumption of destalinization was that social cohesion would be promoted by a policy based on trust, since the social tensions which did in fact exist had been caused or exacerbated by a policy based on distrust. This assumption was implicit in the references to social groups in the resolution on the Central Committee Report to the XX Party Congress (4.5).

The khrushchevist approach to social control was one which denied – at least on the theoretical plane – the existence of social tensions in the new stage of 'intensified construction of communism.' The spirit in which Khrushchev approached social problems was not one of anxiety, but of impatience with expressions of sectional interests detrimental to what he considered to be the long-range general interests of the Soviet Union. There was an element of genuine faith in a communist future in khrushchevism, and an assumption that most people could be brought to share this faith. In contrast with either stalinism or the subsequent phase of conservative reaction, social control under khrushchevism was oriented toward mobilization as well as maintenance of order. It was thus more willing to depart from bureaucratic mechanisms and experiment with group self-regulation. This approach was reflected in the important proposition approved by the XXII Congress and incorporated in the Programme that increasingly, state functions were to be transferred to 'social organizations' (see 4.33). In practice, the khrushchevist approach was embodied in such instrumentalities as permanent production meetings in factories, 'comradely courts,' standing commissions of local soviets (see 4.14), the druzhinas (volunteer police brigades), and a variety of 'social' inspection and check-up organizations.

CONCLUSION

By 1964 khrushchevism had exhausted its momentum and generated serious tensions within the administrative apparatus and economy. Retrospective illumination of these difficulties is provided by steps taken by Khrushchev's successors. The new leadership's stress on food production, industrial efficiency, increased military output, stability of the political structure, and heightened social discipline pointed to felt weaknesses of khrushchevism. The rapid liquidation of production administrations, restoration of raion party committees, and merger of agricultural and industrial obkoms clearly suggested that the 'production principle' had created administrative chaos and was cutting at the root of strong overall party leadership at the local level. Vociferous complaints by party officials revealed how much Khrushchev's economic campaigns, organizational measures, and personnel policy had threatened their professional status and job security. The new leadership's attempt to recreate an atmosphere in which 'ideological' verities once more held sway pointed toward the corrosive effect of Khrushchev's 'practicism.' His opportunistic manipulation of anti-stalinism and downgrading of traditional indoctrination had seriously undermined the public's respect for and fear of orthodox forces in the Soviet system. The rapid approval of large-scale assistance to agriculture, liquidation of the sovnarkhozy, and restoration of the ministerial system of industrial administration, and cautious introduction of more rational planning techniques were responses to major crises in Soviet agriculture produced by the Seven-Year Plan (1959–65) and to the disturbing decline in the rate of increase in industrial output during Khrushchev's last years. Finally, the more overt role of the KGB in post-Khrushchev years points toward general problems bequeathed by Khrushchev to his successors: how to cope with the irrelevance of traditional doctrinal formulas for political integration; how to handle alienation among some intellectuals; how to satisfy working-class demands for a higher standard of living; and how to deal with unrest among the non-Russian nationalities.

G.H.

Documents

4.1
To All Party Members, To All Toilers of the Soviet Union
From the Central Committee of the CPSU, the Council of
Ministers of the USSR, and the Presidium of the Supreme
Soviet of the USSR [On the death of Stalin]   6 March 1953

Stalin's death on 5 March 1953 inevitably led to a crisis of self-confidence among his potential heirs. The dead man had long since come to embody the Soviet state, and there was no well-established mechanism for transmitting legitimate power to any heir or heirs. To justify the new distribution of power, Stalin's lieutenants convened a joint meeting of the Central Committee, Council of Ministers, and Presidium of the Supreme Soviet. A communiqué published in *Pravda* on 7 March at least gave this label to the meeting that evidently occurred on the previous day, although there was hardly time to permit all of the several hundred persons who belonged to these bodies actually to reach Moscow; nor, in view of the communiqué's appeal to avoid 'disorder and panic,' is it clear that it was felt prudent to summon important regional officials from their duty stations at this critical juncture.

The Presidium of the Council of Ministers was to consist of Malenkov as Chairman of the Council of Ministers and Beria, Molotov, Bulganin, and Kaganovich as first deputy-chairmen. Voroshilov was appointed head of state as Chairman of the Presidium of the Supreme Soviet. The former Ministry of State Security (MGB) and Ministry of Internal Affairs (MVD) were combined into a single Ministry of Internal Affairs, headed by Beria. Molotov was appointed Foreign Minister and Bulganin Minister of Defence. In the party, the Bureau of the Presidium was eliminated and membership in the Presidium reduced to ten full and four candidate members. The Secretariat consisted of Malenkov, Khrushchev, Suslov, Mikhailov, Aristov, Ignatiev, Pospelov, and Shatalin. A week later, on 14 March, a plenum of the Central Committee 'satisfied the request of the Chairman of the Council of Ministers of the USSR, Comrade G.M. Malenkov, that he be released from the duties of secretary of the Central Committee of the CPSU.' The Secretariat was reshuffled to include Khrushchev, Suslov, Pospelov, Shatalin, and S.D. Ignatiev.

The last act in the immediate post-Stalin succession struggle was revealed at a plenum of the Central Committee held in early July 1953. On 10 July *Pravda* informed the public: 'The Plenum of the Central Committee of the CPSU, having heard and discussed the report of the Presidium of the Central Committee – of Comrade G.M. Malenkov about the criminal anti-party and anti-state deeds of L.P. Beria aimed at undermining the Soviet state in the interests of foreign capital and manifested in treacherous attempts to place the Ministry of Internal Affairs of the USSR above the government and the CPSU, adopted a decision to remove L.P. Beria from membership in the Central Committee of the CPSU and to expel him from the ranks of the CPSU as an enemy of the Communist Party and of the Soviet People.' The exact time and manner of Beria's execution is still not absolutely clear; but his elimination paved the way for the re-establishment of party control over the security police.

Although the following document was not formally called a resolution, the seventh edition of the official collection of party decisions treated it as one. It was signed by the Central Committee of the party, the Council of Ministers, and the Presidium of the Supreme Soviet. This order and the phrasing of the document suggest, however, that the restoration of the primacy of the party was from the start an element in the politics of the post-Stalin era.

DEAR COMRADES AND FRIENDS

With feelings of the deepest grief the Central Committee of the Communist Party of the Soviet Union, the Council of Ministers of the USSR, and the Presidium of the Supreme Soviet of the USSR inform the party and all toilers of the Soviet Union that Iosif Vissarionovich STALIN, Chairman of the Council of Ministers of the USSR and Secretary of the Central Committee of the Communist Party of the Soviet Union, died on 5 March at 9.50 PM, after a serious illness.

The heart of the comrade-in-arms, the genius who carried on the cause of Lenin, the wise leader and teacher of the Communist Party and the Soviet people – Iosif Vissarionovich STALIN – has stopped beating.

The name of STALIN is infinitely precious to our party, to the Soviet people, to the toilers of the whole world. Together with Lenin, Comrade STALIN created the mighty party of communists, trained and tempered it; together with Lenin, Comrade STALIN inspired and led the Great October Socialist Revolution, founded the first socialist state in the world. Carrying on the immortal cause of Lenin, Comrade STALIN led the Soviet people to the epoch-making victory of socialism in our country to victory over fascism in the Second World War, thus radically changing the whole international situation. Comrade STALIN armed the party and the entire nation with a great and clear programme for building communism in the USSR.

The death of Comrade STALIN, who devoted his whole life to selfless service in the cause of communism, is a grievous loss for the party, the toilers of the Soviet land, and of the whole world.

The news of Comrade STALIN's decease will evoke the deepest sorrow in the hearts of the workers, kolkhozniks, intelligentsia, and all toilers of our motherland, in the hearts of the fighting men of our valiant Army and Navy, in the hearts of the millions of toilers of all countries of the world.

In these sorrowful days all the peoples of our country unite even more closely in our great fraternal family, under the tested leadership of the Communist Party created and fostered by Lenin and Stalin.

The Soviet people has complete confidence, and is imbued with a burning love, for its own Communist Party, since it knows that devotion to the interests of the people is the highest law governing all the party's activities.

Workers, kolkhozniks, the Soviet intelligentsia, all toilers of our country unswervingly follow the policies worked out by our party, which accord with the vital interests of the toilers and are aimed at further strengthening the might of our socialist motherland. Decades of struggle have confirmed the correctness of these policies of the Communist Party; they have led the workers of the Soviet land to the historic victories of socialism. Inspired by these policies the peoples of the Soviet Union confidently advance, under the party's leadership, to new successes of communist construction in our country.

The toilers of our country know that the continuing improvement of the material well-being of all segments of the population – workers, kolkhozniks, and intelligentsia, and the maximal satisfaction of the constantly growing material and cultural demands of the whole of society, have always been and continue to be the object of particular concern of the Communist Party and the Soviet government.

The Soviet people know that the defence capacity and might of the Soviet state are growing and becoming stronger, that the party is reinforcing the Soviet Army and Navy, and the organs of intelligence, constantly to increase our readiness to deal a crushing blow to any aggressor.

The foreign policy of the Communist Party and Soviet government has been and remains an unswerving policy of preserving and consolidating peace, of struggle against the preparation and unleashing of a new war, a policy of international co-operation and development of businesslike relations with all countries.

The peoples of the Soviet Union, loyal to the banner of proletarian internationalism, are consolidating and developing fraternal friendship with the great Chinese people and with the toilers of all the people's democracies, and friendly relations with the toilers of the capitalist and colonial countries struggling for the cause of peace, democracy, and socialism.

Dear comrades and friends!

The great directing and guiding force of the Soviet people in the struggle to build communism is our Communist Party. The iron unity and monolithic solidarity of the party's ranks are the principal conditions of its strength and power. Our task is to preserve this party unity like the apple of our eye, to rear communists as active political fighters for implementing the policies and decisions of the party, and to strengthen still further the party's relations with all the toilers – with the workers, kolkhozniks, and intelligentsia, for it is in this indissoluble tie with the people that our party's strength and invincibility lie.

The party sees as one of its foremost tasks the education of communists and of all the toilers in the spirit of extreme political vigilance, in the spirit of firmness and implacability in the struggle against internal and external enemies.

Appealing in these sorrowful days to the party and the people, the Central Committee of the CPSU, the Council of Ministers of the Union of Soviet Socialist Republics, and the Presidium of the Supreme Soviet of the USSR express their firm conviction that the party and all toilers of our motherland will unite even more closely around the Central Committee and the Soviet government and will mobilize all their strength and creative energy in the great cause of building communism in our country.

The immortal name of STALIN will live forever in the hearts of the Soviet people and of all progressive humanity.

Long live the great, all-conquering teachings of Marx – Engels – Lenin – Stalin!

Long live our mighty socialist motherland!
Long live our heroic Soviet people!
Long live the great Communist Party of the Soviet Union!

Pravda, 6 March 1953

KPSS v rezoliutsiiakh III (7th edition; not included in 8th edition), 600–2

Plenum of the Central Committee   3–7 September 1953

This plenum was the first following the death of Stalin that dealt with an important policy question other than high-level appointments. The tension that existed among the leaders over agriculture was indicated by the absence of any announcement that there had been a plenum until six days after it had ended. Conflict was sharpened by the way in which Khrushchev used the issue of agriculture to advance his own eminence as an authoritative party spokesman and bold reformer – a tactic that had been rebuffed when he attempted to apply it in the early 1950s. Khrushchev's major report (*Current Digest of the Soviet Press*, V, no. 39: 11–12, 24–41), on which the following resolution is based, made it obvious that the abysmal state of agriculture contrasted scandalously with the official propaganda of Stalin and in particular with the claim voiced by Malenkov, before Stalin's death, that the grain problem had been 'solved.' The late leader and his lieutenants responsible for agriculture were attacked only by implication but were clearly held to blame, thus anticipating Khrushchev's later anti-Stalin campaign. At the end of the plenum Khrushchev was elected to the post of 'first secretary,' a new label in party history, which signalled his advancement.

4.2
On Measures Promoting the Further Development of the Agriculture of the USSR   7 September 1953

... VI   ON IMPROVING LEADERSHIP IN AGRICULTURE

1   The plenum of the Central Committee of the CPSU considers that fulfilment of the new and complex tasks in agriculture demands a decisive improvement in the leadership of kolkhozes, MTSs, and sovkhozes by the USSR Ministry of Agriculture and Procurements, the USSR Ministry of Sovkhozes, and the local party, soviet, and agricultural organs.

Successful accomplishment of these tasks demands an improvement in the level of political and organizational work in the countryside; mobilization of the creative activity of communists, komsomols, all kolkhozniks and workers in the MTSs and sovkhozes; the harnessing of all the strengths and resources of socialist agriculture; and a heightening of the responsibility of our cadres for the situation in each kolkhoz, MTS, and sovkhoz, in each raion.

2   The plenum of the Central Committee considers that under the present conditions, when the kolkhozes have become large diversified economic entities, and the MTSs are provided with modern technical equipment and are a decisive force in agricultural production, the task of further strengthening the kolkhozes and MTSs with qualified cadres – capable of providing skilful economic guidance and of guaranteeing the fulfilment of the obligations confronting agriculture – takes on the greatest significance.

The central committees of the union-republic parties, and the krai and oblast party committees, are hereby directed to select in 1953 engineers and mechanics from industry and other branches of the national economy and dispatch them to work in the MTSs and specialized stations as directors, chief engineers, and heads of repair shops; in each MTS these positions are, as a rule, to be occupied by specialists with higher education. MTS directors without specialized education but who have acquired good practical competence and are skilful MTS leaders should be left at their posts and given assistance in improving their qualifications.

The party organizations should conduct explanatory work among tractor drivers and other mechanization cadres, who have left the MTSs to work in industry, construction, and in other organizations, appealing to them to return to the MTSs; they should bear in mind that now – with tractor drivers on the staffs of the MTSs and receiving a high guaranteed wage – many former mechanics will be pleased to return to work in the MTSs.

Engineers and technicians or mechanics coming from other branches of the economy to work in the MTSs, as well as tractor drivers and other mechanics, who have indicated a desire to return to the MTSs, should be discharged without hindrance by their enterprises, institutions, ministries, and departments.

3   The USSR Ministry of Culture is hereby directed in 1954–55 to transfer 6500 mechanical engineers (2500 of these in 1954) to the USSR Ministry of Agriculture and Procurements for work in the MTSs – by releasing young specialists from institutes of agricultural mechanization and other institutions of higher technical education.

4   The plenum of the Central Committee notes that the existing procedure whereby a single agronomist or livestock specialist services several kolkhozes does not meet the increasing problems confronting agriculture. Under this system, in many cases, the livestock and other agricultural specialists do not organize kolkhoz production and are prevented from participating directly in implementing agronomic and veterinary measures, the achievements of science, and the most advanced practices in the kolkhozes.

To intensify agronomic and zootechnical assistance to kolkhozes it is recognized as essential that the agronomists and livestock specialists, instead of being assigned on a district basis, be attached to the MTSs permanently; in this way each kolkhoz should be constantly serviced by one or two agricultural specialists on the staffs of the MTSs. Certain of the largest kolkhozes may be serviced by maintaining on the MTS staffs one specialist for each brigade and farm.

The USSR Ministry of Agriculture and Procurements, the republic councils of ministers, and the krai and oblast executive committees are hereby ordered to dispatch to the MTSs, by the spring of 1954, 100,000 agronomists and livestock specialists with higher and secondary education; these are to be made available by reorganizing the agricultural ministries and their local organs, abolishing the network of district agronomists in the MTSs and the network of district livestock specialists and agronomists in the raion agricultural and procurements administrations, reducing the numbers of specialists working in other institutions and organizations, and also through the influx of young specialists who have just graduated from institutions of higher agricultural and technical education.

5   The party, soviet, and agricultural organizations of oblasts, krais, and republics must cease underestimating the problem of selecting and training leading cadres in kolkhozes; they must strengthen the position of kolkhoz chairman by selecting and promoting to this post specialists with secondary and higher agricultural education who have proven themselves both politically and practically, and other specialists and persons with practical abilities who are familiar with agriculture, possessing great experience as leaders and capable of directing a large kolkhoz.

6   The presently existing practice of leadership of the MTSs and kolkhozes by the agricultural organs does not meet the increasing demands and changes taking place in agriculture. The USSR Ministry of Agriculture and Procurements and its local organs at times work in isolation from the kolkhozes and the MTSs permit a formalistic approach to the solution of many problems of the development of agriculture, fail to analyse the reasons for the neglect of many important branches, and do not give timely necessary assistance to backward raions and kolkhozes.

To improve the leadership of agriculture, and to reinforce the cadres of kolkhozes and MTSs by releasing the largest possible number of specialists from work in the staffs of the agricultural organs, it is essential to reorganize the operation of the USSR Ministry of Agriculture and Procurements and of the local agricultural organs. To this end:

a   the administrative personnel of the USSR Ministry of Agriculture and Procurements and the staffs of its local organs are to be reduced substantially; the specialists so released will be sent to work in MTSs and kolkhozes in order to improve the operational and organizational activities of agricultural organs in the direction of agricultural production;

b   the work of the USSR Ministry of Agriculture and Procurements is to be concentrated on the following matters: planning the development of the fundamental branches of agriculture and supervising the fulfilment of the state plan in agriculture; strengthening agricultural propaganda and directing the scientific institutions working in agriculture, and also making productive application of the achievements of science and most advanced practices; guiding the MTSs in the further development of the mechanization of agricultural production; providing agriculture with material and technical supplies and financing; directing the procurements of agricultural products; selecting, assigning, and training cadres and supervising the observance of the rules of the agricultural artel;

c   the RSFSR Ministry of Agriculture and Procurements is to have leadership of all branches of agriculture, kolkhozes, and MTSs on the territory of the RSFSR, so as to liquidate the existing incorrect situation whereby the RSFSR Council of Ministers and the RSFSR Ministry of Agriculture and Procurements do not bear responsibility for the conduct of fundamental branches of agriculture within the Russian Federation ...

The plenum of the Central Committee considers the inadequacies and errors in the leadership of agriculture to be due in considerable measure to the fact that many oblast and krai committees and central committees of the union-republic parties give unsatisfactory guidance to the raions, are poorly acquainted with the local situation, fail to give effective assistance to backward raions and kolkhozes, have withdrawn from leadership of the MTSs, and have assigned to the raion organizations total responsibility for the operation of the MTSs.

To improve party organizational and party political work in the village the Central Committee plenum resolves:

1 The oblast and krai committees and the central committees of the union-republic parties are directed to strengthen considerably their guidance of mass political work in the countryside; to explain the present resolution to all kolkhoz members and workers in the MTSs and sovkhozes; to develop broad socialist competition in order to solve the tasks of the further development of socialist agriculture, the strengthening and all-around development of the communal economy of the kolkhozes, the increase of total production as well as of the marketed portion, the timely fulfilment of planned deliveries of agricultural products, increasing the incomes of kolkhozes in money and in kind and improving the well-being of kolkhozniks. In all their work party organizations must rely on leading persons in kolkhozes, MTSs, and sovkhozes, experts in agriculture and animal husbandry, whose ranks will henceforth be growing and increasing every day.

Central and local newspapers are obliged to give broad coverage to the progress of socialist competition, to the most advanced practices in kolkhoz development, and to the practice of party and soviet organs in their guidance of agriculture.

2 Oblast and krai committees, and the central committees of union-republic parties, are directed to change their methods of exercising leadership over agriculture; to do away with the superficial bureaucratic approach to the leadership of kolkhozes, MTSs and sovkhozes; to cease acting as administrators in kolkhoz management and to strengthen their connections with the raions and kolkhozes, getting to know the real situation in each raion.

It is essential to increase decisively the responsibility of raion executive committees for the fulfilment of party and government decisions and for the state of agriculture in the raions, to ensure more concrete guidance of the kolkhozes, sovkhozes, and especially the MTSS – considering their enormously increasing role in the development of agriculture.

Measures must be taken to transfer experienced cadres, men who are well acquainted with agriculture and are capable of guiding kolkhozes, MTSS, and sovkhozes correctly and skilfully, to the party's agricultural raion committees and to the raion executive committees. The best workers of the oblast, krai, and republic organizations are to be selected and dispatched to strengthen party and soviet leadership of the raions.

3   Since the existing structure of the party's agricultural raion committees does not meet the demand for improved leadership of the MTSS and the kolkhozes, at the present stage the operation of the raion party apparatus must be restructured so as to eliminate absence of responsibility, or ambiguity about responsibility, in the guidance of kolkhozes and MTSS; to this end the raion committee must have for each MTS a group of workers, headed by the secretary of the party raion committee, whose duty will be to conduct party political work in the MTSS and in the kolkhozes which it services. General guidance of the activities of all of these groups rests with the first secretary of the raion committee. It is not advisable that the MTSS make provision for the position of deputy-director for political affairs.

4   One of the major tasks of the central committees of the union-republic parties, and of the krai, oblast, and raion party committees, is to strengthen the party organizations in the kolkhozes, MTSS, and sovkhozes, intensifying their role in the further development of agriculture. Communists and komsomols must be correctly posted to the decisive sectors of production; well-trained and experienced party workers must be appointed as secretaries of kolkhoz, MTS, and sovkhoz party organizations ...

The Soviet Union is advancing confidently along the road to communism. The practical solution of the task of creating in our country an abundance of agricultural products – on the basis of the mighty growth of socialist industry, as the leading force in the economy – is a very important component of the programme of communist construction. At present this task stands before us as an urgent national task. Its successful solution will also promote the further strengthening of the union between the working class and the kolkhoz peasantry.

The plenum of the Central Committee expresses its firm confidence that under the leadership of the Communist Party the working class, the kolkhoz peasantry, our intelligentsia, and all Soviet people will resolve this problem in a very short time.

Pravda, 13 September 1953   *KPSS v rezoliutsiiakh* VI, 385–429

Plenum of the Central Committee 23 February – 2 March 1954

A further step in Khrushchev's emergence as the outstanding figure in the post-Stalin leadership was his second major report to the Central Committee on the problems of agriculture (*Current Digest of the Soviet Press* VI, no. 12, 3–13). Having described the grim situation in this sector in his report to the plenum of September 1953, he now suggested a bold, indeed risky, major solution: an enormous programme of development of 'virgin lands,' chiefly in Kazakhstan. Despite grave reservations about the plan, voiced privately by his colleagues in the leadership, Khrushchev managed (or was allowed) to proceed with the scheme. The following resolution of the plenum embodied his proposals.

4.3
On the Further Increase of Grain Production in the Country and the Development of Virgin and Unused Lands   2 March 1954

... The plenum of the Central Committee of the CPSU sets before the USSR Ministry of Agriculture, the USSR Ministry of Sovkhozes, the party, soviet, and agricultural organs of Kazakhstan, Siberia, the Urals, the Volga Region, and the North Caucasus, as well as before the MTSs, kolkhozes, and sovkhozes of these regions, a task of major importance for the state – extension of the area sown to grain crops in 1954–55 by opening up not less than 13 million hectares of virgin and unused lands, obtaining from these lands in 1955 1100–1200 puds of grain of which 800–900 million puds will be marketed.

2   The Central Committee of the Communist Party of Kazakhstan, the oblast and krai committees of the CPSU in Siberia, the Urals, the Volga Region, and the North Caucasus, the USSR Ministry of Agriculture, the USSR Ministry of Sovkhozes, the RSFSR Council of Ministers, the Council of Ministers of the Kazakh SSR, the oblast and krai executive committees, and the directors of MTSs and sovkhozes in these regions are directed to increase as follows the grain sowings in kolkhozes and sovkhozes: in 1954, in accordance with the national economic plan, the area sown to wheat and millet is to be increased by 2.3 million hectares, of which 1.8 million hectares will be in kolkhozes and 0.5 million hectares in sovkhozes; in 1955 the area sown to grains will again be increased by not less than 10.7 million hectares.

In the newly opened lands the 1955 grain crop should be sown, as a rule, on well-prepared fallow which has been ploughed early in the autumn.

3   The USSR Ministry of Agriculture, the USSR Ministry of Sovkhozes,

the RSFSR Council of Ministers, the Council of Ministers of the Kazakh SSR, and the local soviet and agricultural organs must in due time, but not later than 1 June 1954, select and mark out suitable pieces of land, mainly from the most fertile virgin and unused lands, pastures and hayfields of low productivity, situated near villages and settlements, for extending grain sowings in kolkhozes and sovkhozes. Lands from the State Land Fund may also be used for organizing new grain sovkhozes and for adding to the lands of sovkhozes and kolkhozes.

4   All the work involved in the cultivation of these grains is to be mechanized so that the ploughing and preliminary tilling of the soil, the sowing, and the harvesting of the crops on these new lands, as well as the threshing, will be on schedule and require minimum labour inputs.

In 1954 the regions where these new lands are being opened up are to be supplied with 120,000 15-horsepower tractors, 10,000 combines, and a suitable number of tractor ploughs, seeding machines, heavy-duty disc harrows, cultivators, and other agricultural machines for use in developing the unused and virgin lands, in ploughing up unproductive meadows and pastures, and in further increasing the area sown to wheat. For the technical maintenance of these tractors and other machines the area must also be supplied with the necessary number of automobiles, transportable repair installations, tank-trucks, oil and gas depots, and other instruments and equipment.

5   The plenum of the Central Committee calls to the attention of all party, soviet, and agricultural organs the fact that the successful development of the unused and virgin lands will depend, above all, upon the correct selection of qualified leaders, engineers, technicians, and agronomists, as well as of machine operators, for the tractor detachments and brigades in the MTSs and sovkhozes, and their dispatch to the new lands.

In view of the urgent need for labour in the MTSs and sovkhozes working to develop the new lands, they must be supplied with skilled cadres from among workers presently employed in MTSs and sovkhozes and also by training tractor drivers and combine operators in trade schools and technical schools of agriculture mechanization, and by setting up courses in the MTSs and sovkhozes themselves. The labour required by the recently organized sovkhozes in the new lands must be made available through organized recruitment.

The plenum of the Central Committee sets before the central committees of the union-republic parties, the CPSU krai and oblast committees, the republic councils of ministers, the oblast and krai executive committees, the USSR Ministry of Agriculture, the USSR Ministry of Sovkhozes, before all party, trade union, and Komsomol organizations, the following task – in 1954, on the basis of an extensive explanatory effort, they are to select persons for leading positions as specialists and qualified workers, sending them to the MTSs and sovkhozes involved in developing the new lands. The selection is to be made both from existing MTSs and sovkhozes and from industry and other branches of the economy. The organized recruitment and dispatch of these persons to the new lands is to be viewed as the fulfilment of an important task set by the party and government, as a great patriotic cause.

In every enterprise, institution, and organization the dispatch of those specialists and qualified workers from among its members who have expressed a desire to go out to work in the new lands should be regarded as a debt of honour.

6   The initiative of the Central Committee of the Komsomol and the local Komsomol organizations in organizing the transfer, on a voluntary basis, of 100,000 machine operators from among the Komsomols and young people, to work in the MTSs and sovkhozes opening up the new lands is to be supported.

7   Engineers, technicians, agronomists, veterinarians, and other agricultural specialists, tractor drivers, combine operators, skilled repair workers, accountants, and others who are sent to the MTSs, sovkhozes, and procurement organizations of the raions developing unused and virgin lands from other MTSs, sovkhozes, industrial enterprises, and organizations are to be paid, at their previous place of work, a bonus of three months' salary and are also to be paid all expenses incurred in their move to their new jobs, in accordance with Article 82 of the Labour Code.

8   To create the necessary living conditions for workers in tractor brigades and detachments of MTSs and sovkhozes opening up new lands, the USSR Ministry of Agriculture, the USSR Ministry of Sovkhozes, and the local party, soviet, and agricultural organs are directed in 1954 to organize field camps provided with wagons and sleeping tents, kitchens, and baths, and furthermore, to organize mess facilities and water supply.

The USSR Ministry of Trade and the Central Union of Consumer Co-operatives are directed to provide for trade in food products and essential supplies in the tractor detachments and brigades, making extensive use of mobile vending counters.

The USSR Ministry of Culture and the All-Union Central Council of Trade Unions must provide cultural services for tractor detachments and brigades of the MTSs and sovkhozes in the new lands (cinema, radio, newspapers, magazines, etc.). The USSR Ministry of Health is to provide medical services for these workers.

9   To increase the material interest of kolkhozes, kolkhozniks, and MTS workers in fulfilling the plan for developing the new lands and obtaining large grain crops from them the following incentives are established:

a   It is recommended that the kolkhozes, by a decision of the general meeting, allow workers in field and tractor brigades additional pay of up to 30 per cent of that part of the harvest collected from the whole sown area in the new lands which is over and above the planned yield for this area;

b It is recommended that the kolkhozes, subject to the discretion of the general meetings of members, issue to their members advances on labour-days to the extent of about 25 per cent of the income derived from the sale to the state – either as compulsory deliveries or as state purchases – of the grain from the newly opened lands;

c The Central Union of Consumer Co-operatives is directed to make available for sale to the kolkhozes delivering grain for state purchase, industrial goods, trucks, automobile trailers, electric motors, construction materials, and other goods for productive and economic use, to the extent of 50 rubles of goods at retail prices for each 100 rubles of grain delivered.

d As an exception, for each centner of grain actually delivered and sold to the state by the kolkhozes the MTS directors may allocate an additional 75 kopeks for distribution as bonuses to MTS tractor brigades and special units. These funds may be allocated as bonuses on the condition that the planned sowing norms have been met and the actual yields from the virgin and unused lands meet the plan targets.

In 1954 and 1955 workers, employees, specialists, and leading personnel of the newly organized sovkhozes on virgin and unused lands are to receive a 15 per cent salary increase.

10 The plenum considers that an increase in grain production demands, over and above the development of virgin and unused lands in Kazakhstan, Siberia, the Urals, the Volga Region, and the North Caucasus, a considerable extension of sown areas in other areas of the country, the non-black-soil belt in particular, through the ploughing up of unused lands, fields, and meadows of low productivity, the clearing of fields overgrown with brush and shrubbery, and the draining of swamps.

Such measures will rapidly make possible the addition of fertile lands to agriculture and an extension of the area sown to grain, vegetables, potatoes, and feed-grains in the heavily populated regions of the country possessing a highly developed industry, thus significantly improving the supply of fresh vegetables, potatoes, milk, and meat available to the populations of urban and industrial centres ...

Pravda, 6 March 1954   *KPSS v rezoliutsiiakh* VI, 430–63.

4.4
**On Errors in the Conduct of Scientific and
Atheistic Propaganda among the Populace**   10 November 1954

In accordance with its Programme, the Communist Party is conducting scientific and educational propaganda of the materialist world view, aimed at a constant increase of the consciousness of the labouring masses and toward their gradual liberation from religious prejudices. In so doing the party has always considered it necessary to avoid offending the feelings of believers in any way.

The Central Committee has information at its disposal that attests that in recent times gross errors have been committed in scientific and atheistic propaganda among the populace in a number of places.

Instead of developing regular, painstaking work in propagandizing natural-scientific knowledge and instead of waging an ideological struggle against religion, certain central and local newspapers as well as speeches of certain lecturers and reporters are permitting offensive attacks against clergy and believers participating in religious observances. There are cases of the ministers of religious cults and believers being represented – without any basis in fact – in the press and in propagandists' speeches as people who are not politically trustworthy. In a number of raions there have been cases of administrative interference in the activities of religious associations and groups, as well as coarseness toward the clergy on the part of local organizations and certain individuals.

Such errors in anti-religious propaganda are fundamentally contrary to the Programme and policy of the Communist Party with respect to religion and believers and are a violation of repeated instructions by the party concerning the inadmissability of offending the feelings of believers.

The Central Committee considers it incorrect that many party organizations have divested themselves of day-to-day leadership of scientific and atheistic propaganda and do not concern themselves with the careful selection of propaganda personnel. Frequently people who are ignorant of science and questions of atheistic propaganda, and at times even hacks, knowing mainly anecdotes and stories about the clergy, are permitted to publish in the press and give lectures and reports. Such an irresponsible approach to the selection of authors of articles and lecturers and reporters and the absence of appropriate supervision by party organizations of the correct trend of scientific and atheistic propaganda is doing serious harm to cultural and educational work among the population.

The Central Committee of the CPSU resolves:

That it is incumbent upon oblast and krai party committees, the central committees of communist parties of the union republics and upon all party organizations resolutely to eliminate errors in atheistic propaganda and in no case to permit in the future any offences whatsoever against the feelings of believers and clergy or to permit administrative interference in the activities of the church. It is necessary to keep in mind that offensive actions with regard to the church, the clergy, and citizens who are believers are incompatible with the line of the party and state on the conducting of scientific and atheistic propaganda and are contrary to the Constitution of the USSR, which accords freedom of conscience to Soviet citizens.

As a result of the profound changes in the socio-economic conditions of life, the liquidation of the exploiting classes, and the victory of socialism in the USSR, and as a result of the successful development of science and the overall growth in the country's cultural level, the majority of the Soviet Union's population has long since freed itself of religious carry-overs from the past; the consciousness of the workers has grown immeasurably. However, one must not fail to keep in mind that there are also citizens who, while actively participating in the life of the country and honestly fulfilling their civic duty to the homeland, are still under the influence of various types of religious beliefs. The party has always demanded, and will continue to demand, a tactful and attentive attitude toward such believers. It is all the more stupid and harmful to consider certain Soviet citizens politically suspect because of their religious convictions. Profound, patient, and properly conceived scientific and atheistic propaganda among believers will help them ultimately to free themselves from their religious errors. On the contrary, all manner of administrative measures and offensive attacks against believers and clergy can only do harm and result in a consolidation and even reinforcement of their religious prejudices.

In conducting scientific and atheistic propaganda, it should be kept in mind that one cannot equate the situation of the church in a socialist country with the situation of the church in an exploitative society. In bourgeois society the church is a support and weapon of the ruling classes, which utilize it for the purpose of enslaving the workers. This does not rule out the possibility that individual clergymen in capitalist society are also capable of going over to, and do go over to, the viewpoint of the workers on a number of basic political questions. However, these clergymen are usually subjected to all manner of persecution on the part of the church and government circles of the capitalist countries because of their behaviour contrary to the interests of the exploiting classes.

In tsarist Russia the church faithfully served the autocracy, the landowners, and the capitalists, justified the harsh exploitation of the masses and supported the exploiters in their struggle against the toilers. It is a known fact too that immediately after the victory of the October Socialist Revolution, during the years of the civil war and afterward, many religious organizations and groups of the clergy maintained a hostile attitude toward the Soviet government. In this connection certain ministers of religious cults were called to account by the state not for their religious activities, but for their anti-government activities directed against the interests of the Soviet people and designed to please internal counter-revolution and international imperialism. It is natural, therefore, that the struggle of the Soviet people against the enemies of the socialist state also included struggle against those reactionary church representatives who conducted activities hostile to the Soviet people. At the present time, as the result of the victory of socialism and the liquidation of the exploitative classes in the USSR, the social roots of religion have been sapped and the base on which the church supported itself has been destroyed. Today, the majority of the clergy, as facts testify, also take a loyal stand with regard to the Soviet government. Therefore the struggle against religious prejudices today must be regarded as an ideological struggle of the scientific, materialist world view against the anti-scientific, religious world view.

Righting of the mistakes committed in anti-religious propaganda must not lead to a weakening of scientific and atheistic propaganda, which is an integral part of the communist education of the working people and has as its aim the dissemination of scientific, materialistic knowledge among the masses and the liberation of believers from the influence of religious prejudices ...

Pravda, 11 November 1954   *KPSS v rezoliutsiiakh* VI, 516–20

XX Party Congress   14–25 February 1956

The 1430 delegates to the XX Party Congress heard reports by Khrushchev on the work of the Central Committee (L. Gruliow, ed., *Current Soviet Policies* II, 1957, 29–62) and Bulganin on the Sixth Five-Year Plan (*ibid.*, 124–42) without unusual incident (4.5, 4.6). Only Mikoyan's speech (*ibid.*, 80–9), among those made in public, introduced explicit criticism of Stalin, and this in mild and limited form. Yet the major event of this congress, which has given the meeting a very special place in history, turned out to be a lengthy speech attacking Stalin, which Khrushchev delivered under the title 'On the Cult of Personality and Its Consequences,' better known as the 'secret speech.' While Stalin's reputation had quietly diminished since 1953 and a majority of the Presidium probably favoured some form of comment on his 'mistakes,' a sweeping condemnation of the late leader was opposed by a majority of the Presidium, who attempted to prevent the delivery of the secret speech. Backstage argument resulted in the postponement of its delivery from the originally scheduled time of 6.00 p.m., 24 February, to midnight of that day. Opponents of the anti-Stalin campaign succeeded in limiting the resolution based on the speech (4.8) to a terse statement about the need to overcome the 'cult,' and extended public comment was postponed until June 1956. During this month a compromise position seems to have been reached by Khrushchev and his opponents, which was reflected in the first major public statement on Stalin, 'On Overcoming the Cult of Personality and Its Consequences' (4.12), dated 30 June 1956. The secret speech itself remains to this day unpublished in the USSR, although it is widely known in a general way as a result of a nation-wide series of closed meetings of party groups in which the contents of the secret speech were revealed. The practice of lending numbered copies to local groups and to foreign communist parties seems to have been followed, leading to a leak, as Khrushchev may have wished. American intelligence agencies acquired the text (or what is generally accepted as such) and it was published in the *New York Times* on 5 June 1956. (The text also may be consulted in L. Gruliow, ed., *Current Soviet Policies* IV, 1957, 172–88; or B. Wolfe, *Khrushchev and Stalin's Ghost*, 1957).

The XX Party Congress also passed resolutions amending the party Rules (4.7) and planning the adoption of a new Programme (4.9).

The Central Committee elected by the Congress had 133 full and 122 candidate members. At its first meeting, immediately following the Congress, A. I. Kirichenko and M. A. Suslov were named members of the Presidium of the Central Committee and A. B. Aristov, N. I. Beliaev, and D. T. Shepilov were appointed secretaries.

4.5
On the Report of the Central Committee   24 February 1956

Having heard and discussed the report of First Secretary of the Central Committee of the CPSU, Comrade N. S. Khrushchev, on the work of the Central Committee, the XX Congress of the CPSU resolves:
total and complete support for the political line and practical activities of the Central Committee of the CPSU;
support for the proposals and conclusions of the Central Committee contained in its report.

The Congress notes with satisfaction that the leninist policy of the Central Committee and of the Soviet government, and the heroic efforts of the Soviet people co-operating closely with all socialist countries, have led to gigantic successes in the struggle to build communism in our country and to bring about peace in the whole world.

The Congress warmly supports the correct and timely measures undertaken during the accounting period by the Central Committee in industry and agriculture, which ensure the continuing growth of the power of our motherland, a new and powerful upsurge of the socialist economy, and a substantial improvement in the well-being of the Soviet people.

The Congress emphasizes that the successful activities of the Central Committee of the CPSU have been founded on the creative application of marxist-leninist teachings, the strictest observance of leninist principles of collective leadership and intra-party democracy, and the unswerving fulfilment of leninist directives on the indissoluble tie between our party and the people. Through all these years the party has held high the great banner of the immortal Lenin ...

The XX Congress of the CPSU notes with profound satisfaction the further consolidation of the Soviet Union's *internal situation*. The Central Committee's consistent implementation of the party's general line during the accounting period has brought about a significant growth of all branches of production, and of the material well-being and cultural level of the population, has further strengthened the moral-political unity of Soviet society, has increased the power of the Soviet state.

A major victory of the party and the people was Soviet industry's fulfilment and overfulfilment of the Fifth Five-Year Plan ahead of time. By 1955 industrial production stood at 185 per cent of the 1950 level, instead of the planned 170 per cent; production of the means of production stood at 191 per cent instead of the planned 180 per cent, and the figure for the production of consumer goods was 176 per cent instead of the planned 165 per cent.

The Congress considers it essential to press forward in the struggle to resolve – through peaceful economic competition in the shortest historical period – the principal economic task of the Soviet Union: namely, relying on the advantages of the socialist economic system, to overtake and surpass the most advanced capitalist countries in per-capita production.

The Communist Party considers it absolutely necessary, in the future as well, to ensure the relatively more rapid growth of heavy industry: in particular, of heavy and light metallurgy, coal and oil production, power, machine building, and the production of chemicals and building materials. At the same time the Congress considers that the level of production attained to date makes possible the rapid development not only of the means of production, but also of consumer goods.

Continued technical progress is the deciding factor in the further growth of industrial production as a whole. The most recent achievements of science, technology, and up-to-date experience must be introduced steadily and in a planned manner into industry and transport; existing equipment must be modernized; the organization of labour and production must be improved and perfected; specialization and co-operation must become more widespread in industry; and on this basis a rapid increase in labour productivity is to be achieved – the decisive factor in the fulfilment of targets for industrial growth and for the further improvement of the well-being of the people.

Continued development of the country's productive forces urgently demands new sources of raw materials, fuel, electricity, and above all, mobilization of the gigantic natural resources of the country's eastern regions. Within the next ten to fifteen years the following must be created in the eastern regions: the largest coal-mining and electricity-generating base in the country, a third high-capacity metallurgical base producing 15-20 million tons of cast iron annually, and also new machine-building centres ...

During the period the CPSU Central Committee has carried out a major political and organizational effort in agriculture. The Central Committee has adopted effective measures to liquidate negligence in a series of branches of agricultural production and to organize a sharp upturn in agriculture.

Of the measures adopted the following are of special importance:
the introduction of a new planning procedure in agriculture which unleashes the creative initiative of the kolkhozniks;
intensification of the material interest of kolkhozes and kolkhozniks in increasing agricultural production;
reinforcing cadres of leaders and specialists in the kolkhozes by dispatching to the villages many thousands of communists and non-party members from the cities and industrial centres;
continuing to strengthen the technical equipment of agriculture, setting up permanent cadres of machine operators in the MTSs and adding to the leaders and engineering-technical cadres in the MTSs;
increasing the amount of state appropriations for the development of agriculture.

In developing its programme for the advance of agriculture the Central Committee decided correctly to concentrate initial efforts on the advance of grain production, as the basis of all of agriculture and of its major branch, animal husbandry. The Central Committee's decisions to open up the virgin lands and to increase sharply the area sown to corn are of enormous significance.

The Congress charges the Central Committee to continue with unflagging energy its work in the advance of agriculture, mobilizing the party and the whole Soviet people for the struggle to create an abundance of foodstuffs for the people and raw material for light industry.

The mechanization of agriculture must be continued, passing in the shortest possible time from the mechanization of individual operations to the complex mechanization of the whole of agricultural production, radically improving propaganda and giving productive application to the achievements of Soviet and foreign science and technology, and of the experience of leading kolkhozes, MTSs, and sovkhozes; on this foundation to effect a sharp reduction in the input of labour and materials in the production of a unit of agricultural production and to increase the yields of all crops and the productivity of animal husbandry.

The Congress considers that at the present time, when the economic capacities of many kolkhozes have significantly increased, it is necessary – along with the general expansion of production that must always be foremost – to devote serious attention to construction in the kolkhozes of dwellings, clubs, kindergartens, and other institutions of cultural and everyday significance.

A decisive factor in the further rapid upsurge of agricultural production is improving the level of agricultural leadership. Here it is necessary to end routine bureaucratic methods, irresponsibility, and ambiguity in the assignment of responsibility. Party, soviet, and agricultural organs must give concrete guidance to each raion, kolkhoz, sovkhoz, and MTS, supporting the initiative of the masses in every way and increasing the material interest of all persons occupied in agriculture, including the leaders, in expanding agricultural production.

The Congress calls upon all party, trade union, economic, and Komsomol organizations to intensify socialist competition on a national scale, to improve its leadership, to heighten still further the creative initiative of workers and kolkhozniks, directing it at solving the tasks set by the party and the government.

The growth of industrial and agricultural production has created genuine possibilities for the steady elevation of the material well-being and cultural level of the Soviet people. During the years of the Fifth Five-Year Plan the national income of the USSR has grown 68 per cent, the real wages of workers and employees have risen by 39 per cent, and the real incomes of kolkhozniks – by one and a half times. The Congress fully supports the measures worked out by the CPSU Central Committee and the USSR Council of Ministers, aimed at a further increase in the real wages of workers and employees and in the incomes of kolkhozniks, at increasing the wages of the lowest-paid groups, and also at bringing order into the wage situation, at intensifying the personal material interest of the individual in the results of his work ...

Substantial successes have been attained in all areas of cultural construction. Universal seven-year education has been introduced, and a ten-year course in the large cities. The conditions are being created for the gradual introduction of a universal ten-year course. The training of specialists in the country's institutions of higher education has been considerably expanded. Benefitting from the constant and effective support of the party and the Soviet government, Soviet scientists are working productively for the economy and for improving the security of our motherland, and have achieved outstanding successes in many areas of science – including nuclear physics, mathematics, mechanics, and certain branches of technical sciences. At the same time the Congress notes serious inadequacies in cultural construction. In the functioning of the schools the principal defect is a certain gap between education and life, the inadequate preparation of graduates for practical affairs. The rapid polytechnization of the school not only demands the introduction of new subjects which will supply the bases of knowledge in matters of industrial and agricultural production, but it also requires that students be familiar in practice with work in enterprises, kolkhozes and sovkhozes, experimental sectors, and school workshops. It is desirable to undertake the establishment of boarding schools, locating them in regions which will be favourable to the health of the children. The network of children's pre-school institutions must also be greatly expanded, and not only must the national educational organs and the state enterprises be involved in this, but also the kolkhozes.

With regard to higher education the principal tasks are the general improvement of the quality of specialist training through an intimate tie between studies and production, the proper location of institutions of higher education in the country – bringing them closer to production, and organizing the curriculum along the lines of contemporary technology. When young engineers and agronomists graduate from their educational institutions, they must possess adequate knowledge about the concrete economics and organization of production.

The Congress regards it as essential that the ties of the country's scientific institutions with production, with the concrete needs of the economy, be reinforced, that their creative efforts be concentrated on the solution of the most important scientific-technical problems, and that the role of science in resolving the practical tasks of communist construction be steadily increased.

In the view of the Congress, one of the major results of the work of the Communist Party during the reporting period has been the continued consolidation of the Soviet social and state order, the further strengthening of the union of the working class and the kolkhoz peasantry, the friendship and fraternal cooperation of all the peoples of the USSR.

The Congress fully supports the measures adopted by the CPSU Central Committee to broaden the rights of the republic organs in economic and cultural matters. While retaining for the all-union ministries general guidance, the definition of plan targets, supervision of their fulfilment, the supplying of equipment, and the financing of capital investment, there must at the same time be an extension of the rights of the republic ministries in the day-to-day administration of enterprises. This will promote an even greater unfolding of creative initiative at the local level, the continued strengthening of the union republics, and the cementing of the friendship of the peoples of our country.

Our party's nationality policy has been and is based on the leninist teaching that socialism not only does not eliminate national differences and characteristics but, on the contrary, ensures the all-round development and flowering of the economies and cultures of all nations and peoples. In the future the party should continue to pay the greatest attention to these characteristics in all its practical work.

The great tasks of communist construction demand a further heightening of the creative activity and initiative of the toilers, even broader mass participation in the state administration and in all its organizational and economic activity. To this end it is necessary to develop Soviet democracy in every way, steadily improving the operation of all soviet organs at the centre and on the local level, strengthening their ties with the masses. The Congress supports the efforts made in recent years by the CPSU Central Committee to reduce the size of the administrative apparatus and cut down on its cost, while at the same time improving the operation of its individual links, and considers it necessary to continue these efforts, conducting in the future as well an implacable struggle with the bureaucratic approach, with instances of an inattentive attitude to the needs of the population.

The Congress fully supports the measures effected by the Central Committee to strengthen Soviet legality, to ensure strict observance of the rights of citizens, as guaranteed by the Soviet Constitution, and places all party and soviet organs under the obligation of vigilantly guarding legality, of putting an end – severely and decisively – to any manifestations of lawlessness, arbitrariness, or violation of the socialist legal order.

The Communist Party and the Soviet state must continue to educate Communists and all toilers in the spirit of extreme political vigilance, must tirelessly strengthen our valiant Armed Forces who so reliably guard the peaceful labour of Soviet people and the security of the socialist motherland.

In the period between the XIX and XX congresses our party gained new and major successes because it was governed by the all-conquering doctrine of marxism-leninism in all its domestic and foreign policy and practical activities, because it held to a firm and consistent course aimed at constructing socialism in our country and strengthening the international socialist camp, because it held high the banner of proleterian internationalism and friendship among peoples.

The period which has elapsed since the XIX Congress has been a period of steady growth in the power and authority of the CPSU, a period in which the leninist unity of the party has been strengthened and its guiding role in Soviet society has been intensified. Ideologically, politically, and organizationally the party has become even stronger, and the marxist-leninist temper of the party masses has become firmer. The party membership – the decisive factor in party and state leadership – has increased substantially.

The XX Congress of the CPSU notes that, confronted with the complex and responsible tasks which arose before the party and country after the XIX Party Congress, the Central Committee met its obligations well, resolved correctly the pressing problems of party, state, and economic construction, and firmly and confidently led the country along the lenininst path.

The Congress notes with satisfaction that in all its activities the Central Committee has unswervingly defended the interests of the party and the people. The Congress fully supports the decisive steps taken by the CPSU Central Committee to end the criminal conspiratorial activities of that dangerous enemy of the party and the people, Beria, and his band. This was at the same time a serious blow to the plans of the imperialist intelligence agencies, and a further strengthening of the party's fighting efficiency was achieved.

The Congress fully supports the great efforts undertaken by the Central Committee to restore leninist norms in party life, to develop intra-party democracy, to inculcate the principles of collective leadership based on the conduct of a marxist-leninist policy, and to improve the style and methods of party work. The struggle for the observance of democratic foundations in party life, against administrative and bureaucratic methods of leadership, for an increase in criticism and self-criticism has heightened the activity of the party masses and the responsibility of Communists for the party cause, for a new political and labour upsurge of the toilers.

A general explanation of the marxist-leninist concept of the role of the individual in history was of major significance for heightening the activity of communists and of all toilers. The Congress considers that the Central Committee was entirely correct in speaking out against the cult of personality, the spread of which diminished the role of the party and the popular masses, belittled the role of collective leadership in the party, and frequently led to serious neglect in work; it charges the Central Committee to continue unswervingly its struggle against the survivals of the cult of personality, in all its activities proceeding from the principle that the true creators of the new life are the popular masses led by the Communist Party. [At the time this resolution was adopted Khrushchev had not yet given his secret speech about Stalin.]

Through its restoration of leninist norms of party life and its development of party democracy, its observance of the principle of collective leadership, and its struggle against the cult of personality, the Central Committee has improved the leadership of industrial and agricultural development, has revealed violations of socialist legality and taken the necessary steps to correct them, has called for a struggle against feelings of smugness and complacency, and has mobilized the whole party, all of our workers – both party and non-party, for an accelerated development of Soviet society, for a continued advance in the material well-being of the Soviet people.

To ensure continued successful forward movement, it will be necessary in the future as well to maintain the party ranks in a high state of fighting efficiency, tirelessly improving and perfecting all our party work. The Congress charges the Central Committee to take steps for the further improvement of all the party's organizational work, emphasizing the organization of economic construction. Party organizations must reorient themselves and become involved in the concrete leadership of economic life, intensifying their study of the technology and economics of industrial enterprises, kolkhozes, MTSs, and sovkhozes, in order to guide their operations skilfully.

The level of organizational work is decisively affected by the way in which its results are verified, the way in which cadres are selected and trained, and by the proper placement of communists in various sectors of economic and cultural construction. The Congress feels that greater attention should be devoted to the promotion of young cadres and women and to increasing the number of communists employed in production.

The Congress views as incorrect the lessened concern for the regulated growth of the party manifested by some party organizations. Since it is not the quantitative, but the qualitative, growth of the party ranks which is important, the Congress directs party organizations to intensify their concern for individual recruitment into the party of outstanding persons, especially workers and kolkhozniks.

The Congress charges the Central Committee to continue improving the organizational structure and the forms of operation of party and soviet organs, in accordance with the changing circumstances.

Particular attention must be devoted to the further strengthening of the raion link. The Congress takes note of the great efforts which the party has displayed in this matter and views as correct the party's reconstruction of the rural raion committees and its creation of instructors' groups headed by the raion committee secretary for the MTS zone.

Nonetheless the level of performance of many raion organizations is still below the requirements facing the party. This is due to the fact that in many raions weak and ineffectual workers, lacking the necessary practical and political qualities, have been made secretaries and raion committee instructors for MTS zones.

Now that the country is faced with gigantic tasks of promoting the advance of agriculture, the reinforcement of the raion organizations with experienced and capable persons has acquired particular significance. Raion party cadres at the present time are working directly in the village primary organizations, in the MTSs, the kolkhozes, the sovkhozes, organizing the toilers of agriculture for carrying out the directives of the party and the government. Thus the level of performance of the raion organizations now determines to a decisive extent the success of the whole national effort to bring about a sharp upturn in agriculture. Therefore energetic organizers of the masses, persons of initiative who are well acquainted with agricultural production, must be appointed to the leading posts in the party raion committees, especially to the posts of secretaries and instructors for the MTS zones, and also as members of the raion soviet executive committees. For this it is necessary to persist in strengthening the raion link, both by promoting the best local workers who have grown up in the kolkhozes and sovkhozes and by attracting people from the cities and industrial centres to work in the raions, creating an immediate material interest on the part of the leaders of raion party and soviet organs in the economic functioning of the MTSs, kolkhozes, and sovkhozes.

At the same time it is necessary to work for the further strengthening of urban party organizations, in every way increasing the responsibility of party city committees and city raion committees for the operation of industrial enterprises and in particular for the productive application of the most recent achievements of science, technology, and most advanced practices, as well as for the functioning of all enterprises and organizations working to satisfy the daily needs of the population.

A most important factor in the successful fulfilment of the tasks confronting the party is the further reinforcement of the ties of the party as a whole, and of each party organization in particular, with the broadest masses of toilers. The Congress directs the attention of party organs to the necessity of stimulating the soviets of workers' deputies and the tradeunion organizations in order to intensify decisively their role in economic and cultural construction, in satisfying the daily needs and requirements of the population, in the communist education of the toilers.

The leninist Komsomol has an important position in the social life of the country, participating actively in economic and cultural construction and helping the party educate youth in the spirit of communism. However, serious inadequacies have been revealed in the functioning of Komsomol organizations, especially in their ideological and educational work. Komsomol organizations are sometimes unable to acquaint youth with practical affairs, and for a vigorous organizational effort they substitute resolutions, showiness, and bustle. These defects will be eliminated if the party's guidance of the Komsomol is improved. Party organizations must display greater concern to create the conditions necessary for educational and mass-cultural work with youth, ensuring the even more active participation of komsomols and of all Soviet youth in state, economic, and cultural construction, in the country's whole socio-political life.

With respect to ideological work the Congress considers one of the most important tasks to be overcoming the gap between propaganda and the practice of communist construction. Our propaganda and agitation must be bound more closely to the tasks of creating the material and productive basis of communism, of producing an abundance of material and cultural wealth, of heightening the communist consciousness of the citizens, putting an end to dogmatism which is alien to the creative spirit of marxism-leninism. The task of propaganda is not only to explain the theory of marxism-leninism, but also to contribute to its practical implementation.

The Congress notes that the Central Committee spoke out in a timely fashion against attempts to deviate from the party's general line favouring the preferential development of heavy industry, as well as against confusion with respect to the construction of socialism in our country and with respect to certain other theoretical questions ...

4.6
On the Sixth Five-Year Plan of Development of the National Economy of the USSR from 1956 to 1960   25 February 1956

The XX Congress of the CPSU hereby notes that the targets of the Fifth Five-Year Plan of development of the economy of the USSR, set by the XIX Party Congress, have been successfully met.

During the past five years industrial production in the USSR has risen by 85 per cent, with production of the instruments of production increasing by 91 per cent, while the total volume of production in machine building and metal working was 2.2 times as great in 1955 as in 1950. Industrial production in 1955 was 3.2 times as great as in 1940. The five-year-plan targets for the major types of heavy industrial production – steel, rolled steel, coal, oil, electricity, cement, aluminum, automobiles, tractors, and many others – have been overfulfilled.

Implementation of the major measures adopted by the party and the government to increase the production of grain and animal products has created the conditions for a sharp upsurge of socialist agriculture. Development of the virgin and unused lands has increased the area sown to grain in 1955 by almost 24 million hectares over 1950. The total harvests of the basic agricultural crops and the production of animal products have increased.

The successful development of heavy industry and the growth in agricultural production have made possible a 76 per cent increase in consumer goods production over the five-year period, which is more than twice the pre-war level. The five-year-plan targets for transport were overfulfilled. The steady advance of technology, the improved organization of production, and the development of socialist competition have raised labour productivity in industry, agriculture, and transport.

During the years of the Fifth Five-Year Plan the USSR national income increased 68 per cent, the real wages of workers and employees increased 39 per cent, and the real incomes of kolkhozniks increased 50 per cent. The targets of the Five-Year Plan for retail trade were overfulfilled. Soviet science and culture have been developing successfully.

At the same time the XX Congress of the CPSU notes the existence of considerable short-comings in some areas of economic activity. The development of certain branches of industry is lagging behind the growing demands of the economy. The five-year-plan target for agricultural production was underfulfilled, and this hampered the development of light industry and food processing – the output of goods for popular consumption.

Many branches of industry are slow to introduce and utilize the newest achievements of contemporary science and technology; there is still insufficient mechanization and automation in industry, agriculture, transport, and construction.

The target for labour productivity in industry and construction is underfulfilled, and labour inputs per unit of production are still high.

Fulfilment of the Fifth Five-Year Plan has increased the economic might of the country, has further strengthened the socialist economic system, has heightened the material and cultural living standard of the Soviet people, has expanded the economic ties between the USSR and the people's democracies, and consolidated the economic position of the Soviet Union and the whole socialist camp.

Now the Soviet Union possesses a powerful and comprehensively developed socialist production, material resources which are much greater than ever before, and skilled cadres.

The level of development of socialized production which has been reached enables the Soviet state to develop at a rapid rate not only production of the means of production – which has been and remains the unshakable foundation of the whole economy – but also production of consumer goods; it makes possible a considerable expansion of social wealth and, thereby, further progress along the path of constructing a communist society in our country.

The XX Congress of the CPSU considers that the Soviet land now affords all the necessary conditions for resolving, through peaceful economic competition and in the historically shortest period, the fundamental economic task of the USSR – catching up with and surpassing the developed capitalist countries in per capita production.

The principal tasks of the Sixth Five-Year Plan of development of the economy of the USSR are to ensure the continued powerful growth of all branches of the economy on the basis of the priority development of heavy industry, continued technical progress, and an increasing of labour productivity; to ensure a sharp advance of agricultural production and on this basis to increase considerably the material well-being and the cultural level of the Soviet people.

The period of the Sixth Five-Year Plan must be one of the continued powerful development of the productive forces of the Soviet land, of the transition of the economy to a higher technical production level, of serious improvement in all qualitative indices and in economic leadership.

Bearing in mind the major tasks confronting the party and the Soviet people, the XX Congress of the CPSU hereby lays down the following directives for the Sixth Five-Year Plan of development of the USSR economy from 1956 to 1960:

I IN INDUSTRY

1   Industrial production during the five years is to increase by approximately 65 per cent.

The primary tasks of the Sixth Five-Year Plan in industry are to be the continued development of heavy and light metallurgy, of the oil, coal, and chemical industries, accelerated rates of construction of power-generating stations, and ensuring the rapid growth of machine building – especially of technically advanced machine tools, drop-presses, and automation instruments and devices. During the five years the production of instruments of production (group A) is to increase by approximately 70 per cent.

The consumer goods industry is to undergo a further considerable expansion. During the five years the production of consumer goods (group B) is to increase by approximately 60 per cent ...

IV IN AGRICULTURE

1   There is to be a sharp advance in agriculture and animal husbandry. By 1960 the total grain crop is to increase to 180 million tons (11 million puds). During the five years the total production of industrial crops, potatoes, vegetables, and animal products is to increase as follows [1960 production as a percentage of 1955]: raw cotton, to 156 per cent; flax fibre, to 135; sugar beets, to 154; potatoes, to 185; vegetables, to 218; meat, to 200; milk, to 195; eggs, to 254; and wool, to 182 per cent.

2   Farming techniques are to be systematically improved through broad application of the achievements of agronomy and of most advanced practices; those crops and plant varieties are to be encouraged which are most productive under local conditions, and the same holds for varieties and breeds of cattle; kolkhozes and sovkhozes are to ensure a correct combination of the various branches of agriculture.

The regionalization of agricultural branches and specialization in agriculture and animal husbandry are to be based on economic advantage with due regard for the natural and economic conditions of each raion – and, within the raion, of each kolkhoz and sovkhoz – the aim being a sharp increase in output per 100 hectares of arable land with minimum inputs of labour and materials.

3   The techniques of cultivating agricultural crops are to be comprehensively improved, extensive use is to be made of the square and square-cluster methods of sowing cotton, sunflower, corn, and other crops which require cultivation between the rows; techniques are to be introduced for the combined mechanization of the growing and harvesting of cultivated crops. Backwardness in seed production is to be eliminated, and an intensified effort is to be made to develop and introduce into production higher-yield and more productive varieties of agricultural crops, high-yield strains of cotton, varieties of sugar beet with a higher sugar content, varieties of sunflower which ripen earlier and have a higher oil content.

The use of mineral fertilizers is to be improved, and also that of local fertilizers, manure, peat, compost, and ash. The industrial mining of peat for agricultural purposes is to be expanded. The production of bacterial fertilizers is to be expanded substantially, and liquid nitrogen fertilizers are to be introduced into production. The industrial production of lime is to be organized on a scale sufficient to cover the needs of agriculture ...

VIII   TO ELEVATE THE MATERIAL AND CULTURAL LIVING STANDARD OF THE PEOPLE

1   In line with the established targets for the development of socialist production and for elevating the productivity of labour, the *national income* (in comparable prices) is to grow by approximately 60 per cent during the five-year period. This is to serve as the basis for the continued growth in the incomes of workers and employees and in the incomes of the peasants; the per-capita consumption of foodstuffs and industrial goods is to be considerably expanded.

2   In 1960 the economy of the USSR will employ approximately 55 million workers and employees.

The real *wages* of workers and employees are to rise by an average of 30 per cent. The wage level of the lowest-paid workers and employees is to be raised.

3   During the Sixth Five-Year Plan it will be necessary to shorten the working day of workers and employees.

The USSR Council of Ministers is charged with working out measures for implementing, during the Sixth Five-Year Plan, the gradual transfer of workers in the leading underground occupations in coal and ore mining to a six-hour working day. The first workers to be transferred to this shorter working day, starting in 1957, will be those working underground and in shops where the temperature is high. The five-hour working day (or the eight-hour day with two days off) is to be instituted in those branches of industry where production conditions make it advisable.

Starting in 1956 the working day preceding a day off or a holiday is to be shortened by two hours for workers and employees.

Starting in 1956 the six-hour working day is to be restored for adolescents between the ages of 16 and 18.

The transition to the shorter working day is to be implemented without any reduction in the wages of workers and employees.

4   The working and living conditions of female workers are to be comprehensively improved. Working mothers are to be granted additional advantages – in particular, longer maternity leaves.

5   Through a substantial increase in the productivity of agriculture and animal husbandry and an increasing labour productivity of kolkhozniks, the *incomes of kolkhozniks*, both in money and in kind, are to rise by an average of not less than 40 per cent – primarily through increased income from the socialized sector; the socialized funds of kolkhozes are to be expanded considerably.

6   State expenditures for allowances and social security payments to workers and employees are to be increased, as are expenditures for social security pensions, for allowances to single mothers and mothers with many children, scholarships for students, free medical assistance, free and reduced-rate passes to sanatoria and rest-homes, expenditures for free education and vocational improvement, for payment of wages during leave, and other payments and benefits to the toilers – from 154 billion roubles in 1955 to about 210 billion roubles in 1960. Pension coverage is to be regularized, the size of the pensions in the lowest categories being substantially increased and that of the unwarrantedly high pensions being lowered; care for the aged is to be improved as are the employment conditions of those invalids who are able to perform socially useful labour without injury to their health.

7   During the five-year period *retail turnover* in the state and cooperative trade networks is to increase by approximately 50 per cent, with retail trade at the village level growing at a faster rate ...

IX   ON ECONOMIC DEVELOPMENT IN THE UNION REPUBLICS AND
     THE DISTRIBUTION OF PRODUCTIVE FORCES

The distribution of productive forces is to be improved by bringing industry closer to sources of raw materials, fuel and power supplies, and to the consumer. The proper specialization and combined development of economic regions is to be ensured through more effective use of their natural and labour resources in order to elevate the productivity of social labour.

Development of the rich natural resources of the country's eastern regions is to be accelerated. Western and eastern Siberia and the Kazakh SSR are to have a higher rate of capital construction than the USSR as a whole. These regions are to establish heavy industrial complexes, especially in those branches with high fuel and power consumption; there is to be extensive construction of heavy and light metallurgical plants, of large hydroelectric and thermal power plants, oil refineries, machine-building and chemical plants, and plants producing construction materials: extensive raw-materials sources are to be developed for the production of heavy and light metals, chemicals, and building materials.

Limitations are to be imposed on the further construction, in European regions of the USSR and in the Urals, of industrial enterprises with high fuel and electricity consumption. In order to liquidate the lag of the fuel industry in the European regions of the USSR behind the growing fuel requirements of these regions and to reduce the distances over which coal has to be hauled, coal mining and oil production in these regions are to increase to the necessary level as are the construction of hydroelectric stations and the development of the gas industry ...

4.7
On Partial Changes in the Rules of the CPSU
[Revises Rules adopted 1952; see 3.45]   24 February 1956

The XX Congress of the CPSU resolves to introduce the following changes in the Rules of the CPSU [see 3.45]:

1   [Revises 3.45, art. 44]   To establish that the plenums of oblast committees, krai committees, and central committees of union republics are convened at least once every four months, and plenums of okrug committees, city committees, and raion committees are convened at least once every three months.

2   [Revises 3.45, art. 40]   Considering the wishes of local party organizations, to establish that congresses of the communist parties of union republics, and party conferences in krai, oblast, okrug, and city committees in cities that are divided into raions, are to be convened once every two years. Congresses of communist parties of union republics that are divided into oblasts (Ukraine, Belorussia, Kazakhstan, Uzbekistan) may be held once every four years.

3   To abrogate point 'c' in article 35 in the CPSU Rules [3.45].

4   [Revises 3.45, art. 56]   In order to broaden the rights of local party organs, to recognize that in large enterprises and institutions, which have over 300 communists, party committees may be established with the approval of oblast committees, krai committees, central committees of union republics.

5   [Revises 3.45, arts. 42 and 50]   To recognize as inadvisable the

retention in the party Rules of the provision concerning the number of secretaries of party committees, considering that their number may change according to the concrete conditions of work. To establish that the number of secretaries in party committees shall be determined by the Central Committee of the CPSU.

6   [Revises 3.45, art. 55]   In view of the task of increasing the influence of party organizations in shops, brigades and sectors of enterprises, kolkhozes, MTSs and sovkhozes, to establish that shop party organizations may be formed with the approval of raion committees, city committees, or corresponding political departments in primary party organizations that have over 50 Communists.

7   To abrogate article 64 [3.45] of the Rules of the CPSU concerning political departments in transport.

4.8
On the Cult of Personality and its Consequences   25 February 1956

Having heard the report by Comrade N.S. Khrushchev on the cult of personality and its consequences, the Congress of the Communist Party of the Soviet Union supports the provisions contained in the report by the Central Committee and charges the CPSU Central Committee to implement thorough measures ensuring that the cult of personality – which is alien to marxism-leninism – will be overcome, that its consequences in all areas of party, state, and ideological work will be liquidated, and that the norms of party life and the principles of collective party leadership worked out by the great Lenin will be strictly implemented.

4.9
On Preparing a New Programme for the CPSU   25 February 1956

The XX Congress commissions the Central Committee to prepare a draft programme of the Communist Party of the Soviet Union, being guided by the fundamental provisions of marxist-leninist theory as creatively developed on the basis of the historical experience of our party, the experience of the fraternal parties of the socialist countries, the experience and achievements of the entire international communist and workers' movement, and also with due regard for the long-range plan being prepared for communist construction and the economic and cultural development of the Soviet Union.

The Congress charges the Central Committee to publish the draft party programme well in advance of the XXI Congress of the CPSU so that an extended discussion of it will be possible. [It was later decided to hold an 'extraordinary' congress, the XXI, sooner than planned – in 1959. Thus the draft of the new party Programme was not published until the summer of 1961, preceding the XXII Party Congress.]

Pravda, 25, 26 February 1956, excepting 4.8, which was first published in *XX s"ezd Kommunisticheskoi Partii Sovetskogo Soiuza* II, 405 (approved for publication on 13 June 1956)

KPSS v rezoliutsiiakh VII, 95–182

**4.10
On the Formation of the RSFSR Bureau
of the Central Committee of the CPSU**   27 February 1956

Separate sections [otdely] for the RSFSR of Party Organs and Agriculture had already existed in the Central Committee apparatus before the XX Congress. The formation of the RSFSR Bureau grouped these and five other sections together as the separate sector of the apparatus responsible for affairs of the Russian Republic. Supervision of the non-Russian union republics was the responsibility of Union Republic sections. In essence the creation of the RSFSR Bureau inserted an additional co-ordinating agency between a part of the Central Committee apparatus and the whole Secretariat and Presidium.

Khrushchev was elected chairman of the new body, which initially consisted of eight members, all regarded as Khrushchev supporters: M.A. Iasnov, I.V. Kapitonov, F.R. Kozlov, V.M. Churaev, V.P. Milarshchikov, A.M. Puzanov, N.G. Ignatov, and A.P. Kirilenko. An additional decision of 14 March 1956 added A.B. Aristov and P.N. Pospelov and established the following sections within the Bureau: party organs, propaganda and agitation, science, schools and culture, agriculture, industry and transport, administrative, trade and financial organs.

To give more concrete leadership to the work of republic organizations, oblast and krai party, soviet, and economic organs, and to provide for more effective solution of problems of economic and cultural growth of the RSFSR, an RSFSR Bureau is hereby established within the Central Committee of the CPSU.

It is recognized as necessary that the post of chairman of the RSFSR Bureau of the Central Committee be combined with that of First Secretary of the Central Committee ...

> *Spravochnik partiinogo rabotnika* (Moscow, 1957), 127 [A slightly different version, not entitled a postanovlenie, as the above was called, appeared in *Pravda*, 29 February 1956.]

4.11
On Measures for Further Improving the Training of Leading Party and Soviet Cadres
26 June 1956

The Central Committee of the CPSU notes that the Higher Party School established in 1946 and the krai and oblast party schools have done much for the training and retraining of party and soviet cadres. During the last ten years more than 55,000 persons have graduated from local party schools, 2843 from the Higher Party School, and more than 6000 from the correspondence division of the Higher Party School. The overwhelming majority of party school graduates are now in party and soviet work. At the same time, the Central Committee considers that there are serious inadequacies in the training of party and soviet workers. The curriculums of the schools devote extremely little time to the concrete economics and organization of industrial and agricultural production – a serious gap in the training of cadres which has a negative effect on their work of economic leadership. Instruction in party affairs, Soviet economics, and the elements of agronomy is often conducted in isolation from the practical work of party organizations and from the up-to-date experience of kolkhozes, sovkhozes, MTSS, and industrial enterprises. Dogmatism and teaching by rote have not yet been eliminated in courses in the social disciplines, and controversial questions of marxism-leninism are not studied in depth. It has sometimes happened that party workers who have not given a satisfactory account of themselves in practice have been sent to study in these schools.

The Central Committee considers that under present conditions, when a considerable part of the party and soviet cadres have undergone training, there is no need for party schools in each oblast and republic; this only leads to the dispersion of cadres and funds and lowers the quality of the training. The existing network of party schools should be cut down, and certain three-year schools should be used as the base for a series of large inter-oblast party schools which would give their students a complete higher party political education as well as extensive knowledge of the workings of the economy.

The Central Committee recognizes the following measures as essential to the continued improvement of the training of leading party and soviet cadres:

ON LOCAL PARTY SCHOOLS

1   On the basis of the existing three-year party schools in the cities of Moscow, Leningrad, Gorky, Kuibyshev, Saratov, Stalingrad, Voronezh, Rostov, Kazan, Sverdlovsk, Perm, Novosibirsk, Barnaul, Krasnoiarsk, Irkutsk, Khabarovsk, Yaroslavl, Ufa, Kharkov, Lvov, Odessa, Dnepropetrovsk, Stalino, Minsk, Vilno, Kishinev, Alma-Ata, Tashkent, and Baku, inter-oblast and inter-republic party schools are to be established with a four-year curriculum giving a higher party political education.

The Moscow, Leningrad, Kiev, Minsk, Khabarovsk, Alma-Ata, and Tashkent party schools are to have sections for training newspaper functionaries.

2   The four-year inter-oblast party schools are to be classified as second-category institutions of higher education. Persons graduating from party schools are to be awarded a diploma from an institution of higher education.

The USSR Ministry of Higher Education (Comrade Eliutin) is directed to place the four-year inter-oblast party schools and the Higher Party Correspondence School of the Central Committee on the list of institutions of higher education.

3   The curriculums of the four-year party schools are approved in accordance with addendum numbers 1 and 2.

As provided in the curriculum, the party schools are to have the following departments: history of the CPSU, party and soviet affairs, dialectical and historical materialism, political economy, historical sciences, soviet economy, agriculture, industrial production, journalism, Russian language and literature (in schools possessing a journalism section).

4   The dean and the departments of the Higher Party School of the CPSU Central Committee are directed to prepare and send out programmes for all subjects on the curriculum of the four-year party schools by 1 August 1956.

5   The four-year party schools are to accept members of the CPSU who have been recommended by the oblast or krai committees or by the central committees of the union-republic parties, who have proved their capacities in party and soviet work, who are less than 35 years of age, and who possess, as a minimum, a secondary education.

Those entering party schools will take entrance examinations in the history of the USSR, Russian language, geography, and in the foundations of marxism-leninism, at the level of the secondary-school graduate. Persons admitted to the entrance examination are granted one month of paid leave by their place of employment to prepare for the examinations.

6   Persons enrolled in four-year party schools are to be paid stipends in the amount of their ordinary salaries, but not less than 1000 rubles, and not more than 1700 rubles, per month. In addition, they are granted allowances in the amount of 100 rubles per month for each dependent.

7   The 1956 entering class of the four-year party schools is hereby approved.

For schools in the oblasts and krais of the RSFSR students are selected by the appropriate oblast and krai party committees; for the schools of the Ukrainian, Belorussian, Lithuanian, Moldavian, Kazakh, Uzbek, Kirgiz, and Azerbaidzhan Soviet Socialist Republics – by the party central committee of the corresponding union-republic. The sections for party organs of the CPSU Central Committee will supervise the staffing of party schools.

8   The oblast and krai committees and the union-republic central committees are permitted to transfer to the four-year course students in the first and second years of the three-year schools on which the inter-oblast party schools will be based, provided these students have completed secondary education, have appropriate experience in party and soviet work, and have done well in their studies.

9   The Higher Party School of the Central Committee of the Ukrainian Communist Party is to pass over to the four-year course based on the curriculum of the inter-oblast party schools.

10   The party organs sections and the Administration of Affairs of the Central Committee are directed, together with the appropriate party oblast and krai committees and the central committees of the union-republic parties, to examine questions connected with ensuring the normal operation of the newly established party schools (staffs, buildings, equipment, etc.) and to submit suitable proposals.

11   The following cities are to retain three-year party schools with the same yearly entering class as before: Kursk, Penza, Smolensk, Tambov, Saransk, Makhachkala, Chkalov, Kurgan, Omsk, Vladivostok, Yerevan, Frunze, and Stalinabad.

12   After 1956 students will no longer be admitted to party schools in the following cities: Arkhangel, Ashkhabad, Vologda, Kirov, Ulianovsk, Cheliabinsk, Kemerovo, Krasnodar, Riga, Tallin, Tula, Ordzhonikidze, Syktyvkar, Chita, Ulan-Ude, Yakutsk, Izhevsk, Riazan, Stavropol, Uzhgorod, Simferopol, Ternopol, Stanislav, and Tbilisi. Students in these schools have the right to complete their studies according to the existing curriculum.

ON THE HIGHER PARTY SCHOOL

13   The Higher Party School of the Central Committee is to be responsible for training cadres for work at the oblast and republic levels, taking in

CPSU members with higher education who have sufficient experience in positions of authority.

The journalism section is to be retained in the Higher Party School.

The course is to be for two years; party, soviet, and newspaper workers not over 40 years of age are accepted for study in the Higher Party School.

In connection with the reorganization of the Higher Party School persons presently in the first and second years are granted the right to complete their studies on the basis of the existing curriculum.

14   The curriculum of the Higher Party School of the Central Committee is hereby approved.

15   The number of matriculants into the Higher Party School in 1956 is set at 200.

16   A special department is to be set up in the Higher Party School of the CPSU Central Committee for training persons sent for study by the communist and workers' parties of foreign countries. This special department will follow the existing three-year curriculum, but in case of necessity the school administration will have the right to introduce small revisions, depending on the composition of the student body and the desires of the communist parties of the various countries concerned.

17   The correspondence division of the Higher Party School and the Higher Party Correspondence School of the Central Committee are to be reorganized. The Higher Party Correspondence School is to adopt the curriculum of the four-year inter-oblast party schools and is to follow a five-year course.

Divisions of the Higher Party Correspondence School are to be set up in the inter-oblast four-year party schools for continuous academic and methodological work with correspondence-school students; the existing consultation points are to be subordinated to these divisions.

The directors of four-year schools are accorded the right to include in the academic load of their teachers work with students of the Higher Party Correspondence School.

18   The number of matriculants into the Higher Party Correspondence School in 1956 is set at 3000.

ON SOVIET-PARTY SCHOOLS AND RETRAINING COURSES

19   The oblast and krai committees and the central committees of the union-republic parties are directed to develop and submit to the CPSU Central Committee, within one month, proposals:

a   for organizing, in oblasts and republics where the need exists, soviet-party schools to prepare cadres for the lower party and soviet levels on the basis of the three-year party schools which will not be receiving new students after 1956;

b for creating continuously operating short-term courses to upgrade the qualifications of party and soviet personnel, in place of the existing one-year courses for training party and soviet personnel.

Spravochnik partiinogo rabotnika (Moscow, 1957), 410–15

4.12
On Overcoming the Cult of Personality and its Consequences 30 June 1956

... In its criticism of the cult of personality the party is guided by the principles of marxism-leninism. For more than three years our party has been struggling consistently against the cult of I.V. Stalin, persistently overcoming its harmful consequences. This matter naturally occupied an important place in the deliberations and decisions of the XX Party Congress. The Congress pointed out that the Central Committee was entirely correct and timely in coming out against the cult of personality, the dissemination of which had detracted from the role of the party and the popular masses, had had a harmful impact on the role of collective leadership in the party, and had frequently led to serious neglect in work, to crude violations of socialist legality. The Congress charged the Central Committee to give effect to consistent measures ensuring that the cult of personality – which is alien to marxism-leninism – will be overcome, that its consequences in all areas of party, state, and ideological work will be liquidated, and that the norms of party life and the principles of collective leadership worked out by the great Lenin will be strictly implemented.

In its struggle against the cult of personality the party is guided by certain well-known principles of marxism-leninism on the role of the popular masses, the party, and the individual in history, on the inadmissibility of a cult of a political leader, however great his services may have been. K. Marx, the founder of scientific communism, emphasized his antipathy 'to any cult of an individual' when he stated that his entry, and that of F. Engels, into the League of Communists 'was on the condition that the statutes would discard everything which contributed to a superstitious bowing before authority.'

In creating our Communist Party V.I. Lenin fought implacably against the anti-marxist concept of the 'hero' and the 'crowds,' resolutely condemning the juxtaposition of lone hero and popular masses. He stated, 'The mind of the tens of millions of the creative masses produces something immeasurably higher than the foresight of the greatest genius.'

In raising the matter of the struggle with the cult of I.V. Stalin, the Central Committee was guided by the fact that the cult of personality contradicts the nature of the socialist order and had become a hindrance to the development of Soviet democracy and to the advance of Soviet society to communism.

On the initiative of the Central Committee the XX Party Congress felt it necessary to disclose boldly and openly the grievous consequences of the cult of personality, the serious errors which were committed during the last period of Stalin's life, and to call upon the entire party for a common effort to do away with everything engendered by the cult of personality [see 4.5, 4.8]. Here the Central Committee realized that a sincere admission of the errors committed would involve certain debits and costs which could be used by enemies. Bold and merciless self-criticism in regard to the cult of personality was new and striking testimony to the strength and solidity of our party and of the Soviet socialist order. It can be confidently stated that not one of the ruling parties of the capitalist countries would ever dare take such a step. On the contrary, they would strive to preserve silence and conceal such unpleasant facts from the people. But the CPSU, educated in the revolutionary principles of marxism-leninism, came out with the whole truth however bitter it may have been. The party took this step solely on its own initiative, guided by considerations of principle. It was motivated by the fact that, although an attack on the cult of Stalin may cause certain temporary difficulties, from the perspective of the vital interests and ultimate goals of the working class an enormous positive result will be attained. This at the same time guarantees firmly that never again, in our party and in our country, will there occur phenomena similar to the cult of personality, that henceforth the party and the country will be led collectively, on the basis of a marxist-leninist policy, in conditions of an expanded party democracy, with the active and creative participation of millions of toilers, with the all-around development of Soviet democracy.

By speaking out resolutely against the cult of personality and its consequences, by openly criticizing the errors which it engendered, the party has once again demonstrated its fidelity to the immortal principles of marxism-leninism, its devotion to the interests of the people, its concern that the best conditions be created for the development of party and Soviet democracy in the interests of the successful construction of communism in our country.

The Central Committee of the CPSU hereby notes that the discussion, in party organizations and at general meetings of the toilers, of the question of the cult of personality and its consequences revealed very active participation by party members and non-party persons and that the line of the CPSU Central Committee was fully approved and supported by the party and the people.

The instances of violation of socialist legality, and other errors associated with the cult of I.V. Stalin disclosed by the party, evoke feelings of grief and profound regret. But Soviet people understand that the condemnation of the cult of personality was necessary for the construction of communism – in which they are active participants. The Soviet people sees that in recent years the party has been persistently implementing practical measures aimed at eliminating the consequences of the cult of personality in all areas of party, state, economic, and cultural activity. Its result has been that the party, whose internal forces have not been unfettered, has drawn even closer to the people and is in a condition of unprecedented creative activity.

How could the cult of Stalin, with all its negative consequences, have arisen and become so widespread in the conditions of the Soviet socialist order?

In examining this question one must bear in mind both the concrete objective historical conditions in which the building of socialism in the USSR occurred and also certain subjective factors associated with Stalin's own personal qualities.

The October Socialist Revolution went down in history as the classic example of the revolutionary transformation of a capitalist society effected under the leadership of the working class. From the example of the heroic struggle of the Bolshevik Party and of the USSR – the first socialist state in the world – the communist parties of other countries and all progressive and democratic forces are learning how to resolve the fundamental social questions raised by the contemporary development of society. During the nearly forty years in which the toilers of our country have been building a socialist society enormous experience has been accumulated which is studied and creatively applied – with due regard for their own concrete conditions – by the toilers of other socialist countries.

This was history's first experiment in building a socialist society, formed by a process of seeking, by testing through practice many truths which before that time had been known to socialists only in outline, in theory. For more than a quarter of a century the Soviet land was the only country building a road to socialism for humanity. In its capitalist encirclement it was like a besieged fortress. After the collapse of the intervention of the fourteen states in 1918–20, the enemies of the Soviet land to east and west continued to prepare new 'crusades' against the USSR. Enemies sent spies and diversionists to the USSR in large quantities, striving in every way to undermine the first socialist state in the world. The threat of new imperialist aggression against the USSR was particularly intensified after the coming to power of fascism in Germany in 1933, as it proclaimed the goal of destroying communism, destroying the Soviet Union – the first toilers' state in the world. All will recall the formation of the so-called 'Anti-comintern Pact,' The 'Berlin-Rome-Tokyo Axis,' which was actively supported by the forces of all international reaction. Faced with the emergent threat of a new war and the rejection by the western states of the measures frequently proposed by the Soviet Union to curb fascism and organize collective security, the Soviet land was compelled to harness all its efforts to strengthening its defence, to fighting against the designs of the hostile capitalist encirclement. Confronted by these external enemies, the party had to educate the whole people in the spirit of constant vigilance and readiness for mobilization.

The designs of international reaction were the more threatening in that a bitter class war had been waged for a long time within the country – deciding the question, 'Who whom?' After the death of Lenin hostile tendencies were activated within the party: trotskyites, right opportunists, bourgeois nationalists – all rejecting the leninist theory of the possibility of the victory of socialism in one country and thus in fact tending toward the restoration of capitalism in the USSR. The party unleashed a merciless struggle against these enemies of leninism.

In carrying out Lenin's precepts the Communist Party set course for the socialist industrialization of the country, the collectivization of agriculture, and the carrying out of the cultural revolution. In the process of resolving these gigantic tasks of building a socialist society in a single isolated country, the Soviet people and the Communist Party had to overcome incredible difficulties and obstacles. In a very short historical period, without any external economic assistance at all, our country had to liquidate its age-old backwardness and reconstruct its whole economy along new socialist lines.

This complex international and domestic situation demanded iron discipline, a ceaseless heightening of vigilance, the most strictly centralized leadership, which could hardly help but have a negative effect on the development of certain democratic forms. During its fierce struggle with the whole world of imperialism our country had to accept certain restrictions on democracy which were justified by the logic of our people's struggle for socialism under conditions of a capitalist encirclement. But even then these restrictions were viewed by the party and the people as temporary, to be removed as the Soviet state became stronger and as the forces of democracy and socialism developed throughout the world. The people consciously accepted these temporary sacrifices, seeing every day new successes of the Soviet social order.

All of these obstacles in the path of the building of socialism were overcome by the Soviet people under the leadership of the Communist Party and its Central Committee, consistently implementing the leninist general line.

The victory of socialism in our country, accomplished under conditions of hostile encirclement and the constant threat of external attack, was a deed of world-historic importance performed by the Soviet people. Through the tense and heroic efforts of the people and the party during the initial five-year plans the economically backward country made a gigantic jump forward in its economic and cultural development. The successes of socialist construction raised the living standard of the toilers and liquidated unemployment for all time. A profound cultural revolution took place in the country. In a short time the Soviet people reared a large technical intelligentsia, reached the level of world technical progress, and advanced Soviet science and technology to one of the leading positions in the world. All of these victories were inspired and organized by the great party of communists. For the toilers of the world the USSR was a graphic and convincing example that the workers and peasants, taking power into their own hands, could get along without capitalists and landowners and successfully build and develop their own socialist state which embodies and protects the interests of the broad popular masses. This all had an enormous inspirational effect on the growth of the influence of communist and workers' parties in all countries of the world.

I.V. Stalin, who for an extended period was general secretary of the party Central Committee, fought actively along with other leading persons for the realization of leninist precepts. He was devoted to marxism-leninism; both as a theoretician and as a major organizer he headed the party's struggle against the trotskyites, the right opportunists, the bourgeois nationalists, and against the designs of the capitalist encirclement. In this political and ideological struggle I.V. Stalin acquired great authority and popularity. However, his name came incorrectly to be linked with all of our great victories. Stalin's head was turned by the successes of the Communist Party and the Soviet land, and by the eulogies addressed to him. In this environment the cult of Stalin gradually took shape.

The development of the cult of personality was enormously favoured by certain of I.V. Stalin's personal qualities, whose negative nature had been noted by V.I. Lenin. In the end of 1922 Lenin sent a letter to the regular party congress which stated:

'Having become general secretary, Comrade Stalin has concentrated immense power in his own hands, and I am not certain that he will succeed at all times in using this power carefully.' In an addendum to this letter, written at the beginning of January 1923, V.I. Lenin again raised the question of certain of Stalin's personal qualities which were intolerable in a leader. 'Stalin is too rude,' wrote Lenin, 'and this quality, which is perfectly tolerable in our private intercourse as communists, becomes intolerable in the position of general secretary. Therefore I propose that comrades give thought to how Stalin may be transferred from his position and another person be appointed to it, a person possessing all of Comrade Stalin's other qualities but superior to him only in this, namely, that he should be more tolerant, more loyal, more polite, and more attentive to comrades, less capricious, etc.'

V.I. Lenin's letters were brought to the attention of the delegates to the XIII Party Congress, which took place shortly after his death. After discussion of these documents it was considered advisable to leave Stalin in the position of general secretary provided, however, that he heeded the criticism of V.I. Lenin and drew from it all necessary conclusions. [These letters of Lenin were not published in the Soviet Union until 1956.]

Remaining in the position of general secretary of the Central Committee, Stalin did heed the criticisms of V.I. Lenin in the first years after his death. Subsequently, however, Stalin greatly overvalued his own services and came to believe in his own infallibility. Certain limitations on party and Soviet democracy which were inevitable under conditions of an intense struggle with the class enemy, and later during the war with the German-Fascist aggressors Stalin started converting into norms of party and state life, crudely violating leninist principles of leadership. Plenary meetings of the Central Committee and party congresses were at first held irregularly, and then for many years were not held at all. Stalin came, in fact, to be above criticism.

Great damage to the building of socialism and the development of democracy within the party and the state was caused by Stalin's erroneous formulation that, as it were, the class struggle became increasingly bitter as the Soviet Union moved toward socialism. This formulation, which was true only for certain stages of the transitional period when the question of 'Who whom?' was being resolved, when a stubborn class battle was being waged to lay the foundations of socialism, was brought to the forefront in 1937 at a time when socialism had been victorious in our country, when the exploiting classes and their economic base had been liquidated. In practice this mistaken formulation served as justification for the crudest violations of socialist legality and for mass repressions.

It was precisely these conditions that gave rise, in particular, to the special position of the organs of state security; they were accorded enormous confidence since they had been of unquestionable service to the people and the country in defending the conquests of the revolution. For an extended time the organs of state security justified this confidence, and their special position did not give rise to any danger. The situation changed after the supervision of these organs by the party and the government gradually came to be replaced by the personal supervision of Stalin; and his individual decisions were frequently substituted for the ordinary administration of the norms of justice. The situation became even more complicated when the criminal band of that agent of international imperialism, Beria, came to be at the head of the organs of state security. Serious violations of Soviet legality were committed, as well as mass repressions. Many honourable communists and non-party Soviet people were defamed and innocently suffered due to the schemes of these enemies.

The XX Congress of the Party and the whole policy of the Central Committee since the death of Stalin have clearly testified to the formation within the party Central Committee of a leninist nucleus of leaders with a correct understanding of the urgent requirements of both domestic and foreign policy. It cannot be said that there was no opposition to the negative phenomena associated with the cult of personality which have hindered the forward movement of socialism. What is more, certain periods such as the war years saw a sharp limitation on the personal actions of Stalin, a substantial weakening of the negative effects of lawlessness, arbitrariness, etc.

As is known, during the war period members of the Central Committee, and also some outstanding Soviet military leaders, took control of certain sectors in the rear and at the front, reaching autonomous decisions, and through their organizational, political, economic, and military efforts – together with local party and Soviet organizations – ensuring the victory of the Soviet people in the war. After the war the negative consequences of the cult of personality again came to be manifested with great force.

Immediately after the death of Stalin the leninist nucleus of the Central Committee undertook a resolute struggle with the cult of personality and its grievous consequences.

The question may be asked: why did these people not come out openly against Stalin and remove him from the leadership? In the existing conditions this could not be done. The facts unquestionably indicate that Stalin was guilty of many lawless acts – especially in the last period of his life. However, it should not at the same time be forgotten that the Soviet people knew Stalin as a person who had always defended the USSR against the plotting of its enemies, a person who always fought for socialism. In this struggle he at times employed unworthy methods, violated leninist principles and the norms of party life. This was Stalin's tragedy. But it also hampered any struggle against the lawless acts which were being committed, for in the prevailing atmosphere of the cult of personality all successes in the building of socialism and the consolidation of the USSR were attributed to Stalin.

Under these conditions an attack on him would not have been understood by the people, and here there was no question of any lack of personal courage. In this situation, clearly, no one attacking Stalin would have elicited popular support. What is more, in these circumstances such an attack would have been seen as an attack on the building of socialism and, in view of the capitalist encirclement, as extremely dangerous and detrimental to the unity of the party and the whole state. And the advances achieved by the toilers of the Soviet Union under the leadership of their Communist Party had instilled in the heart of each Soviet person a justified pride, creating the sort of atmosphere in which isolated errors and inadequacies appeared less significant against the background of the gigantic advances, while the negative consequences of these errors were rapidly offset by the colossal growth in the vitality of the party and of Soviet society.

The fact should also be borne in mind that many of Stalin's deeds and incorrect acts, especially as regards the violation of Soviet legality, became known only later, after his death, mainly through the unmasking of Beria's band and the establishment of party supervision over the organs of state security.

These are the principal conditions and causes of the rise and spread of the cult of I.V. Stalin. Everything stated above explains but, of course, in no way justifies the cult of I.V. Stalin and its consequences, so sharply and justly condemned by our party.

The cult of personality unquestionably inflicted serious damage upon the Communist Party and Soviet society. But to reach conclusions about some sort of change in the social structure of the USSR because of the existence of the cult of personality in the past, or to seek the origins of this cult in the nature of the Soviet social order, would be a crude error. Both one and the other would be absolutely erroneous, would not correspond to reality, would contradict the facts.

Regardless of all the harm which the cult of Stalin caused to the party and the people, it could not and did not change the nature of our social order. No cult of any personality could alter the nature of the socialist state, based as it is on social ownership of the means of production, the alliance of the working class and the peasantry, and the friendship of its peoples, even though this cult did inflict serious damage upon the growth of socialist democracy and upon the rise in the creative initiative of the millions.

To think that any one person, even as forceful a one as Stalin, could alter our socio-political order, would be to fall into a deep contradiction with the facts, with marxism, with the truth, and would be to fall into idealism. This would mean ascribing to a single person such exorbitant and supernatural powers as the capacity to alter the structure of a society, and indeed a social structure in which the many millions of toilers are the decisive force.

As is known, the mode of production – who in society owns the means of production, which class possesses political power – determines the nature of a socio-political order. The whole world knows that in our country, as a result of the October Revolution and the victory of socialism, the socialist mode of production has become established, and that for almost forty years power has been in the hands of the working class and the peasantry. Because of this, the Soviet social order becomes increasingly consolidated, and its productive forces grow steadily, from one year to the next. Even those who wish us harm cannot fail to recognize that.

As is known, the consequences of the cult of personality were certain serious errors in the conduct of various aspects of the activity of the party and the Soviet state, both in the domestic life of the Soviet land and in its foreign policy. One could point, in particular, to Stalin's serious errors in the conduct of agriculture, in organizing the country to repulse the fascist aggressors, to his crude arbitrariness leading to the conflict with Yugoslavia in the post-war period. These errors harmed the development of certain aspects of the life of the Soviet state, hindering – especially in the last years of I.V. Stalin's life – the development of Soviet society, but it goes without saying that they did not deflect it from the correct course of development to communism.

Our enemies claim that the cult of Stalin was not engendered by certain historical conditions which have already passed away but by the Soviet system itself, its – from their viewpoint – undemocratic nature, etc. Such slanderous assertions are refuted by the whole historical development of the Soviet state. The soviets – a new democratic form of state power – arose through the revolutionary creativity of the broadest popular masses who had risen to struggle for their liberty. They were and remain the organs of a genuinely popular sovereignty. It was precisely the Soviet order which enabled the gigantic creative energy of the people to reveal itself. It set in motion the inexhaustible forces contained in the popular masses, involved millions of people in the conscious administration of the state, in active creative participation in the building of socialism. In a short historic period the Soviet state has emerged victorious from the severest tests, passed the trial by fire of the Second World War.

When the last exploiting classes were liquidated in our country, when socialism became predominant throughout the whole economy, and the international situation of our country changed radically, the framework of Soviet democracy expanded immeasurably and continues to expand. Soviet democracy differs from any bourgeois democracy in not only proclaiming, but materially guaranteeing to all members of society without exception, the right to work, education, and leisure, to participation in state affairs, freedom of speech, of the press, and of conscience, and the real opportunity for the free development of individual capacities as well as all other democratic rights and liberties. The essence of democracy lies not in its formal features but in whether or not political power actually serves and reflects the will and the vital interests of the majority of the people, the interests of the toilers. The whole domestic and foreign policy of the Soviet state is evidence that our system is a genuinely democratic and genuinely popular system. The greatest possible increase of the living standard of the people and ensuring them a peaceful existence are the supreme goal and daily concern of the Soviet state.

Testimonies to the continuing development of Soviet democracy are the measures promulgated by the party and the government to expand the rights and competence of the union republics, to ensure the strict observance of legality, to restructure the planning system so as to unshackle local initiative, to activate the local soviets, and to develop criticism and self-criticism.

Regardless of the cult of personality and despite it, the mighty initiative of the popular masses led by the Communist Party and generated by our social order did its great historic work, overcoming all obstacles to the building of socialism. And this is the highest expression of the democratic essence of the Soviet socialist order. The outstanding victories of socialism in our country did not just happen by themselves. They were attained through the mighty organizational and educational efforts of the party and its local organizations, through the party's steadfast education of its cadres and of all communists in the spirit of fidelity to marxism-leninism, in the spirit of devotion to the cause of communism. The strength of Soviet society lies in the consciousness of the masses. Its historic fate has been and is determined by the constructive labour of our heroic working class, our glorious kolkhoz peasantry, our national intelligentsia.

By liquidating the consequences of the cult of personality, restoring bolshevik norms of party life, expanding socialist democracy, our party has further strengthened its ties with the broad masses, has rallied them even more closely to the great banner of leninism.

The fact that the party itself boldly and openly raised the question of liquidating the cult of personality and the unacceptable errors of Stalin is convincing evidence that the party is the unrelenting guardian of leninism, socialism and communism, of socialist legality and the interests of the peoples, of the rights of Soviet citizens. This is the best evidence of the strength and vitality of the Soviet socialist order. At the same time it testifies to the party's resolution to overcome every last consequence of the cult of personality and permit no future repetition of such errors.

Our party's condemnation of the cult of I.V. Stalin and its consequences has evoked support and a broad response in all the fraternal communist parties bespeaks approval and support for our party's measures against the cult of personality and its consequences. In its editorial, 'The Historical Experience of the Dictatorship of the Proletariat,' the organ of the Central Committee of the Communist Party of China, the newspaper *Jen Min Ji Pao*, set forth as follows the outcome of the discussion in the Politburo of the Central Committee of the Chinese Communist Party, of the decisions of the XX Congress of the CPSU: 'The Communist Party of the

Soviet Union, following the precepts of Lenin, takes a serious approach to certain serious errors of Stalin in the guidance of socialist construction, and to their consequences. In view of the seriousness of these errors, the CPSU is confronted with the necessity, while recognizing the great services of Stalin, of disclosing with all severity the essence of the errors committed by Stalin, calling on the whole party to avoid repeating them, resolutely to eradicate the unhealthy consequences of these errors. We, the Communists of China, are deeply convinced that after the sharp criticism which has been developed at the XX Congress of the CPSU, all the active factors which in the past were greatly restrained by certain political errors, will of necessity be set in motion everywhere, that the Communist Party of the Soviet Union and the Soviet people will be even more unified and cohesive than before in the struggle for a great communist society – which is unprecedented in the history of humanity, for a durable peace throughout the world.'

'The service of the leaders of the CPSU,' reads the statement of the Politburo of the French Communist Party, 'has been that they undertook to correct the errors and inadequacies of the cult of personality, this being evidence of the strength and unity of the great party of Lenin, of the confidence placed in it by the Soviet people, and also of its authority in the international workers' movement.' Comrade Eugene Dennis, the General Secretary of the National Committee of the Communist Party of the USA, pointed out in a well-known article the enormous significance of the XX Congress of the CPSU, stating: 'The XX Congress strengthened universal peace and social progress. It marked a new stage in the development of socialism and in the struggle for peaceful coexistence which began in the times of Lenin, was continued in subsequent years, and is now becoming more and more effective and successful.'

At the same time it should be noted that discussions of the cult of personality do not always interpret correctly the reasons for this cult and its consequences for our social order. Comrade Togliatti, for instance, in his lengthy and interesting interview in the magazine, *Nuovi Argomenti*, sets forth, in addition to many extremely important and correct conclusions, certain incorrect propositions. [For a translation of the interview see the Russian Institute (ed.), *The Anti-Stalin Campaign and International Communism* (New York: Columbia University Press, 1956), 97–139.] In particular, one cannot agree with Comrade Togliatti's treatment of the question of whether or not Soviet society manifests 'certain forms of degeneration.' There are no grounds at all for raising such an issue. It is even more incomprehensible in the light of Comrade Togliatti's entirely correct comment elsewhere in the interview: 'It must be concluded that the essence of the socialist order has not been lost since not a single one of the prior gains was lost – above all, the support given to the system by the masses of workers, peasants, and intellectuals who make up Soviet society. This support demonstrates that, despite everything, this society has retained its basically democratic character.'

Indeed, without the support of the Soviet power and the policies of the Communist Party by the broadest national masses, our country could not, in such an unprecedently short period, have created a mighty socialist industry, collectivized agriculture, and emerged victorious from the Second World War, the outcome of which determined the fate of all humanity. The complete crushing of hitlerism, Italian fascism, and Japanese militarism promoted the broad development of the communist movement, enabled the communist parties of Italy, France, and other capitalist countries to grow and obtain mass support, led to the establishment of people's democracies in many countries of Europe and Asia, to the rise and consolidation of the world-wide socialist system, to the unprecedented advances of the national-liberation movement which brought about the collapse of the imperialist system.

By their unanimous support of the decisions of the XX Congress of the CPSU, condemning the cult of personality, all Soviet people view them as testimony to the growing strength of our party, to its leninist position of principle, to its unity and cohesiveness. 'The party of the revolutionary proletariat,' said V.I. Lenin, 'is strong enough to criticize itself openly, calling mistakes and weaknesses by their true names without beating around the bush.' Guided by this leninist principle our party will boldly continue to criticize openly any errors or oversights in its work and to eliminate them vigorously.

The Central Committee considers that the party's work to date on overcoming the cult of personality and its consequences has already yielded positive results.

In the light of the decisions of the XX Party Congress the CPSU Central Committee calls upon all party organizations:
to apply consistently in all our work the major marxist-leninist doctrines on the people as the creator of history and of all the material and spiritual riches of humanity, on the decisive role of the marxist party in the revolutionary struggle to transform society and to bring about the victory of communism;
to persist in the efforts undertaken in recent years by the party Central Committee to ensure strictest observance, in all party organizations from top to bottom, of leninist principles of party leadership and, in particular, the highest such principle – collective leadership, to ensure observance of the norms of party life set forth in the rules of our party, to expand criticism and self-criticism;
to restore in full the principles of Soviet socialist democracy embodied in

the Constitution of the Soviet Union, to rectify every last violation of revolutionary socialist legality;

to mobilize our cadres, all communists and the broadest masses of the toilers, to struggle for practical realization of the goals of the Sixth Five-Year Plan, for this purpose developing in every way the creative initiative and energy of the masses – the true creators of history.

The XX Congress of the CPSU noted that a most important characteristic of our epoch is the transformation of socialism into a world-wide system. The most difficult stage in the development and consolidation of socialism is now behind. Our socialist country has ceased being a solitary island in an ocean of capitalist states. Now, under the banner of socialism, a new life is being built for more than a third of humanity. The ideas of socialism are taking possession of the minds of many millions of people in the capitalist countries. Their influence is gigantic on the peoples of Asia, Africa, and Latin America, who are rising up against all forms of colonialism.

By all partisans of peace and socialism, all democratic and progressive circles, the decisions of the XX Congress of the CPSU are perceived as an inspiring programme for the struggle to consolidate peace throughout the world, for the interests of the working class, for the triumph of socialism.

A broad and inspiring prospect is presently unfolding before the communist parties and the whole international workers' movement – the prevention of a new world war through the combined efforts of all peace-loving forces, checking the monopolies and ensuring the extended peace and security of peoples, ending the arms race and freeing the toilers from the heavy tax burden which it causes, upholding the democratic rights and liberties which enable the toilers to struggle for a better life and a brighter future. This is the vital interest of the millions of ordinary people in all the countries of the world. The successful solution of these problems is to an enormous extent promoted by the peace-loving policies and the increasing advances of the Soviet Union, the Chinese People's Republic, and all the other countries travelling the path of socialism.

Under the new historical conditions such international organizations of the working class as the Comintern and the Cominform have ceased their activities. But this in no way implies that international solidarity has lost its meaning or that the fraternal revolutionary parties holding to the marxist-leninist position no longer need to maintain contact. At the present time, when the forces of socialism and the influence of socialist ideas throughout the world have grown immeasurably and when a multiplicity of roads to socialism are becoming manifest in different countries, marxist parties of the working class must naturally maintain and strengthen their ideological unity and their international fraternal solidarity in the struggle against the threat of a new war, in the struggle against the anti-popular forces of monopoly capital which strive to stifle all revolutionary and progressive movements. The communist parties are united by their great aim of liberating the working class from the yoke of capitalism, by fidelity to the scientific ideology of marxism-leninism, to the spirit of proletarian internationalism, by selfless devotion to the interests of the popular masses.

Under contemporary conditions the activities of all communist parties reflect the national characteristics and conditions of each country, expressing in the fullest possible manner the national interests of their peoples. Realizing, however, that the struggle for the interests of the working class, for peace, and for the national independence of their countries, is at the same time the cause of the whole international proletariat, they rally together and strengthen mutual ties and cooperation. The ideological unity and fraternal solidarity of the marxist parties of the working class in different countries is the more necessary in that the capitalist monopolies are creating their own international aggressive organizations and blocs – such as NATO, SEATO, the Baghdad Pact – which are directed against the peace-loving peoples, the national-liberation movement, the working class, and against the vital interests of the toilers.

At a time when the Soviet Union has done and is doing much to relax international tension – as is now recognized by all – American monopoly capital continues to allocate huge sums for the intensification of subversive activities in the socialist countries. As is known, at the height of the 'cold war' the American Congress officially allocated 100 million dollars for subversion in the people's democracies and the Soviet Union (and this leaves aside the sums which are spent unofficially). Now, when the Soviet Union and the other socialist countries are doing everything possible to slacken international tension, the partisans of the 'cold war' are striving to activate this 'cold war' which stands condemned by the peoples of the whole world. This is seen in the decision of the American Senate to allocate an additional 25 million dollars for subversive activities – this being cynically called 'encouraging freedom' behind the 'iron curtain.'

We must soberly evaluate this fact and draw from it the appropriate conclusions. It is clear, for instance, that the anti-popular outbreaks in Poznan were financed from this source. But the provocateurs and diversionists paid from across the ocean could only keep it up for a few hours. The toilers of Poznan repulsed these hostile sallies and provocations. The plans of the shady knights of the 'cloak and dagger' collapsed, as did their infamous provocation against the people's power in Poland. Any future subversive actions in the people's democracies will collapse in the same way regardless of how generously they are paid with money allocated by the American monopolies. One might say that this money is just spent in vain.

This all goes to show that we cannot tolerate a careless attitude toward the new designs of the agents of imperialism who are striving to penetrate the socialist countries and subvert the achievements of the toilers.

The forces of international reaction are striving to deflect the toilers from the correct way of fighting for their interests, poisoning their souls with disbelief in the success of the cause of peace and socialism. But despite all the plotting of the ideologists of the capitalist monopolies, the working class, headed by its tried and true communist vanguard, will pursue its course which has led to the historic achievements of socialism and will lead to new victories for the cause of peace, democracy, and socialism. One can be confident that the communist and workers' parties of all counties will raise still higher the glorious marxist banner of proletarian internationalism.

Soviet people are justifiably proud that our motherland was the first to set the path to socialism. Now that socialism has become a world-wide system and fraternal cooperation and mutual assistance prevail among the socialist countries, new and favourable conditions have been created for the flowering of socialist democracy, for the continued consolidation of the material-productive base of communism, for the steady advance of the living standard of the toilers, for the all-around development of the new man – the builder of the communist society. Let the bourgeois ideologists invent tales about a 'crisis' of communism, about 'disarray' in the ranks of the communist parties. It is not our custom to listen to such incantations by our enemies. Their prophecies have always burst like soap bubbles. These ill-starred prophets come and go, but the communist movement, the immortal and vivifying ideas of marxism-leninism, have been and are victorious. The same will be true in the future. No malicious and slanderous thrusts by our enemies can halt the invincible historical development of humanity to communism.

Pravda, 2 July 1956   *KPSS v rezoliutsiiakh* VII, 199–218

4.13
On the Party Organizers of the Central Committee of the CPSU   7 August 1956

1   In order to extend democracy within the party still further and to heighten the responsibility of local party organs for the work of large enterprises and the most important institutions, the position of CPSU Central Committee party organizer is hereby abolished in all industrial enter-

prises, in transport, in scientific-research institutes, and in other organizations.

2 Those party organizations of enterprises and institutions in which the position of Central Committee party organizer is abolished are to establish the position of permanent secretary of the party organization, paying him at the rate fixed for Central Committee party organizers.

Spravochnik partiinogo rabotnika (1957), 429

4.14
On Improving the Work of the Soviets of Workers' Deputies and Strengthening their Ties with the Masses   22 January 1957

... In carrying out the decisions of the XX Congress of the CPSU, which set grandiose tasks of communist construction, the party and government are consistently and determinedly realizing the continued development of Soviet democracy, resolutely overcoming the harmful consequences of the personality cult and are assuring the broad participation of the working masses in the management of the state. All this has evoked a definite revival in the work of the soviets of workers' deputies and has increased their role in economic and cultural construction. The soviets have begun to devote attention to questions of improving the material well-being of and cultural and everyday services provided to the Soviet people, training the working masses in a communist spirit, and further strengthening and expanding their ties with the people ...

At the same time, the CPSU Central Committee notes that there are major short-comings in the practical work of the soviets of workers' deputies and of their executive organs and the level of work of many soviets still does not correspond to the tasks set for them by the XX Party Congress.

Many local soviets are doing a feeble job of fulfilling their functions as organizers of the masses in economic and cultural construction, are not showing sufficient concern for the vital needs of the workers, frequently ignore major negligence in housing construction, and show little initiative and persistence in improving the work of schools, hospitals, baths, children's establishments, clubs and libraries, stores, public dining halls, and other enterprises and institutions whose job it is to serve the public.

The facts show that in places where party and soviet organs show true concern for the needs of the people and tackle the matter with the necessary energy, results are quickly achieved. In this regard all manner of praise is due the initiative taken by the party and soviet organizations of the city of Gorky. Early last year the city soviet, with the active participation of the deputies, standing committees, and the soviet aktiv, [the more senior and responsible officials] worked out a detailed plan for housing and cultural construction and for municipal improvement. The plan in question was reviewed and approved at a session of the soviet and broad masses of the public were enlisted in the actual carrying out of the plan. Utilizing existing capabilities and local resources, the people of Gorky almost doubled the construction of housing in the course of a single year, opening 116,000 square metres of housing to tenancy; they laid 22 km of new trolley lines and opened 11 km of trolley-bus lines, brought the roads and sidewalks of 50 streets up to modern standards, and planted 100,000 trees and 200,000 shrubs. The soviets of workers' deputies of Moscow, Leningrad, Kiev, Minsk, Stalingrad, Omsk, Ryazan and Irkutsk are also doing major work in housing construction and urban improvement with the broad participation of the public ...

It is a most important task of the central committees of union-republic communist parties and of krai, oblast, city, and raion party committees to eliminate short-comings in the work of the local soviets in the shortest possible time, and to assure an increased role for the soviets and their executive organs in implementing the policy of the party and government in economic and cultural construction. It is necessary to direct the activities of the soviets on a daily basis toward the solution of urgent problems of economic and cultural life, to expand their ties with the people in every way, and to help the soviets to actually become geniune organizers of the masses in the struggle to further strengthen our socialist state.

In carrying out the decisions of the December [1956] Plenum of the Central Committee, the local soviets and their executive committees must strengthen their influence on, and responsibility for, the work of industry and agriculture, and strive toward fulfilment of production plans and targets by every plant, factory, construction site, kolkhoz, sovkhoz, and MTS. It is necessary that soviet organs constantly concern themselves with the construction and repair of housing, schools, hospitals, children's establishments and municipal enterprises and organizations and with their normal functioning in providing services to the public, with modernization and improvement of the work of urban transportation and communications. The soviets must show greater initiative in seeking out and utilizing local building materials and in expanding private housing construction; they must exercise effective supervision to ensure the correct expenditure of money and materials and not permit them to become overly dispersed or 'frozen,' and resolutely put a stop to all manner of excesses that increase the cost of construction.

Equally responsible tasks confront the soviets in improving state and co-operative trade and in supplying the population with articles of prime necessity. The soviets of workers' deputies must put the work of every store and of public catering enterprises into proper order; they must assure decent service to the consumer, resolutely combat all manner of abuses and take concrete steps to utilize local resources in order to develop the production of food products and consumer goods in every way, while giving all manner of encouragement to initiative and new departures in this matter on the part of soviet, economic, and co-operative organizations.

In the interests of further improvement in the end of work of local soviets and of increasing their responsibility for an upswing in the economy and culture, it is necessary for the central committees, the presidiums of the supreme soviets and the councils of ministers of the union republics to take practical steps in the near future, based on the decisions of the December Plenum of the Central Committee, to increase the powers of the soviets, and to do so above all in matters of planning krai, oblast, city and raion economies; the production and distribution of the output of enterprises of local and cooperative industry; the organization of housing, cultural and highway construction; the extensive development of fuel and building materials production; and in solving financial and budgetary questions ...

The Central Committee considers that the soviets of workers' deptuties are doing a poor job of utilizing the powers granted them under the Constitution in solving questions of economic and cultural construction, in directing the organs of management and enterprises that are subordinated to them, in assuring the safeguarding of public order and of citizens' rights and the observance of socialist legality. These most important questions in the practical work of the soviets are rarely brought before sessions for consideration. Many executive committees, heads of executive committee administrations and departments, and directors of economic organizations are not being held accountable to the soviets, which results in an absence of supervision and a weakening of the directing role of the soviets as the organs of state power at the local level. In many instances sessions of the soviets limit themselves to discussion of minor questions of a current nature, are conducted in a formalistic fashion, at times simply to parade forth approval of the draft decisions prepared by the executive committees. As a consequence, the sessions are conducted in a passive fashion; shortcomings and mistakes in the work of soviet organs and of their executives are not subjected to sharp criticism; proposals made by deputies often receive no attention, while decisions adopted lack concreteness and abound in general appeals and declarations.

Party and soviet organs must take every measure to activize the role of the soviets, increase their militancy, and see to it that they make full use of their powers. It is necessary to ensure that sessions are regularly convened and to broaden substantially the range of questions dealt with at them. The sessions must not be held for purposes of show or for bestowing ceremonious, formal approval on measures worked out beforehand, but for businesslike discussion and solution of topical questions of the economic and cultural life of the krai, oblast, city, and raion, such as economic plans, the budget, the work of industry, the development of agriculture, the state of housing and cultural everyday construction and of municipal affairs, the work of public education organs and public health, trade, public catering, and militia organs, questions of safeguarding socialist property and the personal property of citizens, and of the fight against crime. They must regularly hear and discuss reports from the executive committees as well as from the heads of appropriate branches of the soviet and economic apparatus; and reports on the carrying out of mandates from the electors.

A situation must be created at sessions of soviets in which a broad development of criticism and self-criticism is assured, in order that the deputies may discuss questions thoroughly, without haste, so that they can express their comments and proposals, make inquiries of the executive organs and economic directors and receive exhaustive answers to them. Procedures must be established under which executive committees report at sessions to the deputies on the fundamental aspects of their work in the period between sessions, as well as on fulfilment of the soviet's decisions. Leaders of executive committees and of their administrations and departments are obliged to give detailed replies to, and explanations of measures taken on, the critical remarks, inquiries, and proposals of deputies.

An end must be put to the abnormal situation wherby the population essentially does not know what questions are being dealt with and what decisions taken by the local soviets and their executive organs. The task is one of assuring that the work of soviets is made public, that their work is extensively treated in the local press and on the radio and that the population is informed about decisions which have been taken. After each session, as a rule, the deputies must meet with their constituents, inform them of the decisions taken and conduct organizational work for their fulfilment at the local level ...

There are serious short-comings in the organizational work of soviets among the masses. Many soviets and their executive committees do not base their work on a broad aktiv of workers and have poor ties with the public. Leaders of executive committees and their departments frequently do not consider it their duty to give reports to workers on the work of the soviets, do not regularly receive visitors; and hence in many cases citizens' legitimate grievances are not acted upon. For instance, the chairman and deputy chairman of the Fergana Oblast Executive Committee receive few workers, violate the established procedure for receiving citizens, and are frequently absent on the days when hours are scheduled for receiving the public. The deputies of the Stavropol Krai Soviet are rightly critical of their executive committee for its poor contacts with the localities and for its ignorance of the daily life of the raions, kolkhozes, sovkhozes, and machine tractor stations. Unfortunately, there are similar short-comings in the work of other local soviets' executive committees as well. And there are also quite a few deputies to the soviets who rarely meet with their constituents, with the masses, and in so doing, lose their sense of responsibility to the people.

The Central Committee draws the attention of all party and soviet organizations to the necessity of significantly improving the soviets' organizational work and work with the masses, and for further strengthening their contacts with the public. Particular attention must be devoted to improving work with deputies, to activizing their work in the soviets and among constituents. The deputies to soviets must constantly be in the thick of the people, know the needs, requirements and moods of the masses, regularly meet with constituents, receive them, carefully review statements and complaints from the public, and render assistance in resolving them. Party organizations and soviet executive committees must promote meetings of deputies with their constituents and regular reports by them on their work and the work of the soviet.

In view of the fact that the right, provided for in the Constitution, to recall deputies who have not justified the electorate's confidence is a right that, in fact, is never exercised for want of an established procedure for recalling deputies, the presidiums of the supreme soviets of union and autonomous republics must in the near future work out statutes laying down procedures for the recall of deputies to the local soviets.

Improving the work of soviets depends to a great extent on correctly organizing the work of the executive organs. The executive committees of soviets and their departments are called upon to carry out direct, day to day guidance of cultural, political, and economic construction, to show concern for satisfying the needs and requirements of the working people and to implement the decisions of the soviets and superior state organs. In all their activities the executive committees must rely on the deputies and on a large soviet aktiv; they must scrupulously observe the principle of collectiveness in the work of soviets and not permit the executive committees to supplant the soviets in the solution of questions under consideration at the sessions ...

Standing commissions are of major importance for the practical work of the soviets and for strengthening their ties with the masses. Deserving of approval in this regard is the work of the standing commissions of the Moscow City Soviet of Workers' Deputies, which actively promote the carrying out of the decisions of the soviet and of superior state organs, assist the executive committee in organizing the fulfilment of the plan for the development of the municipal economy. The commissions regularly check the work of the departments and administrations of the Moscow City

Soviet's Executive Committee, and of their subordinate enterprises and establishments; they reveal short-comings in their work and help to eliminate them. Significant work is also being done by the standing commissions of the Dzerzhinsky Raion Soviet of Workers' Deputies in Minsk Oblast. With the broad participation of agronomists, zootechnicians, mechanizers, and the kolkhoz aktiv, the agricultural commission of this soviet regularly prepares and introduces for the consideration of the executive committee and sessions of the soviets important questions concerning the development of the raion's agriculture and conducts persistent organizational work in implementing decisions that have been adopted. However, the standing commissions are still not doing good work everywhere. In many soviets the commissions have only a formal existence and do not enlist an aktiv of workers, collective farmers, and intelligentsia in their work.

Party organs and soviet executive committees must improve seriously the work of standing commissions, must assure their active role in preparing questions for discussion at sessions and at meetings of the executive committees, in overseeing the carrying out of the decisions of soviets and superior organs, and in conducting organizational work among the masses. Standing commissions must participate in the working out of draft decisions; they must deliver co-reports at the sessions, participate in the discussion of economic plans, and oversee the work of enterprises and establishments that are accountable for their work to the soviet. The executive committees, departments, and administrations are obliged to consider the proposals of standing commissions and take practical measures based on them. The powers of the commissions should also be expanded. It is expedient, for instance, to establish a procedure whereby the housing commissions of the soviets conduct a preliminary review of requests for housing and make recommendations on the order in which individual housing needs are to be satisfied, and participate in solving questions concerning the distribution of housing space ...

The Central Committee thinks that a most important task of all party organizations, soviets of workers' deputies, and their executive committees consists in further perfecting the work of the soviet apparatus, in waging a resolute struggle against instances of bureaucratism and red tape, and against inattentive attitudes toward the needs of the public in the work of every establishment and enterprise, and above all in the work of the executive committees themselves and in their administrations and departments.

The facts show that the vital needs of the working people are often poorly satisfied not because the local soviets lack the conditions and material capabilities to do so, but because of bureaucratism and red tape, and because of the irresponsibility of certain staff members of the soviets who have lost their ties with the people and who do not see the living people behind the pieces of papers ...

Our party, as the leading and directing force of Soviet society, is responsible for everything that is done in the country, for the work of the soviets, trade unions, Komsomol, and of all mass public organizations of the working people. Party organizations also bear direct responsibility for the major short-comings that exist in the work of the local soviets. It must be admitted that in many cases party organs, in their practical work of directing the soviets, are guilty of interference in the administrative and managerial functions of the soviet organs, preempt their functions in deciding economic and other questions, and forget the highly important party instruction that 'The functions of party collectives must never be confused with the functions of state organs such as the soviets. The party must implement its decisions through the soviet organs, *within the framework of the Soviet Constitution*. The party strives to guide the work of the soviets, but not to supplant them.' [From a decision of the VIII Party Congress, 1919.]

The Central Committee orders all party organizations resolutely to put an end to needless tutelage over, and petty interference in, the work of the soviets and their executive committees, and to assure a continued development of initiative and independence in the work of the soviets. It should be borne in mind that the raion, city, and oblast party committees cannot take the place of the soviet organs or make up through their own activities for deficiencies in the work of the organs of state management.

Correct guidance of the soviets by party committees consists above all in strengthening soviet organs with experienced, well-trained workers who show initiative and are capable of implementing the party line. It is necessary to patiently instil in the leading cadres of the soviets a spirit of strict responsibility for assigned work, an irreconcilable attitude toward short-comings in the work of the soviet apparatus and the values of strengthening state discipline. It is also necessary to put an end to the practice of co-optation to elective posts in the soviets and of relieving soviet staff workers of their duties without a decision by the soviets of workers' deputies.

The party committees must activate the work of the party groups in the soviets and executive committees and increase their role in, and responsibility for, the work of those organs. At present party groups in soviets are, for the most part, doing an unsatisfactory job of fulfilling their functions as set forth in the CPSU Rules; to a significant degree their work has a formal bent, they seldom meet and do not discuss questions of the work of Communists in the given soviet. This situation cannot be regarded as normal; it is harmful to party guidance of the Soviet organs. It is necessary to see to it that all directives of party organs concerning the work of the soviets are carried out through the Communists who work in the soviets and through the party groups of the executive committees and sessions of the soviets ...

The Central Committees orders party and soviet bodies to take advantage of the forthcoming elections to local soviets of workers' deputies to enliven all the activities of soviets and to assure election to them of worthy representatives of the workers, collective farmers, and intelligentsia.

Elections to the soviets will take place in the setting of the major political and production upsurge occasioned by the decisions of the XX Party Congress. The further development of socialist democratism has increased the activism of the working people and strengthened the control of the masses over the work of the soviets, executive committees, and deputies. In these conditions one can expect that criticism of the organs of state power and of our staff workers will be sharper, that demandingness toward deputies will be increased, and that there will be a significant increase in the vigour with which candidate deputies will be discussed. Party organs and local soviets and their officials must adopt a correct attitude toward the criticism of the masses and take measures to eliminate short-comings in the work of soviet organs.

At the same time it must be borne in mind that certain hostile, anti-Soviet elements are attempting to utilize the electoral campaign for the purpose of slander against the Soviet system and to depict existing, individual bureaucratic distortions as characteristic of the entire state apparatus, as it were, in order to discredit it. Party organizations must deliver a resolute rebuff to hostile and demagogic elements and come to the defense of honest and conscientious workers nominated for the post of deputy ...

In the forthcoming elections the Communist Party, as before, will act together with the trade unions, Komsomol, and other organizations and societies of the working people. Therefore candidates for the post of deputy must be joint candidates of the bloc of communists and non-party members.

There must be no haste in the nomination of candidates; candidacies should first be discussed at workers' meetings by individual shops and at kolkhozniks' meetings by the various brigades; differences should be thrashed out and a consensus arrived at, and only then should a single candidacy be proposed to a general meeting of the collective.

It cannot be regarded as normal when, as in years past, few workers and collective farmers engaged directly in production work were elected to the soviets and when a certain portion of the candidates for deputy were nominated strictly on the basis of the jobs they held and were elected deputies to several soviets concurrently. This situation must be corrected and steps taken to make sure that a broader representation of workers and collective farmers is elected to the soviets ...

Spravochnik partiinogo rabotnika (1957), 448-57

KPSS v rezoliutsiiakh VII, 237-48

4.15
On the Organization of the Publication of Works about V.I. Lenin
11 October 1956

The following decision is unusual in that it specifically countermands earlier party decisions, which were attributed to the Politburo and Secretariat. Although one would assume that these bodies do in fact issue many decisions in the name of the Central Committee, this is a rare public reference to decisions taken in their own name (and taken secretly). In this connection it is also worth noting that in such a sensitive area as the Lenin image even minor literary works had to be submitted to the highest party executive bodies for censorship, and that in Stalin's later years the policy was consciously to diminish publications about Lenin. (This practice did not, however, prevent the fourth edition of Lenin's own works from appearing after the Second World War.) While condemning the former policy in this area, the decision of 1956 did not by any means remove all high-level controls on publications concerning Lenin or on the dissemination of earlier works. For example, the writings of Trotsky on Lenin did not reappear in Soviet libraries.

[Resolved:] To acknowledge that the resolutions of the Politburo of the Central Committee of the VKB (b) of 4 August 1938 'On Marietta Shaginian's novel *Passport to History*, Part I, *The Ulianov Family*' and of the Secretariat of the Central Committee of the VKP (b) of 26 August 1947 'On S. Gil's Booklet *Six Years with V.I. Lenin*' were mistaken and fundamentally incorrect. These resolutions established the organization of publication of works about V.I. Lenin in such a way as to retard the publication of scholarly works, memoirs, and artistic works about V.I. Lenin and actually led to their suppression.

In order to create more favourable conditions for the full and all-round illumination of the life and activities of V.I. Lenin and the popularization of the ideas of leninism, the Central Committee of the CPSU resolves:

1 To revoke ... [the above-noted decisions] as incorrect.
2 To establish the right of publishing houses to decide for themselves

questions concerning the publication of scholarly and artistic works about V.I. Lenin.

To propose to publishing houses that they review anew those works about V.I. Lenin that were formerly rejected for insufficient reason and to decide whether to issue them. It is considered necessary to reissue the more valuable books, brochures, articles, and memoirs about V.I. Lenin that were previously published.

3   To publish memoirs about V.I. Lenin in the form of books, brochures, and scholarly biographies with the consent of the Institute of Marxism-Leninism of the Central Committee of the CPSU.

4   To propose to Glavlit of the USSR, working with the Institute of Marxism-Leninism of the Central Committee of the CPSU, to consider the question of returning to the open collections of libraries those works about V.I. Lenin that were formerly incorrectly removed from circulation.

Spravochnik partiinogo rabotnika
(1956), 364

Plenum of the Central Committee   13–14 February 1957

The February 1957 Plenum of the Central Committee discussed a report by Khrushchev on reorganizing the structure of industrial management in the Soviet Union. This plenum, which laid the groundwork for subsequent enactment by the Supreme Soviet on 10 May 1957 of the law establishing the more than one hundred sovnarkhozes, is considered to have been a major victory for Khrushchev. Only two months before, at the December 1956 Plenum of the Central Committee, the existing system of ministerial control of the economy had, with only minor changes, been reconfirmed. The February Plenum elected F.R. Kozlov a candidate member of the Presidium and re-elected D.T. Shepilov a secretary of the Central Committee.

4.16
On Further Improving the Organization of the
Management of Industry and Construction   14 February 1957

... The development of a socialist economy poses the need for constantly improving the organizational forms and methods of planning and managing industry and construction. A further improvement in the organization of the management of the economy is of immense importance for the unbroken growth of production, for increasing the well-being of the people, and for a fuller utilization of reserves in the economy.

Already in the early years of Soviet government, V.I. Lenin, in mapping out the programme of economic construction, specified that a most important principle of socialist management is the principle of democratic centralism and that socialist construction can be conducted successfully only on the basis of a unified state plan.

The history of the development of the economy of the USSR has confirmed the great vital force of leninist principles of the management of socialist construction, which opened up unlimited possibilities for the active participation of the masses of people in the management of production. The forms of organizational management of economic construction have developed and been improved apace with the growth of the economy and of the country's productive forces. During the transition from solution of the tasks of the restoration period to the implementation of a broad programme of socialist industrialization of the country, when the need arose to create – in a brief period of time – completely new branches of industry, there also arose the need for new organizational forms for the management of economic construction. At that stage people's commissariats and main administrations – and subsequently ministries and departments – specialized according to the major branches of the national economy, were set up. These forms of economic management made it possible to concentrate the efforts of the party and state on creating the decisive branches of heavy industry and on preparing highly qualified engineering and technical cadres, economists, and organizers of production capable of mastering the new technology and of organizing industrial production on a modern scientific and technical level and on a wide scale.

In the post-war years our country's economy made a major step forward and entered into a new and higher stage of development. Over the course of the development of the socialist economy there is an increasingly apparent tendency toward the creation of ever newer branches of industry and construction, toward a further and constantly more profound specialization. This is connected with the growth of new technology, with the tasks of technical progress, with the new achievements of science, which call forth major qualitative changes in the organization of modern industrial production. As industry develops, one is confronted with a question of increasing urgency: should one continue to proceed in the sphere of organizational forms for the management of industry along the line of a further splintering of technical, economic, and administrative management by creating at the center a constant succession of new specialized branch ministries and departments, or should one, rather, seek more flexible forms for managing the economy, forms that are better suited to the features peculiar to the given stage of development?

In recent years the party has carried out a number of important measures to improve the management of the economy. In noting the fundamental short-comings in the practice of state planning, the December 1956 Plenum of the Central Committee pointed out the need to improve the work of the central planning organs and to expand the powers of the union republics and local soviet and party bodies in economic construction.

A major short-coming in the practice of managing industry and construction is the negative influence of the ministries' departmentalism in their approach to the solution of highly important questions in the development of the economy. Departmentalism in the management of industry and construction leads to a weakening and destruction of the normal territorial ties between enterprises of various branches of industry located in a single economic region, and frequently rules out the possibility of solving economic questions locally, in an operative fashion, of utilizing existing material, labour and financial resources in an expedient fashion, and of taking operative measures to do away with short-comings that have come to light during the fulfillment of state plans.

Departmental boundaries hamper extensive specialization and co-operation of production and retard the complex development of the economies of economic regions, republics, krais, and oblasts. As a result, immense enterprise production capacities go unutilized and considerable irrational hauling of freight occurs. The division of construction management among various ministries leads to the creation in a single area of a large number of small construction organizations, to a scattering of construction funds, to freezing of state construction assets, and to increased construction costs.

Ministries and departments, in conducting from the centre the management of enterprises located throughout the country, inevitably spawn a large number of organizations with parallel functions – various sales and supply offices, installations, trusts, etc.

Under the existing management structure, large numbers of talented production organizers and engineering and technical personnel – people who have an expert knowledge of practical work – are diverted from direct participation in production into the central apparatus of the ministries and departments. A significant portion of them settle for ever in the offices of ministries and departments. A big short-coming in the present management structure of industry and construction is the fact that it restricts the opportunities of local party, soviet, and trade union organs in directing economic construction, and hampers their initiative in mobilizing the forces of the enterprises and economic organizations for a fuller and more correct utilization of local reserves and capabilities.

Under present-day conditions, when our industry and construction have undergone immense development, and state enterprises, which number over 200,000, and more than 100,000 construction sites, are located in various republics and regions across the entire expanse of the country – under these conditions it is a practical impossibility to direct the large number of enterprises or construction sites from a single ministry or department in a concrete and operative fashion. With this scale of production, the existing structure for the management of industry and construction does not correspond to the increased demands; it limits possibilities for utilizing the reserves inherent in the socialist economic system.

The interests of further development of the economy confront us with the need to improve the organizational forms of management at all levels of industry and construction, including its very basis, the management of production. In so doing, the organizational structure for the management of industry and construction must be based on the combining of centralized state guidance with an increased role for the local economic, party and trade union organs in the management of the economy. The centre of gravity for the operative management of industry and construction must be transferred to the local level. Keeping in mind the need to eliminate serious short-comings of departmentalism in the management of the economy, it is expedient to organize the management of industry and construction according to basic economic regions, which will bring management closer to production, make it more concrete and operative, and make it possible to enlist the broad masses of the working people in the management of economic construction.

The introduction of a new management structure for industry and construction will make it possible to do a significantly better job of organizing cooperation, to utilize more fully the production capacities of enterprises and the funds allocated for capital construction, and to eliminate more quickly irrational hauling of freight. It will also provide an opportunity to eliminate unnecessary links in management and to bring order into many economic questions that are in a state of confusion today, in particular, the exceptionally important question of the material and technical supply of enterprises and construction sites.

The reorganization of management will exercise a positive influence on the development of science and on unifying the efforts of scientists and specialists from various spheres of learning to serve more efficiently the needs of industry and construction, and will improve the geographic distribution of scientific institutes and higher and secondary educational institutions.

Implementation of the reorganization of the management of industry and construction will assure a further strengthening of the leninist principle of democratic centralism and of the planning principle in the management of the country's economy. V.I. Lenin often stressed that in implementing centralized guidance of socialist construction by the Soviet state and Communist Party, it is necessary to enlist extensively the local bodies in the solution of economic questions ...

Under the new structure for economic management better conditions will be created for enlisting broad circles of workers, engineering and technical intelligentsia, and other strata of society actively in the work of managing enterprises, the various branches of industry and the entire economy. Reorganization of the management of industry and construction will open still broader possibilities for the truly creative participation of our party, soviet, trade union, and Komsomol organizations in the management of the economy.

The management of industry according to the territorial principle, on the basis of distinct economic regions, will make it possible to improve the utilization of local resources for the development of industrial production, fundamentally to set right the question of production specialization and co-operation, more extensively to utilize local initiative both to increase the volume of industrial production and also to improve the qualitative indices of industrial enterprises' work.

Taking into account the fact that the level of development of productive forces of the country, union republics, and economic regions has grown considerably, and that party, soviet, economic, engineering and technical, and trade union cadres have grown up in the localities, the plenum resolves:

1   That it finds it necessary to take measures to further improve the management of industry and construction in order to bring them to a condition that measures up to the tasks and demands of the economy at the present stage of communist construction, the intent being to bring management closer to the economic regions, to expand the powers of the union and autonomous republics, to increase the role of the local party and soviet organizations – as well as trade union and other public organizations – in economic construction, and more extensively to enlist the masses in the management of production.

In view of the fact that the existing forms of management of industry and construction by means of specialized ministries leads to the creation of departmental barriers that impede the full utilization of the immense reserves and possibilities of our economy and that do not provide concrete and operative management of enterprises and construction sites, it is desirable to replace these forms by working out other forms for the management of economic construction, forms that will more fully combine concrete and operative management by economic regions with strict observance of the centralized planning principle on a national scale.

2   To assign to the Central Committee Presidium and the Council of

Ministers the job of working out concrete proposals for reorganizing the management of industry and construction in the sense indicated and, in view of the great state importance of the question, to submit it for consideration by the Supreme Soviet.

In working out practical measures, provision must be made for the need to increase the role of Gosplan in the planning and management of the country's economy, and to reorganize the work of the State Economic Commission; to raise the level of the engineering and technical management of industry and construction and to conduct a proper technical policy on a nation-wide scale; to increase the role of the financial organs in financing and in the mobilization of funds to assure a further upswing in the economy; to assure supervision over the observance of national interests and state discipline; to improve the work of the agencies of state control at the centre and locally, and also to further strengthen the entire system of state statistics.

While continuing to strengthen in every way the planning principle in the development of the country's economy, it is necessary fundamentally to reorganize the work of Gosplan so that it will base itself, in its work, on the bodies being set up in the economic regions and will submit promptly all highly important long-range questions to the government and the Central Committee for their consideration.

While being guided by the general party line of preferential development for heavy industry as the basis for a further upswing in the economy, for strengthening the country's might, increasing its defence capability, and for a continuous growth in the people's material well-being, Gosplan must direct its efforts toward a correct and rational location of our industry, a balanced development of all its branches, and toward specialization and co-operation, proceeding from the concrete conditions of the development of industry in the various regions, the existing historical and cultural experience, and the existing specialization of the regions and prospects for their development.

It is necessary to reorganize the work of the State Economic Commission to simplify its structure and make it less cumbersome; the State Economic Commission must not duplicate the work of Gosplan and other bodies and must not interfere in the functions of administrative management; its responsibility, apart from current planning, is to co-ordinate the work of the directing organs of the economic regions in the fulfillment of the annual plans.

With the aim of assuring constant technical progress in the development of the national economy, the creation of a special body attached to the government of the USSR must be envisaged; it will be the task of this body to follow the trends and level of technological development both within the country and abroad, to make a profound study of everything new and progressive in technology, to work out recommendations for the further improvement of technology and submit them for consideration by the government, and to carry out a number of other measures.

The reorganization of the management of industry and the economy will necessitate a thorough reorganization of the work content and methods of exercising state control. It is essential that the basic work of control be centred on the economic regions so that short-comings in the work of the state and economic apparatus will be brought to light and eliminated locally; the organs of state control, both at the centre and locally, must base themselves in all their work on the broad masses of the working people.

The plenum considers that a reorganization of the management of industry and construction will lead to a further strengthening of the leninist principle of democratic centralism in economic construction, will give still greater scope to the development of the country's productive forces, will make it possible to utilize more fully the immense reserves for a new powerful upswing in the socialist economy of our homeland, to develop fully the creative initiative and activity of the broadest masses of the toilers, and to assure a steady growth of the well-being of the Soviet people.

Pravda, 16 February 1957   *KPSS v rezoliutsiiakh* VII, 249–56

4.17
On the Journal *Voprosy Istorii*   9 March 1957

In the Soviet Union interpretations of past events are directly related to contemporary political tendencies, and intimate the limits of future possibilities. Khrushchev's 'secret speech' and Mikoyan's scathing criticism of party historiography at the XX Party Congress created an opportunity for those specialists on party history interested in restoring objectivity in this key area of history writing to accelerate the demolition of stalinist myths already begun in 1955, and at the same time to challenge the power and privileges of academics and propaganda officials with vested interests in the old dogmas. In the months following the XX Congress the leading history journal, *Voprosy Istorii* (*Problems of History*), published by the Academy of Sciences and guided by its editor Anna Pankratova and outspoken anti-stalinist assistant editor E.N. Burdzhalov, published articles which raised – albeit implicitly, in the historical mode – a series of highly sensitive political issues: the relationship between communism and democratic socialism; treatment of the non-

Russian nationalities; policy toward the peasantry; the question of leadership and participation in the political system; responsibility for crimes of the Stalin era; the right of access to political information, and so forth. As the conservative counter-attack against 'revisionism' gained momentum following the Hungarian Revolution, *Voprosy Istorii* – which had failed to heed informal criticism – became a strategic target. The resolution below which resulted from this shift in political line led to the purging of the journal's editorial board and steered historiography into safer waters.

The Central Committee of the CPSU notes that since the XX Party Congress of the CPSU the journal *Voprosy Istorii* has published a number of interesting materials on questions of historical science. At the same time the journal has committed theoretical and methodological errors revealing a tendency to depart from the leninist principle of a party approach to history.

The leading article entitled 'The Twentieth Congress and the Tasks of Research in Party History' (no. 3, 1956) and the editorial 'On Bugaev's Article' (no. 7), Comrade Moskalenko's article (no. 8), and certain others slur over the differences in principle between the Bolsheviks and the Mensheviks on such an important issue as the hegemony of the proletariat during the revolution, embellish the role of the Mensheviks and belittle the leading role of the Bolsheviks in the revolution of 1905–07, fail to give a leninist criticism of the splitting activities of the Mensheviks and of their opportunism in fundamental revolutionary questions, distort the history of the party's struggle to establish an alliance between the working class and the peasantry. In discussing the party's struggle with the trotskyites and the right opportunists the magazine fails to mention that in their struggle against the party they passed beyond the limits of Soviet legality.

The article, 'Bolshevik Tactics in March-April 1917,' published in issue no. 4 of the journal, and also Comrade Burdzhalov's speeches at readers' conferences, have endeavoured to overemphasize Zinoviev's role in 1917, in the guise of a critique of the cult of personality, taking an objectivist approach to problems of our party's ideological and political struggle. Through unconscientious research in the historical documents he has tried to show that before Lenin's return to Russia the party occupied an essentially semi-Menshevik position and that tendencies toward 'unification' with the Mensheviks were strong in it.

The articles in issues 1 and 7 (1956) of *Voprosy Istorii* in effect have oriented Soviet historians toward a relaxation in the struggle against bourgeois ideology in historiography. Noteworthy is the journal's failure to criticize the revisionist and nationalistic outbursts which have been particularly widespread in the Yugoslav press.

The editor-in-chief of the journal, Comrade Pankratova, and the deputy-editor, Comrade Burdzhalov, for a long time have rejected any criticism of their journal. In his work as editor Comrade Burdzhalov has been crudely violating the principles of collective leadership.

The Central Committee resolves:

1   A number of articles in the journal, *Voprosy Istorii*, which incorrectly elucidate certain matters of principle in the history of the CPSU, are recognized as erroneous.

The editorial board of the journal *Voprosy Istorii* is directed to observe consistently the leninist principle of a party approach to historical science and to struggle resolutely against manifestations of bourgeois ideology and attempts to revise marxism-leninism.

2   The editor-in-chief of the journal, *Voprosy Istorii*, Comrade A. M. Pankratova, is to be shown the serious errors which she has committed in her leadership of the journal.

3   For his mistakes in leadership, the deputy-editor of *Voprosy Istorii*, Comrade E.N. Burdzhalov, is to be relieved of his position.

4   Comrade N.I. Matiushkin is appointed first deputy to the editor-in-chief of *Voprosy Istorii* and is hereby relieved of his position as deputy-editor to deal with problems of the history of foreign countries.

5   The Science, Institutions of Higher Education and Schools Section, and the Propaganda and Agitation Section of the CPSU Central Committee, as well as the Presidium of the USSR Academy of Sciences, are directed to undertake measures to strengthen the editorial board and the editorial staff of the journal.

Spravochnik partiinogo rabotnika
(1957), 381–2

4.18
On Released Secretaries of Primary Party Organizations   21 May 1957

The CPSU Central Committee notes that in all oblasts, krais, and republics the number of released secretaries has in recent years sharply increased in those small primary party organizations in which – according to the CPSU Rules – this work should, as a rule, be done by people not released from their other employment. At the present time the number of paid workers in primary party organizations has increased almost five times since 1940, while the network of party organizations has only approximately doubled in the same period.

Such a situation does not correspond with the party line which calls for the all-round development of the initiative and independent action of communists, for a reduction in the size and expense of the salaried staff. The existence of released secretaries in small primary party organizations inhibits the growth of activity of the communists and creates in their minds the incorrect idea that party work can be successfully conducted only by paid officials. All this hinders the growth and advancement of low-level party cadres and their training in active party political work.

The Central Committee of the CPSU resolves:

1   In establishing the position of released secretary of a primary party organization in an industrial enterprise, an institution, or an institution of higher education, local party organs must be strictly guided by the requirement of the CPSU Rules that party work in primary party organizations containing not more than 100 party members be conducted, as a rule, by persons who have not been released from their productive employment.

2   When the specific working conditions warrant, it shall be possible to retain those released secretaries who have already been appointed to primary party organizations in coal and peat mines, other kinds of mines, oil fields, railroads, water transport organizations, and lumbering and construction undertakings possessing not less than 50 Communists, and of party organizations in sovkhozes and MTSs possessing not less than 25 Communists.

3   The oblast and krai committees and the central committees of the union-republic parties are charged with reviewing the situation and abolishing any unnecessary positions of paid party workers in primary party organizations, bringing their numbers into agreement with paragraphs one and two of this resolution and reporting on their results within one month to the CPSU Central Committee.

4   The CPSU Central Committee decree of 31 August 1949, establishing released secretaries in the party organizations of all sovkhozes in the first and second groups is hereby superseded.

5   The oblast and krai committees and the central committees of the union-republic parties in the future are permitted, in accordance with this decree, to appoint released secretaries of primary party organizations within the limits of existing staff and salary figures for paid party workers at the oblast, krai, or republic level; such appointments are to be reported to the CPSU Central Committee.

Instead of establishing the post of released secretary of a party organization under paragraphs 1 and 2 of this decree, the oblast and krai committees, and the central committees of the union-republic parties may, without exceeding the appropriate account, make supplementary payments to secretaries of party organizations who have not been released from productive work; such payments shall be between one quarter and one half of the salary of a secretary but not more than 700 rubles per month.

6 Requests by local party organizations for approval of additional released party workers in primary party organizations will only be examined by the CPSU Central Committee at the end of the year, during approval of the party budget.

Spravochnik partiinogo rabotnika
(1957), 440–1

Plenum of the Central Committee 22–29 June 1957

The June 1957 Plenum of the Central Committee dealt with the factional fight among the Soviet leaders. The plenum was the climax of a struggle between Khrushchev and his opponents in the party Presidium over power and policy issues. Members of the 'anti-party group,' as the losers in the fight were later labelled, had by no means shared the same views on all questions since 1953. At one or another time individual members of the group are known to have resisted Khrushchev on such major issues as policy toward the West, rapprochement with Yugoslavia, destalinization and rehabilitation of victims of the terror, industrial growth rates, industrial reorganization, the virgin lands' campaign, and nationality policy. Basically, members of the 'anti-party group' were united by a common opposition to Khrushchev's assertive behaviour and non-'ideological' approach to problems, and by fear for their own careers (or even lives). The party Presidium met from 18 June to 22 June to consider the expulsion of Khrushchev from membership. For several days Khrushchev had only minority support – probably from Kirichenko, Mikoyan, and Suslov among the full members. It later became clear that the anti-khrushchevites had for a time included not only Malenkov, Molotov, and Kaganovich, but also Bulganin, Voroshilov, Pervukhin, Saburov, and the candidate member Shepilov. By the 22nd, when the Central Committee plenum was convened, it appears that the anti-Khrushchev front in the Presidium had already cracked – probably because the army and KGB had come to Khrushchev's aid. The plenum expelled 'Comrades' Malenkov, Kaganovich, and Molotov from the Presidium and Central Committee and removed 'Comrade' Shepilov from his posts of Central Committee secretary and candidate member of the Presidium. The voting on the following resolution was not formally unanimous even after it had become apparent that the Khrushchev faction had carried the day. Molotov remained recalcitrant and would not, as his colleagues had, implicitly confess his guilt by voting for the resolution. Instead he abstained, the first recorded breach in unanimity in Central Committee voting since 1927.

Because of the thoroughgoing split in the party leadership culminating in this contest, a new Presidium had to be elected. It consisted of A. B. Aristov, N. I. Beliaev, L. I. Brezhnev, N. A. Bulganin, K.E. Voroshilov, G.R. Zhukov, N.G. Ignatov, A.I. Kirichenko, F.R. Kozlov, O.V. Kuusinen, A.I. Mikoyan, M.A. Suslov, G.A. Furtseva, N.S. Khrushchev, and N.S. Shvernik as full members and N.A. Mukhidinov, P.N. Pospelov, D.S. Korotchenko, Ia. E. Kalnberzin, A.P. Kirilenko, A.N. Kosygin, K.T. Mazurov, V.P. Mzhavanadze, and M.G. Pervukhin as candidates. Kuusinen was also elected to the Secretariat.

4.19
On the Anti-Party Group of Malenkov, G.M., Kaganovich, L.M., and Molotov, V.M. 29 June 1957

At its meeting of 22–29 June 1957 the plenum of the Central Committee of the CPSU considered the matter of the anti-party group of Malenkov, Kaganovich, and Molotov, which had formed within the Presidium of the Central Committee.

At a time when the party, under the leadership of the Central Committee and with the support of the whole people, is making a major effort to carry out the historic decisions of the XX Congress aimed at the further development of the economy and a continued rise in the living standard of the Soviet people, at restoring leninist norms of party life, at liquidating violations of revolutionary legality, at broadening the ties between the party and the popular masses, at developing Soviet socialist democracy, at consolidating friendship among the Soviet peoples, at conducting a correct nationality policy and, as regards foreign policy, at relaxing international tension so as to ensure a durable peace; and at a time when serious advances have already been made in all of these areas, as every Soviet citizen knows – at just this time the anti-party group of Malenkov, Kaganovich, and Molotov came out against the party line.

With the aim of changing the political line of the party, this group sought through anti-party factional methods to replace the leading party organs elected at the plenum of the CPSU Central Committee.

This was no accident.

During the past three to four years in which the party has resolutely set its course at righting the errors and short-comings engendered by the cult of personality, and has been conducting a successful struggle against revisionists of marxism-leninism both in the international arena and within the country, when the party has made a tremendous effort to correct past distortions of the leninist nationality policy, the participants in this antiparty group – now revealed and completely unmasked – continually opposed, either directly or indirectly, the course approved by the XX Congress of the CPSU. This group, in effect, tried to reverse the leninist course toward peaceful coexistence among countries with different social systems, toward relaxing international tension and establishing friendly relations between the USSR and all peoples of the world.

They were against broadening the economic, cultural, and legislative rights of the union republics and also against strengthening the role of the local soviets in resolving these tasks. In this way the anti-party group opposed the party's firm course toward a more rapid economic and cultural development of the union republics, aimed at the further consolidation of leninist friendship among all the peoples of our country. The anti-party group not only failed to understand, but even opposed, the party's measures in the struggle with bureaucratism, aimed at reducing the size of the overinflated state apparatus. In all of these matters they opposed the party's implementation of the leninist principle of democratic centralism.

This group stubbornly opposed, and attempted to wreck, a measure as important as the reorganization of industrial administration and the setting up of sovnarkhozes in the economic regions, which had been supported by the whole party and by the people. They did not want to understand that at the present stage, when socialist industry has developed on such a massive scale and is continuing to grow rapidly – with preference given to the development of heavy industry – it was necessary to discover new and more advanced forms of industrial administration which would disclose large reserves and lead to an even mightier advance of Soviet industry. This group went to the extreme of continuing the struggle against the reorganization of the industrial administration even after these measures had been adopted and were under discussion on a national scale, with subsequent adoption of this legislation at the session of the USSR Supreme Soviet.

With respect to agriculture the participants in this group revealed a failure to understand the new and urgent tasks. They did not recognize the necessity for strengthening the material interest of the kolkhoz peasantry in expanding agricultural production. They objected to abolition of the old bureaucratic planning procedure in the kolkhozes and to introduction of a new procedure which unleashes the initiative of the kolkhozniks in conducting their own economic affairs, which has already led to positive results. They were so cut off from life that they could not perceive the existence of the genuine possibility of abolishing compulsory deliveries of agricultural products from the private plots of kolkhozniks at the end of this year. This measure, of vital significance for millions of toilers of the Soviet land, became possible through the great advance in socialized animal husbandry in the kolkhozes and through development of the sovkhozes. Instead of supporting this urgent measure, the members of the anti-party group came out against it.

They carried on a totally unjustified struggle against the party's appeal to catch up in the near future with the USA in per-capita production of milk, butter, and meat – which was actively supported by the kolkhozes, oblasts, and republics.

The members of the anti-party group thereby manifested their haughty disdain for the urgent and vital interests of the broad popular masses and their disbelief in the enormous potential of the socialist economy, in the popular movement which has arisen for an accelerated advance in the production of milk and meat.

It is no accident that Comrade Molotov, a member of the anti-party group, was sluggish and conservative and not only failed to comprehend the need for opening up the virgin lands but even opposed developing the 35 million hectares of virgin land which has taken on such gigantic significance in our country's economy.

Comrades Malenkov, Kaganovich, and Molotov stubbornly opposed the measures of the Central Committee and our whole party to liquidate the consequences of the cult of personality, to rectify the violations of revolutionary legality which had been committed, and to create conditions which would prevent them from recurring in the future.

At a time when the workers, kolkhozniks, our glorious youth, engineers, technicians, and scientists, writers, and the whole intelligentsia were unanimously supporting the party's measures based on the decisions of the XX Congress of the CPSU, when the entire Soviet people had set to work for the active implementation of these measures, when our country was experiencing a mighty surge of popular activity and an influx of new creative power – the members of the anti-party group remained deaf to this creative movement of the masses.

This group, and Comrade Molotov in particular, were sluggish in foreign affairs and hindered in every way the new and urgent measures aimed at reducing international tension, at consolidating peace throughout the world.

Throughout the lengthy period when Comrade Molotov was Minister of Foreign Affairs, he not only failed to undertake any measures through the Ministry of Foreign Affairs to improve relations between the USSR and Yugoslavia, but he even frequently came out against those measures which were being put through by the Presidium of the Central Committee to improve relations with Yugoslavia. Comrade Molotov's incorrect position on the Yugoslav question was unanimously condemned by the CPSU Central Committee in July, 1955 'as not corresponding to the interests of the Soviet state and the socialist camp and not in line with leninist political principles.'

Comrade Molotov hindered the conclusion of the state treaty with Austria and the improvement of relations with this state, situated in the centre of Europe. The treaty with Austria was of major significance for a general relaxation of international tension. He was also opposed to normalizing relations with Japan at a time when this normalization played a major role in lessening international tension in the Far East. He opposed the principled positions which the party had developed with respect to the possibility of preventing war under contemporary conditions, the possibility of different roads to socialism in different countries, and the need for strengthening contacts between the CPSU and progressive parties abroad.

Comrade Molotov frequently came out against the Soviet governments's new and necessary moves to defend the peace and security of peoples. He rejected, in particular, the advisability of establishing personal contacts between the leaders of the USSR and statesmen of other countries, as is necessary for mutual understanding and for improving international relations.

In many of these matters Comrade Molotov's opinions were supported by Comrade Kaganovich, and in a number of instances by Comrade Malenkov. The Presidium of the Central Committee and the Central Committee as a whole corrected them patiently, struggled against their errors, counting on them to learn from their errors, not to persist in them, and to get into step with the party's leading group. But they continued to maintain their incorrect and un-leninist positions.

Underlying the position of Comrades Malenkov, Kaganovich, and Molotov, which is a departure from the party line, is the fact that they were and are captive to old concepts and methods, are alienated from the life of the party and the country, do not perceive the new conditions and the new environment, are conservative, stubbornly adhere to outworn forms and methods of work which do not correspond to the interests of the movement to communism, rejecting that which is engendered by life and is derived from the interests of the development of Soviet society, from the interests of the whole socialist camp.

In both domestic and foreign affairs they are sectarians and dogmatists, displaying a mechanical and lifeless approach to marxism-leninism. They cannot understand that in contemporary conditions living marxism-leninism – in action, in the struggle for communism, is displayed by implementing the decisions of the XX Party Congress, by persisting in the policy of peaceful coexistence and the struggle for friendship among nations, a policy of the all-round consolidation of the socialist camp, by improving the leadership of industry, by struggling for an all-round advance of agriculture, for an expanding of the rights of the union republics, for a flowering of national cultures, for an all-round development of the initiative of the popular masses.

Having become convinced that their incorrect speeches and acts were steadily being rebuffed in the Presidium of the Central Committee, which has been consistently implementing the line adopted by the XX Party Congress, Comrades Molotov, Kaganovich, and Malenkov took the path of group struggle against the party leadership. In collusion with one another on an anti-party basis they set themselves the goal of changing the party's policy and of returning the party to the incorrect methods of leadership which were condemned by the XX Party Congress. They resorted to techniques of intrigue and reached a secret agreement against the Central Committee. The facts disclosed at the Central Committee plenum show that, by adopting the course of factional struggle, Comrades Malenkov, Kaganovich, and Molotov, and Comrade Shepilov who joined them, violated the party Rules and the resolution 'On Party Unity' of the X Party Congress [2.13], which was drafted by Lenin and which reads:

'In order to ensure strict discipline within the party and in all Soviet work, and to achieve maximum unity while eliminating all factionalism, the Congress gives the Central Committee full powers to apply all measures of party punishment up to and including expulsion from the party in cases of violation of discipline or of a revival or toleration of factionalism, and where Central Committee members are involved, to go as far as to reduce them to candidate status and even – as an extreme measure – to expel them from the party. The condition for the application of such an extreme measure to Central Committee members and candidate members, and to members of the Control Commission, is the convening of a Central Committee plenum, to which all candidate members of the Central Committee and all members of the Control Commission are to be invited. If such a general meeting of the most responsible party leaders decides by a two-thirds majority that it is necessary to demote a Central Committee member to the status of candidate member or to expel him from the party, then such action must be taken immediately.'

This leninist resolution obliges the Central Committee and all party organizations tirelessly to strengthen party unity, to rebuff decisively any manifestation of factionalism or cliquishness, to ensure that work is truly harmonious and truly embodies the unity of will and action of the vanguard of the working class – the Communist Party.

The Central Committee plenum notes with profound satisfaction the monolithic unity and solidarity of all Central Committee members and candidate members and of all members of the CPSU Central Revision Commission – who condemned the anti-party group unanimously. Not one person in the Central Committee plenum supported this group.

When the group was confronted with the unanimous condemnation by the Central Committee plenum of its anti-party activity, the members of the Central Committee plenum unanimously demanding that the members of the group be dropped from the Central Committee and expelled from the party, they admitted their collusion and the harmfulness of their anti-party activity and undertook to submit to the party's decisions.

On the basis of the above, and guided by the interests of the all-around strengthening of the leninist unity of the party, the plenum of the CPSU Central Committee resolves as follows:

1   The factional activity of the anti-party group of Malenkov, Kaganovich, Molotov, and Shepilov who joined them, is condemned as incompatible with the leninist principles of our party.

2   Comrades Malenkov, Kaganovich, and Molotov are dropped from membership in the Central Committee and the Central Committee Presidium; Comrade Shepilov is removed from his position as secretary of the CPSU Central Committee and is dropped as candidate member of the Central Committee Presidium and as member of the Central Committee.

The party Central Committee's unanimous condemnation of the factional activity of the anti-party group of Comrades Malenkov, Kaganovich, and Molotov will serve to strengthen further the unity in the ranks of our leninist party, will strengthen its leadership, and will promote the struggle for the general line of the party.

The party Central Committee calls upon all communists to rally their ranks even more closely around the invincible banner of marxism-leninism, to devote all their energies to the successful fulfilment of the tasks of communist construction.

Pravda, 4 July 1957 *KPSS v rezoliutsiiakh* VII, 267–73

4.20
On Granting to the Central Committees of the Union Republic Parties the Right to Resolve Certain Party-Organizational and Budgetary-Financial Questions 2 August 1957

The central committees of the union republic parties are granted the right to resolve the following questions:

1   They may approve the staffs of city and raion party committees and of other party institutions within their jurisdictions; they may abolish and establish new city and raion party committees; they may classify city and raion party committees with respect to the salaries of their workers; they

may alter the staffing patterns of oblast committees and of the central committees of the union republic parties, provided the structure of the party committee is not affected.

Changes in the staffs of party organs and in the classification of city and raion party committees with respect to salary scale are within the competence of the central committees of the union republic parties, within the limits of the republic's salary account and the staffs of party workers available there. Changes in salary scales and the salary structure require the permission of the CPSU Central Committee.

2   They may form new raions and enlarge or abolish existing ones; they may establish raion centres; they may transform workers' settlements and settlements of the urban type into cities and classify cities as administratively subordinate to the raion, oblast, or republic. Each individual decision of the central committee of a union republic party altering the administrative and territorial structure of the republic is to be communicated to the CPSU Central Committee and, through the soviet organizations, to the Presidium of the USSR Supreme Soviet.

3   They may initiate and terminate publication of raion and city newspapers and also of departmental newspapers and magazines (by agreement with the appropriate ministries and departments); they may determine the size, frequency of publication, and number of copies printed of all newspapers and magazines (without exception) issued on the territory of the republic within the limits of the total appropriations for these purposes and of the paper allocated to the republic; they may confirm the structure and the staffs of political newspapers and magazines issued in the republic or oblast within the limits of the established model staffing patterns and of the salary accounts; they may confirm the business-financial plans of the publishing houses of union-republic central committees; they may decide on the scale of radio broadcasting in republics and oblasts, including broadcasts for the national minorities.

4   They may set up and abolish political education offices and evening schools of marxism-leninism; they may conduct short-term courses for retraining party and propaganda workers within the limits of the allocations in the party budget.

5   They may approve – in accordance with the title list drawn up by the CPSU Central Committee – design and construction estimates for the buildings of party organs and their subordinate institutions, and also for housing within the limits of the allocations approved in the party budget and the standards for estimated costs.

6   In the party's agricultural raion committees they may determine the size of expense accounts for trips, and instead of reimbursing raion committee personnel for these expenses they may decide to pay them a salary increment – within the limits of the allocations for these purposes in the party budget.

7   The central committees of union republic parties are obliged to submit quarterly reports to the CPSU Central Committee on the matters mentioned in paragraphs 1, 3, and 4 of the present resolution, such reports covering the situation as of the first day of the quarter in which the report is submitted.

Spravochnik partiinogo rabotnika
(1957), 440–1

Plenum of the Central Committee   29 October 1957

The October 1957 Plenum of the Central Committee dealt with relationships between the party and the Soviet armed forces. The army, represented by the enormously prestigious Marshal Zhukov, is thought to have played a critical role in the rout of the 'anti-party group.' Zhukov was rewarded for his role in the June crisis by promotion to full membership in the party Presidium. As Minister of Defence, Zhukov had managed to reduce party interference in army operations at the lower echelons. Returning to the Soviet Union on October 26 from a trip to Yugoslavia, he discovered that he had been replaced as Minister of Defence by Marshal Malinovsky. Through this act the party leadership removed from political power the most famous Soviet war hero and set the stage for a subsequent reconsolidation of party controls in the armed forces. After his replacement as Minister of Defence, a plenum of the Central Committee was held on 29 October at which Zhukov was severely criticized and guidelines set for military party work. Zhukov himself was removed by the plenum from both the Presidium and the Central Committee.

To add weight to this rejection of Zhukov an unstated number of military workers and responsible party and Soviet workers were invited to this plenum.

4.21
On Improving Party Political Work in the
Soviet Army and Navy   29 October 1957

By the victory of world-historic importance which they gained in the Great Patriotic War the armed forces of the Soviet Union discharged their responsibilities well and honourably justified the love and trust of the peoples of the USSR.

In the post-war years, thanks to the concern of the Communist Party and the Soviet government, the armed forces of the USSR advanced to a new and higher stage of development on the basis of the general progress of our country's economy, of major successes in the development of heavy industry, science, and technology; they have been supplied with all the latest military equipment and armaments, including nuclear and thermonuclear weapons and rockets. The political morale of the troops is at a high level. The commanding and political officers of the Army and Navy are unreservedly devoted to their people, to the Soviet motherland, and to the Communist Party.

The complex international situation, the arms race in the major capitalist countries, and the requirements of the defence of our motherland demand that commanding officers, political organs, and party organizations continue tirelessly to improve the military preparedness of the troops, to strengthen discipline among the personnel, to train them in the spirit of devotion to the motherland and the Communist Party, and that they endeavour to satisfy the spiritual and material needs of the servicemen.

The plenum of the Central Committee views as especially significant in meeting these tasks the continued improvement of party political work in the Soviet Army and Navy, as this will strengthen the fighting potential of our Armed Forces, rally the servicemen around the Communist Party and the Soviet government, train them in the spirit of selfless devotion to the Soviet motherland, in the spirit of friendship among the peoples of the USSR and of proletarian internationalism. But practical party political work continues to reveal serious defects, and sometimes its importance is even underestimated.

The XX Congress of the CPSU set the party and the people the task of maintaining our defence at the level of contemporary military technology and science, of ensuring the security of our socialist state. An important role in fulfilling this task rests not only with the individual commanding officers but also with the military soviets, the political organs, and the party organizations in the Army and Navy. They must all carry out the policies of the Communist Party firmly and consistently.

The chief source of the might of our Army and Navy is that they are organized, led, and educated by the Communist Party – the leading and directing force of Soviet society. One must always bear in mind Lenin's admonition to the effect that 'the policy of the war department, as of all other departments and institutions, is based precisely on the general directives of the party headed by its Central Committee and under the latter's immediate supervision.'

The plenum of the CPSU Central Committee notes that former Minister of Defence, Comrade G. K. Zhukov, has recently been violating leninist party principles of leadership of the armed forces, has taken the tack of curtailing the work of party organizations, political organizations, and military councils, of liquidating the leadership and supervision of the Army and Navy by the party, its Central Committee, and the government.

The Central Committee plenum has established that a cult of Comrade G.K. Zhukov has started to spread in the Soviet Army, and with his personal complicity. Obsequious persons and flatterers have started to extol him in lectures and reports, articles, films, and pamphlets, unduly exalting his person and his role in the Great Patriotic War. Thus the true history of the war has been distorted to the benefit of Comrade G. K. Zhukov, and the actual situation perverted; this detracts from the gigantic efforts of the Soviet people, the heroism of our armed forces, the role of commanding officers and political workers, the military skill of the commanders of fronts, armies, and navies, the leading and inspiring role of the Communist Party of the Soviet Union.

The party and government estimated highly the services of Comrade G.K. Zhukov in conferring upon him the rank of Marshal of the Soviet Union, four times awarding him the decoration of Hero of the Soviet Union as well as many other decorations. He was accorded great political confidence: at the XX Party Congress he was elected a member of the Central Committee. The Central Committee elected him a candidate member of the Central Committee Presidium, and later a member of the Central Committee Presidium. But Comrade G.K. Zhukov's insufficient party spirit and incorrect understanding of the high valuation that was placed upon his services led him to lose that party modesty which was taught by V.I. Lenin, and he grew conceited – viewing himself as the only hero of all the victories gained by our people and its Armed Forces under the leadership of the Communist Party, and crudely violating the leninist party principles of leadership of the armed forces.

Thus Comrade G. K. Zhukov has not justified the confidence reposed in him by the party. He has revealed himself to be politically unstable and inclined to adventurism both in his understanding of the major tasks of Soviet foreign policy and in his leadership of the Ministry of Defence.

In view of the foregoing the plenum of the CPSU Central Committee has resolved that Comrade G.K. Zhukov be dropped from membership in the Presidium and Central Committee of the CPSU and has directed the Secretariat of the CPSU Central Committee to provide Comrade Zhukov with other work.

The plenum of the CPSU Central Committee expresses its confidence that in carrying out the decisions of the XX Congress of the CPSU the party organizations will continue to devote their efforts to further strengthening the defence capacity of our socialist state.

Pravda, 3 November 1957   *KPSS v rezoliutsiiakh* VII, 295–7

Plenum of the Central Committee   16–17 December 1957

The December 1957 Plenum of the Central Committee heard reports by M.A. Suslov on the results of the Meeting of Representatives of Communist and Workers' parties, and by V.V. Grishin on trade union affairs. At the plenum the Uzbek N.A. Mukhitdinov was elected a full member of the Presidium and secretary of the Central Committee, and N.G. Ignatov and A.I. Kirichenko were also elected secretaries.

4.22
On the Work of the Trade Unions
of the USSR   17 December 1957

... The plenum of the Central Committee of the CPSU considers it necessary to improve significantly the entire work of Soviet trade unions, to increase further their role in the nation-wide struggle to build communism in our country.

The trade unions are called upon to intensify their work of enlisting the working people in the management of production, to increase still further the creative initiative and activism of the working masses in the building of communism in our country, and to rally them still more strongly behind the Communist Party. The central task of the trade unions is to mobilize the masses for the struggle for a further powerful upswing in all branches of the economy, for a continued strengthening of the economic might and defensive power of the Soviet state, for the fulfilment and overfulfilment of the economic plans, for technical progress, for a steady growth in labour productivity, for the strictest economy and thrift in all components of the economy, for maximum utilization of all reserves and possibilities for a rapid growth in industrial and agricultural production and for a further upsurge in the level of the working people's prosperity and culture.

I   ON INCREASING THE ROLE OF THE TRADE UNIONS IN ECONOMIC CONSTRUCTION

In a socialist state the working people, primarily through the soviets of workers' deputies, manage the factories, plants, mines, sovkhozes, MTSS, and other enterprises that comprise national property. In addition, the trade unions play an immense role in drawing workers into participation in the management of production; it is through the trade unions that the working class effect their control over the work of economic managers, who manage production according to the principle of one-man management.

Socialist competition is one of the most important forms for enlisting workers in the management of production; it is a proven method of communist construction. While taking note of the extensive work of the trade unions in developing socialist competition, the Central Committee plenum at the same time calls attention to the fact that there is still a great deal of formalism in the direction of competition, and the obligations assumed are not always backed up by organizing and mass political work with people and by concrete organizational and technical measures ...

Production meetings, which make it possible to combine the principle of one-man management with control from below, are of great importance for the question of enlisting workers in the management of production. However, there are serious short-comings in the way they are being conducted. At many enterprises the role of the production meeting has been downgraded; they are hurriedly convened without the necessary preparation and are held primarily in brigades and sectors. Factory-wide and shop meetings are seldom convened, a fact that narrows the possibilities of the workers and employees for resolving problems related to the work of the shop and the enterprise as a whole. Certain economic managers do not participate in production meetings and do not carry out their decisions, with the result that workers lose interest in the meetings.

The plenum of the Central Committee considers it expedient to transform production meetings at enterprises and construction sites into permanently active institutions that conduct their work with the extensive participation of workers, engineering and technical personnel and office workers, and that include representatives of management, of party and Komsomol organizations, and of scientific and technological societies.

Trade union organizations must improve their guidance of production meetings, enhance their role and authority, and increase the effectiveness of their decisions. The work of production meetings must be subordinated to the tasks of fulfilling and overfulfilling state plans, of making fuller use of internal production reserves, creating working conditions for high labour productivity and perfecting methods for the management of enterprises and construction sites. At the meetings it is expedient to discuss production plans, questions of the organization of production and labour, of improving quality and reducing the unit cost of production and construction, the setting of technical norms, capital construction, improvement of factory management, etc.

Most important questions of production, labour, and everyday and cultural services to the working people are reflected in collective agreements that determine the mutual obligations of the enterprises' collectives and of management. Trade union organizations and economic management must improve the practice of concluding such agreements, assure the unconditional fulfilment of the obligations assumed both by management and by the collective of workers, and must regularly check on their fulfilment with the help of an extensive aktiv and inform the workers and employees of the results of these checks.

It is necessary to intensify the work of the trade unions in enlisting workers and engineering and technical personnel in the ranks of rationalizers and inventors, in directing their creative initiative toward bringing to light reserves in the economy, and in improving machinery, technology, and the organization of production. They must provide strict control over prompt consideration and introduction of rationalizing proposals and inventions and persistently combat instances of inert and bureaucratic attitudes in this matter. They must improve the leadership of scientific and technical societies, increase their role in the study and dissemination of progressive experience and of the latest achievements of science and technology, and in developing creative bonds between workers in the sciences and in production.

The All-Union Central Council of Trade Unions, the central committees of trade unions and republic trade union councils must participate more actively in the discussion of questions of production, labour and everyday life in soviet and economic agencies. In preparing proposals for draft production plans and in considering current questions of labour and everyday life, planning agencies must take into account the opinion of trade union committees. Sovnarkhozes as well as oblast and krai executive committees must provide for participation by representatives of the appropriate trade union committees and councils in their deliberations on draft plans for enterprises, once the drafts have been discussed at general meetings of workers and employees and at conferences or production meetings.

In view of the fact that the work of the USSR Council of Ministers' State Committee on Labour and Wages directly touches on the vital interests of workers and employees, the most important decisions are to be taken jointly by the State Committee on Labour and Wages and the Presidium of the All-Union Central Council of Trade Unions.

II IMPROVING WORKERS' AND EMPLOYEES' CONDITIONS OF WORK AND EVERYDAY LIFE IS A MOST IMPORTANT TRADE UNION TASK

In recent times the party and government, with the active assistance of the trade unions, have carried out a number of important measures for a further increase in the people's well-being: earnings of the lowest-paid workers and employees have been raised; the work day has been shortened on days before holidays and regular days off; the transition to a seven-hour day – and to a six-hour day for work below the earth's surface – is being effected; pensions and benefits have been raised, and the task of eliminating housing shortages within ten to twelve years is being successfully resolved. Each year the socialist state allocates immense resources to labour protection and safety, assuring favourable work conditions for Soviet man, the likes of which do not and cannot exist in a single capitalist country. In the past five years alone, the state has expended over 11,000,000,000 rubles for these purposes.

However, certain economic managers are showing insufficient concern for improving workers' labour conditions, are not making full use of the means available for this purpose, and are tolerating violations of the labour law. At a number of enterprises, the fight for observance of labour safety laws is inadequate, the shielding of technological equipment is incomplete, ventilation is not in good order, and there are frequent instances of enterprises and shops being put into operation with serious gaps in their labour safety provisions and without the requisite complex of sanitary and everyday facilities. There are serious short-comings in the supplying of workers with special work clothing, shoes, and individual protective devices.

It is necessary to increase the responsibility of enterprise and construction site management for labour protection and labor safety measures and for scrupulous and unflagging observance of the labour laws. The task of further improving working conditions and of making them healthier must be regarded as one of state importance. Economic managers who do not fulfill their obligations under collective agreements and who regularly violate the labour laws should be held liable. The trade unions must strengthen their control over the work of the institutions that dispense medical treatment.

The plenum feels that it is necessary to provide, in the long-range plan for the development of the economy in 1959–65, for additional measures to create safe working conditions at mining, metallurgical, and chemical enterprises, in the hot shops of the machine-building industry, and at other production installations, taking into account the latest achievements of science and technology.

The trade unions must make full use of their legal authority to exercise state control over observance of the labour laws, and public control over the status of labour safety; they must persistently demand of economic organs that they unquestioningly implement measures for the further mechanization of arduous and labour-intensive jobs, the introduction of more advanced technology, and the creation of normal sanitary conditions for all workers. In these demands the trade unions will receive the requisite support from party organizations.

In recent times a number of steps have been taken with the direct participation of trade union organizations to adjust wages in construction, in the Donets Basin mines, and at ferrous metallurgy enterprises, as well as those of leading officials and specialists on sovkhozes. However, short-comings in methods of setting norms for labour and wages are still slow in being eliminated. At certain enterprises and construction sites wage increases are outstripping the growth of labour productivity, while the opposite should be the case: the growth of labour productivity must precede wage increases and prepare the way for them.

Trade unions and economic organs must constantly improve the system for recompensing the labour of workers, management, engineering and technical personnel, and office workers and achieve a situation in which wages and the bonus system become powerful levers of material incentive for increasing production output and raising labour productivity, in which they promote the profitable operation of shops and enterprises, an above-plan reduction in the unit cost of production and the application of new technology. They must see to it that every worker knows his output norm, rate norm, and wage scale and has a clear notion of how his earnings are calculated ...

III ON IMPROVING THE EDUCATIONAL AND CULTURAL MASS WORK OF TRADE UNIONS

... The plenum considers it necessary for trade unions to improve their educational and cultural enlightenment work among the working people, intensify their struggle against retrograde views and sentiments, and propagandize healthy practices in everyday living. The trade unions must inculcate in the masses the spirit of Soviet patriotism, socialist internationalism, and friendship among peoples; they must develop in the working people a sense of proprietorship in their country and increase their sense of responsibility to the homeland for the fulfilment of production plans, for technical progress, for the further development of the society's production forces, and for the creation of an abundance of material goods in the country. To this end it is necessary to explain more extensively the domestic and foreign policy of the party and government, and to propagate political and scientific knowledge, making full use of all the means and capabilities of clubs, libraries, the press, motion pictures, radio, television, and amateur work in the arts. It is an important task of the trade union organization to conduct widespread production and technical propaganda and to assist all workers in raising their cultural and technical level ...

IV ON RAISING THE LEVEL OF THE TRADE UNIONS' ORGANIZATIONAL WORK

In connection with the reorganization of the management of industry and construction and the elimination of the dispersion of direction of enterprises among a multiplicity of ministries and departments, the trade unions have carried out a number of measures to improve their organizational work. The centre of operative direction of local trade union organizations has been transferred to the oblasts, krais, and republics; the powers and responsibilities of the trade union councils have been significantly expanded, a number of trade unions have been enlarged and certain superfluous links in the trade union apparatus have been eliminated.

However, the plenum notes that many trade union organizations are still proceeding slowly with the reorganization of their work, are far removed from concrete questions of production, and are devoting little effort to active organizational work. The All-Union Central Council of Trade Unions is exercising feeble control over the implementation of its decisions and is devoting little attention to generalizing and disseminating experience in trade union work.

There are violations of democracy and norms of trade-union life in the trade union organizations: plenums of trade union committees and councils are not regularly convened and their role as organs of collective direction is frequently downgraded. There are also short-comings in the selection and training of trade union cadres. Many trade-union committees and councils do not show sufficient concern for enlisting in trade union work the young and energetic people who have made a good showing in production work and public life and who enjoy the trust of the workers.

The plenum orders the union-republic party central committees, krai, and oblast party committees and the party group of the All-Union Central Council of Trade Unions to make sure that the level of the trade unions' organizational work is raised and to render practical assistance to the trade union councils in organizing their work along the new lines.

In carrying out the tasks that confront the trade unions, a decisive role is to be played by their primary organizations. The All-Union Central Council of Trade Unions and the republic, krai, and oblast trade union councils and committees must improve markedly their guidance of the primary organizations, render them day-to-day assistance, and achieve a situation in which the broad masses feel a sense of closeness and kinship toward them as organizations capable of correctly expressing and defending the interests of the working people and ones which show concern for all aspects of their lives and everyday existence.

The plenum considers it expedient to expand the functions of the factory and plant trade union committees in the sense of giving them the right to participate in the drawing up of the enterprises' industrial and financial plans and in deciding questions of labour norms and pay systems, giving them authority to oversee the observance of labour laws and the fulfilment of collective agreements, to express an opinion on candidates under consideration for managerial positions, and to prevent the firing of workers and office workers without the consent of the local factory or plant trade union committee.

The work of trade union organizations must be organized on the basis of strict observance of the norms of trade union life, of the development of independent action and initiative, the promotion of criticism and self-criticism, the assurance of collective leadership, and the accountability and elected nature of the trade union bodies. It follows that the All-Union Central Council of Trade Unions, and the central and oblast trade union committees and councils should regularly submit reports on their work for broad discussion at meetings and conferences of trade union members. It is necessary to increase the role of the general trade union meetings, and to see to it that the most important questions of production and of everyday and cultural services to the working people are discussed at them. The executives of the trade union and economic bodies are obliged to take active part in the meetings, to promote the development of criticism and self-criticism, to carefully heed the voice of the workers and employees, and to render accounts on the carrying out of proposals made at the meetings ...

VI ON IMPROVING PARTY GUIDANCE OF THE TRADE UNIONS

The strength of Soviet trade unions consists in the fact that they are guided by the leninist policy of the Communist Party, which comprises the vital basis of socialist society. The trade unions can successfully fulfil the tasks that confront them only on condition that they receive guidance from the party and enjoy its help and support.

At present, when the authority of the local trade union bodies has been considerably expanded, the responsibility of party organizations for the work of the trade unions increases still further. Party committees must increase their attention to the trade unions, delve more deeply into the content of their work, assure still more active participation on their part in economic and cultural construction and in the country's entire social and political life.

The plenum notes that certain party committees fail to attach due significance to the growing importance and work of the trade unions, do not delve into the substance of the trade union organizations' work, fail to show the requisite concern for reinforcing them with experienced and politically mature staff, do an insufficient job of inculcating in economic cadres the spirit of scrupulous observance of Soviet labour law, and do not always support the trade union bodies in their rightful demands on economic management.

The plenum orders the union-republic party central committees, the krai, oblast, city and raion party committees and primary party organizations to improve their guidance of the trade unions, to concern themselves above all with the selection and training of trade union cadres, and to recommend for responsible positions in trade union bodies the most capable and best-prepared people, those who have organizational ability and who enjoy authority in the eyes of Communists and non-party members. A Communist promoted to trade union work must consider it a matter of party honour to assure the fulfilment of the tasks confronting the trade union and to win the trust of the masses by his comradely attitude toward them and his solicitude in satisfying their needs.

In their guidance of the trade unions, party organs should always bear in mind the fact that the trade unions are non-party organizations of workers and employees, that all their work is built on the basis of broad democracy and persuasion and that commanding and petty tutelage are all the less permissible where they are concerned. Party committees are obliged to direct the work of the trade union bodies in a capable fashion, to help them constantly in fulfilling their functions, to encourage and develop independent action and initiative on their part in every way and to take appropriate measures with respect to party-member executives who show a lack of concern for trade union organizations and who attempt to downgrade their role.

In view of the fact that the party exercises its influence on all the activities of trade union organizations through the Communist members of the trade unions, to improve the practical work of the party groups set up in the elected trade union organs in accord with the CPSU rules. Through their active participation in the work of the trade unions, Communists must achieve an all-round improvement in their work and at the same time increase their role in solving economic and political tasks ...

Pravda, 19 December 1957   *KPSS v rezoliutsiiakh* VII, 301–15

Plenum of the Central Committee   25–26 February 1958

Since the original collectivization of agriculture in the USSR the MTS had played a fundamental economic and political role in the countryside. Khrushchev's decision to abolish it therefore ranks as one of the most radical of his moves, even though he planned this as a gradual process. He took the first decisive step at the February 1958 Plenum of the Central Committee, at which he delivered the major speech (*Current Digest of the Soviet Press* X, no. 9, 5–13, 40) preparatory to the adoption of the resolution below. Later, following Khrushchev's removal from the leadership, it became clear that many officials had been sceptical of the wisdom of the way in which Khrushchev went about liquidating the MTS. The speed of the operation imposed a severe financial burden on the collective farms and disorganized machinery repair facilities.

4.23
On the Further Development of the Kolkhoz System and the Reorganization of MTSs   26 February 1958

... The improved technical equipment of agricultural production and the rise in the numbers of skilled persons in the kolkhozes, MTSs, and sovkhozes have created the genuine preconditions for a still greater advance of agriculture in the near future.

The party has dispatched several thousand Communists to leading posts in kolkhozes – party and soviet personnel, engineers from industrial enterprises, agronomists, livestock and other specialists. At the beginning of 1957 more than 90 per cent of the kolkhoz chairmen were party members, and more than a third of them possessed secondary and higher specialized education; there has also been an increase in the number of remarkably talented organizers of kolkhoz production who have been promoted because of their practical qualifications. The primary party organizations in the kolkhozes have grown and become stronger. Now the kolkhozes possess capable organizers and qualified specialists who make skilful use of local reserves and opportunities to increase agricultural production.

Production in the kolkhozes has now advanced to a new and higher stage. This new stage in the development of the kolkhoz system is characterized by the increasing economic strength of the kolkhozes which were enlarged during recent years; they have become diversified and technically well-equipped farms with large numbers of skilled cadres; their incomes have considerably increased, and the well-being of the kolkhozniks has risen. The greater material incentives of the kolkhozniks, the introduction of new planning procedure, their newly granted right to change the model rules of the agricultural artel to conform with local conditions – have all unleashed the creative initiative of the kolkhozniks, have caused them to work harder, have strengthened their concern to make better use of the land and equipment, and of all the reserves of kolkhoz production. Kolkhoz members have accumulated great experience in conducting a major socialized enterprise using new technology and the achievements of science.

The MTSs played a gigantic historical role in the establishment and strengthening of the kolkhoz system, in the technical equipment of agriculture, and in consolidating the union between the working class and the peasantry. During the first stage of the development of kolkhozes the party concluded that the most suitable form of state assistance to the kolkhozes for that time was reinforcing their socialized economic operations by setting up the MTSs.

The MTSs were the major political and organizational force around which the peasants united to form kolkhozes and became convinced of the advantages of large-scale mechanized agriculture; the MTSs were the instrument of technical progress in agriculture and of its re-equipping on the basis of new technology, of the training of cadres of skilled machine operators, of the cultural elevation of agriculture and animal husbandry. The MTSs were also of gigantic significance as an important source of grain and other food products, as well as of raw material for industry. In recent years the MTSs served as a major organizational force in the struggle to liquidate the backwardness of certain branches of agricultural production, to implement the party's decisions on agricultural matters.

Now that the majority of the kolkhozes have become organizationally and economically strong, and the kolkhoz economy has made significant progress, the existing form in which kolkhozes have been supplied with production and technical services by the MTSs no longer corresponds to the requirements for the development of agricultural productivity. What is more, in many cases this form has started to hamper the continued advance of leading kolkhozes, hindering the initiative of the kolkhoz cadres and of all kolkhozniks in the better exploitation of kolkhoz production reserves. Increasingly apparent are the negative consequences of a situation in which two socialist enterprises – the kolkhoz and the MTS – are working the same land; this occasionally leads to poor definition of responsibility for the organization of production and detracts from responsibility for increasing crop yields, gives rise to large and unnecessary expenses for maintaining parallel administrations. The MTSs thus accumulate large amounts of unnecessary equipment, and machines are used unproductively.

The plenum of the Central Committee considers that the continuing advance of the country's socialist agriculture and the development of the kolkhoz system make it advisable to change the existing system of supplying kolkhozes with production and technical services and gradually to reorganize the MTSs which, although playing an important and positive role in the past, have now largely exhausted their basic functions. Now that most kolkhozes are in a position to acquire tractors, combines, and other agricultural machinery, and to make correct and more productive use of them, it is advisable to sell these machines to the kolkhozes directly. This will make possible a considerable improvement in the use of modern technical equipment, will accelerate technical progress in agriculture, will increase labour productivity, will increase total production as well as marketed output per hundred hectares of farmland, and reduce its unit cost.

Following different timetables, according to the particular characteristics of the raions and kolkhozes, the MTSs are to be reorganized into technical repair stations (RTSs) which will see to the repair of tractors and other machines, provide the kolkhozes with technical services, sell to the kolkhozes and sovkhozes new technical equipment, spare parts, fuel, fertilizer, chemical pesticides and herbicides, and other materials. In those raions where not all kolkhozes are yet able to acquire tractors and other machinery and, in particular, are not capable of making correct use of this equipment, the existing system for supplying production and technical services to the kolkhozes through the MTSs is to be temporarily maintained.

The sale of tractors and other agricultural machinery to the kolkhozes and the reorganization of the MTSs will strengthen the direct economic ties between industry and agriculture, will further strengthen the alliance between the working class and the peasantry, will elevate the kolkhoz economy, and will promote the better employment of the land, belonging to the whole people, which has been granted to the kolkhozes in perpetuity. On this basis the indivisible funds [capital assets of the kolkhoz] will increase, as will the ties among kolkhozes, and thus kolkhoz property will develop and strengthen and ultimately rise to the level of publicly owned property.

The measures contemplated for the continued development of the kolkhoz system and the reorganization of the MTSs are an intrinsic part of the party's efforts to improve the administration and guidance of the economy. Through implementation of these measures agricultural leadership will rise to a new and higher stage. Like the recent reorganization of the administration of industry and construction, that of the MTS is designed to ensure that maximum benefit will be derived from the advantages of the socialist economic system and productivity reserves, that the creative initiative and activity of the masses will continue to develop, and that the onward movement of Soviet society along the road to communism will accelerate.

The plenum of the CPSU Central Committee considers the measures contemplated for further developing the kolkhoz system and reorganizing the MTSs to be of vital significance for a socialist agriculture and for our whole country. After the collectivization of agriculture, accomplished on the basis of Lenin's genius-like co-operative plan, the implementation of these measures will be a new and exceptionally important and sizable step in developing a socialist agriculture.

Therefore the plenum of the Central Committee of the CPSU resolves:

1   The proposals of the Central Committee for the further development

of the kolkhoz system and the reorganization of the MTSS, designed to implement the decisions of the XX Party Congress on agricultural matters, are recognized as correct and timely.

2   In view of the exceptional importance, for the state, of the continued development of the kolkhoz system and the reorganization of the MTSS, this question is to be placed before the next regular session of the USSR Supreme Soviet. The First Secretary of the Central Committee, Comrade N.S. Khrushchev, is to report on this question at the session of the USSR Supreme Soviet.

Before this matter is examined at the session of the Supreme Soviet, it is advisable that there be a general public discussion of the measures involved – at membership meetings of kolkhozes, in MTSS, sovkhozes, industrial and construction enterprises, in scientific organizations and similar institutions, in military units and institutions, on the pages of newspapers and magazines.

These theses contained in the report of Comrade N.S. Khrushchev, 'On the Further Development of the Kolkhoz System and the Reorganization of the MTSS,' are approved and ordered to be published for general popular discussion.

3   The central committees of the union-republic parties, the krai, oblast, city, and raion party committees, and the primary party organizations are to explain on a broad scale the significance of the contemplated measures, organizing general popular discussion of the theses everywhere. Party and soviet organs must study closely and disseminate all concrete proposals by the toilers in order to find the most advanced and suitable organizational forms for reorganizing the material and technical servicing of kolkhozes to ensure the further development of the kolkhoz system and to create an abundance of agricultural products in the country.

During the course of the general public discussion the party, soviet, trade union, and Komsomol organizations must direct the creative energy and activity of all the toilers to fulfilling and overfulfilling state plans, must mobilize the efforts of male and female kolkhozniks, as well as MTS and sovkhoz workers, for success in the spring sowing in each kolkhoz and sovkhoz, for fulfilment of the obligation to increase agricultural production.

4   The party and soviet organs of union republics and autonomous republics, krais, and oblasts, are directed to determine – on the basis of a thorough study of the economic situation in each raion and kolkhoz – which kolkhozes are economically capable of purchasing tractors and other machinery this year and of using them thriftily, which kolkhozes will need more time to acquire such equipment, and for which kolkhozes it is advisable temporarily to retain the existing system whereby production and technical services are provided through the MTSS.

5   It is advisable to convoke, early in 1959, a Third All-Union Congress of Kolkhozniks to examine urgent problems of kolkhoz development and to make the necessary alterations in the model rules of the agricultural artel ... [This congress was in fact convened in November 1969.]

Pravda, 28 February 1958   KPSS v rezoliutsiiakh VII, 316–22

4.24
On Correcting Errors in the Evaluation of the Operas
'The Great Friendship,' 'Bogdan Khmelnitsky,' and
'With the Whole Heart'   28 May 1958

> The resolution, while affirming the principle of 'socialist realism' in music and the arts, restored the good name of a number of prominent composers and writers who had been attacked under Stalin, and offered some encouragement to creative self-expression in the non-Russian republics of the USSR. (See 3.41.)

The Central Committee of the CPSU hereby notes that the 10 February 1948 Central Committee resolution on V. Muradeli's opera, *The Great Friendship*, on the whole played a positive role in the development of Soviet music. It defined the tasks of developing music on the basis of the principles of socialist realism, emphasized the significance of the tie between art and the best democratic traditions of classical music and of the people's creative work. Formalist tendencies in music were justly condemned, as was the false 'innovativeness' which was withdrawing art from the people and converting it into the property of a narrow clique of aesthetes. The development of Soviet music in recent years has confirmed the correctness and timeliness of these directives of the party.

At the same time the evaluations contained in this resolution of the works of certain composers were in many instances unsubstantiated and unjust. While V. Muradeli's opera, *The Great Friendship* possessed short-comings which merited a businesslike critique, they were not such as to justify declaring the opera an example of formalism in music. The talented composers, Comrades D. Shostakovich, S. Prokofiev, A. Khachaturian, V. Shebalin, G. Popov, N. Miaskovsky, and others – some of whose works manifested incorrect tendencies – were arbitrarily branded representatives of an anti-popular formalist tendency.

Despite historic facts, the resolution criticizing Muradeli's opera drew an artificial contrast between certain peoples of the North Caucasus and others.

Some of the incorrect evaluations in this decree reflected I.V. Stalin's subjective approach to certain artistic and creative works.

I.V. Stalin's subjective approach to the evaluation of certain artistic productions was also manifested in the one-sided and tendentious criticism of the operas *Bogdan Khmelnitsky* by K. Dankevich and *With the Whole Heart* by G. Zhukovsky, that was published on his orders in 1951 *Pravda* editorials. Furthermore, as is known, Molotov, Malenkov, and Beria exerted an extremely negative influence on Stalin in these matters also. Despite the short-comings in both the libretto and the music of *Bogdan Khmelnitsky*, there was no justification for maintaining that the libretto, written by the well-known Soviet writers, V. Vasilevskaia and A. Korneichuk, contained 'major ideological defects,' nor for accusing the composer, K. Dankevich, of lack of principle. The unjust reproaches contained in this article were later repeated in a number of other articles and speeches. The editorial on the opera *With the Whole Heart* was one-sided and contained obvious exaggerations in addition to its correct criticisms of the music and the libretto.

The CPSU Central Committee resolves:

1   The 10 February 1948 Central Committee resolution on V. Muradeli's opera, *The Great Friendship*, which correctly determined the course of development of Soviet art as being one of folk realism and which set forth a just criticism of erroneous and formalist tendencies in music, at the same time contained some unjust and unwarrantedly sharp criticisms of the works of a number of talented Soviet composers, this being a manifestation of the negative features characterizing the period of the cult of personality.

2   The evaluation of the operas, *Bogdan Khmelnitsky* and *With the Whole Heart* given in the *Pravda* editorials is recognized as incorrect and one-sided. The editorial board of *Pravda* (Comrade Satiukov) is charged with preparing, on the basis of this decision, an editorial containing a thorough and profound analysis of the principal issues in the development of Soviet music.

3   The oblast and krai committees, the central committees of the union-republic communist parties, and the USSR Ministry of Culture are ordered to carry out the necessary explanatory work in connection with this resolution in creative unions and artistic institutions with a view to heightening the ideological and artistic level of Soviet music and to increasing the solidarity of the creative intelligentsia on the basis of communist moral principles and by strengthening the bond between art and the life of the people.

Spravochnik partiinogo rabotnika
(1959), 493–5

**4.25
On the Further Expansion of the Rights of the Central
Committees of the Union Republic Parties, of Krai,
Oblast, City, and Raion Party Committees, and of Primary
Party Organizations in Resolving Party-Organizational
and Financial-Budgetary Questions** 30 September 1958

In extension of the resolutions adopted earlier by the Central Committee of the CPSU, the central committees of the union republic parties, the krai, oblast, city, and raion party committees, and primary party organizations are granted the right to resolve the following questions:

The central committees of union republic parties:

1   May approve and alter – when especially necessary and in agreement with the Party Organs Section and the Administration of Affairs of the CPSU Central Committee – the structure of individual city and raion party committees, within the limits of the staff and salary accounts of the republic party organs.

2   May, as an exception, confer on the party committees of large enterprises and organizations, containing more than 1000 Communists, the rights of party raion committees as regards disciplinary affairs of Communists, the registration of members and candidate members, and admission to the CPSU.

3   The central committees of union republic parties must report to the Central Committee all decisions on the matters mentioned in paragraph 2.

Oblast and krai committees, and the central committees of union republic parties:

1   May set the dates by which the city and raion party committees must submit their accounts of party membership dues, bearing in mind that the central committees of the union republic parties and the krai and oblast party committees submit such accounts to the Central Committee once every three months. In this connection the appropriate changes should be made in the wording of sections 9 and 10 of the Instruction on Membership Dues for party members and candidate members.

2   May authorize the establishment of non-staff instructors in party committees in order to involve more Communists in active work and to give more care to the training of young party workers.

3   Whenever necessary, may translate into the local national languages the texts of decisions, letters, and other documents sent to the city and raion party committees, and also to the primary party organizations, by the CPSU Central Committee, ensuring strict observance of the established procedure for the custody and return of such circulated documents.

4   May discuss the advisability of submitting to the oblast and krai party committees, and to the Central Committee, records of meetings of the

bureau or of plenary meetings of the city and raion committees, or of meetings of party members.

City and raion party committees and primary party organizations:

1   May replace the party documents of party members and candidate members who have changed their first or last names through marriage; this is done at the direction of the first secretary of the raion or city party committee (upon submission of proof of marriage) and need not be examined by the bureau of the raion or city committee.

2   City and raion party committees may destroy on the spot any party cards, candidates' cards, or the associated registration forms, which have been mutilated for one reason or another, except for the face of the party or candidate's card which is to be sent, following the established procedure, to the Central Committee of the CPSU.

3   May resolve questions of the advisability of primary party organizations submitting the records of their general meetings or bureau meetings to the city or raion party committee.

4   In accordance with this decree the necessary changes are to be made in Central Committee instructions, 'Procedure for Registering and Issuing Party and Candidate's Cards of the 1954 Format' and 'registration of CPSU Members and Candidate Members.'

Spravochnik partiinogo rabotnika
(1959), 555–6

4.26
On Work with Cadres in the Party Organization of Kirgiziia   21 October 1958

This resolution reflects the general features of personnel policy under Khrushchev. It is also of particular interest from the standpoint of nationality policy. While it suggests – in line with other contemporary official statements – that a hardening of attitudes toward non-Russian culture had occurred after mid-1958, it supports unequivocally the desirability of increasing the percentage of non-Russians among the leadership stratum in the national republics.

Having heard the report of the central committee of the Communist Party of Kirgiziia on its work with cadres, the Central Committee of the CPSU notes that in recent years, and especially since the XX Congress of the CPSU, the party organs of Kirgiziia have implemented a number of measures designed to improve the training of cadres in the most important sectors of party, state, and economic work. The quality of the leading cadres has improved, and the number of workers with secondary and incomplete higher education has increased; quite a few capable and talented organizers, and qualified specialists in science and culture, have been developed from among the indigenous population. This has all exerted a beneficial influence on the development of the republic's economy...

At the same time, work with cadres in the republic is not up to the level of the tasks confronting the Kirgiz party organization in the economic and cultural areas. The attention of the Central Committee and the oblast, city, and raion committees of the party, is not centred on that most important and decisive sector of party work – the selection and promotion of cadres – the result being that serious errors and short-comings have been permitted.

The Communist Party's expansion of the rights of the union republics and the reorganization of leadership in industry, construction, and agriculture, impose new and more stringent demands on the selection of workers. But the party organs do not sufficiently take into account the changed conditions and continue, as before, to study their cadres inadequately; they are frequently unacquainted with rising young workers who deserve promotion and tolerate the continued presence of incapable people in certain responsible positions, persons who are poor organizers and show no promise as leaders.

The party organs of the republic do not effect the necessary supervision of work with cadres in the ministries, departments, and ideological institutions. The party Central Committee and oblast committees have not made sufficient effort to appoint to the rural raions energetic and business-like workers who are capable of providing skilful economic leadership in the new conditions; frequently raion leaders who were not up to their tasks have been replaced by inferior workers devoid of the needed professional and political qualities. This is the principal reason for the slow economic development of many raions – with respect to several important economic indicators the Talass, Uch-Korgon, Kurshab, Batken, and Pokrovsk raions have made no progress in recent years.

The Kirgiz central committee and oblast committees do not give the cadres needed assistance in improving their professional skills and acquiring specialized knowledge.

Many krai and oblast party committees have been insufficiently responsible in selecting cadres for work in the kolkhozes, viewing this as a short-term campaign. The republic contains more than 2000 agronomists, livestock specialists, and veterinarians with higher education, but only 154 of them are working in the kolkhozes. Cadres with low-level qualifications are being trained unsystematically, and too few are being produced for the needs of agriculture, the consequence being that many kolkhozes and sovkhozes are in urgent need of skilled brigadiers, shepherds, and horse-herders. But the raion committees and executive committees do not pay sufficient attention to this important matter. Nor have the party organs of the republic taken energetic measures to improve the placement of party and Komsomol personnel in the decisive production sectors.

These serious short-comings in management of cadres act as a brake on the use of the gigantic reserves in the agriculture of the republic, especially as regards animal husbandry. The enormous areas of natural grazing land and of arable land, the favourable climatic conditions, and the steady increase in the supply of farm machinery to the kolkhozes and sovkhozes permit a large increase in the numbers of cattle, making it possible in the near future to produce two or three times as much meat, milk, and wool. But the republic has not made a suitable effort to improve its meadows and pasturelands, to raise the yields of its perennial grasses. The decisive role of corn as cattle fodder is underestimated ...

Party and soviet organs do not take sufficient pains with cadres for industry and construction. Specialists and qualified workers in the republic are trained unsatisfactorily. One-fifth of the leading and engineering-technical positions in the enterprises, trusts, and administrations of the sovnarkhoz are filled by persons without a technical education, and more than one half of the shop foremen and masters are also in this category. Many factories, mines, and construction sites do not provide adequate housing or cultural conditions, and the result is a high turnover of workers and specialists. This is to a great extent the reason why some enterprises have failed to meet the planned targets for volume of production, for increasing labour productivity, and for reducing unit cost.

The Kirgiz party organs still lag behind in developing cadres of the local nationality for work in the economy, in science, in culture, and in art; they do not make adequate use of the existing institutions of higher education and technical schools, and they do not avail themselves of the educational institutions of the other republics to train the needed specialists of Kirgiz nationality.

The Kirgiz Central Committee and oblast committees are not preparing the necessary reserve of cadres, without which a proper organization of personnel selection and promotion is unthinkable. In many cases the second secretaries of city and raion party committees and the deputy chairmen of executive committees are selected without any thought being given to their growth potential; therefore only a few of them are promoted to first secretary or executive committee chairman. Party organs frequently follow the unjustified course of shifting the same people around from one position to another, thus artificially creating a narrow clique of so-called irreplaceable workers. This all hinders the growth and promotion of capable young workers. The party organization of the republic has slackened its attention to the development and promotion of women, especially Kirgiz women, to leading positions.

The party organs permit considerable short-comings in the selection of cadres for ideological work, make little effort to attract to agitational and propaganda work persons with extensive knowledge of industrial or agricultural economics, literature, or art, provide little guidance of the daily activities of propagandists and agitators. The multinational composition of the population is taken into account insufficiently in mass political work; there are few lectures or speeches on proletarian internationalism, the successes of the leninist nationality policy, or Soviet patriotism; necessary attention is not devoted to propagandizing scientific atheism. Political work often lacks purposefulness and concreteness, is not militant in attacking violators of discipline, private property tendencies, amoral acts, and survivals of the past in everyday life. Leading workers still make too few speeches and lectures to the toilers, do not always know their needs, requests, and feelings, spend little time in the enterprises or visiting the shepherds, horse-herders, and drovers working in isolated pastures.

The central committee and the oblast committees of the Kirgiz Communist Party place little stress on criticism and self-criticism – the major instruments for training cadres, are insufficiently severe and principled in assessing the incorrect and unpartylike conduct of some workers, often fail to discuss their short-comings with them openly, and make a feeble effort to use these errors as a means of training cadres. The party organs inadequately train cadres in the spirit of devotion to ideological principles, adopt a liberal attitude toward party workers who do not meet their obligations, violate the interests of the state, manifest immodest personal behaviour, and misuse their official positions. This is all inimical to the proper training of cadres and weakens state and party discipline.

The Central Committee of the CPSU resolves:

1 The central committee of the Kirgiz Communist Party is directed to eliminate the short-comings mentioned in this resolution and to reorganize its work with cadres to meet the new conditions and tasks. All practical work of party organs with leading cadres is to be centred on increasing their organizational activity, unswerving fulfilment of party and government directives, and the continued development of the economy and culture of the republic.

2 Since the reorganization of the MTSs and the transfer of machinery to the kolkhozes has increased even further the role of the raion organizations in the advance of agriculture, the fundamental task of the Kirgiz Central Committee and oblast committees must be the comprehensive strengthening of the raion party committees, raion executive committees, kolkhozes and sovkhozes by assigning to them experienced and energetic workers who can ensure a sharp increase in the production of meat, milk, wool, cotton, and other agricultural products ...

3 The attention of the central committee of the Kirgiz Communist Party

is directed to the necessity of a bolder promotion to leading positions of young trained workers who are capable organizers and have given a good account of themselves in practical work, ensuring at the same time good collaboration between old, experienced, and young cadres.

At the forthcoming accounting and electoral party conferences and the elections to local soviets of workers' deputies, good and knowledgeable workers are to be selected, whenever this is necessary, as first secretaries of the city and raion party committees and as chairmen of raion and city executive committees. In order to create a cadre reserve, persons of promise are to be proposed as second secretaries of raion and city party committees and as deputy chairmen of raion and city executive committees, and these are to be carefully nurtured and trained for promotion to independent party and soviet work.

4   The party, soviet, and agricultural organs of the Kirgiz SSR are to ensure the correct placement of agricultural specialists, transfering immediately the necessary numbers of agronomists, livestock specialists, and veterinarians from republic and numerous oblast institutions in which they have settled in large numbers, and dispatching them to permanent work in the kolkhozes and sovkhozes. It is necessary to improve considerably the selection and training of kolkhoz cadres with low-level skills. In view of the fact that the number of sheep in the republic is expected to double in the immediate future, a major effort should be made to train shepherds and to supply shepherds' brigades with good, honest, experienced people. Village youth, especially those who have completed secondary education, are to be brought more generally into work on livestock farms. Cadres in animal husbandry are to be seriously strengthened through an influx of Communists and Komsomols.

5   The situation existing in many oblast and city party committees, where supervision and observation of the activities of industrial enterprises is entrusted to persons lacking specialized knowledge and the necessary experience, is to be considered incorrect. The central committee of the Kirgiz Communist Party is directed to strengthen the city and oblast committees by posting to them specialists in industrial production. The efforts of party, economic, and trade union organizations are to be concentrated on the all-round increasing of labour productivity, reduction of the unit cost and improvement of the quality of production, the introduction of new technology and the experience of leading enterprises and production innovators, and fulfilment of the socialist obligations undertaken in honour of the XXI Congress of the CPSU.

The central committee of the Kirgiz Communist Party and the council of ministers of the republic are to develop and implement measures ensuring the more active involvement of the local population, especially the youth, in industry. The turnover of working men and specialists is to be ended through the unconditional fulfilment of housing plans, through improving trade in industrial goods and foodstuffs, especially potatoes, vegetables, meat, and milk; the functioning of dining halls, hospitals, communal and other institutions serving everyday needs is to be upgraded, especially in the cities and workers' settlements.

6   The party organs of Kirgiziia are to bear in mind at all times the need to develop cadres from among the local population for party, governmental, economic, scientific, and cultural-educational work. With an extensive network of higher and secondary specialized educational institutions, the republic possesses the capacity to train on the spot the needed numbers of specialists for most branches of the economy and cultural institutions ...

7   The central committee and the oblast committees of the Kirgiz Communist Party are to intensify their efforts with cadres of ideological and scientific institutions, promoting qualified and politically trained workers to the editorial boards of newspapers and magazines and to work in publishing houses. The Academy of Science of the republic is to be given assistance in improving its training of scientific cadres, especially in the natural science and technical branches of knowledge. Party cadres must work every day to penetrate into the lives and activities of unions of writers, artists, and composers, into theatres, criticizing creative workers from a position of principle, striving for steady improvement in their artistic skills and endeavouring to ensure that their works honestly and clearly reflect the struggle of the Kirgiz people for a new advance in the economy and culture of the republic. The intelligentsia is to be involved more actively in cultural-educational work with the population, and its ties with producers' groups are to be broadened.

8   The party organs of Kirgiziia must eradicate every last trace of formalism and absence of supervision in the marxist-leninist training of communists, improving considerably their study of the theory and history of the CPSU. Cadres are to be educated daily in the spirit of communist devotion to principle, proletarian internationalism, strengthening friendship among peoples, revolutionary vigilance and implacable opposition to short-comings, strict observance of party and state discipline, a high sense of responsibility for the work entrusted to them, and personal modesty. Criticism and self-criticism are to be developed extensively in party organizations, and party workers are to be trained to display a businesslike and concrete approach to work, initiative, persistence and stubbornness in carrying out the directives of the party and government.

Spravochnik partiinogo rabotnika
(1959), 456–70

XXI Extraordinary Party Congress

27 January – 5 February 1959

The XXI Party Congress was attended by 1269 voting delegates. It was convened to approve the main targets of the Seven-Year Plan for 1959–65 – the economic blueprint of khrushchevism. Khrushchev himself delivered the report on this subject (*Current Soviet Policies* III, 41–72). The Congress was officially an 'extraordinary' congress, meaning that it occurred substantially sooner than was necessary under the party Rules. Therefore no report on the work of the Central Committee was delivered and no elections were held. A short resolution calling for the convocation of the next party congress in 1961, as called for in the Rules, was also adopted.

4.27
On the Report by Comrade N.S. Khrushchev 'Control Figures for the Development of the Economy of the USSR in the Years 1959–65'

5 February 1959

The XXI Congress of the CPSU has met at a most important turning-point in history – when the Soviet land, as a result of far-reaching transformations in all aspects of social life, as a result of the victory of socialism, has entered upon a new period in its development, the period of comprehensive building of a communist society. The great goal of building communism, for which many generations have battled, is now being implemented in fact by the Soviet people under the leadership of the Communist Party.

The grandiose scale of the contemplated programme of communist construction in the USSR, the programme of a new and powerful advance of the economy, culture, and material well-being of the people, has no equal in history. The Seven-Year Plan for the development of the economy of the USSR is the concrete embodiment, for the modern era, of the leninist general line of the party ...

The XXI Congress of the CPSU considers the chief tasks of the party in the forthcoming seven years to be:
in economics: a comprehensive development of the country's productive forces; such an increase in production in all branches of the economy, on the basis of the priority development of heavy industry, as will make possible a decisive step forward in creating the material-technical base of communism and ensuring the victory of the USSR in peaceful economic competition with the capitalist countries. The strenthening of the country's economic potential, continued technical progress in all branches of the economy, and a steady increase in the productivity of labour will ensure a considerable rise in the living standard of the people;

in politics: the further consolidation of the Soviet socialist system, of the unity and cohesion of the Soviet people; the development of Soviet democracy, of the activity and spontaneity of the broad popular masses in building communist society; expansion of the functions of social organizations in resolving governmental problems; an enhancing of the organizational and educational role of the party and the socialist state; general consolidation of the union of workers and peasants, of the friendship of the peoples of the USSR;

in ideology: intensification of the party's ideological and educational work; heightening of the communist consciousness of the toilers, and especially of the younger generation, educating them in a communist attitude toward labour, in Soviet patriotism and internationalism; overcoming the remnants of capitalism in the consciousness of individuals; the struggle with bourgeois ideology;

in international relations: consistent implementation of a foreign policy designed to protect and consolidate peace and the security of peoples on the basis of the leninist principle of peaceful coexistence of countries with different social systems; ending the 'cold war' and relaxing international tension; a comprehensive strengthening of the world-wide socialist system and the commonwealth of fraternal peoples.

The fundamental problem of the forthcoming seven years is to gain maximum time in the peaceful economic competition between socialism and capitalism. The economy must develop at a high rate and maintain the necessary proportions.

Attributing primary importance to the development of industry, and especially heavy industry, the XXI Congress of the CPSU considers it essential that the Seven-Year Plan provide for a total increase of about 80 per cent in industrial production, an increase in Group A (production of the means of production) of from 85 to 88 per cent and in Group B (production of consumer goods) – of from 62 to 65 per cent. The average yearly increase in gross output from 1959 to 1965 is to be about 8.6 per cent for industry as a whole – 9.3 per cent for Group A and about 7.3 per cent for Group B ... [Gross industrial output in 1965 was 84 per cent higher than in 1958. Group A was 97 per cent higher while Group B reached 60 per cent; *Narodnoe khoziaistvo SSSR v 1965 g.*]

In agriculture the fundamental task is to reach a level of production which will completely satisfy the food requirements of the population and the needs of industry for raw materials, meeting all other needs of the state for agricultural production. This task is to be resolved primarily through a considerable increase in the yields of all crops, an increase in livestock and continued growth in the productivity of socialized animal husbandry.

During the seven years, gross agricultural output is to increase 1.7 times, and output in the most important categories is to reach the following levels: grain – 10-11 billion puds; sugar beets – 76-84 million tons; raw cotton – 5.7-6.1 million tons; meat (slaughtered weight) – not less than 16 million tons; milk – 100-105 million tons; potatoes – 147 million tons; vegetables – quantities sufficient to satisfy fully the needs of the population. [Gross agricultural output in 1965 was only 15 per cent higher than in 1958. The 1965 production figures were: grain – 7.3 billion puds; sugar beets – 72.3 million tons; raw cotton – 5.66 million tons; meat – 10.0 million tons; milk – 72.6 million tons; potatoes – 88.7 million tons; and vegatables – 17.6 million tons, as against 14.9 in 1958; *Narodnoe khoziaistvo SSSR v 1965 g.*]

The main line in agriculture will henceforth remain a general increase in the production of grain as the foundation of all agricultural production. Today the kolkhozes and sovkhozes are in every way equipped to increase the yield of grain crops everywhere, in the very near future, by an average of three of four centners per hectare. [The average yield of grain crops in kolkhozes and sovkhozes in 1958, the year before the start of the Seven-Year Plan, was 11.1 centners per hectare. In 1965, the last year of the Seven-Year Plan, the average yield was 9.5 centners; *Narodnoe khoziaistvo SSSR v 1965 g.*] The fundamental task in animal husbandry is to increase the production of meat, milk, wool, and eggs; this is to be attained by increasing the numbers of livestock and raising the productivity of all varieties, and also by raising more poultry and rabbits on kolkozes and sovkhozes. The fodder-crop base of agriculture must be strengthened even more persistently, primarily by increasing the production of corn, potatoes, sugar beets, and such leguminous crops as clover, alfalfa, vetch – oats mixtures, peas, lupine, and other crops, with due regard for the characteristics of the different crop zones. The production of soybeans must be increased.

An important task is the successful fulfilment and overfulfilment of the annual plans for procurement of agricultural products of all varieties.

The Congress expresses its confidence that the movement, now developing in the country, for the fulfilment ahead of time of the control-figure targets in agricultural production, especially the production of meat and other livestock products, will make it possible not only to fulfil but also to overfulfil the Seven-Year Plan with respect to target dates and with respect to quantities. Deserving of general approval is the initiative of those republics, krais, and oblasts which have developed concrete measures to increase agricultural production in the immediate future and have undertaken the obligation to increase meat production 2 or 3 times, or more, as early as 1959. By meeting the obligations which they have shouldered, the republics, krais, oblasts, raions, kolkhozes, and sovkhozes will make a worthy contribution to meeting the challenge issued by the leading kolkhozes and sovkhozes – in a short time to catch up with the United

States in the per capita production of meat and other agricultural products. The contribution of each republic, krai, oblast, raion, kolkhoz, and sovkhoz to meeting this challenge is to be evaluated in terms of the production of livestock products per 100 hectares of land.

In order to perform successfully the major tasks which will confront agriculture in the forthcoming seven years, party, soviet, and agricultural organs must in every way consolidate the communal economy of the kolkhozes, must make major strides in the continued mechanization and electrification of agricultural production, in improving the organization of labour, and on this foundation ensure a significant rise in labour productivity and a lowering of the unit cost of agricultural products. The role of the sovkhozes as the leading socialist agricultural enterprises must continue to grow ...

In order to attain a high rate of expanded socialist reproduction the Congress considers it necessary that substantial measures be undertaken in capital construction during the next seven years. In comparison with the preceding seven years the volume of state capital investment will increase 1.8 times and reach the level of approximately 1940-1970 billion rubles, which is almost equal to the total capital investment in the economy in all the years of Soviet power ...

In view of the unprecedented scale of construction in the forthcoming seven years and the need to gain maximum time and achieve the maximum economy of labour, particular attention must be devoted to the correct distribution of productive forces. The further economic development of the country's eastern regions, possessing gigantic natural resources, is to be emphasized. In resolving problems of the continued buildup of productive capacities preference must be accorded to the regions in which investment will have the greatest economic effect. Party organizations must ensure the strictest observance of state interests, eradicating the slightest manifestation of localism.

The Soviet Union is a multinational socialist state founded upon friendship among peoples with equal rights unified by a single will and aspiration to advance along the path of communist construction. Our plans give cogent expression to the leninist nationality policy which provides broad opportunities for the comprehensive development of the economies and cultures of all peoples.

The Seven-Year Plan calls for an enormous growth in the economies of all the union republics. Each republic is to develop primarily those branches of the economy for which the natural and economic conditions are most favourable, so as to make more effective use of the resources of each republic and to ensure the correct combination of the interests of the individual republics and of the Soviet Union as a whole.

In the view of the Congress a major task of the Seven-Year Plan is to effect a substantial rise in labour productivity – the principal source of expanded socialist reproduction and accumulation and the foundation of the further advance of the living standard of the people. During the course of the seven years, labour productivity in industry is to increase by 45-50 per cent, in construction by 60-65 per cent, in railroad transport by 34-37 per cent, in sovkhozes by 60-65 per cent, and in kolkhozes it should approximately double ...

The XXI Congress of the CPSU considers that the gigantic advances in industrial and agricultural development have created all necessary conditions enabling the Soviet people to live still better, with fuller satisfaction of their material and spiritual needs in the near future. To this end the Seven-Year Plan provides for:

a 62-65 per cent increase in national income, which will yield a substantial increase in public consumption; over the seven-year period consumption will increase by 60-63 per cent;

a 40 per cent increase in the real incomes of workers and employees, calculated on the basis of an average worker, and also a real increase of not less than 40 per cent in the real incomes of kolkhoz members; taxes on the population are to be abolished in the near future;

measures to eliminate inconsistencies in pay scales and to raise the pay of the lowest-paid categories of workers and employees, over the seven-year period, from 270-350 rubles per month to 500-600 rubles per month;

an increase in the minimum old-age pension levels from the present 300 rubles to 400 rubles per month in cities, and from 255 to 340 rubles for pensioners living in the countryside and connected with agriculture; also an increase in minimum levels of disability pensions and pensions paid to compensate for loss of the family wage-earner;

a substantial improvement in everyday and other services provided for the population, an expansion of the network of public restaurants, and a reduction in the cost of the food served in them;

an increase in the number of boarding schools, nursery schools, kindergartens, and old-age homes;

a broad surge in housing and communal construction, with about 650-660 million square metres of housing being built, over the seven-year period, in cities and workers' settlements (this being about 15 million apartments); in rural areas the kolkhoz members and the village intelligentsia are to build about 7 million houses;

measures to shorten the working day and the working week. By 1960 all workers and employees are to work a seven-hour day, and those who work underground in the basic occupations connected with coal mining and other kinds of mining are to work a six-hour day. In 1962 workers and employees with a seven-hour working day are to shift to a 40-hour work week. Starting in 1964 persons working underground and in hazardous

occupations are gradually to pass to a 30-hour work week, and all others to a 35-hour week with two days off and a working day of 6-7 hours;
an increase of approximately 62 per cent in state and co-operative retail trade. There is to be a substantial increase in the retail sale of livestock products, vegetable oils, sugar, citrus and other fruits, of such industrial goods as cloth, clothes, underwear, shoes; and also of household and cultural goods, and products of everyday use, especially those which ease the woman's work in the home ...

In defining the tasks presently encountered in the building of communism the XXI Congress of the CPSU is guided by the Soviet Union's entry into a new era of historical development. Socialism in our country has achieved a complete and final victory. The time has passed when the Soviet Union was the only socialist state, and in a hostile capitalist encirclement. Now two world-wide social systems exist: the moribund capitalist system and the socialist one, full of increasing vitality, which engages the sympathies of the toilers of all countries. No power in the world could restore capitalism in our country or overpower the socialist camp.

Under the party's guidance the Soviet people have achieved such victories of socialism in all areas of economic and socio-political life that the creation of the material and technical basis of communist society and the planned transition to communism have become practically realizable tasks. Communism can be attained only if we exceed the level of production of the advanced capitalist countries and ensure higher labour productivity than that of capitalism.

Along with its abundance of material goods, the full-scale building of communism will provide a truly rich spiritual culture satisfying the needs of all in ever-increasing measure, will ensure the continued development of socialist democracy, and will train conscious toilers for the communist society.

With the growth of productive forces there should also be an improvement in socialist social relations, which are based on the principles of comradely cooperation, friendship, and mutual understanding. Technical progress in all branches of the economy and the closer ties between study and production will wipe out substantial differences between mental and physical labour and will raise the cultural and technical level of all toilers. The shortening of the working day and the continued improvement of working conditions through the complex mechanization and automation of production will promote the conversion of labour into a vital necessity for the comprehensive development of the individual.

The kolkhoz system is being consolidated by the measures adopted in recent years to advance agriculture and by the growth in the communal economy of the kolkhozes; its advantages and its enormous potential are becoming increasingly manifest. This all shows that the kolkhoz-cooperative form of production relations serves, and can long continue to serve, the development of the productive forces of agriculture.

With progress in the building of communism there will be a rise in the level of socialization of kolkhoz production, kolkhoz-cooperative property will merge with publicly owned property, and the boundaries between them will be wiped out. The indivisible kolkhoz funds will grow and become consolidated, inter-kolkhoz production ties will develop on a broader scale. Kolkhoz-cooperative property will merge with public property in the future not through curtailment of kolkhoz-cooperative property but through elevation of the degree of its socialization to that of publicly owned property, with the assistance and support of the socialist state.

Under the present conditions of the building of communism the distribution of material goods is based on the governing principle: from each according to his ability, to each according to his work. Distribution according to work gives people a material interest in the results of production, stimulates the growth of labour productivity and of workers' qualifications, improves production technology; it also plays an important educational role, accustoms people to socialist discipline, and makes labour universal and compulsory. Egalitarian distribution would eat into the accumulated funds and would damage the building of communism.

With the development of socialist society and the growth of mass consciousness there will be an increasing rise in the labour enthusiasm of Soviet people, in their concern for the prosperity of society; the striving for gain will die away, and moral stimuli to work for the well-being of society will take on increasing significance.

The transition to distribution according to need will be gradual, in step with the development of productive forces, when an abundance of all necessary consumer goods has been attained and when people will all work willingly according to their capacities and regardless of how much they receive in the way of material goods, knowing that this is necessary for society.

Already today in Soviet society a substantial and increasing share of the material and cultural benefits are distributed free, in the form of pensions, scholarships for students, payments to mothers of large families, funds for building and maintaining schools and hospitals, nursery schools, kindergartens, boarding schools, and also clubs, libraries, and other cultural institutions. The social share in consumption will continue to increase, a major precondition of the gradual transition to the communist principle of distribution.

The Congress notes that at present the chief direction in the development of the socialist state system is the all-round development of democracy, involving all citizens in the guidance of economic and cultural construction and in the administration of public affairs. The role of the soviets as mass organizations of the toilers must be enhanced. Many functions presently fulfilled by organs of the state will be gradually transferred to social organizations. Questions of cultural services, health protection, physical culture, and sports are to be resolved with the active and broad participation of social organizations. In the matter of ensuring observance of the rules of the socialist community an increasingly important role is to be played by the volunteer militia, the comradely courts and other such autonomous organs; together with state institutions they must perform the functions of preserving order in society, defending the rights of citizens, and preventing deeds harmful to society.

The passage of certain functions from state organs to social organizations will not weaken the role of the socialist state in building communism but will broaden and strengthen the political foundation of socialist society, ensuring the continued development of socialist democracy. The Soviet state will be able to devote even greater attention to development of the economy which is the material foundation of our system.

The socialist state has exceptionally important tasks to perform in defending peace, in defending the country from the threat of military attack by the imperialist states. As long as an aggressive imperialist camp continues to exist, the Soviet state is compelled to strengthen and improve its glorious Armed Forces – the Army and the Navy which guard the conquests of socialism and the peaceful labour of the Soviet people. It is necessary to strengthen the organs of state security, whose cutting edge is directed primarily against agents smuggled in by the imperialist states. The function of defending the socialist fatherland at present fulfilled by the state will die out only with the complete disappearance of the threat of an imperialist attack ....

The people's limitless love and confidence in their own party is fully demonstrated by the growth in the ranks of the CPSU through the influx of the best members of the working class, the kolkhoz peasantry, and the Soviet intelligentsia. Since the XX Congress the party has striven consistently to become more democratic, to expand criticism and self-criticism, to increase the activity of the party masses. The Central Committee and the local party organizations have struggled resolutely to restore, and to further develop, Leninist norms of party life and the principles of collective leadership.

All experience in the struggle for the victory of socialism and communism shows that in the process of building a communist society the role of the party, as the tested vanguard of the people and the highest form of social organization, continues to grow ...

The Congress considers that the primary role in implementing the Seven-Year Plan rests with the party and state cadres. There must be an improvement in the distribution and training of cadres; leading positions must be filled by trained persons, persons of principle, persons with a feeling for what is new, who will devote all their strength and knowledge to the well-being of the people, who will approach their work with bolshevik passion, who will be implacable toward short-comings. Young people must be promoted more boldly, must be given the chance to display their abilities in practical work.

The party organizations must send qualified cadres to work in backward enterprises, kolkhozes, sovkhozes, and raions, selecting good organizers and specialists who will be able to draw on the large reserves, organize people, and bring forward the lagging sectors ...

At the present stage of social development the role of the soviets of workers' deputies is further enhanced. The republic, krai, oblast, city, raion, and village soviets must concern themselves every day with the chief aspects of the fulfilment of the Seven-Year Plan targets by industrial enterprises and construction projects, kolkhozes, and sovkhozes, must give thought to elevating the well-being and culture of the toilers. The work of soviet organs will be the more fruitful the more they rely on the activity of the masses and the more resolutely they do away with red tape and bureaucratism.

Certain changes and additions must be made to the Constitution of the USSR. Since the Constitution was adopted important changes have occurred in the political and economic life of the Soviet Union, and the international scene has changed as well. All of these changes should be reflected and embodied legislatively in the Constitution of the Union of Soviet Socialist Republics ...

Today the principal task of the Communist Party and the Soviet people is to ensure the absolute fulfilment of the Seven-Year Plan for development of the economy. Accomplishment of the tasks confronting the party and the government in the ensuing seven years will be of enormous importance for the further consolidation of the might of our country. Furthermore, fulfilment of the Seven-Year Plan for development of the economy of the USSR, which is oriented basically toward the peaceful development of the economy and the advance of public welfare, will further strengthen the country's defensive capacities and heighten its preparedness to deal a crushing rebuff to any encroachments by imperialist aggressors on the great conquests of socialism. The successes of peaceful economic development in the USSR and all the socialist countries will be an additional expression of the advantages of socialism over capitalism and will even further intensify the attraction of the great ideas of marxism-leninism ...

Pravda, 7 February 1959 *KPSS v rezoliutziiakh* VII, 373–495

**4.28
On the State of Mass Political Work among the
Toilers of Stalino Oblast and Measures
for Improving It** 11 March 1959

The XXI Congress of the Communist Party of the Soviet Union has approved a vast programme for building communism in our country. Now that the Soviet Union has entered a new period in its historical development, party organizations must resolutely heighten the level of their ideological-political and organizational efforts, making broad and comprehensive use of all the varied forms and means of communist education of the masses, mobilizing the creative forces of the Soviet people for fulfilment and overfulfilment of the Seven-Year Plan.

Having heard and discussed the report of the Stalino Oblast committee of the Ukrainian Communist Party and that of the Propaganda and Agitation Section of the CPSU Central Committee, entitled 'On the State of Mass Political Work Among the Toilers of Stalino Oblast and Measures for Improving It,' the CPSU Central Committee notes that, through the great organizational and mass political effort which it has exerted in recent years among the toilers, the party organization of Stalino Oblast has achieved serious successes in economic and cultural construction ...

The party organizations of the oblast have raised the level of political agitation. Mass agitational work was especially enlivened in connection with the XXI Congress, becoming more topical and concrete and answering the principal practical questions of the building of communism. Many party, soviet, trade union, and economic leaders participate in mass-political work, as do advanced persons in production, engineers, technicians, and agricultural specialists. A number of city and raion party committees are systematically disseminating and discussing the proposals and critical comments of workers and kolkhozniks, taking the necessary action on them.

At many enterprises, construction sites, kolkhozes and sovkhozes the party organizations, in order to increase the labour activity of workers and kolkhozniks, and to involve them in the solution of basic production problems, make skilful use of diversified forms and methods of work: mass public reviews and surprise inspections to check on the organization of labour, the state of working areas, and the use of machinery; permanent production conferences, economic and technical production conferences, days honouring leading brigades; and mutual verification of the fulfilment of socialist obligations. Much effort is made to generalize the experience of innovators in industrial and agricultural production and to put it into practice.

In educating youth in the revolutionary and labour traditions of the working class an important role is played by meetings with veterans of the

October Revolution, the Civil War, the Great Patriotic War, and with eminent figures in production – such meetings taking place in enterprises, kolkhozes, institutions, and educational institutions. Workers and kolkhozniks are very fond of documentary records and films, satirical leaflets, special programmes on the 'miners' television,' evening universities of culture, and many other forms of mass political work.

This all greatly enriches the content of political agitation, raises the interest of the toilers in the measures being conducted by the party, and has a beneficial effect on the fulfilment of the economic plans by the oblast.

At the same time the CPSU Central Committee notes that the party organizations in Stalino Oblast continue to display serious short-comings in mass political work. Successes in the development of industry, agriculture, and culture could have been considerably greater if all party organizations had conducted daily, extensive political work with the masses. Many party organizations do not maintain constant supervision over the content of political agitation, concern themselves little with its effectiveness. The party oblast committee does not utilize with sufficient persistence the whole gamut of forms and methods of communist education of the toilers, does not take the necessary steps to ensure a broader dissemination of the valuable experience accumulated in some of the party organizations of the oblast.

Major occurrences in the life of the country, questions of international affairs, and decisions of the party and government are not always elucidated for the benefit of workers and kolkhozniks in a timely, intelligible, and convincing manner. Reports and discussions make insufficient use of vivid and vital facts and examples which would help the listeners to gain a more profound grasp of the party's policies. Agitation is frequently declarative, superficial, and formal in character, has little bearing on the concrete tasks of the given enterprise or kolkhoz, is not directed at overcoming difficulties in work, at consolidating labour discipline, and for that reason has no influence on the solution of production problems ...

Many party organizations, agitators, lecturers, and speakers struggle inadequately against manifestations of localism, self-seeking, and disregard for state interests, fail to create the requisite public opinion with respect to people who violate labour and production discipline and the rules of the socialist community. They often turn a blind eye to instances of plunder of public wealth, drunkenness, absenteeism; they do not always react rapidly and severely to manifestations of bourgeois ideology, to various rumours, to slanderous fabrications spread by hostile and philistine elements.

In their mass political work some village party organizations fail to concentrate enough attention on solving fundamental problems of the continued development of the kolkhoz system: raising crop yields, comprehensively developing communal animal husbandry and improving its productivity, reducing the unit input of labour, improving agricultural methods and techniques, using machinery rationally, increasing the size of the kolkhoz indivisible funds, developing inter-kolkhoz enterprises, studying and disseminating most advanced practices. In many kolkhozes lectures and reports are rare, there are no radios, the population has little access to the cinema, and artistic activities are desultory. There are lengthy delays in the deliveries of newspapers and magazines to many kolkhozes, brigades, and farms.

One of the main reasons for the serious short-comings in mass political work is the unsatisfactory selection, assignment, and training of agitators in many party organizations; there is no constant supervision of the activities of agitators, lecturers, and speakers; they are not assisted systematically in their work ...

In the view of the Central Committee of the CPSU the fundamental task of all party and Komsomol organizations is the thorough study and elucidation of the report at the XXI Party Congress on the control figures for the development of the economy of the USSR in the years 1959–65, the decisions of the historic extraordinary XXI Congress of the CPSU, the development of many-sided party political work among the masses to mobilize everyone's efforts to implement these decisions, to fulfil and overfulfil the targets of the Seven-Year Plan for developing the economy of the USSR ...

The Central Committee directs the attention of party organizations to the fundamental importance of mass political work and communist education of the toilers under the present conditions, when our country has entered upon a new and very important period in its development – the period of the expanded construction of a communist society; these become central in the activity of party, soviet, Komsomol, trade union, and other social organizations.

The building of communism is organically linked with a continuous increase in the consciousness of all citizens, with the education of the toilers – and especially of the youth – in the spirit of communist morality and of a correct attitude toward labour, toward their social obligations ...

Party organizations, propagandists, and agitators must explain to the toilers in a clear and intelligible manner precisely what communism is, what great benefits it confers on the people; they must actively and in every way support and develop the beginnings of communism. All Soviet people must be profoundly aware that communist ideals can be realized only in conditions of material and spiritual abundance and that in the creation of these conditions an increase in the production of metal, machinery, in the extraction of oil and coal, the generation of electricity, the production of grain, meat, oil, clothes, and shoes, and in housing construction is of fundamental significance.

A major duty of propagandists and agitators is to bring to the consciousness of each toiler the fact that the most developed capitalist countries can be overtaken and left behind only when we have attained a higher level of labour productivity ...

A closer bond between mass political work and the practical problems of everyday life is the guarantee of its success. The party organizations of industrial enterprises must conduct political agitation in such a way as to ensure the absolute fulfilment of production plans by each enterprise, sector, shop, brigade, and worker; the pace of work must be rhythmical, labour productivity must be raised in every way, the quality of the product must be improved and its unit cost reduced, instruments and materials must be strictly economized, production must be mechanized and automatized on an extensive scale, new technology must be introduced and used even better, most advanced practices must be publicized and incorporated.

The village party organizations are ordered to concentrate on the comprehensive explanation and implementation of the directives of the XXI Congress of the CPSU, and the resolution of the December Plenum of the CPSU Central Committee, 'Results of the Development of Agriculture During the Past Five Years and the Tasks of a Continued Increase in Agricultural Production.' The struggle must be intensified for a continued increase in crop yields, for an expansion in numbers of cattle and for high productivity of communal animal husbandry, for the creation of a firm fodder base in kolkhozes and sovkhozes – mainly through continued extension of the areas sown to corn, for the fullest and most careful use of farm machinery, for an organizational and economic consolidation of the kolkhozes, and for an end to squandering in the expenditure of kolkhoz funds and labour-days ...

Party organizations must intensify their work in educating toilers in the spirit of a collective approach and love for work, of recognition of their social duty, in the spirit of socialist internationalism and patriotism and of observance of the high principles of communist morality. Special attention is to be devoted to the intensified struggle against the remnants of capitalism in the public consciousness, and especially against such shameful manifestations as scorn for socialist labour and discipline, plundering of socialist property, drunkenness, hooliganism, bribetaking, speculation. An implacable struggle is to be conducted against the various manifestations of bourgeois ideology, and all whisperers, intriguers, and spreaders of false rumours and anti-soviet fabrications are to be resolutely unmasked.

All needed steps must be taken to improve the propagandizing of scientific atheism ...

The attention of party organizations is directed to the need for direct participation by leading workers in political agitation, this being a principal determinant of the success of all party efforts at educating the toilers. Whether or not a leader maintains a businesslike day-to-day connection with the masses must be considered a serious criterion for evaluating his work ...

A very important task of party organizations is to improve the selection, assignment, and training of agitators. To this end:

agitators must be carefully selected from among the best prepared communists, Komsomols, outstanding production workers, intellectuals, and persons in leading positions. The best agitators are to be concentrated in the decisive production sectors. The practice is to be reinstituted of confirming agitators and discussing their reports at party meetings and meetings of the party bureau; agitators are not to be overloaded with other assignments;

agitators must be kept regularly informed of the principal issues of domestic and foreign policy, of progress in fulfilling the plans of economic and cultural construction; they must be taught how to give a profound analysis of vital processes, how to connect party policy and the specific tasks confronting the collective of a given enterprise, kolkhoz, or institution. It is essential that agitators be systematically adressed by the first secretaries of oblast, city, and raion party committees, by the chairmen of executive committees of oblast, city, and raion soviets of workers' deputies, by the leaders of economic organizations;

agitators are to conduct regular seminars on various problems of the content and method of mass agitation. Seminars of agitators are to be organized directly in the leading enterprises, in kolkhozes and sovkhozes, wherever there has been positive experience with mass political work;

there must be periodic meetings of agitators from a given city or raion, and also from particular branches of industry or agriculture, for a broader exchange of positive experience in agitational work;

noting that the experience of the Leningrad, Stalino, Azerbaidzhan, Sverdlovsk, and several other party organizations in the creation of schools for agitators has turned out to be justified, party organizations are recommended to make broad use of this technique for training agitators. The curriculums of such schools are to be confirmed by the bureaus of party committees with due regard for the characteristics of each city, raion, enterprise, or kolkhoz;

the leaders of agitation groups may not only be the secretaries of party organizations but also other highly qualified active party members. The city and raion party committees are to convene regular meetings and seminars of leaders of agitation groups for an exchange of experience, for discussion of methods of agitational work, and for evaluation of current themes for lectures and talks with the toilers;

political education centres and offices are to extend assistance to agitators in the selection of the necessary literature and materials, organize individual and group consultations for their benefit, and generalize and disseminate all positive experience with mass political work.

In order to assist party organizers and agitators in their mass political work, the Propaganda and Agitation Section of the Central Committee of the CPSU and Gospolitizdat are directed to publish a popular series entitled *The Agitator's Library*, which will appear periodically and deal with questions of political agitation and with major political issues. A broader effort is to be made to involve party personnel, writers, agitators, and industrial and agricultural specialists in the writing of these pamphlets.

The editorial board of the journal *Agitator* is ordered to devote major attention to assisting agitators in explaining and propagandizing the historic decisions and materials of the XXI Congress of the CPSU, the targets of the Seven-Year Plan, and the domestic and international position of the Soviet Union. Articles and selections containing concrete facts and figures demonstrating the superiority of the socialist system over the capitalist, and the rise in the spontaneous creative activity of the toiling masses, are to be published more frequently. The positive experience of mass political work by party organizations, groups of agitators, and individual agitators is to be given broad treatment. More personnel at the local level are to be involved in the work of the journal.

The editorial boards of the newspaper, *Pravda* and of the journals *Partiinaia zhizn'* (Party Life) and *Agitator* are directed to devote coverage to the experience of the Stalino party organization with mass political work ...

Spravochnik partiinogo rabotnika (1961), 447–60   *KPSS v rezoliutsiiakh* VII, 505–19

4.29
On the Formation in Primary Party Organizations of Industrial and Commercial Enterprises of Commissions to Implement the Right of Party Organizations to Supervise the Administrative Activities of these Enterprises   26 June 1959

The historic targets for the expanded building of a communist society in our country, set by the XXI Congress of the CPSU, can be met successfully if socialist democracy and the creative initiative and spontaneity of the broad popular masses continue to be developed and if social organizations and all toilers are involved even more actively in the administration of state affairs and in the leadership of economic and cultural construction.

The new targets demand an enhancing of the role and responsibility of the party organizations in implementing state plans, in the further expansion of party democracy, and in reinforcing the activity of the party masses. In the contribution of party organizations to the fulfilment of the Seven-Year Plan for development of the economy of the USSR an exceptionally important task is the comprehensive strengthening of the supervision and organization of the execution of party and governmental directives. In this connection particular significance attaches to the extension of social control – as a tested method of improving the operation of all state and economic administrative organs. V.I. Lenin pointed out that one-man management by the individual leader must necessarily be combined with a multiplity of forms and techniques assuring control from below.

The Central Committee notes that the primary party organizations of production and trade enterprises make inadequate use of the right afforded them by the party Rules to supervise the administrative activity of these enterprises, and the existing organizational forms of supervision do not sufficiently meet the demands and targets advanced by the XXI Congress of the CPSU. Such supervision often consists of little more than listening to general reports by economic leaders on the results of the fulfilment of production plans, with many important factors in the functioning of enterprises remaining outside the field of vision of the party organizations. Trade union and Komsomol organizations are still only slightly involved in social control of enterprises.

The Central Committee of the CPSU resolves:

1   In order to eliminate existing short-comings and make fuller use of the right set forth in the CPSU Rules to supervise the administrative activities of enterprises, the primary party organizations of production and commercial enterprises must form commissions, made up of members and candidate members of the CPSU, whose function is to implement the right of party organizations to supervise administrative activities.

Depending upon the character of the enterprise and its conditions of operation the party organizations may set up commissions for supervising the following areas: the promptness and quality of fulfilment of plans and targets for delivery of products to other economic-administrative regions, for export, or to the defence industry; quality of production; introduction of new equipment and technology; mechanization and automation of production, and others. In commercial enterprises commissions are to be set up to supervise the uninterrupted delivery of goods, observance of the rules of Soviet trade, the reduction of trade and production expenses, etc.

The regulation on Commissions in Primary Party Organizations of Production and Trade Enterprises to Implement the Right of Party Organizations to Supervise Administrative Activity is hereby approved.

2   The central committees of the union republic parties, the krai, oblast, city, and raion party committees are hereby directed to extend all neces-

sary assistance to primary party organizations in their establishment of supervision over the functioning of enterprises, and to generalize and disseminate the experience acquired in the operation of these commissions. The directors of sovnarkhozes, enterprises, and other soviet and economic organizations are directed to examine without delay any proposals by primary party organizations and their commissions and their commissions and to take all necessary steps to improve the functioning of enterprises.

Spravochnik partiinogo rabotnika (1961), 555–61   *KPSS v rezoliutsiiakh* VIII, 11–17

4.30
On the Tasks of Party Propaganda under Present Conditions   9 January 1960

At a time of full-scale building of a communist society in our country exceptional significance attaches to our party's ideological work, and especially its decisive area – party propaganda [organized ideological indoctrination, primarily of party members]. The assimilation of a communist outlook, mastery of the fundamentals of marxism-leninism, and a profound understanding of the party's policy become vitally important for each Soviet person. This is determined by the following factors:

in the first place: successful implementation of the programme of communist construction, the creation of the material and technical base of communism, the further strengthening of the economic might of the USSR, and the achievement of an abundance of material goods depend directly upon heightening the level of consciousness of the toilers:

in the second place: as socialist democracy develops and as the socialist state system becomes gradually transformed into communist social self-administration, the method of convincing and educating the masses becomes increasingly the basis for regulating the life of Soviet society;

in the third place: at the present time the formation of the new person with communist character traits, habits, and morality, and the liquidation of the remnants of capitalism in people's consciousness, are among the chief practical tasks;

in the fourth place: the peaceful coexistence of states with different social orders in no way weakens the ideological struggle. Our party has conducted and will conduct an implacable struggle for communist ideology – the most progressive and genuinely scientific ideology of the present age ...

An examination of the state of ideological work in Moscow and

Leningrad, in the Ukrainian, Belorussian, Kazakh, Georgian, and Uzbek Soviet Socialist Republics, in the Sverdlovsk, Saratov, Ulianovsk, and other oblasts of the RSFSR demonstrates that in recent years party organizations have effected a serious reconstruction of party propaganda. A series of measures have been taken to overcome elements of dogmatism – the fundamental defect which became widespread under the influence of the cult of personality and which did considerable harm to ideological and educational work. The abnormal situation in which propaganda was oriented primarily toward the past and based entirely on the *History of the All-Union Communist Party (Bolsheviks). Short Course* with the pre-revolutionary period of the party's development being studied for years, has been basically eliminated. It did not give rise to a profound study of the Soviet people's experience in the struggle for the victory of socialism and was of little assistance in elucidating present problems in the theory and policy of our party.

After the XX and XXI congresses of the CPSU ideological life was considerably activated in our country and rose to a new stage. The propagandizing of communist ideology became more lively and variegated; its effectiveness was heightened, as was its organizing and mobilizing role. The works of K. Marx, F. Engels, and V. I. Lenin, as well as the resolutions of congresses and of plenums of the CPSU Central Committee, were studied more deeply and propagandized more extensively; a number of books were written drawing general conclusions from the practice of socialist construction, and also a series of valuable texts on marxism-leninism; newspapers and magazines improved their propagandizing of the theory and policy of the party.

By applying these new forms party organizations effected a noticeable improvement in the economic education of members, and this in turn had a beneficial impact upon the guidance of enterprises, construction operations, kolkhozes, and sovkhozes. Increased attention was paid to the history of the CPSU, especially to its post-October period, and also to marxist philosophy, to the party's domestic and foreign policy, to major aspects of the building of communism in the people's democracies, and to the world-wide communist, labour, democratic, and national liberation movement. Criticism of bourgeois ideology and modern revisionism became more active and profound. Many-sided experience has been accumulated in ideological work, the number of persons involved in propaganda work has increased, their theoretical and methodological training have improved, and the material basis of party propaganda has been strengthened considerably.

None the less the Central Committee considers that oral and written propaganda still suffer from major short-comings.

The major short-coming of party propaganda remains its failure to overcome completely its isolation from life, from the practice of builders of communism.

Party organizations frequently forget that the basic meaning of propaganda lies in its effectiveness as expressed in concrete results attained in a given sector of communist construction, that the struggle to create the material and technical basis of communism, for an abundance of material and spiritual wealth, for the organization of production on a higher level, remain inalienable elements of ideological work. The fact that success in ideological and educational work itself depends on the development of the material base of society and that the future communist man can be trained only in the course of the struggle to realize certain practical goals, must not be overlooked.

Both oral and printed propaganda are still, as a rule, insufficiently concrete and purposeful, often abstract and purely instructive, limited to general appeals and slogans, and cut off from the acute questions which agitate the popular masses. The living ideas of communism are often presented to the consciousness of the masses as abstractions and not in the form of definite concrete tasks; stress is laid on the mechanical memorizing of bookish formulas and not on a creative understanding of the essence of marxist-leninist theory, not on the struggle to realize communist ideals in life. The instilling of a communist attitude toward labour, the struggle for the practical implementation under modern conditions of the principle 'he who does not work shall not eat,' the campaign against loafers and the remaining parasitic elements who want to live at society's expense without giving anything in return, have not found their proper place in propaganda work.

Both oral and printed propaganda insufficiently reveal the profound theoretical and practical meaning of the measures carried out by the party in recent years; new communist departures in the life of our society are poorly generalized and popularized; most advanced practices in industrial and agricultural production are inadequately disseminated. Propaganda is often diffuse, failing to take into account local conditions and also the age, occupational, education, national, and other characteristics of the different strata of the population.

The advantages of socialism are poorly and sometimes unskilfully elucidated in ideological and educational work, and insufficient use is made of the outstanding achievements of our motherland in all areas of social life to educate Soviet people in the spirit of Soviet patriotism and national pride. This is a serious oversight, especially when it is remembered that the enemies of socialism are intensifying their propaganda in favour of the capitalist way of life and the reactionary ideology of cosmopolitanism. Some party organizations fail to accord due significance to educating the toilers in the spirit of socialist internationalism, to the indestructible and continually strengthening friendship of peoples, to implacable hostility toward the remnants of bourgeois nationalism, toward the restoration, and artificial inculcation as 'national traditions,' of backward reactionary manners and customs, toward the slightest attempt to oppose falsely understood local 'interests' to the overall interests of the Soviet people's struggle for communism.

While decisively condemning dogmatism in ideological work and its isolation from practical tasks, the CPSU Central Committee none the less notes for the benefit of party organizations, the impermissibility of underestimating theory, and calls attention to occasions when a superficial elucidation and analysis of problems of economic construction, of concrete economics and current politics, without their creative comprehension, without drawing profound theoretical generalizations and conclusions, could have been damaging to the formation of a communist outlook among the toilers.

Another serious short-coming of party propaganda is that its sphere of influence is too narrow, it has too little mass appeal, and is not always presented in an accessible form.

All the conditions have now been created for expanding the framework of party propaganda, for bringing it within the reach of every worker, kolkhoznik, and intellectual, of every Soviet person. But party organizations do not make sufficient use of these conditions. As before, oral and printed propaganda (party education, lectures, political literature, a considerable part of the periodical press) is directed primarily at party members and candidates, at non-party activists, and intellectuals. Some population groups are entirely outside daily ideological and political influence. Party organizations are still little concerned at ensuring that the system of ideological and educational work among the broad toiling masses should be many-sided and flexible and fully in accord with modern conditions.

Mass exercises designed to reach the broad layers of toilers: lectures and reports, question-and-answer evenings, creative discussions, theoretical conferences, comradely talks, study evenings, Sunday readings, etc., are infrequent and sometimes pitched at a low level. Nor does ideological and educational work make full use of such instruments of propaganda as the press, the radio, television, the cinema, clubs, libraries, and other cultural-educational institutions, and of the best works of literature and art.

Sufficient continuous attention is not devoted to ensuring that lectures, talks, articles, pamphlets, and political exercises are comprehensible and popular. Every party organization is still not concerned to train capable propagandists who love their work, to increase their theoretical competence and methodological skill. Therefore propaganda speeches are occasionally marked by drabness, dryness, and lack of expressiveness; they do not stir up their listeners and readers.

While noting the considerable significance and the positive role of social sciences and those who pursue them for developing and popularizing marxist-leninist theory, for the ideological training of Soviet people, the CPSU Central Committee nonetheless feels that many of the inadequacies in the content of party propaganda are to be explained by a certain lag of social science workers behind the practice of communist construction and the tasks of ideological work. Many economists, philosophers, historians, and other scholars have not yet overcome elements of dogmatism, do not take a bold and creative approach to life, to the experience of the struggle of the masses, poorly elaborate current theoretical and practical questions, are often the prisoners of outmoded and sterile problems.

The social science institutes of the USSR Academy of Sciences, the Institute of Marxism-Leninism of the Central Committee and its branches, the Academy of Social Sciences, and the Higher Party School of the Central Committee, the theoretical journals, and many social science departments of institutes of higher education still have too little contact with the daily lives of party organizations and do not always give active and creative assistance to ideological work.

The Central Committee views as the principal reason for the inadequacies in party propaganda the fact that some central committees of union republic parties, krai, and oblast party committees, as well as the departments and institutions occupied with ideological work, give poor leadership to this major sector of party activity.

The party committees and their propaganda and agitation sections frequently get carried away by the showy side of propaganda, evaluate it mainly by the number of measures implemented instead of by their results, by their consequences for increasing labour and socio-political activity, the communist consciousness of the masses. In many cases party, soviet, and economic leaders rely on the generally satisfactory indices of economic activity of the oblast, raion, enterprise, and kolkhoz, and do not devote due attention to training toilers in a communist spirit. The leaders of some party organizations fail to struggle perseveringly against alien ideology, do not give proper rebuff to manifestations of nationalism, cosmopolitanism, and apoliticalness, are sometimes passive and on the defensive with respect to idealistic religious ideology, which is so hostile to marxism-leninism, react mildly and belatedly to crude violations of labour discipline and of communist moral principles, are conciliatory toward remnants of the past in the consciousness of Soviet people.

Considerable numbers of leading party, soviet, and economic personnel still fail to participate personally in propaganda activities, forgetting that the stubborn effort to increase one's own ideological and theoretical level, close day-to-day contact with people, the active explanation of the great ideas of marxism-leninism to the masses, and the mobilization of the toilers for implementing the party's policy – are the inalienable qualities and the most important duty of every Communist and, even more, of every leading Communist ...

The effectiveness of party propaganda is manifested first of all in concrete production results. An effort should be made to have less political twaddle in propaganda and more concrete struggle for an accelerated tempo of communist construction. Oral and printed propaganda must serve to mobilize the masses for the successful fulfilment of the Seven-Year Plan and of the whole programme of communist construction in the USSR, to increase labour productivity and promote technical progress in the economy, to disclose new reserves and apply most advanced practices, to economize and be thrifty with state instruments and wealth, to further the struggle against stagnation and conservatism, and to inculcate intolerance toward short-comings.

The duty of party propaganda is to use striking examples from life to set forth the advantages of the socialist order and marxist-leninist ideology, to give outstanding case histories from communist work and life, to form ideologically convinced and comprehensively developed members of communist society. The toilers must be trained in a spirit of unshakable faith in the cause of the party and the people, of collectivism and love for work, of socialist internationalism and Soviet patriotism, of lofty moral principles of the new society; an implacable struggle must be waged against occasional manifestations of apoliticalness, nationalism, and cosmopolitanism which are still encountered in our Soviet reality, against remnants of the past: contempt for work and for one's social obligations, the plundering of public property, bureaucratism, bribe-taking, speculation, toadyism, drunkenness, hooliganism, and other phenomena alien to our social order.

An active offensive operation must be conducted against bourgeois ideology, which is so hostile to marxism-leninism, and against its right-socialist and revisionist advocates; the political vigilance of Soviet people must be ceaselessly heightened.

Under contemporary conditions thorough explanation of the foreign policy of the Soviet Union takes on major significance. Party propaganda must avail itself of the concrete facts of the struggle to implement leninist principles of peaceful coexistence in order to instil pride in the toilers for their great motherland, that stands in the vanguard of the forces of peace and progress, to arouse in each Soviet person a burning desire to strengthen the might of the Soviet Union and of the whole socialist camp through his own selfless labour, to participate actively in the great competition between socialism and capitalism, in every way to promote the consolidation of peace throughout the world. It will be necessary, in the future as well, to unmask resolutely the imperialist partisans of a continuation of the 'cold war,' all those who are striving to maintain and exacerbate international tension and the arms race.

The basic content of party propaganda must consist in a profound study and extensive elucidation of the marxist-leninist classics, of the theoretical problems and practical tasks set forth in the decisions of the XX and XXI Party congresses, the plenums of the Central Committee, in the speeches of party and governmental leaders, in the major documents of the international communist movement; it must also include a study of the history of the CPSU, of political economy, of marxist philosophy. Under modern conditions, when marxist-leninist theory has fused with the practice of communist construction, when the resolution of practical tasks of the building of communism is at the same time the resolution of major theoretical questions, life itself must be studied in depth and the practice of communist construction generalized, so that on this basis marxism-leninism may be studied and revolutionary theory may be developed and propagandized.

The CPSU Central Committee emphasizes that the *results of party propaganda, its effectiveness and educational role, will be the greater the more closely it is connected with the creativity of the people, with their life, with the practice of communist construction.* It is necessary to reject once and for all the view that it suffices to set before the listener the sum total of knowledge, supported with quotations, to fulfil the function of a Bolshevik propagandist. Education during the labour process, during the course of the struggle for communism – is the main direction of ideological work under contemporary conditions and one which has entirely justified itself in practice. Party propaganda must be concrete and purposeful; it must enhance the drive of the toilers to resolve pressing economic and political tasks ...

Considering that under contemporary conditions *a mastery of the ideas of marxism-leninism, a profound understanding of the party's policy and the struggle for its realization are a vital need not only of communists but of all toilers*, the framework of propaganda must be expanded so that it reaches each Soviet person ...

The Central Committee calls to the attention of party committees and organizations the necessity for a differentiated approach to propaganda which takes into account all occupational, age, educational, national, and other characteristics of the various strata of the population ...

Party committees are directed to raise the ideological level of *party education*, viewing the creative study of marxism-leninism as the decisive link in all propaganda work.

Considering that a knowledge of the history of the CPSU is of major significance for forming a marxist-leninist outlook, for the communist education of the toilers, the study of party history is to be organized on an extensive basis, differentiated with respect to methods and periods, in the political education system. Primary attention is to be concentrated on the study of the party's activities in the years of the Great Patriotic War, in the pre-war and post-war years, and expecially since the XX Party Congress.

While introducing material generally from the history of local party organizations, it is necessary at the same time to stress the international content of our party's history, to study and elaborate the history of the union republic communist parties as a component part of the history of the CPSU. The organic relationship between the history of the CPSU and that of the world communist movement must be brought to light.

Under contemporary conditions the attention of party organizations must be concentrated on propagandizing economic knowledge, on a profound study of the laws of development of the socialist form of production, especially the ways of creating the material and technical basis of communism, and of further improving production relations in the city and the country. More attention must be devoted to a study of the basic tasks of the development of socialist economics, as outlined by the XX and XXI party congresses and the plenums of the CPSU Central Committee, and also of the urgent economic problems of industry, agriculture, construction, transport, and other branches of the economy.

In the system of political education an important place must be allotted to questions of marxist philosophy, the dialectical-materialistic elaboration of present-day processes in social life, especially the laws governing the transition from socialism to communism and new data in the natural sciences ...

The Central Committee considers that *in organizing political education the centre of gravity must truly be switched to political self-education*, this being the fundamental method of mastering marxism-leninism which has entirely justified itself in practice. At the present time when there has occurred a significant expansion of the general educational, cultural, and political horizon of the toilers, and when theoretical and political literature is being published in mass editions, steps must be taken to ensure that only those enrol in political circles and schools who really lack the necessary training for independent study.

In political self-education *primary attention is to be centred on collective, seminar forms of independent study* ... They must end the practice whereby Communists either entirely cease improving their ideological-political qualifications or else spend year after year chewing over the same old questions which are, as a rule, rather far removed from contemporary reality.

In recent years a flexible system of political education has arisen within the party. In improving it, party organizations must be guided by the fact that no system of political education can be regarded as perfect, as given once and for all. The principal task is to maintain the voluntary principle in selecting the form of political education while at the same time fully satisfying all the numerous demands and interests of Communists and non-party people.

The following model system of political education is recommended for adoption by party organizations:

a the political school as the elementary stage of marxist-leninist education;

b circles and theoretical seminars for studying the history of the CPSU;

c circles and theoretical seminars for studying the fundamentals of marxism-leninism;

d theoretical seminars and circles for studying marxist-leninist philosophy, political economy, concrete economic problems, questions of atheism, current politics, international affairs, the world communist movement, economic schools;

e universities of marxism-leninism; individual specialized study and work in theoretical seminars for the study of particular marxist-leninist classics, particular problems in history of the CPSU and political economy, dialectical and historical materialism, ethics, aesthetics, atheism, in the world communist, labour, democratic, and national-liberation movement, and others ...

Considering that the level of party propaganda depends decisively upon *propaganda cadres*, party organizations are to improve the selection, education, and theoretical and methodological training of the leaders of political schools, circles, and theoretical seminars, of consultants and lecturers. To this end:

a party personnel, engineers, agronomists, and other specialists working in the economy are to be more broadly involved in propaganda activities. It must be borne in mind that propagandizing the ideas of marxism-leninism can be successfully conducted only by comprehensively trained and convinced persons who can set forth the most important doctrines of marxism-leninism creatively, graphically, and intelligibly, with examples from everyday life, who are knowledgeable in concrete economic problems and know well the practical needs of enterprises, kolkhozes, and sovkhozes. More care must be taken to expand the horizons and increase the cultural level of propagandists, to improve their mastery of method;

b the seminars and propaganda courses given by party committees must be improved;

c more information must be given about the experience of propagandists in newspapers, magazines, pamphlets, and books, on the radio and on television. The *Library of the Propagandist* is to be published, being a series of pamphlets on the practice and method of propaganda work;

d the power of public opinion must be brought to bear more actively in propaganda work, more effort must be made to increase the authority of propagandists and give them moral encouragement. The practice of overloading propagandists with social tasks must be forbidden as incorrect and harmful. Propaganda is to be regarded as a fundamental and highly important party assignment ...

Party committees are to promote the activity of *political education houses and offices*, intensifying their role in generalizing and disseminating outstanding case histories in propaganda work, in organizing theoretical and methodological assistance to persons occupied in the independent study of theory, and to propagandists. The practice of establishing, in large primary party organizations, political education offices with broad public involvement, and also methodological councils and groups, is to be encouraged ...

Since the ideological level and scope of political education depend to a considerable extent upon the availability of *textbooks, handbooks of methodology, and visual aids*, their development must continue. It is necessary, in the first place, to issue a variety of short popular handbooks on the component elements and major problems of marxism-leninism, making general use of the proven practice of organizing open competitions.

Popular texts on philosophy, atheism, the economics of industrial and agricultural enterprises, on the history of the international communist movement, and on the history of the national liberation movements of the peoples of Asia, Africa, and Latin America are to be developed for the system of party education and readied for publication in 1960–61; other works to be prepared for the same purpose are various collections of readings (each on a single component of marxism-leninism), works on problems of communist education, on marxist-leninist ethics and aesthetics, on philosophical problems of natural science, and a series of visual aids each designed for a particular form of political education ...

Party committees must extend the scope and raise the ideological level of *propaganda lectures*. The tendency noted in some party organizations to cut down on the number of lectures devoted to marxist-leninist theory is erroneous. A struggle must be waged against the tendency to devote them to generalized abstractions, offensive repetition of truisms, or a superficial enumeration of facts, instead of to serious analysis of the major processes of contemporary social development. The quality of lectures must be systematically supervised. Regular lectures, tailored to the particular audience, which are profound in content and both graphic and intelligible in form, must be given on theory, party history, and party policy in all towns and villages, enterprises, construction sites, kolkhozes, and sovkhozes.

The groups of lecturers attached to the central committees of the union republic parties, the krai, oblast, city, and raion party committees, and the party committees of large primary party organizations must be strengthened. The functioning of the local branches of the All-Union Society for the Dissemination of Political and Scientific Knowledge must be improved, as must that of Komsomol lecture groups, and party supervision over them must be increased. Scientists and scholars, persons active in literature and art, specialists of alll kinds, party, soviet, trade union, Komsomol, and economic personnel, must all be involved more actively in lecturing on a voluntary basis ...

The role of the *press* must be enhanced in the communist education of the people. Now that the task of setting up a varied network of newspapers and magazines, and of issuing books in massive editions, has been basically resolved, the main problem is steadily to increase their ideological level, to use them skilfully to resolve the pressing tasks of communist construction. To this end it is necessary:

a to use the press more frequently to raise, elaborate, and propagandize current political, economic, ideological, moral, and ethical problems as well as new and highly effective forms and methods of party organizational and political work. Newspapers and magazines must become a genuine forum of the people, giving answers to all burning questions; they must intrude more actively into life and give effective assistance to the party in resolving concrete tasks of communist construction and the education of the toilers;

b to improve radically the content and quality of propaganda materials and to show that the theoretical propositions of marxism-leninism are indissolubly connected with the historical creativity of the popular masses. Propaganda in the press should avoid general discussions and repetition, should provide more precise and graphic data and better organized and cogent arguments; the ways in which the materials are presented in the press must become more varied (special columns, reviews, creative discussions, etc.). Militant party journalism should be employed generally; there should be effective explanations and comments on party and governmental measures, on the major events of the country's domestic and international life, and ideology which is alien to Soviet society should be severely unmasked. It is especially important to teach the masses from positive examples, giving broad press coverage to the gigantic successes of the Soviet people, to new communist departures in the life of our society;

c to end the harmful practice whereby only a narrow group of authors participates in press propaganda, and to have press contributions written by party and soviet personnel, scientists and scholars, specialists of all sorts, innovators in industry and agriculture, literary and artistic figures, persevering in the development of new journalists and writers from among persons who are familiar with life and have experience working in the party, the state apparatus, or in the economy, from worker or peasant correspondents. Each newspaper and magazine should have its own tightly knit group of publicists and propagandists, skilful popularizers of revolutionary theory who are capable of responding effectively to topical questions with graphic and forceful press articles;

d to elevate the role of the propaganda sections in the editorial boards of newspapers, assigning to them well-trained and knowledgeable persons. The practice of creating non-staff propaganda sections in raion and city newspapers, and other ways of involving the public in the activity of the press, are to be supported;

e to disseminate more broadly and deeply, in newspapers, magazines, pamphlets, and books, the experience of party organizations and of the best propagandists in ideological educational work; to raise and discuss questions of the practice and method of oral and printed propaganda;

f to issue more mass political literature aimed at the millions of workers and peasants; this literature must present in an accessible and expressive manner present problems in theory and in party policy, must generalize experience in the building of communism and in educating the new man, must clarify the important events of the present. The format of such literature must be small, it must be attractively printed, and it should not be expensive ...

The central committees of the union republic parties, the krai, and oblast party committees, and all party organizations are ordered to make wider use of *radio and television* for propagandizing the ideas of marxism-leninism and for mobilizing the toilers to carry out the plans for building communism. They must elevate the ideological level of radio and television, must regularly transmit short and pithy talks and lectures on the basic problems of marxist-leninist theory and the major questions of the party's domestic and external policy, which are capable of interesting the broadest circles of listeners. Leading persons in the party, the soviets, and in economic life must give systematic lectures and reports on the radio and on television which answer the questions of greatest concern to the toilers ...

The role of social sciences in communist education and in propaganda must be enhanced. Party propaganda can be truly profound and effective only when it is steadily enriched through contributions from imaginative research, when the best scholars participate in it directly and actively. In its turn, social science can carry out its tasks only when organically connected with the practice of communist construction and ideological work, with the urgent demands of party propaganda.

Persons occupied in the social sciences must investigate and describe the struggle of the party and people for the victory of communism, must penetrate into life and creatively develop fundamental contemporary theoretical problems, the fundamental laws of the transition from socialism to communism. It is the honourable duty of Soviet scholars to compile and publish, in the immediate future:

a a multi-volume history of the CPSU which must discuss in comprehensive fashion the multifaceted activity of our party and the world-historic significance of its experience for the world communist movement. [The first of six projected volumes of the new *History of the Communist Party of the Soviet Union*, produced by the Institute of Marxism-Leninism of the Central Committee under the editorship of a board chaired by P.N. Pospelov, was published in 1964. As of 1974 all the volumes of the work had still not appeared in print];

b joint investigations by philosophers, economists, and historians on the major and most pressing problems of the building of communism in the USSR;

c scientific works on the techniques of communist construction, on the laws of development of the world system of socialism, on the world communist, labour, and democratic movement, on the present stage in the general crisis of capitalism, on the collapse of the colonial system of imperialism and the development of the national-liberation struggle of the peoples of Asia, Africa, and Latin America;

d scientific works exposing the pseudoscientific theories of bourgeois, right-socialist, and revisionist defenders of capitalism ...

The Central Committee of the CPSU calls to the most serious attention of party committees and organizations the need for the continued improvement of *ideological education work in secondary and higher educational institutions*, considering that the fusion of study and socially useful labour creates particularly favourable conditions for forming a marxist-leninist outlook and high communist consciousness in student youth.

The quality of instruction in marxist-leninist science must be improved in institutions of higher learning, instructors capable of setting forth the fundamentals of marxism-leninism in a creative and attractive manner must be appointed to work in social science departments, a love for the study of revolutionary theory must be instilled in the students. A persistent effort must be made to ensure that each student master marxist-leninist theory as a creative doctrine and one indissolubly connected with his life and that he be able to guide his practical activity by the principal propositions of this theory. Student youth must be brought to active participation in social life; it must assimilate the concrete skills of propaganda work.

The role of the secondary schools and the secondary specialized educational institutions, which are called upon to educate comprehensively trained builders of the communist society, has increased substantially in connection with the reconstruction of the national educational system. For that reason the concern for forming a communist outlook and for a high level of consciousness among the pupils and students of secondary educational institutions takes on particular significance at the present time. The effort must be made to ensure that while assimilating their academic disciplines the pupils and students master the materialist outlook and the communist ideology, learn to understand the party's policy and to struggle for its realization.

It is advisable to introduce, during the 1961–62 academic year, in the upper years of secondary schools and secondary specialized schools, a popular course in the fundamentals of political knowledge. A special text is to be prepared for use in this course ...

The Central Committee of the CPSU demands that party organizations intensify their guidance of ideological work, and in particular its decisive sector – party propaganda. Questions of party propaganda must be continually at the centre of attention of party committees and primary party organizations and must be systematically discussed at bureau meetings, at plenums, at party membership meetings, and in primary party organizations.

The CPSU Central Committee emphasizes that an indispensable condition for improving the guidance of party propaganda is the correct selection, assignment, and training of cadres. There must be constant improvement in the selection and training of the leading personnel of party committees who are concerned with ideological work; young and well-trained persons must be promoted more boldly.

Party propaganda, political education, and the ideological tempering of Communists and of the toilers generally, is a major task of all Communists and, in the first place, of leading party personnel. It is their duty to be deeply versed in propaganda work, to keep in touch with from day to day, and to participate in it personally; they must serve as examples of stubborn improvement in ideological competence, of the mastery of marxism-leninism. All party organizations must strive to ensure that ideological life is in full swing ...

Pravda, 9 January 1960   *KPSS v rezoliutsiiakh* VIII, 37–58

4.31
On the Experimental Creation of Party Commissions in the City and Raion Party Committees of Moscow, Leningrad, and Moscow Oblast   13 December 1960

1   The Moscow city party committee and the Moscow and Leningrad oblast party committees are hereby permitted to set up, on an experimental basis, in large city and raion party committees, non-staff party commissions for the preliminary examination of questions relating to admission to the party, and to disciplinary affairs of Communists.

2   Each such party commission is to consist of not more than 15 persons taken from the corresponding party committee and from the party mem-

bership; it is approved by the bureau of the city or raion party committee and functions under its immediate guidance.

Communists who have been party members for at least three years are to be approved as chairmen of party commissions.

3   The tasks of the party commission are to include the preliminary study and examination of all disciplinary matters of Communists upon which primary party organizations have taken decisions, and also the summoning of such Communists to discuss these matters at the bureau of the party, city, or raion committee. If the Communist is in agreement with the decision of the primary party organization and with the conclusion of the commission, his disciplinary case may be examined in his absence by the bureau of the city or raion party committee.

With respect to admission to the CPSU, the commission is to obtain preliminary information on those filing applications for party membership, verify the documents to ensure their correctness, and report its conclusions to the bureau of the city or raion party committee.

The bureaus of city or raion party committees approve the decisions of primary party organizations with due regard to the proposal on admission made by the commission in the presence of the applicant.

Partiinaia zhizn', 15 January 1962   *KPSS v rezoliutsiiakh* VIII, 121–2

XXII Party Congress   17–31 October 1961

The XXII Party Congress was attended by 4408 voting delegates, an increase of almost fourfold over the number attending the XXI Congress. Khrushchev delivered both the Central Committee Report and the Report on the Draft Party Programme (*Current Soviet Policies* IV, 42–77, 83–116). This document (4.33), which called for the substantial completion of the construction of communist society in twenty years, had been the subject of enormous publicity and controlled discussion before the Congress, and was the focal point of party propaganda after its adoption at the Congress. The Programme was perhaps the principle monument to khrushchevism, and did not altogether survive his retirement in 1964, although it was not explicitly renounced in any authoritative party pronouncement.

Frol Kozlov gave the report on changes in the party Rules (4.34). The Congress also witnessed the emergence into the open of Sino-Soviet rivalry, and was the occasion for renewed attacks upon stalinism and the 'anti-party group.' Resistance by some party leaders to Khrushchev's attempts to undermine domestic opposition to his own policies was suggested by several speeches delivered at the Congress, as well as by the symbolically important decision (4.35) to remove Stalin's body from the mausoleum in Red Square – an act also directed against the Chinese. After the Congress, G.I. Voronov was raised from candidate to full membership in the Presidium, and Sh. R. Rashidov and V.V. Shcherbitsky became candidate members; P.N. Demichev, L.F. Ilichev, B.N. Ponomarev, and I.V. Spiridonov were appointed secretaries of the Central Committee. The Congress elected a Central Committee of 175 full and 155 candidate members.

4.32
On the Report of the Central Committee   31 October 1961

The XXII Congress of the CPSU meets at a time when our motherland has entered the period of full-scale construction of a communist society, when socialism has become solidly established in the people's democracies, and when the forces of progress and peace are growing rapidly throughout the world.

The years which have elapsed since the XX Congress of the CPSU were of exceptional significance for the life of our party, the Soviet people, and all humanity. In carrying out the leninist general line, the party mobilized all the toilers to fulfil the tasks of communist construction along the whole broad front where this great work is being done. The extraordinary XXI Congress of the CPSU, which adopted the Seven-Year Plan for the development of the economy, was a major milestone in the development of the USSR toward communism.

The XXII Congress of the CPSU takes great satisfaction in summing up the world-historic victories of the Soviet people. The land of the Soviets has travelled the road of heroic struggle and is now in the full flower of its creative efforts. The power of the Soviet Union has increased even further, and there has been an immeasurable growth in its international authority as a fighter for peace and progress, for friendship among peoples, for the happiness of humanity.

The whole course of events confirms the correctness of the theoretical conclusions and the political line of our party. The course set by the XX Congress, which was dictated by life itself, by concern for the popular welfare, and is permeated with the spirit of leninist revolutionary creativity, has triumphed completely.

Having heard and discussed the report by Comrade N.S. Khrushchev, First Secretary of the Central Committee – the Report of the CPSU Central Committee – the XXII Congress of the Communist Party of the Soviet Union resolves:

The political course and practical actions of the CPSU Central Committee in both domestic and foreign policy are fully and completely approved. The conclusions and proposals contained in the Report of the CPSU Central Committee are also approved ...

The Congress notes with satisfaction that, through steady implementation of the *domestic policy* elaborated by the XX Congress, great successes have been achieved in the development of all branches of the economy during the accounting period. Industry and agriculture have been advancing rapidly, the economic might and defence capacity of our motherland have become even greater, and the material and spiritual demands of Soviet people are coming to be satisfied more fully. The creation of the material and technical base of communism is now established on a firm basis.

A very important trait of the period since the XX Congress is the accelerated rate of communist construction.

During the past six years industrial production has risen by almost 80 per cent. The Seven-Year Plan is being carried out successfully. For the first three years of the seven-year period the average annual increase in industrial production has been 10 per cent, instead of the projected 8.3 per cent. New and substantial reserves in the socialist economy have been disclosed and harnessed, which has made possible an increment of about 19 million rubles of industrial production over and above the targets of the first three years of the Seven-Year Plan. Much work has been done on the technical re-equipment of all branches of material production. Thousands of the most modern types of machines, machine tools, instruments, and automation devices have been developed.

The Congress notes that the rearmament of the Soviet Army with nuclear missiles has been effected thanks to the ceaseless concern of the party and the government and to the selfless labour of the Soviet people. In the hands of our people this powerful military technology serves reliably to defend the conquests of socialism and to strengthen peace throughout the world.

Since the XX Congress there have been serious *qualitative changes* in industry, construction, and transport. There has been a radical improvement in the structure of the fuel balance; electrical power engineering has been given a new technical foundation; the rate of development of the chemical industry and the technical reconstruction of all types of transportation have been accelerated substantially. The party and the government have taken steps to develop light industry and food processing, to increase the production of consumer goods; this has already had a beneficial impact on the improved living standard of Soviet people, and the benefits will be even greater in the future.

Capital construction has developed on an unprecedented scale due to the introduction of new technology in construction and to the general use of pre-cast concrete. Between 1956 and 1961, 156 billion rubles were invested in the economy, this exceeding the volume of capital construction during all the years of the Soviet power up to the XX Party Congress. About six thousand new state enterprises have been brought into production, and these include the largest hydroelectric stations, metallurgical, chemical, and machine-building plants, and textile mills in the world. The reconstruction and expansion of existing enterprises – which is an economical and effective way of increasing productive capacity – have also been extensively practiced.

The course outlined by the party for accelerating the development of the country's *eastern regions* is also being consistently implemented. Mighty power-generating installations are being constructed to utilize the rich hydroelectric resources and cheap coal of the area; rich deposits of iron ore and natural gas are being tapped; a third metallurgical base is being successfully created; light metallurgy, machine-building, and the chemical and construction industries are being developed; new cities and industrial centres are rising.

The Congress fully approves the *reconstruction of the administration of industry and construction* effected by the Central Committee and the Soviet government. This revolutionary and vitally necessary measure broke down the departmental barriers which had become a brake on the further development of the country's productive force, elevated the role of the union republics and of the local party, soviet, and economic organs in economic and cultural development, and unleashed the creative initiative of the masses. As a result of this reconstruction of the administration of industry and construction, all branches of the economy are working better and more effectively and are making fuller use of existing production reserves.

The task of overtaking and surpassing the most advanced capitalist countries in per capita production is being successfully accomplished. The Soviet Union has already overtaken the most advanced capitalist country – the United States of America – not only in the rate, but also in the absolute annual increase, of production. At the present time the USSR leads the USA in the production of iron ore and coal, in the manufacture of coke, pre-cast concrete, main-line electrical and steam locomotives, timber, wool fibres, animal oils, sugar, fish, and a number of other articles and products.

The fulfilment of the Seven-Year Plan will advance the economy of the Soviet Union to the point at which only a little time will be needed to surpass the USA in per capita production as well. This will signal the world-historic victory of socialism over capitalism.

The Congress notes the major effort undertaken by the Central Committee in the advancement of *agriculture*. The effects of the war, and also certain past errors and short-comings of agricultural leadership, had placed the country in a serious situation. The low level of agricultural production could have hindered the development of the Soviet economy, with a serious impact on the welfare of the people.

Having disclosed the reasons for the lag in agriculture, the Central Committee developed and put through the urgent measures needed for the continued development of agriculture. With the active participation of the whole population, the party strengthened the material and technical base of the kolkhozes and sovkhozes, reorganized the MTSs, elevated the role of the sovkhozes in communist construction, introduced a new planning procedure for agriculture, restored the leninist principle of the material interest of kolkhozniks and sovkhoz workers in increasing agricultural production, assigned leading cadres and specialists to the kolkhozes and sovkhozes, reorganized the functioning of the agricultural organs, and increased the role of science in agriculture.

Opening up the virgin and unused lands was of outstanding importance for increasing grain production and developing all of agriculture; these now yield more than 40 per cent of all grain procurements in the country. *The opening up of the virgin lands was a great labour exploit of the Soviet people; it will live down through the centuries.*

The party's measures for advancing agriculture have already yielded concrete results, and these results will be even more significant in the future. In the last five years total agricultural production was 43 per cent greater than during the preceding five-year period. Whereas the state formerly purchased only about two billion puds of grain every year, recently it has been purchasing three billion puds a year and more. State purchases of other agricultural products have also risen significantly. Radical changes have also been introduced into animal husbandry, which was for so many years in a state of neglect. In recent years the number of cattle in kolkhozes and sovkhozes has increased 68 per cent, and that of pigs has risen two and a half times; procurements of animal products have risen sharply.

Noting the fundamental significance of the decisions of the January (1961) Plenum of the CPSU Central Committee, which condemned smugness and complacency and the slackened attention paid to agriculture in many oblasts and republics – leading to lowered growth rates in the production of grain, meat, and milk in 1959–60 and causing them to lag behind the Seven-Year Plan targets – the Congress fully approves the concrete measures developed by the Central Committee for the continued increase in agricultural production. As is seen from the preliminary results of this year, these measures have had a beneficial impact. Kolkhozes and sovkhozes have raised their production of grain. The state will purchase much more grain this year than last. There has also been an increase in the production of cotton, sugar beets, sunflowers, and other crops. The number of cattle has increased, as have the production and state purchases of animal products. However, the rate of growth in the production of meat and milk is still far from what is needed.

On the basis of their accumulated experience kolkhozes and sovkhozes must now take another large stride forward and successfully meet the targets of the Seven-Year Plan. Efforts by kolkhozes and sovkhozes to revise crop structures and replace low-yield crops by those with higher yields such as, in particular, legumes and corn, are especially important for resolving the pressing problems of agriculture. It is also necessary to make persistent use of the potential of agriculture in order successfully to accomplish one of the major tasks of communist construction – the creation of an abundance of agricultural products for the people.

The *material well-being of the toilers* is steadily rising. On the basis of the growth in the national income of the USSR the real incomes of workers and employees (calculated in terms of the income of a single worker) have risen 27 per cent over the past five years, and that of kolkhozniks 33 per cent. Retail state and co-operative trade has increased more than one and a half times. All workers and employees now work either a seven-hour or a six-hour day. Pay levels have been regularized and, especially in the case of the lowest-paid categories of workers and employees, raised; the excessively high rates of pay in certain categories have been eliminated. Pensions have been increased; the average old-age pension has more than doubled. The gradual abolition of personal taxes started in 1960. Public funds play an increasing role in advancing public welfare. Payments and benefits to the population from these funds amounted to 24.5 billion rubles in 1960, as against 4.2 billion in 1940, and by the end of the Seven-Year Plan they will increase to 40 billion rubles. The 1956–60 programme for state housing construction has been successfully fulfilled: during these five years more housing was built than during the previous fifteen years, with about 50 million persons receiving new housing.

The period between the XX and XXII congresses has been marked by outstanding achievements in *Soviet science and culture*. A new and brilliant epoch was opened in the development of man's scientific knowledge by the victories of the Soviet Union in the conquest of space, the unprecedented flights of the first cosmonauts in history, Yurii Gagarin and German Titov. Soviet scientists also made considerable advances in the peaceful use of atomic energy, in cybernetics and the design of high-speed computers, in polymer chemistry, in the development of automation and telemechanics, radio, electronics, in social sciences, and in other areas of science and technology.

The Congress views as correct the measures adopted to *reorganize education and strengthen the tie between school and life*, to organize boarding schools as well as schools and groups with a longer academic day, to develop correspondence schools and night schools, to train highly skilled specialists for all branches of economic and cultural construction.

Recent years have seen the creation of a number of significant works of *literature and art*, correctly reflecting our reality and setting forth the character traits of the new man – the builder of communism.

Socialist social relations are steadily improving with the development of the productive forces and the multiplication of the material and spiritual riches of Soviet society. The Congress approves the policy of continuing the consolidation and merger of the public and kolkhoz-cooperative forms of socialist property, of consistently implementing the principle of material self-interest, of developing socialist democracy, of bringing together and promoting the all-round mutual enrichment of the cultures of the Soviet socialist nations, of consolidating the moral and political unity of our society, of actively shaping communist principles in labour, in life, and in the consciousness of Soviet people.

The great successes achieved by our people under the party's leadership gladden Soviet people and inspire them with confidence that in the future our country will continue to progress even more rapidly and successfully along the road to communism. Faithful to leninism, the party never tolerates conceit or complacency, sees not only the successes but also the short-comings of party, soviet, and economic organs, concentrates its efforts on the resolution of unsolved problems. All efforts must be aimed at ensuring an even more rapid growth in the economy, a rise in the public welfare, and consolidation of the power of the Soviet state. The more actively all that is new and progressive is supported, and the more generally it is applied in production, the more strikingly will short-comings be disclosed, the more rapidly will they be eliminated, and the more successfully will the tasks confronting us be resolved. The cause of communist construction is the great cause of the millions, the cause of the whole people.

The Congress charges the Central Committee to continue to direct the forces of the party and the people to accelerating the rate of communist construction, to making even fuller use of the gigantic inner potential of all branches of the socialist economy.

The attention of the party and people must be concentrated primarily on accomplishing the following major tasks:

Ensuring the fulfilment and overfulfilment of the Seven-Year Plan targets, which will have decisive significance for creating the material and technical base of communism, for our victory in the peaceful economic competition with capitalism. Heavy industry must continue to develop at an accelerated pace, especially electrical power engineering, metallurgy, chemistry, machine building, the fuel and construction industries. The Congress places all party organizations under the obligation to mobilize the toilers for the struggle to fulfil the Seven-Year Plan targets which have now been adjusted upwards. A general expansion of the production of consumer goods is recognized as necessary. The funds accumulated through industry's overfulfilment of the plan targets are to be directed mainly into agriculture, light industry, and food processing;

Continued technical progess is to stimulate a *comprehensive growth of labour productivity in industry, construction, agriculture, and transport.* The increasing of labour productivity is the key to the policy and practice of communist construction, the unfailing condition of an advance in public welfare, of creating an abundance of material and cultural benefits for the toilers;

The organization of economic management is to be persistently improved, so that ultimately the greatest increase in production will be attained with the least expenditure. For this it is necessary to select the most progressive and economically advantageous directions of industrial development; to improve specialization and co-operation; to effect the all-around mechanization and automation of production processes; to introduce into production more rapidly the newest achievements of science and technology, progressive methods, and most advanced practices; to make better use of the internal reserves of economic regions, enterprises, and construction sites; to consolidate state discipline in all links of the economic apparatus, to struggle mercilessly against wastefulness, squandering, sluggishness, conservatism. The reduction of production costs and improvement of quality, universal thrift and economy, increasing profitability, and the growth of socialist accumulation must be the operational law of each Soviet enterprise;

The planning and organization of capital construction must be decisively improved, the effectiveness of capital investment must be sharply raised, and the anti-state localistic practice of dissipating funds as well as material, technical, and labour resources must be ended. Particular attention must continue to be directed to developing the productive forces of the eastern regions, to the opening up and combined exploitation of their natural riches;

Concrete and skilful leadership must be given to *agriculture*, the achievements of science and advanced experience must be persistently applied, better use must be made of the land; sowings must be structured more effectively; corn, peas, fodder legumes, and other high-yield crops must be planted more extensively; more fertilizer must be made available, and it must be used more efficiently; the quality of agricultural work must be improved, and on this basis a significant increase in the yield and total harvest of grain and other agricultural crops must be attained; the number of cattle and the production of animal products must be systematically increased. In the view of the Congress the urgent tasks are to extend the mechanization and electrification of agriculture, to satisfy fully the needs of kolkhozes and sovkhozes for modern equipment, to increase the production of mineral and organic fertilizers as well as of herbicides and other chemical weapons against weeds, pests, and crop diseases. This comprehensive mechanization is to ensure a growth in labour productivity and a reduction in the unit cost of agricultural production. Maximum production with minimum labour input is the major principle of communist construction in the countryside. In the immediate future state purchases of grain are to increase to 4 billion, 200 million puds; of meat, to 13 million tons; of milk, to 50 million tons per annum; the production of sugar beets, cotton, flax, potatoes, vegetables, fruits, tea, and other agricultural products is to increase significantly. *The development of agriculture is the business of the whole party, of the whole Soviet people*;

The *living standard of the people* is to grow steadily on the basis of the continued growth of industrial and agricultural production. The Congress feels that it is necessary to carry out further measures to shorten the working day and the working week and also to abolish personal taxes. The wage and salary rates in all categories are to be standardized; housing is to be built at an even faster rate, its quality is to be improved, and its cost is to be lowered; the construction of nurseries, kindergartens, and other institutions servicing the daily needs of the population is to be accelerated; there is to be an improvement in pensions, in the organization of trade and public eating places, and in the medicinal and day-to-day services provided for the population; all aspects of the public educational system are to be steadily improved;

Purposeful scientific investigations are to be conducted, and youth is to be granted an easier entry into science. The Congress sets Soviet scientists the major task of ensuring that Soviet science advances to the level at which it can win an advanced position in every major direction of world science and technology;

The literature and art of socialist realism are to be developed, their ideological and artistic level is to be raised, and their connection with the practice of communist construction – with the life of the people – is to be consolidated;

The defence capacity of our motherland – the bulwark of peace throughout the world – is to be maintained at the requisite level; the Soviet Army's weaponry is to be improved; the level of the military and ideological-political training of its personnel is to be increased; the vigilance of the people is to be increased; the constructive labour and peaceful lives of Soviet people – the builders of communism – are to be reliably safeguarded;

Socialist social relations are to be developed and perfected: through consolidating the public and kolkhoz-cooperative forms of socialist property; through the correct combination of material and moral incentives to work;

through broadening the participation by the popular masses in the administration of all the country's affairs; through strengthening the friendship of peoples; through giving comprehensive support to the desire of Soviet people to work and live in a communist manner.

The creation of the material and technical base of communism, the development of socialist social relations, the moulding of the member of communist society – these are the major domestic tasks confronting the party during the period of the full-scale construction of communism.

Our country's successes in foreign and domestic policy are the result of the heroic labour of the Soviet people and of the gigantic organizational and educational effort of the Communist Party, the result of the consistent implementation of its leninist line which was profoundly and creatively expressed in the historic decisions of the XX Congress of the CPSU. The party has still further consolidated its ties with the people. With the victory of socialism and the consolidation of the unity of Soviet society, the Communist Party, which arose as the party of the working class, has become the party of the whole people and extended its guiding influence in all areas of social life. The Communist Party has come to its XXII Congress united and cohesive, full of creative power and with an invincible will to go forward under the marxist-leninist banner to the total victory of communism.

The Congress notes that a very important aspect of the party's activity during the accounting period has been the *restoration and continued development of leninist norms of party life and leninist principles of collective leadership in all elements of the party and state.*

The open and bold condemnation by the party and the Central Committee of the cult of I.V. Stalin was of enormous significance for the building of socialism and communism, for the whole international communist movement. The party told the people the whole truth about the abuses of power which took place during the period of the cult of personality and resolutely condemned the errors, distortions, and methods alien to the spirit of leninism which were engendered in the atmosphere of the cult of personality. The party has subjected the cult of personality to a thorough criticism, has overcome the distortions and errors of the past, and is steadily implementing measures designed to eliminate completely any possible future repetition of such errors. These measures have found expression in the party Programme and Rules.

The XXII Congress completely and wholeheartedly approves the extensive and fruitful efforts of the Central Committee to restore and develop leninist principles in all areas of party, state, and ideological work; these have opened up broad prospects for the creative initiative of the party and the people, have promoted the broadening and strengthening of the party's ties with the masses, and have increased its fighting efficiency.

The Congress is in complete agreement with, and fully supports, the Central Committee's resolute measures to unmask, and to crush ideologically, the anti-party group of Molotov, Kaganovich, Malenkov, Bulganin, Pervukhin, Saburov, and Shepilov who joined them, which came out against the leninist course outlined by the XX Congress, opposed the measures designed to overcome the cult of personality and its consequences, attempted to maintain discredited forms and methods of leadership, and to slow down the development of the new in our life. During the factional struggle of the anti-party group Comrade Voroshilov committed serious errors in siding with this group against the party's leninist policy. During the June Plenum of the Central Committee, Comrade Voroshilov recognized his errors and condemned the factional activity of the anti-party group, thus making a certain contribution to the unmasking of the anti-party renegades. Having cast aside these unprincipled factionists, intriguers, and careerists, the party has closed ranks even more tightly, strengthened its ties with the people, and mobilized all its forces for the successful implementation of its general line.

Speaking for the whole party, the XXII Congress condemns with indignation such subversive, anti-party, factional activity as incompatible with the leninist principle of party unity. Anyone taking the course of factional struggle, intrigue behind the scenes, and machinations against the leninist party line and party unity is acting against the interests of the whole people, the interests of building communism. Expressing the will of all communists, the Congress states that the party will steadily continue to implement the leninist law that the unity and purity of the party's ranks are to be maintained and that an implacable struggle is to be conducted against any manifestations of cliquishness or factionalism.

The restoration and development of leninist principles of collective leadership were of particular significance for the party and the Soviet state. The regular convocation of party congresses and plenary sessions of the Central Committee, regular meetings of all electoral organs of the party, general public discussion of the major issues of state, economic, and party development, extensive consultations with persons employed in various branches of the economy and in cultural affairs, have become standard in party and state life. All the major issues of domestic and foreign policy have been subjected to broad discussion in our party and are the expression of its collective wisdom and experience.

The indissoluble nature of the tie between the party and the people is graphically manifested in the growth of the party's ranks, in the constant influx of fresh forces into the party. During the accounting period the party's membership increased by two and a half million and now numbers almost ten million Communists.

The XXII Congress orders the Central Committee to continue to strengthen party unity, to struggle for the purity of its marxist-leninist outlook, to reinforce its ranks by bringing in the leading members of the working class, the kolkhoz peasantry, and the intelligentsia, to elevate even higher the title of Communist – as the active, steadfast, and conscious fighter for the well-being of the people, for communism.

The Congress notes that in recent years *the party has effected a decisive turn toward a concrete form of economic leadership*. The Central Committee has directed the attention of party organizations and leading persons to the fulfilment of economic plans, to mobilizing the unused potential of our economy, to studying most advanced practices and disseminating them broadly, and has used concrete positive examples of correct economic management for purposes of instruction. The Congress emphasizes that the strength of party leadership lies in its ability to organize the efforts of the masses and direct them to the accomplishment of major tasks, in the capacity to combine the talents, knowledge, and experience of numerous persons in order to accomplish great things. While ever bearing in mind Lenin's instruction that our party is strong in the consciousness and activity of the masses, it is necessary even more energetically to heighten the communist consciousness and political activity of the toilers, to rally them even more closely around the party.

The Congress directs particular attention to the *necessity for improving work with cadres, their selection and training*, for striking the proper balance between the old and experienced party workers and young, energetic, and capable organizers. There is no room in leadership positions for out-of-date and conceited persons who have lost their feel for life, who are devoid of ideas and principles. The party has struggled and will continue to struggle implacably against violators of party and state discipline, against those who undertake to deceive the party and the state, against toadies, yes-men, deceitful persons, and bureaucrats. In the struggle against short-comings in work it is necessary to make full use of criticism and self-criticism – as this is our sharpest weapon.

The Congress attributes great significance to the principle of renovating electoral organs, as this will open up new opportunities for the extensive use of the creative forces of the party and the people in the building of communism. The systematic renovation of electoral organs should become the inviolable norm of party, state, and social life in our country.

Life itself, practical activity, is the best school for the training and political tempering of cadres. The character traits of a party and state figure of the leninist type are forged in the struggle to carry out the party line, in practical work, in performing concrete tasks of communist construction. The mass of active party members must be brought more boldly to work in party organs on a voluntary basis.

Under present conditions *party, state, and public supervision of the correct organization of affairs, of the precise fulfilment of the requirements of the* CPSU *Programme and Rules, of the directives and instructions of the party and the Soviet government by every person in every position, is of fundamental significance*. The system of supervision is an effective means of improving the leadership of communist construction on the basis of genuinely democratic principles, a reliable weapon in the struggle against bureaucratism and red tape, a school for the communist training of the masses.

In order to strengthen the supervision and verification of the de facto execution of tasks it is necessary to establish a strict procedure through which local party organs can give an account to higher ones, to the masses of communists, of their fulfilment of party decisions. The XXII Congress directs the Central Committee to come forward with effective measures for improving and perfecting the system of party, state, and public supervision.

The Congress attributes great significance to the *activity of the mass organizations of the toilers* – the soviets, the trade unions, the Komsomol, the co-operatives. Now that communist self-administration is increasingly developing, the role of these organizations in the life of socialist society is steadily growing ...

A continued rise in the level and intensity of *ideological work* is one of the primary tasks of the party and an important condition of the success of all of its practical activity. The interests of the building of communism demand that questions of the communist education of the toilers and, in particular, of the younger generation, be at the focus of the activity of each party organization, of the whole Soviet community.

At present the primary trends in ideological work are: propagandizing of marxist-leninist doctrine and the shaping of a scientific outlook among all members of society; the struggle against the remnants of capitalism in the consciousness of individuals and against the influence of the hostile bourgeois ideology; the education of toilers in the noble moral principles embodied in the moral code of the builders of communism; the forming of comprehensively developed members of the communist society. Training the individual for work, instilling in him the love and respect for labour as the primary necessity of life, are the essence and the core of any effort of communist education.

Ideological work at the present time must stress the profound explanation of the CPSU *Programme, arming the toilers of Soviet society with a great plan governing the struggle for the victory of communism, mobilizing all the toilers for implementation of the new party Programme.* To the accomplishment of this task must be subordinated all the party's instruments for exerting ideological influence on the masses: propaganda, agitation, the press, radio, television, the cinema, cultural-educational efforts, literature, and art.

Ideological work is the main instrument for performing the tasks of communist construction. It must further the growth of the political and labour activity, the communist consciousness of the Soviet people. The profound study by party and state cadres of marxist-leninist theory, of the world-historic experience of the struggle of the Communist Party and the Soviet people for the victory of socialism and communism, elevating the level of educational work and intensifying its influence on the lives and deeds of the people, remain the primary tasks of the party in propaganda and ideological work. It is necessary to be guided by the very important party principle of the unity of ideological and organizational work.

In recent years the scope and significance of the party's and the Central Committee's theoretical activity have greatly increased. Waging a struggle on two fronts – against revisionism as the main danger and against the dogmatic petrification of revolutionary theory – the party has firmly defended and creatively developed the doctrine of marxism-leninism. The accounting period in the history of the party has been marked by creative solutions to major theoretical problems of the building of communism in our country and to urgent problems of the international communist movement. The XXII Congress unanimously and with great satisfaction approves the fruitful theoretical work of the CPSU Central Committee which has received its fullest expression in the new Programme of our party.

The Congress emphasizes the necessity of continuing to hold high the all-conquering banner of marxism-leninism, guarding its purity, and enrichening its theory with new conclusions and propositions generalizing the experience acquired in communist construction. Guided by the leninist principle of the unity of theory and practice, the party must consider the defense and the creative development of marxism-leninism as its chief duty ...

Expressing the will of the whole Soviet people, the XXII Congress states in the name of ten million Communists:

The CPSU will continue to hold high the victorious banner of marxism-leninism, will fulfil its international duty to the toilers of all countries, will devote all its strength to struggling for the interests of all people, for reaching the great historic goal – the building of a communist society.

The party solemnly proclaims: the present generation of Soviet people will live under communism!

4.33
Programme of the CPSU 31 October 1961

INTRODUCTION

The Great October Socialist Revolution ushered in a new era in the history of mankind, the era of the downfall of capitalism and the establishment of communism. Socialism has triumphed in the Soviet Union and has achieved decisive victories in the people's democracies; socialism has become the practical cause of hundreds of millions of people, and the banner of the revolutionary movement of the working class throughout the world.

More than a hundred years ago Karl Marx and Frederick Engels, the great teachers of the proletariat, wrote in the Communist Manifesto: 'A spectre is haunting Europe, the spectre of communism.' The courageous and selfless struggle of the proletarians of all countries brought mankind nearer to communism. First dozens and hundreds of people, and then thousands and millions, inspired by the ideals of communism, stormed the old world. The Paris Commune, the October Revolution, the socialist revolutions in China and in a number of European and Asian countries are the major historical stages in the heroic battles fought by the international working class for the victory of communism. A tremendously long road, a road drenched in the blood of fighters for the happiness of the people, a road of glorious victories and temporary reverses, had to be traversed before *communism, which was once no more than a dream, became the greatest force of modern times, a society that is being built up over vast areas of the globe.*

In the early twentieth century the centre of the international revolutionary movement shifted to Russia. Russia's heroic working class, led by the Bolshevik Party headed by Vladimir Ilyich Lenin, became its vanguard. The Communist Party inspired and led the socialist revolution; it was the organizer and leader of the first workers' and peasants' state in history. The brilliant genius of Lenin, the great teacher of the working people of the world, whose name will live for ever, illumines mankind's road to communism.

On entering the arena of political struggle, the leninist Communist Party raised high the banner of revolutionary marxism over the world. Marxism-leninism became a powerful ideological weapon for the revolutionary transformation of society. At every historical stage the party, taking guidance from the theory of Marx-Engels-Lenin, accomplished the tasks scientifically formulated in its programmes.

In adopting its *first Programme* at its Second Congress in 1903, the Bolshevik Party called on the working class and all the working people of Russia to fight for the overthrow of the tsarist autocracy and then of the bourgeois system and for the establishment of the dictatorship of the proletariat. In February 1917 the tsarist regime was swept away. In October 1917 the proletarian revolution abolished the capitalist system so hated by the people. *A socialist country came into being for the first time in history. The creation of a new world began.*

The first Programme of the party had been carried out.

Adopting its *second Programme* at its Eighth Congress in 1919, the party promulgated the task of building a socialist society. Treading on unexplored ground and overcoming difficulties and hardships, the Soviet people under the leadership of the Communist Party put into practice the plan for socialist construction drawn up by Lenin. *Socialism triumphed in the Soviet Union completely and finally.*

The second Programme of the party had likewise been carried out.

The gigantic revolutionary exploit accomplished by the Soviet people has roused and inspired the masses in all countries and continents. A mighty purifying thunderstorm marking the springtime of mankind is raging over the earth. *The socialist revolutions in European and Asian countries have resulted in the establishment of the world socialist system.* A powerful wave of national liberation revolutions is sweeping away the colonial system of imperialism.

One-third of mankind is building a new life under the banner of scientific communism. The first contingents of the working class to shake off capitalist oppression are facilitating victory for fresh contingents of their class brothers. The socialist world is expanding; the capitalist world is shrinking. Socialism will inevitably succeed capitalism everywhere. Such is the objective law of social development. Imperialism is powerless to check the irresistible process of emancipation.

Our epoch, whose main content is the transition from capitalism to socialism, is an epoch of struggle between the two opposing social systems, an epoch of socialist and national liberation revolutions, of the breakdown of imperialism and the abolition of the colonial system, an epoch of the transition of more and more peoples to the socialist path, of the triumph of socialism and communism on a world-wide scale. The central factor of the present epoch is the international working class and its main creation, the world socialist system.

Today the Communist Party of the Soviet Union (CPSU) *is adopting its third Programme, a programme for the building of communist society.* The new Programme is a constructive generalization of the experience of socialist development, it takes account of the experience of the revolutionary movement throughout the world and, giving expression to the collective opinion of the party, defines the main tasks and principal stages of communist construction.

The supreme goal of the party is to build a communist society on whose banner will be inscribed: 'From each according to his ability, to each according to his needs.' The party's motto, 'Everything for the sake of man, for the benefit of man,' will be put into effect in full.

The Communist Party of the Soviet Union, true to proletarian internationalism, always follows the militant slogan 'Workers of all countries, unite!' *The party regards communist construction in the* USSR *as the Soviet people's great internationalist task*, in keeping with the interests of the world socialist system as a whole and with the interests of the international proletariat and all mankind.

Communism accomplishes the historic mission of delivering all men from social inequality, from every form of oppression and exploitation, from the horrors of war, and proclaims *Peace, Labour, Freedom, Equality, Fraternity, and Happiness for all peoples of the earth.*

Part one
The transition from capitalism to
communism is the road of
human progress

I THE HISTORICAL NECESSITY OF THE
TRANSITION FROM CAPITALISM TO SOCIALISM

The epoch-making turn of mankind from capitalism to socialism, initiated by the October Revolution, is a natural result of the development of society. Marxism-leninism discovered the objective laws of social development and revealed the contradictions inherent in capitalism, the inevitability of their bringing about a revolutionary explosion and of the transition of society to communism.

Capitalism is the last exploiting system. Having developed its productive forces to an enormous extent, it became a tremendous obstacle to social progress. Capitalism alone is responsible for the fact that the twentieth century, a century of colossal growth of the productive forces and of great scientific progress, has not yet put an end to the poverty of hundreds of millions of people, has not provided an abundance of material and spiritual values for all men on earth. The growing conflict between productive forces and production relations imperatively demands that mankind should break the decayed capitalist shell, release the powerful productive forces created by man, and use them for the good of society as a whole.

Whatever the specific character of the rise and development of capitalism in any country, that system has everywhere common features and objective laws.

The development of world capitalism and of the revolutionary struggle of the working class has fully confirmed the correctness of the marxist-leninist analysis of capitalism and its highest stage, imperialism, given in the first and second programmes of the party. The basic propositions of this analysis are also given below in the present Programme.

Under capitalism, the basic and decisive means of production belong to the numerically small class of capitalists and landowners, while the vast majority of the population consists of proletarians and semi-proletarians, who own no means of production and are therefore compelled to sell their labour-power and by their labour create profits and riches for the ruling classes of society. The bourgeois state, whatever its form, is an instrument of the domination of labour by capital.

The development of large-scale capitalist production – production for profit, for the appropriation of surplus value – leads to the elimination of small independent producers, makes then wholly dependent on capital. Capitalism extensively exploits female and child labour. The economic laws of its development necessarily give rise to a huge army of unemployed, which is constantly replenished by ruined peasants and urban petty bourgeoisie. The exploitation of the working class and all working people is continuously increasing, social inequality is becoming more and more marked, the gulf between the haves and have-nots is widening, and the sufferings and privations of the millions are growing worse.

Capitalism, by concentrating millions of workers in its factories, socializing the process of labour, imparts a social character to production; nevertheless, it is the capitalists who appropriate the fruits of labour. This fundamental contradiction of capitalism – the contradiction between the social character of production and the private-capitalist form of appropriation – manifests itself in production anarchy and in the fact that the purchasing power of society falls short of the expansion of production and leads periodically to destructive economic crises. Crises and periods of industrial stagnation, in turn, are still more ruinous to small producers, increase the dependence of wage-labour on capital, and lead more rapidly to a relative, and sometimes an absolute, deterioration of the condition of the working class.

The growth and development of the contradictions of bourgeois society are accompanied by the growing discontent of the working people and the exploited masses with the capitalist system, by an increase in the number of proletarians and their greater unity, and by a sharpening of their struggle against the exploiters. At the same time there is an accelerated *creation of the material conditions that make possible the replacement of capitalist by communist production relations, that is, the accomplishment of the social revolution which is the aim of the Communist Party, the politically conscious exponent of the class movement of the proletariat.*

The working class, which is the most consistent revolutionary class, is the chief motive force of the revolutionary transformation of the world. In the course of class struggles it becomes organized, sets up its trade unions and political parties, and wages an economic, political and theoretical struggle against capitalism. In fulfilling its historic mission as the revolutionary remaker of the old society and creator of a new system, the working class becomes the exponent, not only of its own class interests, but of the interests of all working people. It is the natural leader of all forces fighting against capitalism.

The dictatorship of the proletariat and the leadership of the marxist-leninist party are indispensable conditions for the triumph of the socialist revolution and the building of socialism. The firm alliance of the working class and the working peasant masses under the leadership of the working class is the supreme principle of the dictatorship of the proletariat.

The process of concentration and centralization of capital, while destroying free competition, led in the early twentieth century to the establishment of powerful capitalist monopoly associations – syndicates, cartels, and trusts – which acquired decisive importance in the economy, led to the merging of bank capital and immensely concentrated industrial capital, and to intensive export of capital. The trusts, which encompassed entire groups of capitalist powers, began the economic division of a world already divided territorially among the wealthiest countries. Capitalism had entered its final stage, the stage of monopoly capitalism, of imperialism.

The period of a more or less smooth spread of capitalism all over the globe gave way to spasmodic, cataclysmic development causing an unprecedented growth and aggravation of all the contradictions of capitalism – economic, political, class, and national. The imperialist powers' struggle for markets, for spheres of capital investment, for raw materials and labour, and for world domination became more intense than ever. In an epoch of the undivided rule of imperialism, that struggle necessarily led to devastating wars.

Imperialism is decaying and moribund capitalism; it is the eve of the socialist revolution. *The world capitalist system as a whole is ripe for the social revolution of the proletariat.*

The exceedingly high degree of development of world capitalism in general; the replacement of free competition by state monopoly capitalism; the establishment, by banks as well as associations of capitalists, of machinery for the social regulation of production and the distribution of products; the growing cost of living and the oppression of the working class by the syndicates, connected with the growth of capitalist monopolies; the enslavement of the working class by the imperialist state, and the immensely increased difficulty of the economic and political struggle of the proletariat; and the horrors, hardships, and ruination brought about by imperialist war have all made inevitable the downfall of capitalism and the transition to a higher type of social economy.

The revolutionary break-up of imperialism does not take place all over the world simultaneously. The uneven character of the economic and political development of the capitalist countries under imperialism leads to revolutions occurring at different periods in different countries. V.I. Lenin developed the theory of the socialist revolution in new historical conditions, elaborated the theory of the possibility of socialism triumphing first in one capitalist country taken singly.

Russia was the weakest link in the imperialist system and the focal point of all its contradictions. On the other hand, all the conditions necessary for the victory of socialism arose in her. Her working class was the most revolutionary and best organized in the world and had considerable experience of class struggle. It was led by a marxist-leninist party armed with an advanced revolutionary theory and steeled in class battles.

The Bolshevik Party brought together in one revolutionary torrent the struggle of the working class for socialism, the country-wide peace movement, the peasants' struggle for land, and the national liberation movement of the oppressed peoples of Russia, and directed these forces to the overthrow of capitalism.

II THE HISTORIC SIGNIFICANCE OF THE OCTOBER REVOLUTION AND OF THE VICTORY OF SOCIALISM IN THE USSR

The Great October Revolution breached the imperialist front in Russia, one of the world's largest countries, firmly established the dictatorship of the proletariat, and created a new type of state – the Soviet socialist state – and a new type of democracy – democracy for the working people.

Workers' and peasants' power, born of the revolution, took Russia out of the bloodbath of the imperialist war, saved her from the national catastrophe to which the exploiting classes had doomed her, and delivered her peoples from the danger of enslavement by foreign capital.

The October Revolution undermined the economic basis of a system of exploitation and social injustice. Soviet power nationalized industry, the railways, banks, and the land. It abolished the landlord system and fulfilled the peasants' age-long dream of land.

The October Revolution smashed the chains of national oppression; it proclaimed and put into effect the right of nations to self-determination, up to and including the right to secede. The revolution completely abolished the social-estate and class privileges of the exploiters. For the first time in history, it emancipated women and granted them the same rights as men.

The socialist revolution in Russia shook the entire structure of world capitalism to its very foundations; the world split into two opposing systems.

For the first time there emerged in the international arena a state which put forward the great slogan of peace and began carrying through new principles in relations between peoples and countries. Mankind acquired a reliable bulwark in its struggle against wars of conquest, for peace and the security of peoples.

The October Revolution led the country on to the road to socialism. The path which the Soviet people were to traverse was an unexplored and arduous one. The reactionary forces of the old world did all they could to strangle the Soviet state at its birth. The young Soviet Republic had to cope with intervention and civil war, economic blockade and disruption, conspiracies, sabotage, subversion, terrorism, and numerous other trials. Socialist construction was rendered incredibly difficult by the socio-economic, technical, and cultural backwardness of the country. The victorious workers and peasants lacked knowledge of state administration and the experience necessary for the construction of a new society. The difficulties of socialist construction were greatly increased by the fact that for almost thirty years the USSR was the world's only socialist state, and was subjected to incisive attacks by the hostile capitalist encirclement. The class struggle in the period of transition from capitalism to socialism and therefore acute.

The enemies of leninism maintained that Russia was not mature enough for a socialist revolution, that it was impossible to build socialism in one country. But the enemies of leninism were put to shame.

A wise, discerning policy, the greatest staunchness, organization, and deep faith in their own strength and in the strength of the people were required of the party of the working class. It was necessary to steer the right course in socialist construction and ensure the victory of socialism, despite the highly complicated international situation and a relatively weak industrial basis, in a country whose economy had been badly ravaged by war and where small-commodity production was overwhelmingly predominant.

The party proved equal to that historic task. Under the leadership of Lenin it worked out a plan for the radical transformation of the country, for the construction of socialism. On the basis of a thorough scientific analysis, Lenin elaborated the policy of the proletarian state for the entire period of transition from capitalism to socialism. He evolved the New Economic Policy (NEP), designed to bring about the victory of socialism. The main elements of the Lenin plan for the building of a socialist society were industrialization of the country, agricultural co-operation, and the cultural revolution.

The party upheld that plan in an acute struggle against sceptics and capitulators, against the trotskyists, right opportunists, nationalist deviators, and other hostile groups. It rallied the whole of the Soviet people to the struggle to put Lenin's programme into practice.

The point at issue at the time was: either perish or forge full steam ahead and overtake the capitalist countries economically.

The Soviet state had first of all to solve the problem of *industrialization*. In a historically brief period, without outside help, the Soviet Union built up a large-scale modern industry. By the time it had fulfilled three five-year plans (1929–41) the Soviet Union had become a mighty industrial power that had achieved complete economic independence from the capitalist countries. Its defence capacity had increased immeasurably. *The industrialization of the USSR was a great exploit performed by the working class and the people as a whole*, for they spared no effort or means, and consciously made sacrifices to lift the country out of its backward state.

The destiny of socialism in a country like the USSR largely depended on the solution of a most difficult problem, namely, the transition from a small-scale, dispersed peasant economy to *socialist co-operation*. Led by the party, aided and fully supported by the working class, the peasantry took the road to socialism. Millions of small individual farms went into voluntary association to form collective farms. A large number of Soviet state farms and machine and tractor stations were established. The introduction in the Soviet countryside of large-scale socialist farming meant a *far-reaching revolution in economic relations, in the entire way of life of the peasantry*. Collectivization forever delivered the countryside from kulak bondage, from class differentiation, ruin, and poverty. The real solution of the eternal peasant question was provided by the Lenin co-operative plan.

To build socialism it was necessary to raise the cultural level of the people; this too was successfully accomplished. A *cultural revolution* was carried out in the country. It freed the working people from spiritual slavery and ignorance and gave them access to the cultural values accumulated by mankind. The country, the bulk of whose population had been illiterate, made breath-taking progress in science and culture.

Socialism, which Marx and Engels scientifically predicted as inevitable and the plan for the construction of which was mapped out by Lenin, has become a reality in the Soviet Union.

Socialism has done away for ever with the supremacy of private ownership of the means of production, that source of the division of society into antagonistic classes. Socialist ownership of the means of production has become the solid economic foundation of society. Unlimited opportunities have been afforded for the development of the productive forces.

Socialism has solved a great social problem – it has abolished the exploiting classes and the causes engendering the exploitation of man by man. There are now two friendly classes in the USSR – the working class and the peasantry. And these classes, furthermore, have changed. The common character of the two forms of socialist property has brought the working class and the collective-farm peasantry close together; it has strengthened their alliance and made their friendship indestructible. A new intelligentsia, coming from the people and devoted to socialism, has emerged. The one-time antithesis between town and countryside, between labour by hand and by brain, has been abolished. The indestructible socio-political and ideological unity of the Soviet people has been built on the basis of the common vital interests of the workers, peasants, and intellectuals.

The socialist principle 'From each according to his abilities, to each according to his work' has been put into effect in the Soviet Union. This principle ensures that the members of society have a material interest in the fruits of their labour; it makes it possible to harmonize personal and social interests in the most effective way and serves as a powerful stimulus for increasing productivity of labour, developing the economy, and raising the people's standard of living. The awareness that they work for themselves and their society and not for exploiters inspires the working people with labour enthusiasm; it encourages their effort for innovation, their creative initiative, and mass socialist competition. Socialism is creative effort by the working masses. The growing activity of the people in the building of a new life is a law of the socialist epoch.

The aim of socialism is to meet the growing material and cultural requirements of the people ever more fully by continuously developing and improving social production.

The entire life of socialist society is based on the principle of broad *democracy*. Working people take an active part, through the Soviets, trade unions, and other mass organizations, in managing the affairs of the state and in solving problems of economic and cultural advancement. Socialist democracy includes both political freedoms – freedom of speech, of the press, and of assembly, the right to elect and to be elected, and also social rights – the right to work, to rest and leisure, to free education and free medical services, to material security in old age and in case of illness or disability; equality of citizens of all races and nationalities; equal rights for women and men in all spheres of political, economic and cultural activity. Socialist democracy, unlike bourgeois democracy, does not merely proclaim the rights of the people, but guarantees that they are really implemented. Soviet society ensures the real liberty of the individual. The highest manifestation of this liberty is man's emancipation from exploitation, which is what primarily constitutes genuine social justice.

Socialism has created the most favourable conditions for the rapid progress of science. The achievements of Soviet science clearly show the superiority of the socialist system and testify to the unlimited possibilities of scientific progress and to the growing role of science under socialism. It is only logical that the country of victorious socialism should have ushered in the era of the utilization of atomic energy for peaceful purposes, and that it should have blazed a trail into outer space. The man-made satellites of the earth and the sun, powerful space rockets and interplanetary spaceships, atomic power stations, and the first triumphal orbitings of the globe, accomplished by Soviet citizens, which are a source of pride to all mankind, have become symbols of the creative energy of ascendant communism.

The solution of the *national question* is one of the greatest achievements of socialism. This question is of especial importance to a country like the Soviet Union, inhabited by more than a hundred nations and nationalities. Socialist society has not only guaranteed the political equality of nations and created Soviet national statehood, but has also abolished the economic and cultural inequality inherited from the old system. With reciprocal fraternal assistance, primarily from the great Russian people, all the Soviet non-Russian republics have set up their own modern industries, trained their own national working class and intelligentsia, and developed a culture that is national in form and socialist in content. Many peoples who in the past were backward have achieved socialism bypassing the capitalist stage of development. The union and consolidation of equal peoples on a voluntary basis in a single multinational state – the Union of Soviet Socialist Republics – their close co-operation in state, economic, and cultural development, their fraternal friendship and flourishing economy and culture constitute the most important result of the leninist national policy.

To the Soviet people fell the historic role of starting on a new road, of blazing a new path of social development. This required special efforts of them, a continuous quest for forms and methods of building the new society that had to be tested in the crucible of life. For nearly two out of little more than four decades, the Soviet people were compelled to devote their energies to the repulsion of invasions by the imperialist powers and to post-war economic rehabilitation. The Soviet system was put to a particularly severe test during the Great Patriotic War, the most trying war in history. By winning that war, the Soviet people proved that there are no forces in the world capable of stopping the progress of socialist society.

What are the principal lessons to be learned from the experience of the Soviet people?

Soviet experience has shown that the peoples are able to achieve socialism only as a result of the *socialist revolution and the establishment of the dictatorship of the proletariat*. Despite certain specific features due to the concrete historical conditions of socialist construction in the Soviet Union, then in a hostile capitalist encirclement, this experience has fully confirmed the fundamental principles of socialist revolution and socialist construction, principles which are of universal significance.

Soviet experience has shown that socialism alone can put an end to the exploitation of man by man, production anarchy, economic crises, unemployment, and the poverty of the people, and ensure planned, continuous, and rapid development of the economy and steady improvement of the people's standard of living.

Soviet experience has shown that the working class can fulfil its historic mission as the builder of a new society only in a firm *alliance with the non-proletarian working masses*, primarily the peasantry.

Soviet experience has shown that the victory of the socialist revolution alone provides all possibilities and conditions for the abolition of all national oppression, *for the voluntary union of free and equal nations and nationalities in a single state*.

Soviet experience has shown that the *socialist state* is the main instrument for the socialist transformation of society. The state organized and unites the masses, exercises planned leadership of economic and cultural construction, and safeguards the revolutionary gains of the people.

Soviet experience has shown that *socialism and peace are inseparable*. The might of socialism serves peace. The Soviet Union saved mankind from fascist enslavement. The Soviet state, which champions peace and implements the leninist principle of the peaceful coexistence of states with different social systems, is a mighty barrier to imperialist aggression.

Soviet experience has fully borne out the marxist-leninist theory that *the Communist Party plays a decisive role in the formation and development* of a socialist society. Only a party that steadfastly pursues a class, proletarian policy, and is equipped with progressive, revolutionary theory, only a party solidly united and closely linked with the masses, can organize the people and lead them to the victory of socialism.

Soviet experience has shown that fidelity *to the principles of marxism-leninism, of proletarian internationalism*, their firm and unswerving implementation and defence against all enemies and opportunists, are imperative conditions for the victory of socialism.

The world's greatest revolution and the socialist reorganization of society, which has attained unprecedented heights in its development and prosperity, have confirmed in practice *the historical truth of leninism* and have delivered a crushing blow to social reformist ideology.

As a result of the devoted labor of the Soviet people and the theoretical and practical activities of the Communist Party of the Soviet Union, *there exists in the world a socialist society that is a reality, and a science of socialist construction that has been tested in practice. The highroad to socialism has been paved*. Many peoples are already marching along it, and it will be taken sooner or later by all peoples.

III   THE WORLD SOCIALIST SYSTEM

The Soviet Union is not pursuing the tasks of communist construction alone but in fraternal community with the other socialist countries.

The defeat of German fascism and Japanese militarism in the Second World War, in which the Soviet Union played the decisive part, created favourable conditions for the overthrow of capitalist and landlord rule by the peoples in a number of European and Asian countries. The peoples of Albania, Bulgaria, China, Czechoslovakia, the Democratic Republic of Vietnam, the German Democratic Republic, Hungary, the Korean People's Democratic Republic, Poland and Rumania, and still earlier the people of the Mongolian People's Republic, adopted the path of socialist construction and, together with the Soviet Union, have formed the socialist camp. Yugoslavia likewise took the socialist path. But the Yugoslav leaders by their revisionist policy contraposed Yugoslavia to the socialist camp and the international communist movement, thus threatening the loss of the revolutionary gains of the Yugoslav people.

The socialist revolutions in Europe and Asia dealt imperialism a further powerful blow. The victory of the revolution in China was of special importance. The revolutions in European and Asian countries are the biggest event in world history since October 1917.

A new form of political organization of society, *people's democracy*, a variety of the dictatorship of the proletariat, emerged. It reflected the distinctive historical and national features of the various countries.

There emerged a world socialist system, a social, economic, and political community of free sovereign peoples pursuing the socialist and communist path, united by an identity of interests and goals and the close bonds of international socialist solidarity.

In the People's Democracies socialist production relations are dominant and the socio-economic possibility of capitalist restoration has been eliminated. The successes of these countries have conclusively proved that true progress in all lands, irrespective of the level of their economic development, their area, and population, is feasible only under socialism.

The combined forces of the socialist camp guarantee each socialist country against encroachments by imperialist reaction. The consolidation of the socialist countries in a single camp, its increasing unity and steadily growing strength, ensures the complete victory of socialism and communism within the framework of the system as a whole.

The countries of the socialist system have accumulated considerable collective experience in the remodelling of the lives of hundreds of millions of people and have contributed many new and specific features to the forms of political and economic organization of society. This experience is a most valuable asset to the international revolutionary movement.

It has been borne out in practice and recognized by all marxist-leninist parties that the processes of socialist revolution and construction are founded on a number of *basic objective laws* applicable to all countries entering upon the socialist path.

The world socialist system is a *new type of economic and political relationship between countries*. The socialist countries have the same type of economic basis – social ownership of means of production; the same type of political system – rule of the people with the working class at their head; a common ideology – marxism-leninism; common interests in the defence of their revolutionary gains and national independence from encroachments by the imperialist camp; and a great common goal – communism. This socio-eonomic and political community constitutes the objective groundwork for lasting and friendly intergovernmental relations within the socialist camp. The distinctive features of the relations existing between the countries of the socialist community are complete equality, mutual respect for independence and sovereignty, and fraternal mutual assistance and co-operation. In the socialist camp, or which is the same thing, in the world community of socialist countries, none have, or can have, any special rights or privileges.

The experience of the world socialist system has confirmed the need for the *closest unity* of countries that fall away from capitalism, for their united effort in the building of socialism and communism. The line of socialist construction in isolation, detached from the world community of socialist countries, is theoretically untenable because it conflicts with the objective laws governing the development of socialist society. It is harmful economically because it causes waste of social labour, retards the rates of growth of production, and makes the country dependent upon the capitalist world. It is reactionary and dangerous politically because it does not unite, but divides the peoples in face of the united front of imperialist forces, because it nourishes bourgeois nationalist tendencies and may ultimately lead to the loss of the socialist gains.

As they combine their effort in the building of a new society, the socialist states give active support to and extend their political, economic, and cultural co-operation with countries that have cast off colonial rule. They maintain – and are prepared to maintain – broad, mutually advantageous trade relations and cultural contacts with the capitalist countries.

The development of the world socialist system and of the world capitalist system is governed by diametrically opposed laws. The world capitalist system emerged and developed in fierce struggle between the countries composing it, through the subjection and exploitation of the weaker countries by the strong, through the enslavement of hundreds of millions of people and the reduction of entire continents to the status of colonial appendages of the imperialist metropolitan countries. The formation and development of the world socialist system, on the other hand, proceeds on the basis of sovereignty and free will and in conformity with the fundamental interests of the working people of all the countries of that system.

Whereas the world capitalist system is governed by the law of uneven economic and political development that leads to conflicts between countries, the world socialist system is governed by opposite laws, which ensure the steady and balanced growth of the economies of all countries belonging to that system. Growth of production in a country belonging to the capitalist world deepens the contradictions between countries and intensifies competitive rivalries. The development of each socialist country, on the other hand, promotes the general progress and consolidation of the world socialist system as a whole. The economy of world capitalism develops at a slow rate, and goes through crises and upheavals. Typical of the economy of world socialism, on the other hand, are high and stable rates of growth and the common steady economic progress of all socialist countries.

All the socialist countries make their contribution to the building and development of the world socialist system and the consolidation of its might. The existence of the Soviet Union greatly facilitates and accelerates the building of socialism in the people's democracies. The marxist-leninist parties and the peoples of the socialist countries proceed from the fact that the successes of the world socialist system as a whole depend on the contribution and effort made by each country, and therefore consider the greatest possible development of the productive forces of their country an internationalist duty. The co-operation of the socialist countries enables each country to use its resources and develop its productive forces to the full and in the most rational manner *A new type of international division of labour* is taking shape in the process of the economic, scientific, and technical co-operation of the socialist countries, the co-ordination of their economic plans, the specialization and combination of production.

The establishment of the Union of Soviet Socialist Republics and, later, of the world socialist system is the commencement of the historical process of all-round association of the peoples. With the disappearance of class antagonisms in the fraternal family of socialist countries, national antagonisms also disappear. The rapid cultural progress of the peoples of the socialist community is attended by a progressive mutual enrichment of the national cultures and an active moulding of the internationalist features typical of man in socialist society.

The experience of the peoples of the world socialist community has confirmed that their fraternal *unity and co-operation* conform to the supreme national interests of each country. The strengthening of the unity of the world socialist system on the basis of proletarian internationalism is an imperative condition for the further progress of all its member countries.

The socialist system has to cope with certain difficulties, deriving chiefly from the fact that most of the countries in that system had a medium or even low level of economic development in the past, and also from the fact that world reaction is doing its utmost to impede the building of socialism.

The experience of the Soviet Union and the people's democracies has confirmed the accuracy of Lenin's thesis that the class struggle does not disappear in the period of the building of socialism. The general trend of class struggle within the socialist countries in conditions of successful socialist construction leads to consolidation of the position of the socialist forces and weakens the resistance of the remnants of the hostile classes.

But this development does not follow a straight line. Changes in the domestic or external situation may cause the class struggle to intensify in specific periods. This calls for constant vigilance in order to frustrate in good time the designs of hostile forces within and without who persist in their attempts to undermine the people's power and sow strife in the fraternal community of socialist countries.

Nationalism is the chief political and ideological weapon used by international reaction and the remnants of the domestic reactionary forces against the unity of the socialist countries. Nationalist sentiments and national narrow-mindedness do not disappear automatically with the establishment of the socialist system. Nationalist prejudice and survivals of former national strife are an area in which resistance to social progress may be most protracted and stubborn, bitter, and insidious.

The Communists consider it their prime duty to educate working people in a spirit of internationalism, socialist patriotism, and intolerance of all possible manifestations of nationalism and chauvinism. Nationalism is harmful to the common interests of the socialist community and, above all, to the people of the country where it obtains, since isolation from the socialist camp holds up that country's development, deprives it of the advantages deriving from the world socialist system, and encourages the imperialist powers to make the most of nationalist tendencies for their own ends. Nationalism can gain the upper hand only where it is not consistently combated. The marxist-leninist internationalist policy and determined efforts to wipe out the survivals of bourgeois nationalism and chauvinism are an important condition for the further consolidation of the socialist community. Yet while they oppose nationalism and national egoism, Communists always show utmost consideration for the national feelings of the masses.

The world socialist system is advancing steadfastly towards decisive victory in its economic competition with capitalism. It will shortly surpass the world capitalist system in aggregate industrial and agricultural production. Its influence on the course of social development in the interests of peace, democracy, and socialism is growing more and more.

The magnificent edifice of the new world being built by the heroic labours of the free peoples on vast areas of Europe and Asia is a prototype of the new society, of the future of all mankind.

IV CRISIS OF WORLD CAPITALISM

Imperialism has entered the period of decline and collapse. An inexorable process of decay has seized capitalism from top to bottom – its economic and political system, its politics and ideology. Imperialism has for ever lost its power over the bulk of mankind. The main content, main trend and main features of the historical development of mankind are being determined by the world socialist system, by the forces fighting against imperialism, for the socialist reorganization of society.

The First World War and the October Revolution ushered in the general crisis of capitalism. The second stage of this crisis developed at the time of the Second World War and the socialist revolutions that took place in a number of European and Asian countries. World capitalism has now entered a new, third stage of that crisis, the principal feature of which is that its development was not connected with a world war.

The break-away from capitalism of more and more countries, the weakening of imperialist positions in the economic competition with socialism; the break-up of the imperialist colonial system; the intensification of imperialist contradictions with the development of state-monopoly capitalism and the growth of militarism; the mounting internal instability and decay of capitalist economy evidenced by the increasing inability of capitalism to make full use of the productive forces (low rates of production growth, periodic crises, continuous undercapacity operation of production plant, and chronic unemployment); the mounting struggle between labour and capital; an acute intensification of contradictions within the world capitalist economy; and unprecedented growth of political reaction in all spheres, rejection of bourgeois freedoms, and establishment of fascist and despotic regimes in a number of countries; and the profound crisis of bourgeois policy and ideology – all these are manifestations of the *general crisis of capitalism*.

In the imperialist stage *state-monopoly capitalism* develops on an extensive scale. The emergence and growth of monopolies leads to the direct intervention of the state, in the interests of the financial oligarchy, in the process of capitalist reproduction. It is in the interests of the financial oligarchy that the bourgeois state institutes various types of regulation and resorts to the nationalization of some branches of the economy. World wars, economic crises, militarism, and political upheavals have accelerated the development of monopoly capitalism into state-monopoly capitalism.

The oppression of finance capital keeps growing. Giant monopolies controlling the bulk of social production dominate the life of the nation. A handful of millionaires and multimillionaires wield arbitrary power over the entire wealth of the capitalist world and make the life of entire nations mere small change in their selfish deals. The financial oligarchy is getting fabulously rich. The state has become a committee for the management of the affairs of the monopoly bourgeoisie. The bureaucratization of the economy is rising steeply. State-monopoly capitalism combines the strength of the monopolies and that of the state into a single mechanism whose purpose is to enrich the monopolies, suppress the working-class movement and the national liberation struggle, save the capitalist system, and launch agressive wars.

The right-wing socialists and revisionists are making out state-monopoly capitalism to be almost socialism. The facts give the lie to this contention. State-monopoly capitalism does not change the nature of imperialism. Far from altering the position of the principal classes in the system of social production, it widens the rift between labour and capital, between the majority of the nation and the monopolies. Attempts at state regulation of the capitalist economy cannot eliminate competition and anarchy of production, cannot ensure the planned development of the economy on a nation-wide scale, because capitalist ownership and exploitation of wage labour remain the basis of production. The bourgeois theories of 'crisis-free' and 'planned' capitalism have been laid in the dust by the development of contemporary capitalist economy. The dialectics of state-monopoly capitalism is such that instead of shoring up the capitalist system as the bourgeoisie expects, it aggravates the contradictions of capitalism and undermines its foundations. State-monopoly capitalism is the fullest material preparation for socialism.

The new phenomena in imperialist development corroborate the accuracy of Lenin's conclusions on the principal objective laws of capitalism in its final stage and on its increasing decay. Yet this decay does not signify complete stagnation, a palsy of its productive forces, and does not rule out growth of capitalist economy at particular times and in particular countries.

All in all, capitalism is increasingly impeding the development of contemporary productive forces. Mankind is entering the period of a scientific and technical revolution bound up with the conquest of nuclear energy, space exploration, the development of chemistry, automation, and other major achievements of science and engineering. But the relations of production under capitalism are much too narrow for a scientific and technical revolution. Socialism alone is capable of effecting it and of applying its fruits in the interests of society.

Technical progress under the rule of monopoly capital is turning against the working class. By using new forms, the monopolies intensify the exploitation of the working class. Capitalist automation is robbing the worker of his daily bread. Unemployment is rising, the living standard is dropping. Technical progress is continuously throwing more groups of small producers overboard. Imperialism is using technical progress chiefly for military purposes. It is turning the achievements of human genius against humanity. As long as imperialism exists, mankind cannot feel secure about its future.

Modern capitalism has made the *market problem* extremely acute.

Imperialism is incapable of solving it, because lag of effective demand behind growth of production is one of its objective laws. Moreover, it retards the industrial development of the underdeveloped countries. The world capitalist market is shrinking relative to the more rapidly expanding production capacity. It is partitioned by countless customs barriers and restrictive fences and split into exclusive currency and finance zones. An acute competitive struggle for markets, spheres of investment, and sources of raw materials is underway in the imperialist camp. It is becoming doubly acute since the territorial sphere of capitalist domination has been greatly narrowed.

Monopoly capital has, in the final analysis, doomed bourgeois society to low rates of production growth that in some countries barely keep ahead of the growth of population. A considerable part of the production plant stands idle, while millions of unemployed wait at the factory gates. Farm production is artificially restricted, although millions are underfed in the world. People suffer want in material goods, but imperialism is squandering material resources and social labour on war preparations.

Abolition of the capitalist system in a large group of countries, the developing and strengthening of the world socialist system, the disintegration of the colonial system and the collapse of old empires, the commencing reorganization of the colonial economic structure in the newly free countries, and the expanding economic connections between the latter and the socialist world – all these factors intensify *the crisis of world capitalist economy*.

State-monopoly capitalism stimulates militarism to an unheard-of degree. The imperialist countries maintain immense armed forces even in peacetime. Military expenditures devour an ever-growing portion of the state budgets. The imperialist countries are turning into militarist, military-police states. Militarization pervades the life of bourgeois society.

While enriching some groups of the monopoly bourgeoisie, militarism leads to the exhaustion of nations, to the ruin of the peoples languishing under an excessive tax burden, mounting inflation, and a high cost of living. Within the lifetime of one generation imperialism plunged mankind into the abyss of two destructive world wars. In the First World War the imperialists annihilated ten million and crippled twenty million people. The Second World War claimed nearly fifty million human lives. In the course of these wars entire countries were ravaged, thousands of towns and villages were demolished, and the fruits of the labour of many generations were destroyed. The new war being hatched by the imperialists threatens mankind with unprecedented human losses and destruction. Even the preparations for it bring suffering and privation to millions of people.

The progress achieved in the development of the productive forces and the socialization of labour is being usurped by the contemporary capitalist state in the interests of the monopolies.

The monopoly bourgeoisie is a useless growth on the social organism, one unneeded in production. The industries are run by hired managers, engineers, and technicians. The monopolists lead a parasitical life and with their menials consume a substantial portion of the national income created by the toil of proletarians and peasants.

Fear of revolution, the successes of the socialist countries, and the pressure of the working-class movement compel the bourgeoisie to make partial concessions with respect to wages, labour conditions, and social security. But more often then not mounting prices and inflation reduce these concessions to nought. Wages lag behind the daily material and cultural requirements of the worker and his family, which grow as society develops. Even the relatively high standard of living in the small group of capitalistically developed countries rests upon the plunder of the Asian, African, and Latin American peoples, upon non-equivalent exchange, discrimination against female labour, brutal oppression of Negroes and immigrant workers, and also upon the intensified exploitation of the working people in those countries. The bourgeois myth of 'full employment' has proved to be sheer mockery, for the working class is suffering continuously from mass unemployment and insecurity. In spite of some successes in the economic struggle, the condition of the working class in the capitalist world is, on the whole, deteriorating.

The development of capitalism has dissipated the legend of the stability of small peasant farming once and for all. The monopolies have seized dominant positions in agriculture as well. Millions of farmers and peasants are being driven off the land, and their farms are being brought under the hammer. Small farms survive at the price of appalling hardships, the peasants' underconsumption, and excessive labour. The peasantry is groaning under the burden of mounting taxes and debts. Agrarian crises are bringing ever greater ruin to the countryside. Unspeakable want and poverty fall to the lot of the peasantry in the colonial and dependent countries; it suffers the dual oppression of the landlords and the monopoly bourgeoisie.

The monopolies are also ruining small urban proprietors. Handicrafts are going under. Small-scale industrial and commercial enterprises are fully dependent upon the monopolies.

Life has fully confirmed the marxist thesis of increasing proletarization in capitalist society. The expropriated masses have no other prospect of acquiring property than the revolutionary establishment of the social ownership of means of production, that is, making them the property of the whole people.

The uneven development of capitalism alters the balance of forces between countries and makes the contradictions between them more acute. The economic and with it the political and military centre of imperialism, has shifted from Europe to the United States. US monopoly capital, gorged on war profits and the arms race, has seized the most important sources of raw materials, the markets and the spheres of investment, has built up a unique kind of colonial empire, and has become the biggest *international exploiter*. Taking cover behind spurious professions of freedom and democracy, US imperialism is in effect performing the function of *world gendarme*, supporting reactionary dictatorial regimes and decayed monarchies, opposing democratic, revolutionary changes, and launching aggressions against peoples fighting for independence.

The US monopoly bourgeoisie is the mainstay of international reaction. It has assumed the role of 'saviour' of capitalism. The US financial tycoons are engineering a 'holy alliance' of imperialists and founding aggressive military blocs. American troops and war bases are stationed at the most important points of the capitalist world.

But the facts reveal the utter incongruity of the US imperialist claims to world domination. Imperialism has proved incapable of stemming the socialist and national liberation revolutions. The hopes which American imperialism pinned on its atomic weapons monopoly fell through. The United States has not been able to retain its share in the economy of the capitalist world, although it is still capitalism's chief economic, financial, and military force. The United States, the strongest capitalist power, is past its zenith and has entered the stage of decline. Imperialist countries such as Great Britain, France, Germany, and Japan have also lost their former power.

The basic contradiction of the contemporary world, that between socialism and imperialism, does not eliminate the *deep contradictions* rending the capitalist world. The aggressive military blocs founded under the aegis of the USA are time and again faced with crises. The international state-monopoly organizations springing up under the motto of 'integration,' the mitigation of the market problem, are in reality new forms of the redivision of the world capitalist market and are becoming seats of acute strain and conflict.

The contradictions between the principal imperialist powers are growing deeper. The economic rehabilitation of the imperialist countries defeated in the Second World War leads to the revival of the old and the emergence of new knots of imperialist rivalry and conflict. The Anglo-American, Franco-American, Franco-West German, American-West German, Japanese-American, and other contradictions are becoming especially acute. Fresh contradictions will inevitably arise and grow in the imperialist camp.

The American monopolies and their British and French allies are openly assisting the West German imperialists who are cynically advocating aggressive aims of revenge and preparing a war against the socialist countries and other European states. A dangerous centre of aggression, imperilling the peace and security of all peoples, is being revived in the heart of Europe. In the Far East the American monopolies are reviving Japanese militarism, which is in a certain way dependent on them. This constitutes another dangerous hotbed of war threatening the countries of Asia and, above all, the socialist countries.

The interests of the small group of imperialist powers are incompatible with the interests of all other countries, the interests of all peoples. Deep-rooted antagonism divides the imperialist countries from the countries that have won national independence and those that are fighting for their liberation.

Contemporary capitalism is inimical to the vital interests and progressive aspirations of all mankind. Capitalism with its exploitation of man by man, with its chauvinist and racist ideology, with its moral degradation, its rampage of profiteering, corruption, and crime is defiling society, the family, and man.

The bourgeois system came into being with the alluring slogans of liberty, equality, fraternity. But the bourgeoisie made use of these slogans merely to elbow out the feudal gentry and to assume power. Instead of equality a new gaping abyss of social and economic inequality appeared. Not fraternity but ferocious class struggle reigns in bourgeois society.

Monopoly capital is revealing its reactionary, anti-democratic substance more and more strikingly. It does not tolerate even the former bourgeois-democratic freedoms, although it proclaims them hypocritically. In the current stage of historical development it is getting harder for the bourgeoisie to propagate slogans of equality and liberty. The upswing of the international labour movement restricts the manoeuvres of finance capital. Finance capital can no longer quash the revolutionary sentiments of the masses and cope with the inexorably growing revolutionary, anti-imperialist movement by means of the old slogans and by bribing the labour bureaucracy.

Having taken full possession of the principal material values, monopoly capital refuses to share political power with anyone. It has established a dictatorship, the dictatorship of the minority over the majority, the dictatorship of the capitalist monopolies over society. The ideologists of imperialism hide the dictatorship of monopoly capital behind specious slogans of freedom and democracy. They declare the imperialist powers to be countries of the free world and represent the ruling bourgeois circles as opponents of all dictatorship. In reality, however, freedom in the imperialist world signifies nothing but freedom to exploit the working class, the working people, not only at home, but in all other countries that fall under the iron heel of the monopolies.

The bourgeoisie gives extensive publicity to the allegedly democratic nature of its election laws, singing special praise to its multi-party system and the possibility of nominating many candidates. In reality, however, the monopolists deprive the masses of the opportunity to express their will and elect genuine champions of their interests. Being in control of such potent means as capital, the press, radio, television, and using their henchmen in the trade unions and other mass organizations, they mislead the masses and impose their own candidates upon the electorate. The different bourgeois parties are usually no more than different factions of the ruling bourgeoisie.

The dictatorship of the bourgeoisie also grossly violates the will of the electorate. Whenever the bourgeoisie sees that the working people are likely, by using their constitutional rights, to elect a considerable number of the champions of their interests to the legislative organs, it brazenly alters the election system and arbitrarily limits the number of working people's representatives in parliament.

The financial oligarchy resorts to the establishment of fascist regimes, banking on the army, police, and gendarmerie as a last refuge from the people's wrath, especially when the masses try to make use of their democratic rights, albeit curtailed, to uphold their interests and end the all-pervading power of the monopolies. Although the vicious German and Italian fascism has crashed, fascist regimes still survive in some countries and fascism is being revived in new forms in others.

Thus, *the world imperialist system is rent by deep-rooted and acute contradictions*. The antagonism of labour and capital, the contradictions between the people and the monopolies, growing militarism, the break-up of the colonial system, the contradictions between the imperialist countries, conflicts and contradictions between the young national states and the old colonial powers, and – most important of all – the rapid growth of world socialism, are sapping and destroying imperialism, leading to its weakening and collapse.

Not even nuclear weapons can protect the monopoly bourgeoisie from the unalterable course of historical development. Mankind has learned the true face of capitalism. Hundreds of millions of people see that capitalism is a system of economic anarchy and periodic crises, chronic unemployment, poverty of the masses, and indiscriminate waste of productive forces, a system constantly fraught with the danger of war. Mankind does not want to, and will not, tolerate the historically outdated capitalist system.

V THE INTERNATIONAL REVOLUTIONARY MOVEMENT
   OF THE WORKING CLASS

The international revolutionary movement of the working class has achieved epoch-making victories. *Its chief gain is the world socialist system.* The example of victorious socialism is revolutionizing the minds of the working people of the capitalist world; it inspires them to fight against imperialism and greatly facilitates their struggle.

Social forces that are to ensure the victory of socialism are taking shape, multiplying and becoming steeled in the womb of capitalist society. A new contingent of the world proletariat – the young working-class movement of the newly free, dependent, and colonial countries of Asia, Africa, and Latin America – has entered the world arena. Marxist-leninist parties have arisen and grown. They are becoming a universally recognized national force enjoying ever greater prestige and followed by large sections of the working people.

The international revolutionary movement has accumulated vast experience in the struggle against imperialism and its lackeys in the ranks of the working class. It has become more mature ideologically and possesses great organized strength and a militantly dynamic spirit. The trade union movement, which unites vast masses of working people, is playing an increasing role.

The capitalist countries are continuously shaken by class battles. Militant actions of the working class in defence of its economic and political interests are growing in number. The working class and all working people have frequently imperilled the class rule of the bourgeoisie. In an effort to maintain its power, the finance oligarchy, in addition to methods of suppression, uses diverse ways of deceiving and corrupting the working class and its organizations, and of splitting the trade-union movement on a national and international scale. It bribes the top stratum of trade unions, co-operatives, and other organizations and swells the labour bureaucracy, to which it allots lucrative positions in industry, the municipal bodies, and the government apparatus. Anti-communist and anti-labour legislation, the banning of communist parties, wholesale dismissal of Communists and other progressive workers, blacklisting in industry, 'loyalty' screening of employees, police reprisals against the democratic press, and the suppression of strikes by military force have all become routine methods of action for the governments of the imperialist bourgeoisie in its efforts to preserve its dictatorship.

The reactionary forces in individual capitalist countries can no longer cope with the growing forces of democracy and socialism. Struggle and competition between the capitalist states do not preclude, however, a certain unity among them in the face of the increasing strength of socialism and the working-class movement. The imperialists form reactionary alliances; they enter into mutual agreements and set up military blocs and bases spearheaded not only against the socialist countries, but also against the revolutionary working-class and national liberation movement. The reactionary bourgeoisie in a number of European states have in peacetime opened the doors of their countries to foreign troops.

The bourgeoisie seeks to draw definite lessons from the October Revolution and the victories of socialism. It is using new methods to cover up the ulcers and vices of the capitalist system. Although all these methods render the activities of the revolutionary forces in the capitalist countries more dificult, they cannot reduce the contradictions between labour and capital.

The world situation today is more favourable to the working class movement. The achievements of the USSR and the world socialist system as a whole, the deepening crisis of world capitalism, the growing influence of communist parties among the masses, and the ideological breakdown of reformism have brought about a substantial change in the conditions of class struggle that is to the advantage of the working people. Even in those countries where reformism still holds strong positions, appreciable shifts to the left are taking place in the working-class movement.

In the new historical situation, the working class of many countries can, even before capitalism is overthrown, compel the bourgeoisie to carry out measures that transcend ordinary reforms and are of vital importance to the working class and the progress of its struggle for the victory of the revolution, for socialism, as well as to the majority of the nation. By uniting the democratic and peace-loving forces, the working class can make ruling circles cease preparations for a new world war, renounce the policy of starting local wars, and use the economy for peaceful purposes. By uniting the working people, the masses, the working class can beat back the offensive of fascist reaction and bring about the implementation of a national programme for peace, national independence, democratic rights, and a certain improvement of the living conditions of the people.

The capitalist monopolies are the chief enemy of the working class. They are also the chief enemy of the peasants, handicraftsmen, and other small urban proprietors, of most office workers and intellectuals, and even of a section of the middle capitalists.

The working class directs its main blow against the capitalist monopolies. All the main sections of a nation have a vital interest in abolishing the unlimited power of the monopolies. This makes it possible to unite all the democratic movements opposing the oppression of the finance oligarchy in a mighty *anti-monopoly torrent*.

The proletariat advances a programme for combating the power of the monopolies with due regard to the present as well as the future interests of its allies. It advocates broad nationalization on terms most favourable to the people. It backs the peasants' demands for radical land reforms and works for the realization of the slogan 'The land to those who till it.'

The proletariat, together with other sections of the people, wages a resolute struggle for broad democracy. It mobilizes the masses for effective action against the policy of the finance oligarchy, which strives to abolish democratic freedoms, restrict the power of parliament, revise the constitution with the aim of establishing the personal power of the henchmen of monopoly, and to go over from the parliamentary system to some variety of fascism.

It is in this struggle that the alliance of the working class and all working people is shaped. The working class unites the peasantry, its chief ally, to combat the survivals of feudalism and monopoly domination. Large sections of the office workers and a considerable section of the intelligentsia, whom capitalism reduces to the status of proletarians and who realize the need of changes in the social sphere, become allies of the working class.

General democratic struggles against the monopolies do not delay the socialist revolution but bring it nearer. *The struggle for democracy is a component of the struggle for socialism.* The more profound the democratic movement, the higher becomes the level of the political consciousness of the masses and the more clearly they see that only socialism clears for them the way to genuine freedom and well-being. In the course of this struggle, right socialist, reformist illusions are dispelled and a political army of the socialist revolution is brought into being.

Socialist revolutions, anti-imperialist national liberation revolutions, people's democratic revolutions, broad peasant movements, popular struggles to overthrow fascist and other despotic regimes, and general democratic movements against national oppression – all these merge in a single world-wide revolutionary process undermining and destroying capitalism.

The proletarian revolution in any country, being part of the world socialist revolution, is accomplished by the working class of that country and the masses of its people. The revolution is not made to order. It cannot be imposed on the people from without. It results from the profound internal and international contradictions of capitalism. The victorious proletariat cannot impose any 'felicity' on another people without thereby undermining its own victory.

Together with the other marxist-leninist parties, the Communist Party of the Soviet Union regards it as its internationalist duty to call on the peoples of all countries to rally, muster all internal forces, take vigorous action, and drawing on the might of the world socialist system, forestall or firmly repel imperialist interference in the affairs of the people of any country risen in revolt and thereby prevent imperialist export of counter-revolution. It will be easier to prevent export of counter-revolution if the working people, defending the national sovereignty of their country, strive to bring about the abolition of foreign military bases on their territory and to make their country dissociate itself from aggressive military blocs.

Communists have never held that the road to revolution lies necessarily through wars between countries. Socialist revolution is not necessarily connected with war. Although both world wars, which were started by the imperialists, culminated in socialist revolutions, revolutions are quite feasible without war. The great objectives of the working class can be realized without world war. Today the conditions for this are more favourable than ever.

The working class and its vanguard – the marxist-leninist parties – seek to accomplish the socialist revolution *by peaceful means*. This would meet the interests of the working class and the people as a whole, it would accord with the national interests of the country.

In the conditions prevailing at present, in some capitalist countries the working class, headed by its forward detachment, has an opportunity to unite the bulk of the nation, win state power without a civil war, and achieve the transfer of the basic means of production to the people upon the basis of a working-class and popular front and other possible forms of agreement and political co-operation between different parties and democratic organizations. The working class, supported by the majority of the people and firmly repelling opportunist elements incapable of renouncing the policy of compromise with the capitalists and landlords, can defeat the reactionary, anti-popular forces, win a solid majority in parliament, transform it from a tool serving the class interests of the bourgeoisie into an instrument serving the working people, launch a broad mass struggle outside parliament, smash the resistance of the reactionary forces, and provide the necessary conditions for a peaceful socialist revolution. This can be done only by extending and continuously developing the class struggle of the workers and peasants and the middle strata of the urban population against big monopoly capital and reaction, for far-reaching social reforms, for peace and socialism.

Where the exploiting classes resort to violence against the people, the possibility of a *non-peaceful transition to socialism* should be borne in mind. Leninism maintains, and historical experience confirms, that the ruling classes do not yield power of their own free will. Hence, the degree of bitterness of the class struggle and the forms it takes will depend not so much on the proletariat as on the strength of the reactionary groups' resistance to the will of the overwhelming majority of the people, and on the use of force by these groups at a particular stage of the struggle for socialism. In each particular country the actual applicability of one method of transition to socialism or the other depends on concrete historical conditions.

It may well be that as the forces of socialism grow, the working-class movement gains strength and the positions of capitalism are weakened, there will arise in certain countries a situation in which it will be preferable for the bourgeoisie, as Marx and Lenin foresaw, to agree to the basic means of production being purchased from it and for the proletariat to 'pay off' the bourgeoisie.

The success of the struggle which the working class wages for the victory of the revolution will depend on how well the working class and its party master the use of *all forms* of struggle – peaceful and non-peaceful, parliamentary and extra-parliamentary – and how well they are prepared for any swift and sudden replacement of one form of struggle by another form of struggle. While the principal regularities of the socialist revolution are common to all countries, the diversity of the national peculiarities and traditions that have arisen in the course of history creates specific conditions for the revolutionary process, the variety of forms and rates of the proletariat's advent to power. This predetermines the possibility and necessity, in a number of countries, of *transition stages* in the struggle for the dictatorship of the proletariat, and a *variety of forms* of political organization of the society building socialism. But whatever the form in which the transition from capitalism to socialism is effected, that transition can come about only through revolution. However varied the forms of a new, people's state power in the period of socialist construction, their essence will be the same – *dictatorship of the proletariat*, which represents genuine democracy, democracy for the working people.

A bourgeois republic, however democratic, however hallowed by slogans purporting to express the will of the people or nation as a whole (or extra-class will), inevitably remains in practice – owing to the existence of private capitalist ownership of the means of production – a dictatorship of the bourgeoisie, a machine for the exploitation and suppression of the vast majority of the working people by a handful of capitalists. In contrast to the bourgeoisie, which conceals the class character of the state, the working class does not deny the class character of the state.

The dictatorship of the proletariat is a dictatorship of the overwhelming majority over the minority; it is directed against the exploiters, against the oppression of peoples and nations, and is aimed at abolishing all exploitation of man by man. The dictatorship of the proletariat expresses not only the interests of the working class, but also those of all working people; its chief content is not violence but creation, the building of a new, socialist society, and the defence of its gains against the enemies of socialism.

Overcoming the split in its ranks is an important condition for the working class to fulfil its historic mission. No bastion of imperialism can withstand a closely-knit working class that exercises unity of action. The communist parties favour co-operation with the social-democratic parties not only in the struggle for peace, for better living conditions for the working people, and for the preservation and extension of their democratic rights and freedoms, but also in the struggle to win power and build a socialist society.

At the same time Communists criticize the ideological positions and right-wing opportunist practice of social democracy and expose the right social democratic leaders, who have sided openly with the bourgeoisie and renounced the traditional socialist demands of the working class.

The communist parties are the vanguard of the world revolutionary movement. They have demonstrated the vitality of marxism-leninism and their ability not only to propagate the great ideals of scientific communism, but also to put them into practice. Today the international communist movement is so powerful that the combined forces of reaction cannot crush it.

The communist movement grows and becomes steeled as it fights against various opportunist trends. Revisionism, right opportunism, which is a reflection of bourgeois influence, is the chief danger within the communist movement today. The revisionists, who mask their renunciation of marxism with talk about the necessity of taking account of the latest developments in society and the class struggle, in effect play the role of pedlars of bourgeoise-reformist ideology within the communist movement. They seek to rob marxism-leninism of its revolutionary spirit, to undermine the faith which the working class and all working people have in socialism, to disarm and disorganize them in their struggle against imperialism. The revisionists deny the historical necessity of the socialist revolution and of the dictatorship of the proletariat. They deny the leading role of the marxist-leninist party, undermine the foundations of proletarian internationalism, and drift to nationalism. The ideology of revisionism is most fully embodied in the programme of the League of Communists of Yugoslavia.

Another danger is dogmatism and sectarianism, which cannot be reconciled with a creative development of revolutionary theory, which lead to the dissociation and isolation of Communists from the masses, doom them to passive expectation or incite them to leftist adventurist actions in the revolutionary struggle, and hinder a correct appraisal of the changing situation and the use of new opportunities for the benefit of the working class and all democratic forces. Dogmatism and sectarianism, unless steadfastly combated, can also become the chief danger at particular stages in the development of individual parties.

The Communist Party of the Soviet Union holds that an uncompromising struggle against revisionism, dogmatism, and sectarianism, against all departures from leninism, is a necessary condition for the further strengthening of the unity of the world communist movement and for the consolidation of the socialist camp.

The communist parties are independent and they shape their policies with due regard to the specific conditions prevailing in their own countries. They base relations between themselves on equality and the principles of proletarian internationalism. They co-ordinate their actions, consciously and of their own free will, as components of a single international army of labour. The Communist Party of the Soviet Union, like all the other communist parties, regards it as its internationalist duty to abide by the appraisals and conclusions which the fraternal parties have reached jointly concerning their common tasks in the struggle against imperialism, for peace, democracy and socialism, and by the Declaration and the Statement adopted by the communist parties at their international meetings [in 1957 and 1960].

Vigorous defence of the unity of the world communist movement in line with the principles of marxism-leninism and proletarian internationalism, and the prevention of any action likely to disrupt that unity are an essential condition for victory in the struggle for national independence, democracy and peace, for the successful accomplishment of the tasks of the socialist revolution, for the construction of socialism and communism.

The CPSU will continue to concentrate its efforts on strengthening the unity and cohesion of the ranks of the great army of communists of all countries.

VI THE NATIONAL LIBERATION MOVEMENT

The world is experiencing a period of stormy national liberation revolutions. Imperialism suppressed the national independence and freedom of the majority of the peoples and put the fetters of brutal colonial slavery on them, but *the rise of socialism marks the advent of the era of emancipation of the oppressed peoples*. A powerful wave of national liberation revolutions is sweeping away the colonial system and undermining the foundations of imperialism. Young sovereign states have arisen, or are arising, in one-time colonies or semi-colonies. Their peoples have entered a new period of development. They have emerged as makers of a new life and as active participants in world politics, as a revolutionary force destroying imperialism.

But the struggle is not yet over. The peoples who are throwing off the shackles of colonialism have attained different degrees of freedom. Many of them, having established national states, are striving for economic and durable political independence. The peoples of those formally independent countries that in reality depend on foreign monopolies politically and economically are rising to fight against imperialism and reactionary pro-imperialist regimes. The peoples who have not yet cast off the chains of colonial slavery are conducting a heroic struggle against their foreign enslavers.

The young sovereign states do not belong either to the system of imperialist states or to the system of socialist states. But the overwhelming majority of them have not yet broken free from the world capitalist economy even though they occupy a special place in it. They constitute that part of the world which is still being exploited by the capitalist monopolies. As long as they do not put an end to their economic dependence on imperialism, they will be playing the role of a 'world countryside,' and will remain objects of semi-colonial exploitation.

The existence of the world socialist system and the weakening of imperialism offer the peoples of the newly free countries the prospect of a national renascence, of ending age-long backwardness and poverty, and achieving economic independence.

The interests of a nation call for the eradication of the remnants of colonialism, the elimination of the roots of imperialist power, the ousting of foreign monopolies, the founding of a national industry, the abolition of the feudal system and its survivals, the implementation of radical land reforms with the participation of the entire peasantry and in its interests, the pursuit of an independent foreign policy of peace, the democratization of the life of society and the strengthening of political independence. All patriotic and progressive forces of the nation are interested in the solution of national problems. That is the basis on which they can be united.

Foreign capital will retreat only before a broad union of patriotic, democratic forces pursuing an anti-imperialist policy. The pillars of feudalism will crumble only under the impact of a general democratic movement. Only far-reaching agrarian reforms and a broad peasant movement can sweep away the remnants of medievalism that fetter the development of the productive forces, and solve the acute food problem that faces the peoples of Asia, Africa, and Latin America. Political independence can be made secure only by a people that has won democratic rights and freedoms and is taking an active part in governing the state.

Consistent struggle against imperialism is a paramount condition for the solution of national tasks. Imperialism seeks to retain one-time colonies and semi-colonies within the system of capitalist economy and perpetuate their underprivileged position in it. US *imperialism is the chief bulwark of modern colonialism.*

The imperialists are using new methods and new forms to maintain colonial exploitation of the peoples. They resort to whatever means they can (colonial wars, military blocs, conspiracies, terrorism, subversion, economic pressure, bribery) to control the newly free countries and to reduce the independence they have won to mere form, or to deprive them of that independence. Under the guise of 'aid,' they are trying to retain their old positions in those countries and capture new ones, to extend their social basis, lure the national bourgeoisie to their side, implant military despotic regimes, and put obedient puppets in power. Using the poisoned weapon of national and tribal strife, the imperialists seek to split the ranks of the national liberation movement; reactionary groups of the local exploiting classes play the role of allies of imperialism.

Imperialism thus remains the chief enemy and the chief obstacle to the solution of the national problems facing the young sovereign states and all dependent countries.

A national liberation revolution does not end with the winning of political independence. Independence will be unstable and will become fictitious unless the revolution brings about radical changes in the social and economic spheres and solves the pressing problems of national rebirth.

The working class is the most consistent fighter for the consummation of this revolution, for national interests and social progress. As industry develops, its ranks will swell and its role on the socio-political scene will increase. The alliance of the working class and the peasantry is the fundamental condition for the success of the struggle to carry out far-reaching democratic changes and achieve economic and social progress. This alliance must form the core of a broad national front. The extent to which the national bourgeoisie will take part in the anti-imperialist and anti-feudal struggle will depend in considerable measure on the solidity of the alliance of the working class and the peasantry. The national front embraces the working class, the peasantry, the national bourgeoisie, and the democratic intelligentsia.

In many countries, the liberation movement of the peoples that have awakened proceeds under the flag of nationalism. Marxist-leninists draw a distinction between the nationalism of oppressed nations and that of the oppressor nations. The nationalism of an oppressed nation contains a *general democratic element* directed against oppression, and Communists support it because they consider it historically justified at a given stage. That element finds expression in the striving of the oppressed peoples to free themselves from imperialist oppression, to gain national independence and bring about a national renascence. But the nationalism of an oppressed nation has yet another aspect, one expressing the ideology and interests of the reactionary exploiting top stratum.

The national bourgeoisie is dual in character. In modern conditions the national bourgeoisie in those colonial, one-time colonial, and dependent countries where it is not connected with the imperialist circles is objectively interested in accomplishing the basic tasks of an anti-imperialist and anti-feudal revolution. Its progressive role and its ability to participate in the solution of pressing national problems are, therefore, not yet spent.

But as the contradictions between the working people and the propertied classes grow and the class struggle inside the country becomes more acute, the national bourgeoisie shows an increasing inclination to compromise with imperialism and domestic reaction.

The development of the countries which have won their freedom may be a complex multi-stage process. By virtue of varying historical and socio-economic conditions in the newly free countries, the revolutionary effort of the masses will impart many distinctive features to the forms and rates of their social progress.

One of the basic questions confronting these peoples is, which road of development should the countries that have freed themselves from colonial tyranny take, the capitalist road or the non-capitalist?

What can capitalism bring them?

Capitalism is the road of suffering for the people. It will not ensure rapid economic progress nor eliminate poverty; social inequality will increase. The capitalist development of the countryside will ruin the peasantry still more. The workers will be fated either to engage in back-breaking labour to enrich the capitalists, or to swell the ranks of the disinherited army of the unemployed. The petty bourgeoisie will be crushed in competition with big capital. The benefits of culture and education will remain out of reach of the people. The intelligentsia will be compelled to sell its talent.

What can socialism bring the peoples?

Socialism is the road to freedom and happiness for the peoples. It ensures rapid economic and cultural progress. It transforms a backward country into an industrial country within the lifetime of one generation and not in the course of centuries. A planned socialist economy is an economy of progress and prosperity by its very nature. Abolition of the exploitation of man by man does away with social inequality. Unemployment disappears completely. Socialism provides all peasants with land, helps them to develop farming, combines their labour efforts in voluntary co-operatives and puts modern agricultural machinery and agronomy at their disposal. Peasant labour is made more productive and the land is made more fertile. Socialism provides a high material and cultural standard of living for the working class and all working people. Socialism lifts the people out of darkness and ignorance and gives them access to modern culture. The intelligentsia is offered ample opportunities for creative effort for the benefit of the people.

It is for the peoples themselves to decide which road they will choose. In view of the present balance of world forces and the actual feasibility of powerful support from the world socialist system, the peoples of the former colonies can decide this question in their own interest. Their choice will depend on the balance of class forces. The non-capitalist road of development is ensured by the struggle of the working class and the masses of the people, by the general democratic movement, and meets the interests of the absolute majority of the nation.

The establishment and development of *national democracies* opens vast prospects for the peoples of the economically underdeveloped countries. The political basis of a national democracy is a bloc of all the progressive, patriotic forces fighting to win complete national independence and broad democracy, and to consummate the anti-imperialist, anti-feudal, democratic revolution.

A steady growth of the class and national consciousness of the masses is a characteristic of the present stage of social development. The imperialists persist in distorting the idea of national sovereignty, in emasculating it of its main content and in using it as a means of fomenting national egoism, implanting a spirit of national exclusiveness and increasing national antagonisms. The democratic forces establish the idea of national sovereignty in the name of equality for the peoples, of their mutual trust, friendship, and assistance and of closer relations between them, in the name of social progress. The idea of national sovereignty in its democratic sense becomes more and more firmly established; it acquires increasing significance and becomes an important factor in the progressive development of society.

The communist parties are steadfastly carrying on an active struggle to consummate the anti-imperialist, anti-feudal, democratic revolution, to establish a state of national democracy and achieve social progress. *The Communists' aims are in keeping with the supreme interests of the nation.* The attempts of reactionary circles to disrupt the national front under the guise of anti-communism and their persecution of Communists lead to the weakening of the national liberation movement and run counter to the national interests of the peoples; they imperil the gains achieved.

The national states become ever more active as an independent force on the world scene; objectively, this force is in the main a *progressive, revolutionary, and anti-imperialist force*. The countries and peoples that are now free from colonial oppression are to play a prominent part in the prevention of a new world war – the focal problem of today. The time is past when imperialism could freely use the manpower and material resources of those countries in its predatory wars. The time has come when the peoples of those countries, breaking the resistance of the reactionary circles and those connected with the colonialists, and overcoming the vacillation of the national bourgeoisie, can put their resources at the service of universal security and become a new bulwark of peace. This is what their own fundamental interests and the interests of all peoples demand.

The joining of the efforts of the newly free peoples and of the peoples of the socialist countries in the struggle against the war danger is a cardinal factor of world peace. This mighty front, which expresses the will and strength of two-thirds of mankind, can force the imperialist aggressors to retreat.

The socialist countries are sincere and true friends of peoples fighting for their liberation and of those that have freed themselves from imperialist tyranny, and render them all-round support. They stand for the abolition of all forms of colonial oppression and vigorously promote the strengthening of the sovereignty of the states rising on the ruins of colonial empires.

The CPSU considers fraternal alliance with the people who have thrown off the colonial or semi-colonial yoke to be a corner-stone of its international policy. This alliance is based on the common vital interests of world socialism and the world national liberation movement. The CPSU regards it as its internationalist duty to assist the peoples who have set out to win and strengthen their national independence, all peoples who are fighting for the complete abolition of the colonial system.

VII THE STRUGGLE AGAINST BOURGEOIS AND REFORMIST IDEOLOGY

A grim struggle is going on between two ideologies – communist and bourgeois – in the world today. This struggle is a reflection, in the spiritual life of mankind, of the historic process of transition from capitalism to socialism.

The new historical epoch has brought the revolutionary world outlook of the proletariat a genuine triumph. Marxism-leninism has gripped the minds of progressive mankind.

Bourgeois doctrines and schools have failed in the test of history. They have been and still are unable to furnish scientific answers to the questions posed by life. The bourgeoisie is no longer in a position to put forward ideas that will induce the masses to follow it. More and more people in the capitalist countries are renouncing the bourgeois world outlook. *Bourgeois ideology is experiencing a grave crisis.*

A revolutionary change in the minds of vast masses is a long and complex process. The more victories the world socialist system achieves, the deeper the crisis of world capitalism and the sharper the class struggle, the more important becomes the role of marxist-leninist ideas in unifying and mobilizing the masses to fight for communism. The ideological struggle is a most important element of the class struggle of the proletariat.

Imperialist reaction mobilizes every possible means to exert ideological influence on the masses as it attempts to denigrate communism and its noble ideas and to defend capitalism. The chief ideological and political weapon of imperialism is anti-communism, which consists mainly in slandering the socialist system and distorting the policy and objectives of the communist parties and marxist-leninist theory. Under the false slogans of anti-communism, imperialist reaction persecutes and hounds all that is progressive and revolutionary; it seeks to split the ranks of the working people and to paralyse the proletarians' will to fight. Rallied to this black banner today are all the enemies of social progress: the finance oligarchy and the military, the fascists and reactionary clericals, the colonialists and landlords, and all the ideological and political supporters of imperialist reaction. Anti-communism is a reflection of the extreme decadence of bourgeois ideology.

The defenders of the bourgeois system, seeking to keep the masses in spiritual bondage, invent new 'theories' designed to mask the exploiting character of the bourgeois system and to embellish capitalism. They assert that modern capitalism has changed its nature, that it has become 'people's capitalism' in which property is 'diffused' and capital becomes 'democratic,' that classes and class contradictions are disappearing, that 'incomes are being equalized' and economic crises eliminated. In reality, however, the development of modern capitalism confirms the accuracy of marxist-leninist theory of the growing contradictions and antagonisms in capitalist society and of the aggravation of the class struggle within it.

The advocates of the bourgeois state call it a *'welfare state.'* They propagate the illusion that the capitalist state opposes monopolies and can achieve social harmony and universal well-being. But the masses see from their own experience that the bourgeois state is an obedient tool of the monopolies and that the vaunted 'welfare' is welfare for the magnates of finance capital, and suffering and torment for hundreds of millions of working men.

The 'theoreticians' of anti-communism describe the imperialist countries as the 'free world.' In reality the 'free world' is a world of exploitation and lack of rights, a world where human dignity and national honour are trampled underfoot, a world of obscurantism and political reaction, of rabid militarism and bloody reprisals against the working people.

Monopoly capital engenders *fascist ideology* – the ideology of extreme chauvinism and racism. Fascism in power is an overt terroristic dictatorship of the most reactionary, most chauvinistic, and most imperialist elements of finance capital. Fascism begins everywhere and always with vicious anti-communism to isolate and rout the parties of the working class, to split the forces of the proletariat and defeat them piecemeal, and then to do away with all the other democratic parties and organizations and turn the people into the blind tool of the policy of the capitalist monopolies. Fascism strikes first of all at the communist parties since they are the most consistent, staunch, and incorruptible defenders of the interests of the working class and all working people.

Imperialist reaction makes extensive use of *chauvinism and racism* to incite nationalist and racial conflicts, persecute entire nationalities and races (anti-semitism, racial discrimination against Negroes and the peoples of the underdeveloped countries), blunt the class consciousness of the working people and divert the proletariat and its allies from the class struggle.

Clericalism is acquiring ever greater importance in the political and ideological arsenal of imperialism. The clericals do not confine themselves to using the Church and its ramified machinery. They now have their own big political parties which in many capitalist countries are in power. By setting up its own trade union, youth, women's, and other organizations clericalism splits the ranks of the working class and all working people. The monopolies lavishly subsidize clerical parties and organizations, which exploit the religious sentiments of the working people and their superstitions and prejudices.

Bourgeois ideology assumes a variety of forms and uses the most diverse methods and means of deceiving the working people. But they all boil down to the same thing – defence of the declining capitalist system. The ideas running through the political and economic theories of the modern bourgeoisie, through its philosophy and sociology, through its ethics and aesthetics, substantiate monopoly domination, justify exploitation, defame social property and collectivism, glorify militarism and war, whitewash colonialism and racism, and foment enmity and hatred among the peoples.

Anti-communism is becoming the main instrument of reaction in its struggle against the democratic forces of Asia, Africa, and Latin America. It is the meeting ground of imperialist ideology and the ideology of the feudal, pro-imperialist elements and the reactionary groups of the bourgeoisie of the countries which have gained their freedom from colonial tyranny. The anti-popular circles of those countries seek to tone down the general democratic content of nationalism, to play up its reactionary aspect, to push aside the democratic forces of the nation, to prevent social progress, and to hinder the spread of scientific socialism. At the same time they advance theories of 'socialism of the national type,' propagate socio-philosophical doctrines that are, as a rule, so many variations of the petty-bourgeois illusion of socialism, an illusion which rules out the class struggle. These theories mislead the people, hamper the development of the national liberation movement, and imperil its gains.

National-democratic, anti-imperialist ideas are becoming widespread in the countries which have liberated themselves from colonial oppression. The Communists and other proponents of these ideas patiently explain to the masses the untenability of the illusion that national independence and social progress are possible without a determined struggle against imperialism and internal reaction. They come out actively against chauvinism and other manifestations of reactionary ideology, which justifies despotic regimes and the suppression of democracy. At the same time the Communists act as exponents of socialist ideology, rallying the masses under the banner of scientific socialism.

The ideological struggle of the imperialist bourgeoisie is spearheaded primarily against the working class and its marxist-leninist parties. Social democratism in the working-class movement and revisionism in the communist movement reflect the bourgeois influence on the working class.

The contemporary right-wing social democrats are the most important ideological and political prop of the bourgeoisie within the working-class movement. They eclectically combine old opportunist ideas with the 'latest' bourgeois theories. The right wing of social democracy has completely broken with marxism and contraposed so-called democratic socialism to scientific socialism. Its adherents deny the existence of antagonistic classes and the class struggle in bourgeois society; they forcefully deny the necessity of the proletarian revolution and oppose the abolition of the private ownership of the means of production. They assert that capitalism is being 'transformed' into socialism.

The right-wing socialists began by advocating social reforms in place of the socialist revolution and went so far as to defend state-monopoly capitalism. In the past they impressed on the minds of the proletariat that their differences with revolutionary marxism bore not so much on the ultimate goal of the working-class movement as on the ways of achieving it. Now they openly renounce socialism. Formerly the right-wing socialists refused to recognize the class struggle to the point of recognizing the dictatorship of the proletariat. Today they deny, not only the existence of the class struggle in bourgeois society, but also the very existence of antagonistic classes.

Historical experience has shown the bankruptcy of both the ideology and the policy of social democracy. Even when reformist parties come to power they limit themselves to partial reforms that do not affect the rule of the monopoly bourgeoisie. Anti-communism has brought social reformism to an ideological and political impasse. This is one of the main reasons for the crisis of social democracy.

Marxism-leninism is winning more and more victories. It is winning them because it expresses the vital interests of the working class, of the vast majority of mankind, which seeks peace, freedom, and progress, and because it expresses the ideology of the new society succeeding capitalism.

VIII PEACEFUL COEXISTENCE AND THE STRUGGLE FOR WORLD PEACE

The CPSU considers that the chief aim of its foreign-policy activity is to provide peaceful conditions for the building of a communist society in the USSR and developing the world socialist system, and together with the other peace-loving peoples to deliver mankind from a world war of extermination.

The CPSU maintains that forces capable of preserving and promoting universal peace have arisen and are growing in the world. Possibilities are arising for essentially new relations between states.

Imperialism knows no relations between states other than those of domination and subordination, of oppression of the weak by the strong. It bases international relations on *diktat* and intimidation, on violence and arbitrary rule. It regards wars of aggression as a natural means of settling international issues. For the imperialist countries diplomacy has been, and remains, a tool for imposing their will upon other nations and preparing wars. At the time of the undivided rule of imperialism the issue of war and peace was settled by the finance and industrial oligarchy in the utmost secrecy from the peoples.

Socialism contrasts imperialism with *a new type of international relations*. The foreign policy of the socialist countries, which is based on the principles of peace, the equality and self-determination of nations, and respect for the independence and sovereignty of all countries, as well as the fair, humane methods of socialist diplomacy, are exerting a growing influence on the world situation. At a time when imperialism no longer plays the dominant role in international relations, while the socialist system is playing an increasing role, and when the influence of the countries that have won national independence and of the masses of the people in the capitalist countries has grown very considerably, it is becoming possible for the new principles advanced by socialism to gain the upper hand over the principles of aggressive imperialist policy.

For the first time in history, a situation has arisen in which not only the big states, but also the small ones, the countries which have chosen independent development, and all the states which want peace, are in a position, irrespective of their strength, to pursue an independent foreign policy.

The issue of war and peace is the principal issue of today. Imperialism is the only source of the war danger. The imperialist camp is making preparations for the most terrible crime against mankind – a world thermonuclear war that can bring unprecedented destruction to entire countries and wipe out entire nations. The problem of war and peace has become a life-and-death problem for hundreds of millions of people.

The peoples must concentrate their efforts on curbing the imperialists in good time and preventing them from making use of lethal weapons. *The main thing is to ward off a thermonuclear war, to prevent it from breaking out*. This can be done by the present generation.

The consolidation of the Soviet state and the formation of the world socialist system were historic steps towards the realization of mankind's age-old dream of banishing wars from the life of society. In the socialist part of the world there are no classes or social groups interested in starting a war. Socialism, outstripping capitalism in a number of important branches of science and technology, has supplied the peace-loving peoples with powerful material means of curbing imperialist aggression. Capitalism established its rule with fire and sword, but socialism does not require war to spread its ideals. Its weapon is its superiority over the old system in social organization, political system, economy, the improvement of the standard of living, and spiritual culture.

The socialist system is a natural centre of attraction for the peace-loving forces of the globe. The principles of its foreign policy are gaining ever greater international recognition and support. A vast *peace zone* has taken shape on earth. In addition to the socialist countries, it includes a large group of non-socialist countries that for various reasons are not interested in starting a war. The emergence of those countries in the arena of world politics has substantially altered the balance of forces in favour of peace.

There is a growing number of countries that adhere to a policy of neutrality and strive to safeguard themselves against the hazards of participation in aggressive military blocs.

In the new historical epoch the masses have a far greater opportunity of actively intervening in the settlement of international issues. The peoples are taking the solution of the problem of war and peace into their own hands more and more vigorously. The anti-war movement of the masses, which takes various forms, is a major factor in the struggle for peace. The international working class, the most uncompromising and most consistent fighter against imperialist war, is the great organizing force in this struggle of the people as a whole.

It is possible to avert a world war by the combined efforts of the mighty socialist camp, the peace-loving non-socialist countries, the international working class, and all the forces championing peace. The growing superiority of the socialist forces over the forces of imperialism, of the forces of peace over those of war, will make it actually possible to banish world war from the life of society even before the complete victory of socialism on earth, with capitalism surviving in a part of the world. The victory of socialism throughout the world will do away completely with the social and national causes of all wars. *To abolish war and establish everlasting peace on earth is a historic mission of communism.*

General and complete disarmament under strict international control is a radical way of guaranteeing a durable peace. Imperialism has imposed an unprecedented burden of armaments on the peoples. Socialism sees its duty towards mankind in delivering it from this absurd waste of national wealth. The solution of this problem would have historic significance for mankind. By an active and determined effort the peoples can and must force the imperialists into disarmament.

Socialism has offered mankind the only reasonable principle of maintaining relations between states at a time when the world is divided into two systems – the principle of the peaceful coexistence of states with different social systems, put forward by Lenin.

Peaceful coexistence of the socialist and capitalist countries is an *objective necessity* for the development of human society. *War cannot and must not serve as a means of settling international disputes.* Peaceful coexistence or disastrous war – such is the alternative offered by history. Should the imperialist aggressors nevertheless venture to start a new world war, the peoples will no longer tolerate a system which drags them into devastating wars. They will sweep imperialism away and bury it.

Peaceful coexistence implies renunciation of war as a means of settling international disputes, and their solution by negotiation; equality, mutual understanding, and trust between countries; consideration for each other's interests; non-interference in internal affairs; recognition of the right of every people to solve all the problems of their country by themselves; strict respect for the sovereignty and territorial integrity of all countries; promotion of economic and cultural co-operation on the basis of complete equality and mutual benefit.

Peaceful coexistence serves as a basis for the peaceful competition between socialism and capitalism on an international scale and constitutes a specific form of class struggle between them. As they consistently pursue the policy of peaceful coexistence, the socialist countries are steadily strengthening the positions of the world socialist system in its competition with capitalism. Peaceful coexistence affords more favourable opportunities for the struggle of the working class in the capitalist countries and facilitates the struggle of the peoples of the colonial and dependent countries for their liberation. Support for the principle of peaceful coexistence is also in keeping with the interests of that section of the bourgeoisie which realizes that a thermonuclear war would not spare the ruling classes of capitalist society either. The policy of peaceful coexistence is in accord with the vital interests of all mankind, except the big monopoly magnates and the militarists.

The Soviet Union has consistently pursued, and will continue to pursue, the policy of the peaceful coexistence of states with different social systems.

The Communist Party of the Soviet Union advances the following *tasks in the field of international relations:*

to use, together with the other socialist countries, peaceful states and peoples, every means of preventing world war and providing conditions for the complete abolition of war from the life of society;

to pursue a policy of establishing sound international relations, and work for the dissolution of all military blocs opposing each other, the discontinuance of the 'cold war' and the propaganda of enmity and hatred among nations, and the abolition of all air, naval, rocket, and other military bases on foreign territory;

to work for general and complete disarmament under strict international control;

to strengthen relations of fraternal friendship and close co-operation with the countries of Asia, Africa, and Latin America which are fighting to attain or consolidate national independence, with all peoples and states that advocate the preservation of peace;

to pursue an active and consistent policy of improving and developing relations with all capitalist countries, including the United States of America, Great Britain, France, the Federal Republic of Germany, Japan, and Italy, with a view to safeguarding peace;

to contribute in every way to the militant solidarity of all contingents and organizations of the international working class, which oppose the imperialist policy of war;

steadfastly to pursue a policy of consolidating all the forces fighting against war. All the organizations and parties that strive to avert war, the neutralist and pacifist movements and the bourgeois circles that advocate peace and normal relations between countries will meet with understanding and support on the part of the Soviet Union;

to pursue a policy of developing international co-operation in the fields of trade, cultural relations, science, and technology;

to be highly vigilant with regard to the aggressive circles, which are intent on violating peace; to expose, in good time, the initiators of military adventures; to take all necessary steps to safeguard the security and inviolability of our socialist country and the socialist camp as a whole.

The CPSU and the Soviet people as a whole will continue to oppose all wars of conquest, including wars between capitalist countries, and local wars aimed at strangling people's emancipation movements, and consider it their duty to support the sacred struggle of the oppressed peoples and their just anti-imperialist wars of liberation.

The Communist Party of the Soviet Union will hold high the banner of peace and friendship among the nations.

Part two
The tasks of the
Communist Party of the Soviet Union
in building a communist society

COMMUNISM— THE BRIGHT FUTURE OF ALL MANKIND

The building of a communist society has become an immediate practical task for the Soviet people. The gradual development of socialism into communism is an objective law; it has been prepared by the development of Soviet socialist society throughout the preceding period.

What is communism?

Communism is a classless social system with one form of public ownership of the means of production and full social equality of all members of society; under it, the all-round development of people will be accompanied by the growth of productive forces through continuous progress in science and technology; all the springs of co-operative wealth will flow more abundantly, and the great principle 'From each according to his ability, to each according to his needs' will be implemented. Communism is a highly organized society of free, socially conscious working people in which public self-government will be established, a society in which labour for the good of society will become the prime vital requirement of everyone, a necessity recognized by one and all, and the ability of each person will be employed to the greatest benefit of the people.

A high degree of communist consciousness, industry, discipline, and devotion to the public interest are qualities typifying the man of communist society.

Communism ensures the continuous development of social production and rising labour productivity through rapid scientific and technological progress; it equips man with the best and most powerful machines, greatly increases his power over nature and enables him to control its elemental forces to an ever greater extent. The social economy reaches the highest stage of planned organization, and the most effective and rational use is made of the material wealth and labour reserves to meet the growing requirements of the members of society.

Under communism there will be no classes, and the socio-economic and cultural distinctions, and differences in living conditions, between town and countryside will disappear; the countryside will rise to the level of the town in the development of productive forces and nature of work, forms of production relations, living conditions, and well-being of the population. With the victory of communism, mental and physical labour will merge organically in the production activity of people. The intelligentsia will no longer be a distinct social stratum. Manual labourers will have risen in cultural and technological standards to the level of workers by brain.

Thus, communism will put an end to the division of society into classes and social strata, whereas the whole history of mankind, with the exception of its primitive period, was one of class society. Division into opposing classes led to the exploitation of man by man, class struggle, and antagonisms between nations and states.

Under communism all people will have equal status in society, will stand in the same relation to the means of production, will enjoy equal conditions of work and distribution, and will actively participate in the management of public affairs. Harmonious relations will be established between the individual and society on the basis of the unity of public and personal interests. For all their diversity, the requirements of people will express the sound, reasonable requirements of the fully developed person.

The purpose of communist production is to ensure uninterrupted progress of society and to provide all its members with material and cultural benefits according to their growing needs, their individual requirements and tastes. People's requirements will be satisfied from public sources. Articles of personal use will be in the full ownership of each member of society and will be at his disposal.

Communist society, which is based on highly organized production and advanced technology, alters the character of work, but it does not release the members of society from work. It will by no means be a society of anarchy, idleness, and inactivity. Every able-bodied person will participate in social labour and thereby ensure the steady growth of the material and spiritual wealth of society. Thanks to the changed character of labour, its better technical equipment and the high degree of consciousness of all members of society, the latter will work willingly for the public benefit according to their own inclinations.

Communist production demands high standards of organization, precision and discipline, which are ensured, not by compulsion, but through an understanding of public duty, and are determined by the whole pattern of life in communist society. Labour and discipline will not be a burden to people; labour will no longer be a mere source of livelihood – it will be a genuinely creative process and source of joy.

Communism represents the highest form of organization of public life. All production units and self-governing associations will be harmoniously united in a common planned economy and a uniform rhythm of social labour.

Under communism nations will draw closer and closer together in all spheres on the basis of a complete identity of economic, political and spiritual interests, of fraternal friendship and co-operation.

Communism is a system under which the abilities and talents of the free man, his best moral qualities, blossom forth and reveal themselves in full. Family relations will be freed once and for all from material considerations and will be based solely on mutual love and friendship.

In defining the basic tasks to be accomplished in building a communist society, the party is guided by Lenin's great formula: *'Communism is Soviet power plus the electrification of the whole country.'*

The CPSU, being a party of scientific communism, proposes and fulfils the tasks of communist construction in step with the preparation and maturing of the material and spiritual prerequisites, considering that it would be wrong to jump over necessary stages of development, and that it would be equally wrong to halt at an achieved level and thus check progress. The building of communism must be carried out by successive stages.

In the current decade (1961-70) the Soviet Union, in creating the material and technical basis of communism, will surpass the strongest and richest capitalist country, the USA, in production per head of population; the people's standard of living and their cultural and technical standards will improve substantially; everyone will live in easy circumstances; all collective and state farms will become highly productive and profitable enterprises; the demand of Soviet people for well-appointed housing will, in the main, be satisfied; hard physical work will disappear; the USSR will have the shortest working day.

The material and technical basis of communism will be built up by the *end of the second decade* (1971-80), ensuring an abundance of material and cultural values for the whole population; Soviet society will come close to a stage where it can introduce the principle of distribution according to needs, and there will be a gradual transition to one form of ownership – public ownership. Thus, *a communist society will in the main be built in the USSR*. The construction of communist society will be fully completed in the subsequent period.

The majestic edifice of communism is being erected by the persevering effort of the Soviet people – the working class, the peasantry, and the intelligentsia. The more successful their work, the closer the great goal – communist society.

I THE TASKS OF THE PARTY IN THE ECONOMIC FIELD AND IN THE CREATION AND PROMOTION OF THE MATERIAL AND TECHNICAL BASIS OF COMMUNISM

The main economic task of the party and the Soviet people is to create *the material and technical basis of communism* within two decades. This means complete electrification of the country and perfection on this basis of techniques, technologies, and organization of social production in all the fields of the economy; comprehensive mechanization of production operations and a growing degree of their automation; widespread use of chemicals in the economy; vigorous development of new, economically effective brandhes of production, new types of power, and new materials; all-round and rational utilization of natural, material and labour resources; organic fusion of science and production, and rapid scientific and technical progress; a high cultural and technical level for the working people; and substantial superiority over the more developed capitalist countries in productivity of labour, which constitutes the most important prerequisite for the victory of the communist system.

As a result, the USSR will possess productive forces of unparalleled might; it will surpass the technical level of the most developed countries and occupy first place in the world in per capita production. This will serve as a basis for the gradual transformation of socialist social relations into communist relations and for a development of production that will make it possible to meet in abundance the requirements of society and all its members.

In contrast to capitalism, the planned socialist system of economy combines accelerated technical progress with the full employment of all able-bodied citizens. Automation and comprehensive mechanization serve as a material basis for the gradual development of socialist labour into communist labour. Technical progress will require higher standards of production and a higher level of vocational and general education of all working people. The new machinery will be used to improve radically the Soviet people's working conditions, and make them much easier, to reduce the length of the working day, to improve living conditions, eliminate hard physical work and, subsequently, all unskilled labour.

The material and technical basis will develop and improve continuously together with the evolution of society towards the complete triumph of communism. The level of development of science and technology, and the degree of mechanization and automation of production operations, will steadily rise.

The creation of the material and technical basis of communism will call for huge investments. The task is to utilize these investments most rationally and economically, with the maximum effect and gain of time.

1 *The development of industry, construction, transport, and their role in creating the productive forces of communism*
The creation of the material and technical basis of communism, the task of making Soviet industry technologically the best and strongest in the world call for the further development of heavy industry. On this basis, all the other branches of the economy – agriculture, the consumer goods industries, the construction industry, transport and communications, as well as the branches directly concerned with services for the population – trade, public catering, health, housing, and communal services – will be technically re-equipped.

A first class heavy industry, the basis for the country's technical progress and economic might has been built up in the Soviet Union. The CPSU will continue to devote unflagging attention to the growth of heavy industry and its technical progress. The main task of heavy industry is to meet all the needs of the country's defence and to ensure the development of industries producing consumer goods, so as to satisfy better and in full the requirements of the people, the vital demands of Soviet man, and to effect the development of the country's productive forces.

With these aims in view, CPSU plans the following increases in *total industrial output*:

within the current ten years, by approximately 150 per cent, exceeding the level of US industrial output;

within twenty years, by not less than 500 per cent, leaving the present overall volume of US industrial output far behind.

To achieve this, it is necessary to raise *productivity of labour* in industry by more than 100 per cent within ten years, and by 300–350 per cent within twenty years. In twenty years' time labour productivity in Soviet industry will exceed the present level of labour productivity in the USA by roughly 100 per cent, and considerably more in terms of per-hour output, due to the reduction of the working day in the USSR.

Such an intensive development of industry will call for major progressive changes in its *structure*. The role of new branches ensuring the greatest technical progress will grow very considerably. The less effective fuels, types of power, raw and semi-manufactured materials will be increasingly superseded by highly effective ones, and their comprehensive use will increase greatly. The share of synthetic materials, metals, and alloys with new properties will increase considerably. New types of automatic and electronic machinery, instruments, and apparatus will be rapidly introduced on a large scale.

Electrification, which is the pivot of the economic construction of communist society, plays a key role in the development of all economic branches and in the effecting of all modern technological progress. It is therefore important to ensure the priority development of *electric power* output. The plan for the electrification of the country provides for an almost threefold increase in the power capacity per industrial worker within the present decade; a considerable expansion of industries with a high rate of power consumption through the supply of cheap power; and extensive electrification of transport, agriculture, and the household in town and countryside. The electrification of the country will on the whole be completed in the course of the second decade.

The annual output of electricity must be brought up to about 900,000–1,000,000 million kwh by the end of the first decade, and to 2,700,000–3,000,000 million kwh by the end of the second decade. For this it will be necessary in the course of twenty years to increase accordingly the installed capacities of electric power plants and to build hundreds of thousands of kilometres of high-tension transmission and distribution lines throughout the country. A single power grid for the whole USSR will be built and will have sufficient capacity reserves to transmit electric power from the eastern regions to the European part of the country; it will link up with the power grids of other socialist countries.

As atomic energy becomes cheaper, the construction of atomic power stations will be expanded, especially in areas poor in other power sources, and the use of atomic energy for peaceful purposes in the economy, in medicine and science will increase.

The further rapid expansion of the output of *metals and fuels*, the basis of modern industry, remains one of the major economic tasks. Within twenty years metallurgy will develop sufficiently to produce about 250 million tons of steel a year. Steel output must cover fully the growing requirements of the economy in accordance with the technological progress achieved in that period. The output of light, non-ferrous, and rare metals will grow very appreciably; the output of aluminum and its use in electrification, engineering, construction, and the household will considerably increase. A steady effort will be made to ensure priority development of oil and gas production as these items will be used increasingly as raw materials for the chemical industry. Coal, gas, and oil extraction must meet the requirements of the economy in full. The most progressive and economic methods of extracting mineral fuels are to be applied extensively.

One of the most important tasks is the all-round development of the *chemical* industry, and the full use in all economic fields of the achievements of modern chemistry. This provides greater opportunities to increase the national wealth and the output of new, better and cheaper capital and consumer goods. Metal, wood, and other materials will be increasingly replaced by economical, durable, light synthetic materials. The output of mineral fertilizers and chemical weed and pest killers will rise sharply.

Of primary importance for the technical re-equipment of the entire economy is the development of *mechanical engineering*, with special stress laid on the accelerated production of automated production lines and machines, automatic, telemechanic and electronic devices, and precision instruments. The designing of highly efficient machines consuming less raw materials and power and leading to higher productivity of labour will make rapid progress. The requirements of the economy in all types of modern machines, machine tools and apparatus, as well as spare parts and instruments will be met in full.

The development of mechanical engineering in the first decade will serve as the basis of *comprehensive mechanization* in industry, agriculture, construction, transport, and in the municipal economy. Comprehensive mechanization will exclude manual loading and unloading jobs and strenuous labour in both the basic and auxiliary operations.

In the twenty years comprehensive *automation* will be effected on a mass scale, with increasing emphasis on fully automated shops and factories, making for high technical and economic efficiency. Introduction of the very latest systems of automated control will be speeded up. Cybernetics, electronic computers, and control systems will be widely applied in production processes in industry, building and transport, in scientific research, planning, designing, accounting, statistics, and management.

The vast scope of capital construction calls for the rapid development and technological modernization of the *construction and building materials industry* up to a level meeting the requirements of the economy, for a maximum reduction of construction schedules and costs, and an improvement of the quality of construction through its continuous industrialization; it is essential to go over completely at the earliest possible time to erecting wholly prefabricated buildings and structures of standard design made of large prefabricated elements.

The CPSU will concentrate its efforts on ensuring a rapid increase in the output of *consumer goods*. The growing resources of industry must be used more and more to fully meet all the requirements of Soviet people and to build and equip enterprises and establishments catering to the household and cultural needs of the population. Along with the accelerated development of all branches of the light and food industries, the share of consumer goods in the output of heavy industry will also increase. More electricity and gas will be supplied to the population.

The growth of the economy will call for the accelerated development of *all transport facilities*. The most important tasks in the sphere of transport are: expansion of transport and road construction to meet in full the requirements of the economy and the population in all modes of transport; further modernization of the railways and other transport systems; a considerable increase of the speed of rail, sea and river traffic; the co-ordinated development of all types of transport as components of a single transport network. The share of pipeline transport will increase.

A single deep-water system will link the main inland waterways of the European part of the USSR.

A network of modern roads will be built throughout the country. The automobile fleet will increase sufficiently to fully meet freight and passenger requirements; car hire centres will be organized on a large scale. Air transport will become a means of mass passenger traffic extending to all parts of the country.

Up-to-date *jet* engineering will develop rapidly, above all in air transport, as well as in space exploration.

All means of *communication* (post, radio and television, telephone and telegraph) will be developed still more. All regions of the country will have reliable communications and a grid system of television stations.

Full-scale communist construction calls for a more rational *geographic distribution* of industries in order to save social labour and ensure the comprehensive development of areas and specialization of their industries, do away with the overpopulation of big cities, facilitate the elimination of essential distinctions between town and countryside, and further equalize the economic levels of different parts of the country.

To gain time, priority will be given to developing easily exploited natural resources that provide the greatest economic effect.

Industry in the areas to the *east of the Urals*, where there are immense natural riches, raw material, and power resources, will expand greatly.

The following must be achieved within the next twenty years: in Siberia and Kazakhstan – the creation of new power bases using deposits of cheap coal or the waterpower resources of the Angara and Yenisei rivers; the organization of big centres of energy-intensive industries, the development of new rich ore, oil, and coal deposits; and the construction of a number of new large machine-building centres; in areas along the Volga, in the Urals, north Caucasus, and Central Asia – the rapid development of the power, oil, gas and chemical industries, and the development of ore deposits. Alongside the development of the existing old metallurgical centres in the Urals and the Ukraine, completion is envisaged of the country's third metallurgical base in Siberia, and the building of two new ones: in the central European part of the USSR, utilizing the iron ore of the Kursk ironfields, and in Kazakhstan. Soviet people will be able to carry out daring plans to change the courses of some northern rivers and regulate their discharge for the purpose of utilizing vast water resources for the irrigation and watering of arid areas.

The economy in the European part of the USSR which contains the bulk of the population and where there are great opportunities for increased industrial output, will make further substantial progress.

The maximum acceleration of scientific and engineering progress is a major national task which calls for daily effort to reduce the time spent on designing new machinery and introducing it in industry. It is necessary to promote in every way the initiative of economic councils, enterprises, social organizations, scientists, engineers, designers, workers, and kolkhozniks in creating and applying new technical improvements. Of utmost importance is the material and moral stimulation of mass invention and rationalization movements, of enterprises, shops, sovkhozes and kolkhozes, teams, and innovators who master the production of new machinery and utilize it skilfully.

The party will do everything to *enhance the role of science* in the building of communist society; it will encourage research to discover new possibilities for the development of the productive forces, and the rapid and extensive application of the latest scientific and technical achievements; a decisive advancement in experimental work, including research directly at enterprises, and the efficient organization of scientific and technical information and of the whole system of studying and disseminating progressive Soviet and foreign methods. Science will itself in full measure become a direct productive force.

Constant *improvement in the technology* of all industries and production branches is a requisite for their development. Technological progress will make man's labour easier, facilitate substantial intensification and acceleration of production and give it the highest degree of precision, will facilitate the standardization of mass production items and maximum use of production lines. Machining will be supplemented and, when necessary, replaced by chemical methods, the technological use of electricity, electrochemistry, etc.; radio-electronics, semiconductors, and ultrasound will occupy an increasingly important place in production techniques. The construction of new, technically up-to-date enterprises will proceed side by side with the reconstruction of those now in existence and the replacement and modernization of their equipment.

Development of *specialization and co-operation, and the appropriate combination of related enterprises*, is a most important condition for technical progress and the rational organization of social labour. Articles of similar type should be manufactured mainly at large specialized plants, with provision for their most rational geographic distribution.

New techniques and the reduction of the working day call for *a higher level in the organization of work*. Technical progress and better organization must be fully utilized to increase labour productivity and reduce production costs at every enterprise. This implies a higher rate of increase in labour productivity as compared with the rate of growth of wages, better rate-fixing, prevention of loss of working time, and operation on a profitable basis in all sectors of production.

Most important will be systematic improvement of the qualifications of those working in industry and other branches of the economy in connection with technical progress. The planned training, instruction, and rational employment of those released from various jobs and transferred to other jobs due to mechanization and automation are essential.

Existing enterprises will be improved and developed into enterprises of communist society. Typical of this process will be new machinery, high standards of production organization and efficiency through increased automation of production operations, and the introduction of automation into control; an improvement of the cultural and technical standards of the workers, the increasing fusion of physical and mental labour and the growing proportion of engineers and technicians in every industrial enterprise; the expansion of research, and closer links between enterprises and research institutes; promotion of the competition movement, application of the achievements of science and the best forms of labour organization and best methods of raising labour productivity, the extensive participation of workers' collectives in the management of enterprises, and the spreading of communist forms of labour.

2 *The development of agriculture and social relations in the countryside*

Along with a powerful industry, a flourishing, versatile, and highly productive agriculture is an imperative condition for the building of communism. The party is organizing a great development of productive forces in agriculture, which will make it possible to accomplish two basic, closely related tasks: *a/* to build up an abundance of high-quality food products for the population and of raw materials for industry, and *b /* to effect the gradual transition of social relations in the Soviet countryside to communist relations and eliminate, in the main, the distinction between town and country.

The chief means of achieving progress in agriculture and satisfying the growing needs of the country in farm produce are comprehensive mechanization and consistent *intensification*: high efficiency of crop farming and stock breeding based on science and progressive experience in all kolkhozes and sovkhozes, a steep rise in the yields of all crops, and greater output per hectare with the minimum outlay of labour and funds. On this basis, it is necessary to achieve a steady growth of agricultural production in keeping with the needs of society. Agriculture will approach the level of industry in technical equipment and the organization of production; farm labour will turn into a variety of industrial labour, and the dependence of agriculture upon the elements will decrease considerably, and ultimately drop to a minimum.

The development of virgin and unused land and establishment of new large-scale sovkhozes, the reorganization of the MTSs, the sale of implements of production to the kolkhozes, introduction of new planning procedures, and the enhancement of material incentives for agricultural workers – all constituted an important stage in the development of agriculture. The party will continue to devote considerable attention to the development of agriculture in the virgin and unused land development areas.

The further advance of the countryside to communism will proceed through the development and improvement of the two forms of socialist farming – the kolkhozes and sovkhozes.

The kolkhoz system is an integral part of Soviet socialist society. It is the path charted by V.I. Lenin for the gradual transition of the peasantry to communism; it has stood the test of history and conforms to the distinctive features of the peasantry.

Kolkhoz farming accords in full with the level and needs of the development of modern productive forces in the countryside, and makes possible effective use of new machinery and the achievements of science, and rational employment of manpower. The kolkhoz blends the personal interests of the peasants with common, nation-wide interests, individual with collective interest in the results of production, and offers extensive opportunities for raising the incomes and the well-being of peasants on the basis of rising labour productivity. It is essential to make the most of the possibilities and advantages of the kolkhoz system. By virtue of the social form of its economy – its organizational structure and its democratic foundations – which will develop more and more, the kolkhoz ensures that production is run by the kolkhoz members themselves, that their creative initiative is enhanced and that the kolkhozniks are educated in the communist spirit. The kolkhoz is a school of communism for the peasantry.

Economic advancement of the kolkhoz system creates conditions for the gradual *rapprochement* and, in the long run, also for the merging of kolkhoz property and the property of the whole people into one communist property.

The *sovkhozes*, which are the leading socialist agricultural enterprises, play an ever-increasing role in the development of agriculture. The sovkhozes must serve the kolkhozes as a model of progressive, scientifically managed, economically profitable social production, of high efficiency and labour productivity.

The CPSU proceeds from the fact that the further consolidation of the *unbreakable alliance of the working class and the kolkhoz peasantry* is of crucial political and socio-economic importance for the building of communism in the USSR.

A *Building up an abundance of agricultural produce*
In order fully to satisfy the requirements of the entire population and the economy for agricultural produce, the task is to increase the *aggregate volume of agricultural production* in ten years by about 150 per cent, and in twenty years by 250 per cent. Agricultural output must keep ahead of the growing demand. In the first decade the Soviet Union will outstrip the United States in per capita output of the key agricultural products.

Accelerated growth of *grain* production is the chief link in the further development of all agriculture and a basis for the rapid growth of stock breeding. Aggregate grain crops will more than double in twenty years, and their yield will double. The output of wheat, corn, cereal, and leguminous crops will increase substantially.

Livestock breeding will develop at a rapid rate. The output of animal products will rise: meat about threefold in the first ten years and nearly fourfold in twenty years, and milk more than double in the first decade and nearly threefold in twenty years. The planned increase in the output of animal products will be achieved by increasing the cattle and poultry population, improving stock and productivity, and building up reliable fodder resources, chiefly corn, sugar beet, fodder beans, and other crops.

Productivity of labour in agriculture will rise not less than 150 per cent in ten years, and five- to six-fold in twenty years. The rapid rise of the productivity of farm labour – at a higher rate than in industry – will serve to eliminate the lag of agriculture behind industry and will turn it into a highly developed branch of the economy of communist society.

Further mechanization of agriculture, introduction of *comprehensive mechanization*, and use of automatic devices and highly efficient and economical machinery adapted to the conditions of each zone will be the basis for the growth of productivity of farm labour.

The party considers rapid *electrification* of agriculture one of the most important tasks. All sovkhozes and kolkhozes will be supplied electric power for production and domestic purposes, from the state power grid and from power stations to be built in the countryside.

The technical re-equipment of agriculture must be combined with the most progressive forms and methods of the organization of labour and production and the maximum improvement of the cultural and technical education of farm workers. There will be increasingly more qualified workers with special agricultural training and proficient in the use of new machinery in the kolkhozes and sovkhozes. Good care and maintenance of agricultural machinery and its highly efficient use are extremely important.

To ensure high, stable, steadily increasing harvests, to deliver agriculture from the baneful effects of the elements, especially droughts, to steeply raise land fertility, and to rapidly advance livestock breeding, it is necessary:

to effect a scientifically expedient distribution of agriculture by natural economic zones and districts, and a more thorough and stable *specialization* of agriculture with priority given to the type of farm product where the best conditions for it exist and the greatest saving in outlay is achieved;

to introduce on all kolkhozes and sovkhozes a *scientifically based system of land cultivation and animal husbandry* consistent with local conditions and with the specialization of each farm, ensuring the most effective use of the land and the most economically expedient combination of branches, the best structure of crop acreage with the substitution of high-yielding and valuable crops for crops of little value and those giving low yields; to ensure that every kolkhoz and sovkhoz masters the most advanced methods of farming with the application of efficient crop rotation and sows high-grade seed only; to build up reliable fodder resources in all districts and to introduce the foremost stock-breeding techniques in kolkhozes and sovkhozes;

to effect a rational *introduction of chemicals* in all branches of agriculture, to meet all its needs in mineral fertilizers and chemical and biological means of combating weeds, blights, diseases, and plant and animal pests, and to ensure the best use of local fertilizers in all kolkhozes and sovkhozes; to apply broadly biological achievements, and especially microbiology, which is assuming ever-greater importance for the improvement of soil fertility;

to carry through a far-flung *irrigation programme*; to irrigate and water millions of hectares of new land in the arid areas and improve existing irrigated farming; to expand field-protective afforestation, building of water reservoirs, watering of pastures and draining of marshy land; and to combat systematically the water and wind erosion of soil. Considerable attention will be devoted to the conservation and rational use of forests, water reservoirs, and other natural resources, and to their re-stocking and development.

The party will promote the development of *agricultural science*, focus the creative efforts of scientists on the key problems of agricultural progress, and work for the practical application and extensive introduction of the achievements of science and progressive production experience in crop farming and stock breeding. Research institutions and experimental stations are to become important links in agricultural management, and scientists and specialists must become the direct organizers of farm production. Each region or group of regions of the same zonal type should have agricultural research centres, with their own large-scale farms and up-to-date material and technical resources, to work out recommendations for collective and state farms applicable to the given district. Agricultural research and educational establishments and institutions must be chiefly located in rural areas and be directly associated with farm production, so that students may learn while working and work while learning.

B *Kolkhozes and sovkhozes on the road to communism; remoulding social relations in the countryside*

The economic basis for the development of kolkhozes and sovkhozes lies in the continuous growth and best use of their productive forces, improvement of the organization of production and methods of management, steady rise of labour productivity and strict observance of the principle: higher payment for good work, for better results. On this basis the kolkhozes and sovkhozes will become to an increasing degree enterprises of the communist type in production relations, character of labour, and the living and cultural standards of their personnel.

The policy of the party in relation to the kolkhozes is based on blending country-wide interests with the material interest of the kolkhozes and their members in the results of their labour. The state will promote the growth of the productive forces of the kolkhoz system and the economic advancement of all kolkhozes; concurrently, the kolkhoz peasantry must contribute more widely to the building of communist society.

The state will ensure the full satisfaction of the needs of the kolkhozes for modern machinery, spare parts, chemicals, and other means of production, will train new hundreds of thousands of skilled farm workers, and will considerably increase capital investments in the countryside, in addition to the greater investments which the kolkhozes will themselves make. The amount of manufactured goods made available to the countryside will increase greatly.

Strict observance of their contractual commitments to the state by the kolkhozes and their members is an inviolable principle of their participation in the development of the economy.

The system of state purchasing must aim at increasing the amount and improving the quality of agricultural products bought, on the basis of an all-round advancement of kolkhoz farming. It is essential to co-ordinate the planning of state purchases and the production plans of the kolkhozes, with utmost consideration for the interests of agricultural production, its proper distribution, and specialization.

Policy in the sphere of state purchasing prices of agricultural produce and state selling prices of means of production to the countryside must take account of the interests of extended reproduction in both industry and agriculture and of the need to accumulate funds in the kolkhozes. It is essential that the level of state purchasing prices encourage the kolkhozes to raise labour productivity and reduce production expenses, since greater farm output and lower production costs are the basis of greater incomes for the kolkhozes.

The proper ratio of *accumulation and consumption* in the distribution of incomes is a prerequisite of successful kolkhoz development. The kolkhozes cannot develop without continuously extending their commonly owned assets for production, insurance, cultural, and community needs. At the same time, it must be a standing rule for every kolkhoz to raise its members' incomes from collective farming and to enhance their living standards as labour productivity rises.

Great importance attaches to improved methods of rate-setting and labour remuneration in kolkhozes, supplementary remuneration of labour, and other incentives to obtain better production results. Increasingly equal economic conditions must be provided to improve the incomes of kolkhozes existing under unequal natural economic conditions in different zones, and also within zones, in order to put into effect more consistently the principle of equal pay for equal work on a scale embracing the entire kolkhoz system. Farming on all kolkhozes must be based on the principle of profitability.

In its organizational work and economic policy, the party will strive to overcome the lag of the economically weak kolkhozes and to turn all kolkhozes into economically strong, high-income farms in the course of the next few years. The party sets the task of continuously improving and educating kolkhoz personnel, of ensuring the further extension of kolkhoz democracy, and promoting the principle of collectivism in management.

As the kolkhozes develop, their basic production facilities will expand, and modern technical means will become dominant.

The economic advancement of the kolkhozes will make it possible to perfect *kolkhoz internal relations*: to raise the degree to which production is socialized; to bring the rate setting, organization, and payment of labour closer to the level and the forms employed at state enterprises and effect a transition to a guaranteed monthly income; to develop community services more broadly (public dining, kindergartens and nurseries, and other services, etc.).

At a certain point the collective production in kolkhozes will achieve a level at which it will fully satisfy members' requirements. On this basis, supplementary private farming will gradually become economically unnecessary. When collective production in the kolkhozes is able to replace in full production on the supplementary private plots of the kolkhoz members, when the collective farmers see for themselves that their supplementary private farming is unprofitable, they will give it up of their own accord.

As productive forces increase, inter-kolkhoz production ties will develop and the socialization of production will transcend the limits of individual kolkhozes. The building, jointly by several kolkhozes, of enterprises and cultural and welfare institutions, state-kolkhoz power stations, and enterprises for the primary processing, storage, and transportation of farm products, for various types of building, the manufacture of building materials and elements, etc., should be encouraged. As communally owned assets increase, the kolkhozes will participate more and more in establishing enterprises and cultural and welfare institutions for general public use, boarding schools, clubs, hospitals, and holiday homes. All these developments, which must proceed on a voluntary basis and when the necessary economic conditions are available, will gradually impart to kolkhoz-cooperative property the nature of public property.

The *sovkhozes* have a long way to travel in their development – to increase production and improve its quality continuously, to concentrate on attaining high rates of growth of labour productivity, and steadily to reduce production costs and raise farm profitability. This calls for the economically expedient specialization of sovkhozes. Their role in supplying food to the urban population will grow. They must become mechanized and well-organized first-class factories of grain, cotton, meat, milk, wool, vegetables, fruit, and other products, and must develop seed farming and pure-strain animal husbandry to the utmost.

The material and technical basis of the sovkhozes will be extended and improved, and living and cultural conditions on sovkhozes will approach those in towns. Sovkhoz management should follow a more and more democratic pattern which will allot a greater role to personnel, to general meetings, and production conferences in deciding production, cultural, and other community issues.

As the kolkhozes and sovkhozes develop, their production ties with each other and with local industrial enterprises will grow stronger. The practice of jointly organizing various enterprises will expand. This will ensure a fuller and more balanced use of manpower and production resources throughout the year, raise the productivity of social labour and enhance the living and cultural standards of the population. Agrarian-industrial associations will gradually emerge wherever economically expedient, in which, given appropriate specialization and co-operation of agricultural and industrial enterprises, agriculture will combine organically with the industrial processing of its produce.

As production in kolkhozes and sovkhozes develops and social relations within them advance, agriculture rises to a higher level, affording the possibility of transition to communist forms of production and distribution. The kolkhozes will draw level in economic conditions with the nationally owned agricultural enterprises. They will turn into highly developed mechanized farms. By virtue of high labour productivity all kolkhozes will become economically powerful. Kolkhoz members will be adequately provided and their requirements fully satisfied out of kolkhoz production. They will have the service of dining establishments, bakeries, laundries, kindergartens, and nurseries, clubs, libraries, and sports grounds. The payment of labour will be the same as at nationally owned enterprises; they will enjoy all forms of social security (pensions, holidays, etc.) out of kolkhoz and state funds.

Gradually, the kolkhoz villages will grow into amalgamated urban communities with modern housing facilities, public amenities and services, and cultural and medical institutions. The rural population will ultimately draw level with the urban population in cultural and living conditions.

Elimination of socio-economic and cultural distinctions between town and country and of differences in their living conditions will be one of the greatest gains of communist construction.

3 *Management of the economy and planning*
The building of the material and technical basis of communism calls for a continuous improvement in economic management and planning. Chief emphasis at all levels of planning and economic management must be laid on the most rational and effective use of the material, labour, and financial resources and natural wealth, and on the elimination of excessive expenditure and of losses. The immutable law of economic development is to

achieve in the interests of society the highest results at the lowest cost. In the improvement of economic management utmost stress is to be laid on making the apparatus of management simpler and cheaper to run.

Planning must at all levels concentrate on the rapid development and introduction of new techniques. It is essential that progressive, scientifically substantiated norms for the use of means of production be continuously improved and strictly observed in all sectors of the economy.

The party attaches prime importance to more *effective investments*, the choice of the most profitable and economical trends in capital construction, achievement of the maximum growth of output per invested ruble, and reduction of the time lapse between investment and return. It is necessary continuously to improve the structure of capital investments and to expand that portion of them which is spent on equipment, machinery, and machine tools.

It should be an immutable condition of planning and economic organization to concentrate investments in the decisive sectors of industry, to eliminate scattering of allocations, and to accelerate the completion of construction projects.

Continuous improvement of the *quality of output* is an imperative requirement of economic development. The quality of goods produced by Soviet enterprises must be considerably higher than that of the best capitalist enterprises. For this purpose, it is necessary to apply a wide range of measures, including public control, and to enhance the role of quality indexes in planning, in the assessment of the work of enterprises, and in socialist competition.

Communist construction presupposes the maximum development of *democratic principles of management* coupled with a strengthening and improvement of *centralized economic management by the state*. The economic independence and the rights of local organs and enterprises will continue to expand within the framework of the single national economic plan. Plans and recommendations made at lower levels, beginning with enterprises, must play an increasing role in planning.

Centralized planning should chiefly concentrate on working out and ensuring the fulfilment of the key targets of the economic plans with the greatest consideration paid to recommendations made at lower levels; on co-ordinating and dovetailing plans drawn up locally; on spreading scientific and technical achievements and advanced production experience; on enforcing a single state policy in the spheres of technical progress, capital investment, distribution of industry, payment of labour, prices, and finance, and a unified system of accounting and statistics.

It is essential that the economy develop on a strictly *proportionate* basis, that economic disproportions be prevented in good time, ensuring sufficient economic reserves as a condition for stable high rates of economic development, uninterrupted operation of enterprises and continuous improvement of the people's well-being.

The growing scale of the economy, the rapid development of science and technology call for an improvement of the scientific level of planning, designing, accounting and statistics. A better scientific, technical and economic substantiation of plans will ensure their greater stability, which also presupposes timely correction and amendment of plans in the course of their fulfilment. Planning must be continuous, the annual and long-term plans must be organically integrated, and funds and material and technical resources must be provided for.

Firm and consistent discipline, day-to-day control, and determined elimination of elements of localism and of a narrow departmental approach in economic affairs are necessary conditions for successful communist construction.

There must be further expansion of the role and responsibility of *local bodies* in economic management. The transfer of a number of functions of economic management by the all-union bodies to those of the republics, by republican bodies to those of the oblasts, and by oblast bodies to those of the raions should be continued. It is necessary to improve the work of the sovnarkhozy as the most viable form of management in industry and construction conforming to the present level of productive forces. Improvement of the work of sovnarkhozy within economic administrative regions will also be accompanied by greater co-ordination of the work of economic bodies, in order better to organize the planned, comprehensive economic development of such major economic regions as the Urals, the Volga area, west Siberia, the Far East, east Siberia, Transcaucasia, the Baltic area, Central Asia, etc.

Extension of the operative independence and *initiative of enterprises* on the basis of state-plan targets is essential in order to mobilize untapped resources and make more effective use of capital investments, production facilities, and finances. It is necessary to enhance the role of enterprises and stimulate their interest in introducing the latest machinery and using production capacities to the utmost.

The selection, training, and promotion of people who directly head enterprises and kolkhozes, who organize and manage production, are of decisive importance in economic management. The sphere of material production is the main sphere in the life of society; the most capable people must, therefore, be given leading posts at enterprises.

The direct and most active participation of *trade unions* in elaborating and realizing economic plans, in matters concerning the labour of factory and office workers, in setting up organs of economic administration of management of enterprises, must be extended more and more in the big centres and at the local level. The role of collectives of factory and office workers in matters concerning the work of enterprises must be enhanced.

In the process of communist construction economic management will make use of material and moral incentives for high production figures. The proper combination of material and moral labour incentives is a great creative factor in the struggle for communism. In the course of the advance to communism the importance of moral labour incentives, public recognition of achieved results, and the sense of responsibility of each for the common cause will become continuously greater.

The entire system of planning and assessing the work of central and local organizations, enterprises, and kolkhozes must stimulate their interest in higher plan targets and the maximum dissemination of progressive production experience. Initiative and successes in finding and using new ways of improving the quantitative and qualitative indexes of production should be specially encouraged.

There must be a continuous improvement in norm setting, the system of labour payments and bonuses, in financial control over the quantity and quality of work, in the elimination of wage levelling, and the stimulation of collective forms of material incentives raising the interest of each employee in the high efficiency of the enterprise as a whole.

It is necessary in communist construction to make full use of commodity-money relations in keeping with their new content in the socialist period. Here such instruments of economic development as cost accounting, money, price, production cost, profit, trade, credit, and finance play a big part. With the transition to a single communist form of people's property and a communist system of distribution, commodity-money relations will become economically outdated and will wither away.

The important role of the state budget in distributing the social product and national income will prevail throughout the period of full-scale communist construction. There will be a further strengthening of the monetary and credit system, a consolidation of Soviet currency, a steady rise of the purchasing power of the ruble, and an increase in the importance of the ruble in the international arena.

It is necessary to promote profitable operation of enterprises, to work for economy and thrift, reduction of losses, lower production costs, and higher profitability. The price system should be continuously improved in conformity with the tasks of communist construction, technical progress, growth of production and consumption, and the reduction of production expenditures. Prices must, to a growing extent, reflect the socially necessary outlays of labour, ensure return of production and circulation expenditures and a certain profit for each normally operating enterprise. Systematic, economically justified price reductions based on growth of labour productivity and reduction of production costs are the main trend of the price policy in the period of communist construction.

Soviet society possesses immense national assets. For this reason, the role of accounting and control over the maintenance and proper use of the national wealth increases. Thrift, the proper use of every ruble belonging to the people, competent expenditure of funds, the continuous improvement of planning and methods of management, improvement of organization and conscious discipline, and development of the initiative of the people are powerful means of accelerating the advance of Soviet society to communism.

II THE TASKS OF THE PARTY IN IMPROVING THE LIVING STANDARD OF THE PEOPLE

The heroic labor of the Soviet people has produced a powerful and versatile economy. There is now every possibility to improve rapidly the living standards of the entire population – the workers, peasants, and intellectuals. The CPSU sets the historically important task of *achieving in the Soviet Union a living standard higher than that of any of the capitalist countries*.

This task will be effected by: *a* / raising individual payment according to the quantity and quality of work done, coupled with reduction of retail prices and abolition of taxes paid by the population; *b* / increase of the public consumption fund intended for the satisfaction of the requirements of members of society irrespective of the quantity and quality of their labour, that is, free of charge (education, medical treatment, pensions, maintenance of children at children's institutions, transition to cost-free use of public amenities, etc.).

The rise of real income of the population will be outstripped by a rapid increase in the amount of commodities and services, and by extensive construction of dwellings and cultural and service buildings.

Soviet people will be more prosperous than working people in the developed capitalist countries even if average incomes will be equal, because in the Soviet Union the national income is distributed in the interests of all members of society and there are no parasitic classes as in the bourgeois countries which appropriate and squander immense wealth plundered from millions of working people.

The party acts upon Lenin's thesis that communist construction must be based upon the principle of material incentives. In the coming twenty years payment according to one's work will remain the principal source for satisfying the material and cultural needs of the working people.

The disparity between high and comparatively low incomes must be steadily reduced. Increasingly greater numbers of unskilled personnel will become skilled, and the diminishing difference in proficiency and labour productivity will be accompanied by a steady reduction of disparities in levels of pay. As the living standard of the entire population rises, low-income levels will approach the higher, and the disparity between the incomes of peasants and workers, low-paid and high-paid personnel, and of the populations of different parts of the country, will gradually shrink.

At the same time, as the country advances towards communism, personal needs will be increasingly met out of public consumption funds, whose rate of growth will exceed the rate of growth of payments for labour. The transition to communist distribution will be completed after the principle of distribution according to one's work outlives itself, that is, when there is an abundance of material and cultural wealth and labour becomes a prime necessity of life for all members of society.

a *Provision of a high level of income and consumption for the whole population; expansion of trade*

The national income of the USSR in the next ten years will increase nearly 150 per cent, and about 400 per cent in twenty years. The real income per capita will increase by more than 250 per cent in twenty years. In the first decade already the real income of all factory, professional, and office workers (including public funds) per employed person will, on the average, be almost doubled, and the incomes of the low-paid categories of factory and office workers will increase approximately threefold. Thus, by the end of the first decade there will be no low-paid categories of factory and office workers in the country.

By virtue of higher rates of growth of the labour productivity of kolkhozniks, their real incomes will grow more rapidly than the incomes of factory workers, and will, for the average employed person, more than double in the next ten years and increase more than fourfold in twenty years.

The wages of such numerically large sections of the Soviet intelligentsia as engineers and technicians, agronomists and stock-breeding experts, teachers, medical and cultural workers, will rise considerably.

As the income of the population grows, *the general level of public consumption will rise rapidly*. The entire population will be able adequately to satisfy its need for high-quality and varied foodstuffs. The share of animal products (meat, fats, dairy produce), fruit, and high-grade vegetables in public consumption will rise substantially in the near future. The demand of all sections of the population for high-quality consumer goods – attractive and durable clothes, footwear, and goods improving and adorning the daily life of Soviet people, such as comfortable modern furniture, up-to-date household goods, a wide range of goods for cultural purposes, etc. – will be amply satisfied. Production of motorcars will be considerably extended to service the population.

Output of consumer goods must meet the growing consumer demand in full, and must conform to its changes. Timely output of goods in accordance with the varied demand of the population, with consideration for local, national, and climatic conditions, is an imperative requirement for all the consumer industries.

Soviet trade will be further developed as a necessary condition to meeting the growing requirements of the people. Good shopping facilities will be made available throughout the country, and progressive forms of trading will be widely applied. The material and technical basis of Soviet trade – the network of shops, warehouses, refrigerators, and vegetable stores – will be extended.

Consumer cooperatives, which are to improve trade in the countryside and organize the sale of surplus agricultural produce, will develop. Kolkhoz trade will lose none of its importance.

An abundance of material and cultural benefits for the whole population will be attained in the course of the second decade, and material prerequisites will be created for the transition in the period to follow to the communist principle of distribution according to need.

b Solution of the housing problem and improvement of living conditions

The CPPSU sets the task of solving the most acute problem in the improvement of the well-being of the Soviet people – the housing problem. In the course of the first decade an end will be put to the housing shortage in the country. Families that are still housed in overcrowded and substandard dwellings, will get new flats. At the end of the second decade, every family, including newly-weds, will have a comfortable flat conforming to the requirements of hygiene and cultural living. Peasant houses of the old type will, in the main, give place to new modern dwellings, or – wherever possible – they will be rebuilt and appropriately improved. In the course of the second decade housing will gradually become rent-free for all citizens.

Town building, architecture, and planning aimed at designing modern, comfortable towns and communities, industrial projects, dwellings and public buildings economical to build and to maintain, are acquiring great importance. Towns and communities must constitute a rational and comprehensive organization of industrial zones, residential areas, public and cultural institutions, communal services, transport, engineering equipment, and power sources ensuring the best possible conditions for labour, life, and leisure.

An extensive programme of public services construction and of improvements in all towns and workers' estates will be carried out in the coming period, which will involve completion of their electrification, the necessary gasification, provision of telephone communications, public transport facilities, waterworks, sewerage, and measures for the further improvement of sanitary conditions in towns and other populated localities, including tree planting, pond building, and effective measures to combat air, soil, and water pollution. Well-appointed small and middle-size towns will be increasingly developed, making for better and healthier living conditions.

Public transport facilities (trolleys, buses, trolley-buses, and subways) will become free in the course of the second decade, and at the end of it such public amenities as water, gas, and heating will also be free.

c *Reduction of working hours and the further improvement of working conditions*

In the coming ten years the country will go over to *a six-hour working day* with one day off a week, or *a 35-hour working week* with two days off, and on underground jobs and enterprises with harmful working conditions to a five-hour working day or a 30-hour five-day working week.

By virtue of a corresponding rise in labour productivity, transition to a still shorter working week will be begun in the second decade.

The Soviet Union will thus have the world's shortest and, concurrently, the most productive and highest paid working day. Working people will have much more leisure time, and this will add to their opportunities of improving their cultural and technical level.

The length of the annual paid holidays of working people will be increased together with the reduction of the working day. Gradually the minimum length of leave for all industrial, professional and office workers will increase to three weeks and subsequently to one month. Paid holidays will be gradually extended also to kolkhozniks.

All-round measures to make working conditions healthier and lighter constitute an important task in improving the well-being of the people. Modern means of labour safety and hygiene designed to prevent occupational injuries and diseases will be introduced at all enterprises. Night shifts will be gradually abolished at enterprises, save those where round-the-clock operation is required by the production process or the need to service the population.

d *Health services and measures for increased longevity*

The socialist state is the only state which undertakes to protect and continuously improve the health of the whole population. This is provided for by a system of socio-economic and medical measures. There will be an extensive programme designed to prevent and sharply reduce diseases, wipe out mass infectious diseases, and further increase longevity.

The needs of the urban and rural population for all forms of highly qualified *medical services* will be met in full. This will call for the extensive building of medical institutions, including hospitals and sanatoria, the equipment of all medical institutions with modern appliances, and regular medical check-ups for the entire population. Special emphasis must be laid on extending in town and country the network of mother-and-child health institutions (maternity homes, medical consultation centres, children's health homes and hospitals, forest schools, etc.).

In addition to the existing free medical services, accommodation of sick persons at sanatoria and the dispensing of medicines will become gratuitous.

In order to afford the population an opportunity to rest in an out-of-town environment, holiday homes, boarding houses, country hotels, and tourist camps will be built, where working people will be accommodated at a reasonable charge or by way of a bonus, as well as at a discount or gratis.

The party considers it a most important task to ensure the education from early childhood of a sound young generation harmoniously developed physically and spiritually. This calls for utmost encouragement of all forms of mass sport and physical training, specifically at schools, and for drawing greater and greater sections of the population, particularly the youth, into sports.

e *Improvement of family living conditions and of the position of women; maintenance of children and incapacitated people at public expense*

The remnants of the unequal position of women in domestic life must be totally eliminated. Social and living conditions must be provided to enable women to combine happy motherhood with increasingly active and creative participation in social labour and social activities, and in scientific and artistic pursuits. Women must be given relatively lighter and yet sufficiently well-paid jobs. Confinement leave will be extended.

It is essential to provide conditions to reduce and lighten the domestic work of women, and later to make possible the replacement of domestic work by public forms of satisfying the daily needs of the family. Up-to-date inexpensive domestic machinery, appliances, and electrical devices will be made extensively available for this purpose; the needs of the population for service establishments will be fully met in the next few years.

The extension of *public dining*, including canteens at enterprises, institutions, and in big dwelling houses, until it meets the demands of the population, calls for special attention. Service at dining establishments and the quality of catering must be radically improved, so that meals at public dining establishments may be tasty and nourishing and cost the family less than meals cooked at home. Price reductions in public dining will keep ahead of price reductions for foodstuffs in the shops. By virtue of all this public dining will be able to take precedence over home cooking within 10–15 years.

The transition to free public dining (midday meal) at enterprises and institutions, and for kolkhozniks at work, will begin in the second decade.

A happy childhood for every child is one of the most important and noble aspects of communist construction. The development of a ramified network of children's institutions will make it possible for more and more families, and in the second decade for every family, to keep children and adolescents free of charge at children's establishments if they so desire. The party considers it essential that everything should be done to fully meet in the next few years the demand for children's pre-school institutions.

In town and country there will be: full and cost-free satisfaction of the population's need for nurseries, kindergartens, playgrounds, daycare schools, and young pioneer camps; the mass provision of an extensive network of boarding schools with free maintenance of children; free hot meals at all schools, introduction of after-school hours with free dinners for school children, and free issue of uniforms and school supplies.

In keeping with the growth of national income, state organs, the trade unions, and the kolkhozes will in the course of the twenty years gradually undertake maintenance of all citizens incapacitated through old age or some disability. Sickness and disability grants and old-age pensions will be extended to kolkhoz members; old-age and disability pensions will be steadily raised. The number of comfortable homes for old people and invalids providing free accommodation for all applicants will be greatly increased in town and country.

By fulfilling the tasks set by the party for the improvement of the well-being of the people, the Soviet Union will make considerable headway towards the practical realization of the communist principle of distribution according to need.

At the end of the twenty years public consumption funds will total about half of the aggregate real income of the population. This will make it possible to effect at public expense:
free maintenance of children at children's institutions and boarding schools (if parents wish);
maintenance of disabled people;
free education at all educational establishments;
free medical services for all citizens, including the supply of medicines and the treatment of sick persons at sanatoria;
rent-free housing and free communal services;
free municipal transport facilities;
free use of some types of public services;
steady reduction of charges for and, partially, free use of holiday homes, boarding houses, tourist camps, and sports facilities;
increasingly broad provision of the population with benefits, privileges and scholarships (grants to unmarried mothers, mothers of many children, scholarships for students);
gradual introduction of free public dining (midday meals) at enterprises and institutions, and for kolkhozniks at work.

The Soviet state will thus demonstrate to the world a truly full satisfaction of the growing material and cultural requirements of man. The living standard of Soviet people will improve all the faster, the faster the productive forces of the country develop and labour productivity grows, and the more broadly the creative energy of the Soviet people comes into play.

The programme set forth can be fulfilled with success under conditions of peace. Complications in the international situation and the resultant necessity to increase defence expenditures may hold up fulfilment of the plans for raising the living standard of the people. An enduring normalization of international relations, reduction of military expenditures and, in particular, the realization of general and complete disarmament under an appropriate agreement between countries, would make it possible greatly to surpass the plans for raising the people's living standard.

The fulfilment of the grand programme of improving the living standard of the Soviet people will have a world-wide historic impact. The party calls on the Soviet people to work perseveringly, and with inspiration. Every one of the working people of the Soviet Union must do his duty in the building of a communist society and in the effort to fulfil the programme for the improvement of the people's living standard.

II THE TASKS OF THE PARTY IN THE SPHERES OF STATE DEVELOPMENT AND THE FURTHER PROMOTION OF SOCIALIST DEMOCRACY

The dictatorship of the proletariat, born of the socialist revolution, played an epoch-making role by ensuring the victory of socialism in the USSR. In the course of socialist construction, however, it underwent changes. After the exploiting classes had been abolished, the function of suppressing their resistance ceased to exist. The chief functions of the socialist state – organization of the economy, culture and education – developed in full measure. The socialist state entered a new period of its development. The state began to grow over into a nation-wide organization of the working people of socialist society. Proletarian democracy was growing more and more into a socialist democracy of the people as a whole.

The working class is the only class in history that does not aim to perpetuate its power. Having brought about the complete and final victory of socialism – the first phase of communism – and the transition of society to the full-scale construction of communism, the dictatorship of the proletariat has fulfilled its historic mission and has ceased to be indispensable in the USSR from the point of view of the tasks of internal development. The state, which arose as a state of the dictatorship of the proletariat, has in the new contemporary stage, become a state of the entire people, an organ expressing the interests and will of the people as a whole. Since the working class is the foremost and best organized force of Soviet society, it plays a leading role also in the period of the full-scale construction of communism. The working class will have completed its role of leader of society after communism is built and classes disappear.

The party holds that the dictatorship of the working class will cease to be necessary before the state withers away. The state as an organization of the entire people will survive until the complete victory of communism. Expressing the will of the people, it must organize the building up of the material and technical basis of communism, and the transformation of socialist relations into communist relations, must exercise control over the measure of work and the measure of consumption, promote the people's welfare, protect the rights and freedoms of Soviet citizens, socialist law and order and socialist property, instil in the people conscious discipline and a communist attitude to labour, guarantee the defence and security of the country, promote fraternal co-operation with the socialist countries, uphold world peace, and maintain normal relations with all countries.

All-round extension and perfection of socialist democracy, active participation of all citizens in the administration of the state, in the management of economic and cultural development, improvement of the government apparatus, and increased control over its activity by the people constitute the main direction in which socialist statehood develops in the period of the building of communism. As socialist democracy develops, the organs of state power will gradually be transformed into organs of public self-government. The leninist principle of democratic centralism, which ensures the proper combination of centralized leadership with the maximum encouragement of local initiative, the extension of the rights of the union republics and greater creative activity of the masses, will be promoted. It is essential to strengthen discipline, constantly control the activities of all sections of the administrative apparatus, check the execution of the decisions and laws of the Soviet state, and heighten the responsibility of every official for the strict and timely implementation of these laws.

1 *The soviets and development of the democratic principles of government*

The role of the soviets, which are an all-inclusive organization of the people embodying their unity, will grow as communist construction progresses. The soviets, which combine the features of a government body and a mass organization of the people, operate more and more like social organizations, with the masses participating extensively and directly in their work.

The party considers it essential to perfect the forms of popular representation and promote the democratic principles of the Soviet electoral system.

In nominating candidates for election to the soviets, it is necessary to guarantee the widest and fullest discussion of the personal qualities and suitability of the candidates at meetings and in the press to ensure the election of the worthiest and most authoritative of them.

To improve the work of the soviets and bring fresh forces into them, it is advisable that at least one-third of the total number of deputies to a soviet should be elected anew each time so that *fresh millions of working people may learn to govern the state.*

The party considers *systematic renewal of the leading bodies* necessary to bring a wider range of able persons into them and rule out abuses of authority by individual government officials. It is advisable to introduce the principle that the leading officials of the union, republican and local bodies should be elected to their offices, as a rule, for not more than three consecutive terms. In those cases in which the personal gifts of the official in question are generally believed to make his further activity within a leading body useful and necessary, his re-election may be allowed. His election shall be considered valid if not a simple majority, but not less than three-quarters of the votes are cast in his favour.

The party regards the perfection of the principles of socialist democracy and their rigid observance as a most important task. It is necessary to ensure in full: regular accountability of soviets and deputies to their constituents and the right of the electorate to recall ahead of term deputies who have not justified the confidence placed in them; publicity and the free and full discussion of all important questions of government and of economic and cultural development at the meetings of soviets; regular accountability of executive government bodies to meetings of soviets – from top to bottom; checking the work of these bodies and control over their activity; systematic discussion by the soviets of questions raised by deputies, criticism of short-comings in the work of government, economic, and other organizations.

Every deputy to a soviet must take an active part in government affairs and carry on definite work. The role of the standing committees of the soviets will become greater. The standing committees of the supreme soviets must systematically control the activities of ministers, departments, and sovnarkhozy; they must actively contribute to the implementation of the decisions adopted by the respective supreme soviets. To improve the work of the legislative bodies and increase control over the executive bodies, deputies shall be periodically released from their regular employment for committee work.

An increasing number of questions which now come under the jurisdiction of the departments and sections of executive bodies must be gradually referred to the standing committees of the local soviets for decision.

The rights of the local soviets of working people's deputies (local self-government) will be extended. Local soviets will make final decisions on all questions of local significance.

Special attention should be paid to the strengthening of government bodies at the raion level. As kolkhoz-cooperative and public property draw closer together, a single democratic body administering all enterprises, organizations, and institutions at the raion level will gradually take shape.

The participation of social organizations and associations of the people in the legislative activity of the representative bodies of the Soviet state will be extended. The trade unions, the Komsomol and other mass organizations as represented by their all-union and republican bodies must be given the right to take legislative initiative, that is, to propose draft laws.

Discussion by the people of draft laws and other decisions of both national and local significance must become the rule. The most important draft laws should be put to a nation-wide referendum.

The CPSU attaches great importance to improving the work of the government apparatus, which is largely responsible for the proper utilization of all the resources of the country and the timely settlement of all questions relating to the cultural and everyday needs of the people. The Soviet government apparatus must be simple, qualified, inexpensive, efficient, and free of bureaucracy, formalism, and red tape.

Constant state and public control is an important means of accomplishing this task. In keeping with Lenin's directions, control bodies must function permanently to combine state control with public inspection at the centre and the local level. The party regards inspection by people's control bodies as an effective means of drawing large sections of the people into the management of state affairs and control over the strict observance of legality, as a means of perfecting the government apparatus, eradicating bureaucracy, and promptly realizing proposals made by the people.

The government apparatus of the socialist state serves the people and is accountable to them. Negligence, abuse of power, and red tape by an official must be resolutely combated and the official concerned must be severely punished regardless of the position he holds. It is the duty of Soviet people to see to it that legality and law and order are rigidly enforced; they must not tolerate any abuses, and must combat them.

The party holds that democratic principles in *administration* must be developed further. The principle of electivity and accountability to representative bodies and to the electorate will be gradually extended to all the leading officials of state bodies.

An effort should be made to ensure that the salaried government staffs are reduced, that ever larger sections of the people learn to take part in administration and that work on government staffs eventually cease to constitute a profession.

While every executive must be held strictly and personally responsible for the job entrusted to him, it is necessary consistently to exercise the principle of collective leadership at all levels of the government and economic apparatus.

The broadest democracy must go hand in hand with strict observance of comradely discipline by the working people, and should promote such discipline and control from above and from below. The important thing in the activity of all government bodies is organizational work among the masses, proper selection, testing and appraisal of officials on the strength of their practical work, and control over the actual fulfilment of the assignments and decisions of the leading bodies.

The further *promotion of socialist law and order* and the improvement of legal rules governing economic organization, cultural, and educational work and contributing to the accomplishment of the tasks of communist construction and to the all-round development of the individual are very important.

The transition to communism means the fullest extension of personal freedom and the rights of Soviet citizens. Socialism has brought the working people the broadest guaranteed rights and freedoms. Communism will bring the working people further great rights and opportunities.

The party's objective is to enforce strict observance of socialist legality, eradicate all violations of law and order, abolish crime and remove all the causes of crime.

Justice in the USSR is exercised in full conformity with the law. It is based on truly democratic lines: election and accountability of the judges and people's assessors, the right to recall them before expiry of their term, the publicity of court proceedings, and the participation of prosecutors and advocates from the general public in the work of the courts, with the courts and investigating and prosecuting bodies strictly observing legality and all the norms of judicial procedure. The democratic foundations of justice will be developed and improved.

There should be no room for law breakers and criminals in a society building communism. But as long as there are criminal offences, it is necessary severely to punish those who commit crimes dangerous to society, violate the rules of the socialist community, and refuse to live by honest labour. Attention should be mainly focused on crime prevention.

Higher standards of living and culture, and greater social consciousness of the people, pave the way to the abolition of crime and the ultimate replacement of judicial punishment by measures of public influence and education. Under socialism, anyone who has strayed from the path of the working man can return to useful activity.

The whole system of government and social organizations educates the people in a spirit of voluntary and conscientious fulfilment of their duties and leads to a natural fusion of rights and duties to form unified standards of communist behaviour.

2 *The further heightening of the role of social organizations; the state and communism*
The role of social organizations increases in the period of the full-scale

construction of communism. The *trade unions* acquire particular importance as schools of administration and economic management, as schools of communism. The party will help the trade unions to take a growing share in economic management and to make the standing production conferences increasingly effective in improving the work of enterprises and exercising control over production. The trade unions shall:

work constantly to increase the communist consciousness of the masses; organize a competition movement for communist labour and help the working people in learning to manage state and social affairs; take an active part in controlling the measure of labour and the measure of consumption; encourage the activity of factory and office workers, enlisting their aid in the work for continuous technical progress, for higher productivity of labour, for the fulfilment and overfulfilment of state plans and assignments;

work steadfastly for the improvement of the skill of factory and office workers and their working and living conditions; protect the material interests and rights of the working people;

ensure that housing and cultural development plans are fulfilled and that public dining, trade, social insurance, and health resort services are improved;

ensure control over the spending of public consumption funds and over the work of all enterprises and institutions serving the people;

improve cultural services and recreation facilities for the working people; encourage physical training and sports.

The Komsomol, an independently acting public organization of youth which helps the party to educate young people in a communist spirit, enlist them in the practical job of building the new society and train a generation of harmoniously developed people who will live, work, and manage public affairs under communism, will play a greater role. The party regards youth as a great creative force in the Soviet people's struggle for communism.

The Komsomol must display still greater initiative in all spheres of life and must encourage the activity and labor heroism of youth. Komsomol organizations must concentrate on educating young people in a spirit of utmost devotion to their country, the people, the Communist Party and the communist cause, constant preparedness for labour for the good of society and for overcoming all difficulties and improving the general education and technical knowledge of all young men and women. It is the sacred duty of the Komsomol to prepare young people for the defence of their socialist country, to educate them as selfless patriots capable of firmly repelling any enemy. The Komsomol educates the youth in a spirit of strict adherence to communist moral principles and standards. Its activities in the schools and Young Pioneer organizations must contribute to the moulding of a buoyant, industrious, and physically and morally sound generation.

A greater role will be played by *co-operatives* – kolkhozes, consumers', housing, and other co-operative organizations – as a form of drawing the masses into communist construction, as media of communist education and schools of public self-government.

Other social associations of the working people – scientific, scientific-technical and popular-science societies, rationalizers' and inventors' organizations, associations of writers, artists, and journalists, cultural education organizations, and sports societies – will likewise be developed.

The party regards it as a major task of the social organizations to promote labour competition in every possible way, and to encourage communist forms of labour, to stimulate the activity of working people in building a communist society, to work for the improvement of the living conditions of the people and the satisfaction of their growing spiritual requirements. Mass organizations should be given a greater part in managing cultural, health, and social insurance institutions; within the next few years they should be entrusted with the management of theatres and concert halls, clubs, libraries, and other state-controlled cultural education establishments; they should be encouraged to play a greater part in promoting law and order, particularly through the people's volunteer squads and comradely courts.

To extend the independent activities of mass organizations, the party considers it necessary further to reduce their salaried staffs from top to bottom, to renew each elective body by roughly as many as one-half of its membership at the regular election. It is advisable for the leading functionaries of social organizations not to be elected, as a general rule, for more than two consecutive terms.

As socialist statehood develops, it will gradually become *communist self-government* of the people which will embrace the soviets, trade unions, co-operatives, and other mass organizations of the people. This process will represent a still greater development of democracy, ensuring the active participation of all members of society in the management of public affairs. Public functions similar to those performed by the state today in the sphere of economic and cultural management will be preserved under communism and will be modified and perfected as society develops. But the character of the functions and the ways in which they are carried out will be different from those under socialism. The bodies in charge of planning, accounting, economic management, and cultural advancement, now government bodies, will lose their political character and will become organs of public self-government. Communist society will be a highly organized community of working men. Universally recognized rules of the communist way of life will be established whose observance will become an organic need and habit with everyone.

Historical development inevitably leads to the withering away of the state. To ensure that the state withers away completely, it is necessary to provide both internal conditions – the building of a developed communist society – and external conditions – the victory and consolidation of socialism in the world arena.

3 *The strengthening of the armed forces and the defence potential of the Soviet Union*
With the wholehearted support of the entire Soviet people, the Communist Party of the Soviet Union steadfastly upholds and defends the gains of socialism and the cause of world peace, and works tirelessly to deliver mankind for all time from wars of aggression. The leninist principle of peaceful coexistence of states with different social systems always has been, and remains, the general principle of the foreign policy of the Soviet state.

The Soviet Union perseveringly seeks to bring about the realization of its proposals for general and complete disarmament under strict international control. But the imperialist countries stubbornly refuse to accept these proposals, and feverishly build up their armed forces. They refuse to reconcile themselves to the existence of the world socialist system, and openly proclaim their insane plans for the liquidation of the Soviet Union and the other socialist states through war. This obliges the Communist Party, the armed forces, the state security organs, and all the peoples of the USSR to be keenly vigilant with regard to the aggressive intrigues of the enemies of peace, always to protect peaceful labour, and to be constantly prepared to take up arms in defence of their country.

The party maintains that as long as imperialism exists the threat of aggressive wars will remain. The CPSU regards the defence of the socialist motherland, and the strengthening of the defence potential of the USSR, of the might of the Soviet armed forces, as a sacred duty of the party and the Soviet people as a whole, as a most important function of the socialist state. The Soviet Union sees it as its internationalist duty to guarantee, together with the other socialist countries, the reliable defence and security of the entire socialist camp.

In terms of internal conditions, the Soviet Union needs no army. But since the danger of war coming from the imperialist camp persists, and since complete and general disarmament has not been achieved, the CPSU considers it necessary to maintain the defensive power of the Soviet state and the combat preparedness of its armed forces at a level ensuring the decisive and complete defeat of any enemy who dares to encroach upon the Soviet Union. The Soviet state will see to it that its armed forces are powerful, that they have the most up-to-date means of defending the country – atomic and thermonuclear weapons, rockets of every range, and that they keep all types of military equipment and all weapons up to standard.

The party educates communists and all Soviet people in the spirit of constant preparedness for the defence of their socialist country, of love of their armed forces. It will promote in every way the further development of voluntary mass defence organizations. Defence of the country, and service in the Soviet armed forces, is the lofty and honourable duty of Soviet citizens.

The CPSU is doing everything to ensure that the Soviet armed forces are a well-knit and smoothly operating organism, that they have a high standard of organization and discipline, carry out in exemplary fashion the tasks assigned them by the party, the government, the people, and are prepared at any moment to administer a crushing rebuff to imperialist aggressors. One-man leadership is a major principle of the organization of the Soviet Armed Forces.

The party will work indefatigably to train Army and Navy officers and political and technical personnel fully devoted to the communist cause and recruited among the finest representatives of the Soviet people. It considers it necessary for the officer corps tirelessly to master marxist-leninist theory, to possess a high standard of military-technical training, meet all the requirements of modern military theory and practice, and strengthen military discipline. All Soviet soldiers must be educated in the spirit of unqualified loyalty to the people, to the communist cause, of readiness to spare no effort and, if necessary, to give their lives in the defence of their socialist country.

Party leadership of the armed forces, and the increasing role and influence of the party organizations in the Army and Navy are the bedrock of military development. The party works unremittingly to increase its organizing and guiding influence on the entire life and activity of the Army, Air Force, and Navy, to rally the servicemen round the Communist Party and the Soviet government, to strengthen the unity of the armed forces and the people, and to educate the soldiers in the spirit of courage, bravery, heroism, and comradeship with the armies of the socialist countries, of readiness at any moment to take up the defence of their Soviet country, which is building communism.

IV   THE TASKS OF THE PARTY IN THE FIELD OF NATIONAL RELATIONS

Under socialism nations flourish and their sovereignty grows stronger. The development of nations does not proceed along lines of strengthening national strife, national narrow-mindedness and egoism, as it does under capitalism, but along lines of their association, fraternal mutual assistance, and friendship. The appearance of new industrial centres, the prospecting and development of mineral deposits, virgin land development, and the growth of all modes of transport increase the mobility of the population and promote greater intercourse between the peoples of the Soviet Union.

People of many nationalities live together and work in harmony in the Soviet republics. The boundaries between the union republics of the USSR are increasingly losing their former significance, since all the nations are equal, their life is based on a common socialist foundation, the material and spiritual needs of every people are satisfied to the same extent, and they are all united in a single family by common vital interests and are advancing together to the common goal – communism. Spiritual features deriving from the new type of social relations and embodying the finest traditions of the peoples of the USSR have taken shape and are common to Soviet men and women of different nationalities.

Full-scale communist construction constitutes a new stage in the development of national relations in the USSR in which the nations will draw still closer together until complete unity is achieved. The building of the material and technical basis of communism leads to still greater unity of the Soviet peoples. The exchange of material and spiritual values between nations becomes more and more intensive, and the contribution of each republic to the common cause of communist construction increases. Obliteration of distinctions between classes and the development of communist social relations make for a greater social homogeneity of nations and contribute to the development of common communist traits in their culture, morals, and way of living, to a further strengthening of their mutual trust and friendship.

With the victory of communism in the USSR, nations will draw still closer together, their economic and ideological unity will increase, and the communist traits common to their spiritual make-up will develop. However, the obliteration of national distinctions, and especially of language distinctions, is a considerably longer process than the obliteration of class distinctions.

The party approaches all questions of national relationships arising in the course of communist construction from the standpoint of proletarian internationalism and firm pursuance of the leninist nationalities policy. The party neither ignores nor exaggerates national characteristics.

The party sets the following tasks in the sphere of national relations:

a to continue the all-round economic and cultural development of all the Soviet nations and nationalities, ensuring their increasingly close fraternal co-operation, mutual aid, unity, and affinity in all spheres of life, thus achieving the utmost strengthening of the Union of Soviet Socialist Republics; to make full use of, and advance the forms of, national statehood of the peoples of the USSR;

b in the economic sphere, it is necessary to continue the line of comprehensive development of the economies of the Soviet republics, effect a rational geographic location of production and planned working of natural wealth, and promote socialist division of labour among the republics, unifying and combining their economic efforts, and properly balancing the interests of the state as a whole and those of each Soviet republic. The extension of the rights of the union republics in economic management having produced substantial positive results, such measures may also be carried out in the future with due regard to the fact that the creation of the material and technical basis of communism will call for still greater interconnection and mutual assistance among the Soviet republics. The closer the intercourse between nations and the greater the awareness of country-wide tasks, the more successfully can manifestations of localism and national egoism be overcome.

In order to ensure successful accomplishment of the tasks of communist construction and the co-ordination of economic activities, inter-republican economic organs may be set up in some zones (notably for such matters as irrigation, power grids, transport, etc.).

The party will continue its policy ensuring the actual equality of all nations and nationalities with full consideration for their interests and devoting special attention to those areas of the country which are in need of more rapid development. Benefits accumulating in the course of communist construction must be fairly distributed among all nations and nationalities;

c to work for the further all-round development of the socialist cultures of the peoples of the USSR. The large scale of communist construction and new victories of communist ideology are enriching the cultures of the peoples of the USSR, which are socialist in content and national in form. There is a growing ideological unity among the nations and nationalities and a greater rapprochement of their cultures. The historical experience of socialist nations shows that national forms do not ossify; they change, advance, and draw closer together, shedding all outdated traits that contradict the new conditions of life. An international culture common to all the Soviet nations is developing. The cultural treasures of each nation are increasingly augmented by works acquiring an international character.

Attaching decisive importance to the development of the socialist content of the cultures of the peoples of the USSR, the party will promote their further mutual enrichment and rapprochement, the consolidation of their international basis, and thereby the formation of the future single world-wide culture of communist society. While supporting the progressive traditions of each people, and making them the property of all Soviet people, the party will in all ways further new revolutionary traditions of the builders of communism common to all nations;

d to continue promoting the free development of the languages of the peoples of the USSR and the complete freedom for every citizen of the USSR to speak, and to bring up and educate his children, in any language, ruling out all privileges, restrictions or compulsions in the use of this or that language. By virtue of the fraternal friendship and mutual trust of peoples, national languages are developing on a basis of equality and mutual enrichment.

The voluntary study of Russian in addition to the native language is of positive significance, since it facilitates reciprocal exchanges of experience and access by every nation and nationality to the cultural gains of all the other peoples of the USSR, and to world culture. The Russian language has, in effect, become the common medium of intercourse and co-operation between all the peoples of the USSR;

e to pursue consistently as heretofore the principles of internationalism in the field of national relations; to strengthen the friendship of peoples as one of the most important gains of socialism; to conduct a relentless struggle against manifestations and survivals of nationalism and chauvinism of all types, against trends of national narrow-mindedness and exclusiveness, idealization of the past and the veiling of social contradictions in the history of peoples, and against customs and habits hampering communist construction. The growing scale of communist construction calls for the continuous exchange of trained personnel among nations. Manifestations of national aloofness in the education and employment of workers of different nationalities in the Soviet republics are impermissible. The elimination of manifestations of nationalism is in the interests of all nations and nationalities of the USSR. Every Soviet republic can continue to flourish and strengthen only in the great family of fraternal socialist nations of the USSR.

V THE TASKS OF THE PARTY IN THE SPHERES OF IDEOLOGY,
EDUCATION INSTRUCTION, SCIENCE, AND CULTURE

Soviet society has made great progress in the socialist education of the masses, in the moulding of active builders of socialism. But even after the socialist system has triumphed there persist in the minds and behaviour of people survivals of capitalism, which hamper the progress of society.

In the struggle for the victory of communism, ideological work becomes an increasingly powerful factor. The higher the social consciousness of the members of society, the more fully and broadly their creative activities come into play in the building of the material and technical basis of communism, in the development of communist forms of labour and new relations between people, and consequently, the more rapidly and successfully the building of communism proceeds.

The party considers that the paramount task in the ideological field in the present period is to educate all working people in a spirit of ideological integrity and devotion to communism, and cultivate in them a communist attitude to labour and the public economy; to eliminate completely survivals of bourgeois views and morals; to ensure the all-round, harmonious development of the individual; to create a truly rich spiritual culture. Special importance is attached by the party to the moulding of the rising generation.

The moulding of the new man is effected through his own active participation in communist construction and the development of communist principles in the economic and social spheres, under the influence of the educational work carried out by the party, the state, and various social organizations – work in which the press, radio, cinema, and television play an important part. As communist forms of social organization are created, communist ideas will become more firmly rooted in life and work and in human relations, and people will develop the ability to enjoy the benefits of communism in a rational way. Joint planned labour by the members of society, their daily participation in the management of state and public affairs, and the development of communist relations of comradely cooperation and mutual support, recast the minds of people in a spirit of collectivism, industry, and humanism.

Increased communist consciousness of the people furthers the ideological and political unity of the workers, kolkhozniks, and intellectuals and promotes their gradual fusion in the single collective of the working people of communist society.

The party sets the following tasks:

1 *In the field of development of communist consciousness*
a *The shaping of a scientific world outlook*

Under socialism and at a time when a communist society is being built, when spontaneous economic development has given way to the conscious organization of production and social life as a whole, and when theory is a daily translated into practice, it is of prime importance that a scientific world outlook be shaped in all working people of Soviet society on the basis of marxism-leninism, an integral and harmonious system of philosophical, economic, and socio-political views. The party calls for the education of the population as a whole in the spirit of scientific communism and strives to ensure that all working people fully understand the course and perspectives of world development, that they take a correct view of international and domestic events and consciously build their life on communist lines. Communist ideas and communist deeds should blend organically in the behaviour of every person and in the activities of all collectives and organizations.

The theoretical elaboration and timely practical solution of new problems raised by life are essential to the successful advance of society to communism. Theory must continue to illumine the road of practice, and help detect and eliminate obstacles and difficulties hindering successful communist construction. The party regards it as one of its most important duties to further elaborate marxist-leninist theory by studying and generalizing new phenomena in the life of Soviet society and the experience of the world revolutionary working-class and liberation movements, and creatively to combine the theory and the practice of communist construction.

b Labour education

The party sees the development of a communist attitude to labour in all members of society as its chief educational task. Labour for the benefit of society is the sacred duty of all. Any labour for society, whether physical or mental, is honourable and commands respect. Exemplary labour and management in the social economy should serve to educate all working people.

Everything required for life and human progress is created by labour. Hence every able-bodied man must take part in creating the means which are indispensable for his life and work and for the welfare of society. Anyone who receives any benefits from society without doing his share of work, is a parasite living at the expense of others.

It is impossible for a man in communist society not to work, for neither his social consciousness nor public opinion will permit it. Work according to one's ability will become a habit, a prime necessity of life, for every member of society.

c The affirmation of communist morality

In the course of the transition to communism, the moral principles of society become increasingly important; the sphere of action of the moral factor expands and the importance of the administrative control of human relations diminishes accordingly. The party will encourage all forms of conscious civic self-discipline leading to the assertion and promotion of the basic rules of the communist way of life.

Communists reject the class morality of the exploiters; in contrast to the perverse, selfish views and morals of the old world, they promote communist morality, which is the noblest and most just morality, for it expresses the interests and ideals of the whole of working mankind. Communism makes the elementary standards of morality and justice, which were distorted or shamelessly flouted under the rule of the exploiters, inviolable rules for relations both between individuals and between peoples. Communist morality encompasses the fundamental norms of human morality which the masses of the people evolved in the course of millenniums as they fought against vice and social oppression. The revolutionary morality of the working class is of particular importance to the moral advancement of society. As socialist and communist construction progresses, communist morality is enriched with new principles, a new content.

The party holds that *the moral code of the builder of communism* should comprise the following principles:

devotion to the communist cause; love of the socialist motherland and of the other socialist countries;

conscientious labour for the good of society – he who does not work, neither shall he eat;

concern on the part of everyone for the preservation and growth of public wealth;

a high sense of public duty; intolerance of actions harmful to the public interest;

collectivism and comradely mutual assistance: one for all and all for one;

humane relations and mutual respect between individuals – man is to man a friend, comrade, and brother;

honesty and truthfulness, moral purity, modesty, and unpretentiousness in social and private life;

mutual respect in the family, and concern for the upbringing of children;

an uncompromising attitude to injustice, parasitism, dishonesty, careerism and money-grubbing;

friendship and brotherhood among all peoples of the USSR; intolerance of national and racial hatred;

an uncompromising attitude to the enemies of communism, peace, and the freedom of nations;

fraternal solidarity with the working people of all countries, and with all peoples.

d The promotion of proletarian internationalism and socialist patriotism

The party will untiringly educate Soviet people in the spirit of proletarian internationalism and will vigorously promote the international solidarity of the working people. In fostering the Soviet people's love of their country, the party maintains that with the emergence of the world socialist system the patriotism of the members of socialist society is expressed in devotion and loyalty to their own country and to the entire community of socialist countries. Socialist patriotism and socialist internationalism necessarily imply proletarian solidarity with the working class and all working people of all countries. The party will continue perseveringly to combat the reactionary ideology of bourgeois nationalism, racism, and cosmopolitanism.

e All-round and harmonious development of the individual

In the period of transition to communism, there are greater opportunities for *educating a new man, who will harmoniously combine spiritual wealth, moral purity, and a perfect physique.*

All-round development of the individual has been made possible by historic social gains – freedom from exploitation, unemployment, and poverty, from discrimination on account of sex, origin, nationality, or race. Every member of society is provided with equal opportunities for education and creative labour. Relations of dependence and inequality between people in public affairs and in family life disappear. The personal dignity of each citizen is protected by society. Each is guaranteed an equal and free choice of occupation and profession with due regard to the interests of society. As less and less time is spent on material production, the individual is afforded ever greater opportunities to develop his abilities, gifts, and talents in the fields of production, science, engineering, literature, and the arts. People will increasingly devote their leisure to public pursuits, cultural intercourse, intellectual and physical development, scientific, technical, and artistic endeavour. Physical training and sports will become part and parcel of the everyday life of people.

f Elimination of the survivals of capitalism in the minds and behaviour of people

The party considers it an integral part of its communist education work to combat manifestations of bourgeois ideology and morality, and the remnants of private-owner psychology, superstitions, and prejudices.

The general public, public opinion, and extensive criticism and self-criticism must play a big role in combating survivals of the past and manifestations of individualism and selfishness. Comradely censure of anti-social behaviour will gradually become the principal means of doing away with manifestations of bourgeois views, customs, and habits. The power of example in public affairs and in private life, in the performance of one's public duty, acquires tremendous educational significance.

The party uses ideological media to educate people in the spirit of a scientific materialist world conception, to overcome religious prejudices without insulting the sentiments of believers. It is necessary to conduct regularly broad atheistic propaganda on a scientific basis, to explain patiently the untenability of religious beliefs, which were engendered in the past when people were overawed by the elemental forces and social oppression and did not know the real causes of natural and social phenomena. This can be done by making use of the achievements of modern science, which is steadily solving the mysteries of the universe and extending man's power over nature, leaving no room for religious inventions about supernatural forces.

g The exposure of bourgeois ideology

The peaceful coexistence of states with different social systems does not imply an easing of the ideological struggle. The Communist Party will go on *exposing the anti-popular, reactionary nature of capitalism* and all attempts to paint bright pictures of the capitalist system.

The party will *steadfastly propagate the great advantages of socialism and communism over the declining capitalist system.*

The party advances the scientific ideology of communism in contrast to reactionary bourgeois ideology. Communist ideology, which expresses the fundamental interests of the working class and all working people, teaches them to struggle, to live and work, for the happiness of all. It is the most humane ideology. Its ideals are to establish truly human relations between individuals and peoples, to deliver mankind from the threat of wars of extermination, and bring about universal peace and a free, happy life for all men on earth.

2 *In the field of public education*

The transition to communism implies training that will make people communist-minded and highly cultured, people fitted for both physical and mental labour, for active work in various social, governmental, scientific, and cultural spheres.

The system of public education is so organized as to ensure that the instruction and education of the rising generation are closely bound up with life and productive labour, and that the adult population can combine work in the sphere of production with further training and education in keeping with their vocations and the requirements of society. Public education along these lines will make for the moulding of harmoniously developed members of communist society and for the solution of the cardinal social problem, namely the elimination of substantial distinctions between mental and physical labour.

The main tasks in the field of instruction and education are:

a Introduction of universal compulsory secondary education

In the next decade compulsory secondary general and polytechnical eleven-year education is to be introduced for all children of school age, and eight-year education for young people engaged in the national economy who have not had appropriate schooling; in the subsequent decade everyone will have the opportunity to receive a complete secondary education. Universal secondary education is guaranteed by the development of general and polytechnical education, professional training combined with socially useful labour of school children to the extent of their physical capacity, and a considerable expansion of the network of all types of general schools, including evening schools, which provide a secondary education in off-work hours.

Secondary education must furnish a solid knowledge of the fundamentals of the basic sciences, an understanding of the principles of the communist world outlook, and a labour and polytechnical training in accordance with the rising level of science and engineering, with due regard to the needs of society and to the abilities and inclinations of the students as well as the moral, aesthetic, and physical education of a healthy rising generation.

In view of the rapid progress of science and engineering, the system of industrial, professional, and vocational training should be improved continuously, so that the skills of those engaged in production may develop together with their better general education in the social and natural sciences and with the acquisition of specialized knowledge in engineering, agronomy, medicine, and other fields.

b   The public upbringing of children of pre-school and school age
The communist system of public education is based on the public upbringing of children. The educational influence which the family exerts on children must be brought into ever greater harmony with their public upbringing.

The growing number of pre-school institutions and boarding schools of different types will fully meet the requirements of all working people who wish to give their children of pre-school and school age a public upbringing. The importance of the school, which is to cultivate love of labour and knowledge in children and to raise the younger generation in the spirit of communist consciousness and morality, will increase. An honourable and responsible role in this respect falls to teachers, and to the Komsomol and Young Pioneer organizations.

c   Creation of conditions for high-standard instruction and education of the rising generation
The party plans to carry out an extensive programme for the construction of schools and cultural-education establishments to meet fully the needs of education and instruction. All schools will be housed in good buildings and will go over to a one-shift timetable. They will all have study workshops and chemistry, physics, and other laboratories; rural schools will also have their own farming plots; large factories will have production training shops for school children. Modern facilities – cinema, radio, and television – will be widely used in schools.

For physical training and aesthetic education, all schools and extra-scholastic establishments will have gymnasiums, sports grounds, and facilities for the creative endeavour of children in music, painting, sculpture, etc. The network of sports schools, sports grounds, tourist camps, skiing centres, aquatic stations, swimming pools, and other sports facilities will be expanded in town and countryside.

d   Higher and secondary special education
In step with scientific and technical progress, higher and secondary special education, which must train highly skilled specialists with a broad theoretical and political background, will be expanded.

Shorter working hours and a considerable improvement in the standard of living of the entire population will provide everyone with an opportunity to receive a higher or secondary special education if he so desires. The number of higher and secondary specialized schools, evening and correspondence schools in particular, as well as higher schools at factories, agricultural institutes (on large sovkhozes), studios, conservatories, etc., must be increased in all areas of the country with the support of factories and trade unions and other social organizations. The plan is to considerably increase every year the number of students at higher and secondary specialized schools; specialized education will be afforded to tens of millions of people.

3 *In the field of science*
Under the socialist system of economy, scientific and technical progress enables man to employ the riches and forces of nature most effectively in the interests of the people, to discover new forms of energy and to create new materials, to develop means of weather control, and to master outer space. Application of science in production becomes a decisive factor of rapid growth of the productive forces of society. Scientific progress and the introduction of scientific achievements into the economy will remain an object of special concern to the party.

Most important are the following tasks:
a Development of theoretical investigations
The further perspectives of scientific and technical progress depend in the present period primarily on the achievements of *the key branches of natural science*. A high level of development in *mathematics, physics, chemistry, and biology* is a necessary condition for the advancement and the effectiveness of the technical, medical, agricultural, and other sciences.

Theoretical research will be promoted to the utmost, primarily in such decisive fields of technical progress as electrification of the whole country, comprehensive mechanization and automation of production, transport and communications, the application of chemistry to the leading branches of the economy, industrial uses of atomic energy. This applies to:
studying the power and fuel balance of the country, finding the best ways and means of utilizing natural sources of power, working out scientific fundamentals of a single power grid, discovering new power sources and developing methods of direct conversion of thermal, nuclear, solar, and chemical energy into electric power, and solving problems related to control of thermonuclear reactions;
working out the theory and principles of designing new machines, automatic and telemechanical systems, intensively developing radio-electronics, elaborating the theoretical foundations of computing, control, and information machines, and technically improving them;
investigating chemical processes, working out new, more efficient technologies, and creating inexpensive high-quality artificial and synthetic

materials for all branches of the economy: mechanical engineering, building, the manufacture of household goods and mineral fertilizers, and creating new preparations for use in medicine and agriculture;
improving existing methods and devising new, more effective methods of prospecting minerals and making comprehensive use of natural wealth.

Big advances are to be made in the development of all biological sciences in order to solve medical problems successfully and to achieve further progress in agriculture. The main tasks to be solved by these sciences in the interests of mankind are: ascertainment of the essence of the phenomena of life, the biological laws governing the development of the organic world, study of the physics and chemistry of living matter, elaboration of various methods of controlling vital processes, in particular, metabolism, heredity, and directed changes in organisms. It is essential to develop more broadly and deeply the Michurin line in biology, which is based on the proposition that conditions of life are primary in the development of the organic world. Medicine must concentrate on discovering means of preventing and conquering cancer, virulent, cardio-vascular, and other dangerous diseases. It is important to study and extensively use micro-organisms in the economy and the health services, among other things for the production of foods and foodstuffs, vitamins, antibiotics, and enzymes, and for the development of new agricultural techniques.

Artificial earth satellites and spaceships have, by enabling man to penetrate into outer space, provided great opportunities of discovering new natural phenomena and laws and of investigating the planets and the sun.

In the age of rapid scientific progress, the elaboration of the philosophical problems of modern natural science on the basis of dialectical materialism, the only scientific method of cognition, becomes still more urgent.

There must be intensive development of research work in the *social sciences*, which constitute the scientific basis for the guidance of the development of society. Most important in this field is the study and theoretical generalization of the experience gained in communist construction; investigation of key objective laws governing the economic, political, and cultural progress of socialism and its development into communism, and elaboration of the problems of communist education.

The task of economic science is to generalize new phenomena in the economic life of society, and to work out the national economic problems whose solution promotes successful communist construction. Economists must concentrate on finding the most effective ways of utilizing material and labour resources in the economy, the best methods of planning and organizing industrial and agricultural production, and elaborating the principles of a rational distribution of the productive forces and of the technical and economic problems of communist construction.

The investigation of problems of world history and contemporary world development must disclose the law-governed process of mankind's advance towards communism, the change in the balance of forces in favour of socialism, the aggravation of the general crisis of capitalism, the break-up of the colonial system of imperialism and its consequences, and the upsurge of the national liberation movement of peoples.

It is important to study the historical experience of the Communist Party and the Soviet people, tried and proved successful in practice, the objective laws of development of the world socialist system and the world communist and working-class movement.

It is essential, in the future as well, to firmly defend and develop dialectical and historical materialism as the science of the most general laws of development of nature, society, and human thinking.

The social sciences must continue to struggle with determination against bourgeois ideology, against right socialist theory and practice, and against revisionism and dogmatism; they must uphold the purity of the principles of marxism-leninism.

b *Ties between science and production*

Close ties with the creative labour of the people and practical construction are an earnest of a fruitful development of science.

In conformity with the requirements of economic and cultural development, it is essential to extend and improve the network of research institutions, including those attached to the central bodies directing economic development and those attached to the sovnarkhozy, and the network of research laboratories and institutes at the major industrial plants and in farming areas; to develop research at higher educational establishments; to improve the geographical distribution of research institutions and higher educational establishments, and to ensure the further development of science in all the union republics and major economic areas.

Research institutions must plan and co-ordinate their work in the most important fields of research in accordance with the plans of economic and cultural development. The role of the collective opinion of scientists in directing scientific work will increase. Free comradely discussions promoting the creative solution of pressing problems are an essential condition for scientific development.

The party will adopt measures to extend and improve the material facilities of science and to enlist the most capable creative forces in scientific pursuits.

It is a point of honour for Soviet scientists to consolidate the advanced positions which Soviet science has won in major branches of knowledge and to take *a leading place in world science* in all key fields.

4 *In the field of cultural development, literature, and art*
Cultural development during the full-scale construction of communist society will constitute the closing stage of a great cultural revolution. At this stage all the necessary ideological and cultural conditions will be created for the victory of communism.

The growth of the productive forces, progress in engineering and in the organization of production, increased social activity of the working people, development of the democratic principles of self-government, and a communist reorganization of everyday life depend in very large measure on the cultural advancement of the population.

Absorbing and developing all the best that has been created by world culture, communist culture will be a new, higher stage in the cultural progress of mankind. It will embody the versatility and richness of the spiritual life of society, and the lofty ideals and humanism of the new world. It will be the culture of a classless society, a culture of the entire people, of all mankind.

a All-round advancement of the cultural life of society
In the period of transition to communism, creative effort in all fields of culture becomes particularly fruitful and accessible to all members of society. Soviet literature, music, painting, cinema and theatre, television, and all the other arts will attain higher standards in their ideological make-up and artistry. People's theatres, mass amateur art, technical invention, and other forms of creative endeavour by the people will become widespread. The advancement of artistic and creative activities among the masses will ensure the appearance of new gifted writers, artists, musicians, and actors. The development and enrichment of the arts are based on a combination of mass amateur endeavour and professional art.

The party will work unremittingly to ensure that literature, art, and culture flourish, that every individual is given full scope to apply his abilities, that the people are educated aesthetically and develop a fine artistic taste and cultural habits. The artistic element will ennoble labour still more, make living conditions more attractive, and lift man up spiritually.

To provide the material basis for cultural development on a grand scale:
book publishing and the press will be vigorously developed, and the printing and paper industries will be expanded accordingly;
there will be more libraries, lecture halls and reading rooms, theatres, houses of culture, clubs, and cinemas;

the country-wide radio diffusion network will be completed; television stations covering all industrial and agricultural areas will be built;

people's universities, people's theatrical companies, and other amateur cultural organizations will be widely developed;

a large network of scientific and technical laboratories and of art and cinema studios will be provided for the use of all who have the inclination and ability.

The party considers it necessary to distribute cultural institutions evenly throughout the country in order gradually to bring the cultural standard of the countryside level with that of the town and achieve rapid cultural progress in all the newly developed areas.

b *Enhancement of the educational role of literature and art*

Soviet literature and art, imbued with optimism and dynamic communist ideas, are great factors in ideological education and cultivate in Soviet people the qualities of builders of a new world. They must be a source of joy and inspiration to millions of people, express their will, their sentiments and ideas, enrich them ideologically and educate them morally.

The highroad of literature and art lies through the strengthening of their bond with the life of the people, through faithful and highly artistic depiction of the richness and versatility of socialist reality, inspired and vivid portrayal of all that is new and genuinely communist, and exposure of all that hinders the progress of society.

In the art of socialist realism, which is based on the principles of partisanship and kinship with the people, bold pioneering in the artistic depiction of life goes hand in hand with the cultivation and development of the progressive traditions of world culture. Writers, artists, musicians, theatrical workers, and film makers have every opportunity of displaying creative initiative and skill, using manifold forms, styles, and genres.

The Communist Party shows solicitude for the proper development of literature and art and their ideological and artistic standards, helps social organizations and literary and art associations in their activities.

c *The expansion of international cultural relations*

The party considers it necessary to expand the Soviet Union's cultural relations with the countries of the socialist system and with all other countries for the purpose of pooling scientific and cultural achievements and of bringing about mutual understanding and friendship among peoples.

VI COMMUNIST CONSTRUCTION IN THE USSR AND CO-OPERATION OF THE SOCIALIST COUNTRIES

The CPSU regards communist construction in the Soviet Union as a component of the building of communist society by the peoples of the entire world socialist system.

The fact that socialist revolutions took place at different times and that the economic and cultural levels of the countries concerned are dissimilar, predetermines the non-simultaneous completion of socialist construction in those countries and their non-simultaneous entry into the period of the full-scale construction of communism. Nevertheless, the fact that the socialist countries are developing as members of a single world socialist system and utilizing the objective laws and advantages of this system *enables them to reduce the time necessary for the construction of socialism and offers them the prospect of effecting the transition to communism more or less simultaneously, within one and the same historical epoch.*

The first country to advance to communism facilitates and accelerates the advance of the entire world socialist system to communism. In building communism, the peoples of the Soviet Union are breaking new roads for mankind, testing their correctness by their own experience, bringing out difficulties, finding ways and means of overcoming them, and selecting the best forms and methods of communist construction.

Since the social forces – the working class, the co-operative peasantry, and the people's intelligentsia – and the social forms of economy (enterprises based on the two forms of socialist property) in the Soviet Union and in the other socialist countries are of one type, there will be common basic objective laws for communist construction in the USSR and in those countries, with due allowance made for the historical and national peculiarities of each country.

The construction of communism in the USSR promotes the interests of every country of the socialist community, for it increases the economic might and defence potential of the world socialist camp and provides progressively favourable opportunities for the USSR to expand its cultural and economic co-operation with the other socialist countries and increase the assistance and support it renders them.

The CPSU maintains that the existing forms of economic relations between the socialist countries – foreign trade, co-ordination of economic plans, and specialization and combination of production – will be developed and perfected more and more.

The socialist system makes possible abolition of the disparities in the economic and cultural development of countries inherited from capitalism, the more rapid development of the countries whose economy lagged behind under capitalism, and the steady promotion of their economies and cultures with the purpose of evening up the general level of development of the countries of the socialist community. This is ensured by the advantages of the socialist economic system and by equality in economic relations; by mutual assistance and the sharing of experience, specifically, by reciprocal exchanges of scientific and technological achievements and by co-ordinated research; by the joint construction of industrial projects and by co-operation in the development of natural resources. All-round fraternal co-operation benefits every socialist country and the world socialist system as a whole.

It is in the best interest of socialist and communist construction that each socialist country combines the effort to strengthen and develop its economy with the effort to expand economic co-operation of the socialist community as a whole. The development and levelling of the economy of the socialist countries must be achieved primarily by every country using its internal resources to the full, by improving the forms and methods of economic leadership, steadily applying the leninist principles and methods of socialist economic management, and making effective use of the advantages of the world socialist system.

Material prerequisites for the construction of communism are created by the labour of the people of the country concerned and by its steadily growing contribution to the common cause – the consolidation of the socialist system. This purpose is served by the application in socialist construction of the law of planned, proportionate development; encouragement of the creative initiative and labour activity of the masses; continuous perfection of the system of the international division of labour through the co-ordination of national economic plans, specialization, and combination of production within the world socialist system on the basis of voluntary participation, mutual benefit, and an overall improvement of the level of science and engineering; the study of collective experience; the promotion of co-operation and fraternal mutual assistance; strict adherence to the principles of material incentive and the all-round promotion of moral stimuli to work for the good of society; control over the measure of labour and rate of consumption.

Socialism brings peoples and countries together. In the course of extensive co-operation in all economic, socio-political, and cultural fields, the common economic basis of world socialism will be consolidated.

The objective laws of the world socialist system, the growth of the productive forces of socialist society, and the vital interests of the peoples of the socialist countries predetermine an increasing affinity of the various national economies. As Lenin foresaw, tendencies develop toward the future creation of a world communist economy regulated by the victorious working people according to one single plan.

The CPSU, in community with the communist parties of the other socialist countries, regards the following as its tasks:
in the *political* field, the utmost strengthening of the world socialist system; promotion of fraternal relations with all the socialist countries along the lines of complete equality and voluntary co-operation; political consolidation of the countries of the socialist community for joint struggle against

imperialist aggressors, for universal peace and for the complete triumph of communism;

in the *economic* field, expansion of trade between the socialist countries; development of the international socialist division of labour; increasing co-ordination of long-range economic plans of the socialist countries to ensure a maximum saving of social labour and an accelerated development of the world socialist economy; the promotion of scientific and technical co-operation;

in the *cultural* field, steady development of all forms of cultural co-operation and intercourse between the peoples of the socialist countries; exchanges of cultural achievements; encouragement of joint creative effort by scientists, writers, and artists; extensive measures to ensure the mutual enrichment of national cultures and bring the mode of life and the spiritual cast of the socialist nations closer together.

The CPSU and the Soviet people will do everything in their power to support all the peoples of the socialist community in the construction of socialism and communism.

VII   THE PARTY IN THE PERIOD OF FULL-SCALE COMMUNIST CONSTRUCTION

As a result of the victory of socialism in the USSR and the consolidation of the unity of Soviet society, the Communist Party of the working class has become the vanguard of the Soviet people, a party of the entire people, and extended its guiding influence to all spheres of social life. The party is the mind, honour, and conscience of our epoch, of the Soviet people, the people effecting great revolutionary transformations. It looks keenly into the future and shows the people scientifically based paths along which to advance, arouses titanic energy in the masses, and leads them to the accomplishment of great tasks.

The period of full-scale communist construction is characterized by a further *enhancement of the role and importance of the Communist Party as the leading and guiding force of Soviet society*.

Unlike all preceding socio-economic formations, communist society does not develop spontaneously, but as a result of the conscious and purposeful efforts of the masses led by the marxist-leninist party. The Communist Party, which unites the foremost representatives of the working class, of all working people, and is closely connected with the masses, which enjoys unbounded prestige among the people and understands the laws of social development, provides proper leadership in communist construction as a whole, giving it an organized, planned, and scientifically based character.

The enhancement of the role of the party in the life of Soviet society in the new stage of its development derives from:

the growing scope and complexity of the tasks of communist construction, which call for a higher level of political and organizational leadership;

the growth of the creative activity of the masses and the participation of fresh millions of working people in the administration of state affairs and of production;

the further development of socialist democracy, the enhancement of the role of social organizations, the extension of the rights of the union republics and local organizations;

the growing importance of the theory of scientific communism, of its creative development and propaganda, the necessity for improving the communist education of the working people and struggling to overcome the survivals of the past in the minds of people.

There must be a new higher stage in the development of the party itself and of its political, ideological, and organizational work that is in conformity with the full-scale building of communism. The party will continuously improve the forms and methods of its work, so that its leadership of the masses, of the building of the material and technical basis of communism, of the development of society's spiritual life will keep pace with the growing requirements of the epoch of communist construction.

Being the vanguard of the people building a communist society, the party must also be in the vanguard in the organization of internal party life and serve as an example and model in developing the most advanced forms of public communist self-government.

Undeviating observance of the leninist standards of party life and the principle of collective leadership, enhancement of the responsibility of party organs and their personnel to the party rank and file, promotion of the activity and initiative of all Communists and of their participation in elaborating and realizing the policy of the party, and the development of criticism and self-criticism, are a law of party life. This is an imperative condition of the ideological and organizational strength of the party itself, of the unity and solidarity of party ranks, of an all-round development of inner-party democracy, and an activization on this basis of all party forces, and of the strengthening of ties with the masses.

The cult of the individual, and the violations of collectivism in leadership, of intra-party democracy and socialist legality arising out of it, are incompatible with the leninist principles of party life. The cult of the individual belittles the role of the party and the masses and hampers the development of the ideological life of the party and the creative activity of the working people.

In order to effect the leninist principle of collective leadership consistently, to ensure a greater influx of fresh party forces into the leading party organs, to combine properly old and young cadres, and to rule out the possibility of an excessive concentration of power in the hands of individual officials and prevent cases of their getting beyond the control of the collective, the party considers it necessary to carry out the following measures:

a To introduce in practice a regular renewal, in certain proportions, of the members of all elected party bodies – from primary organizations to the Central Committee, at the same time preserving continuity of leadership.

At all regular elections, not less than one-quarter of the members of the Central Committee of the CPSU and its Presidium shall be renewed. Presidium members may, as a rule, be elected for not more than three consecutive terms. Particular party workers may, by virtue of their generally recognized authority and high political, organizational, and other abilities, be successively elected to the leading bodies for a longer period. In that case, the respective candidate is considered elected, provided not less than three-quarters of the votes are cast for him by secret ballot.

Members of the Central Committees of the communist parties of union republics, of krai and oblast committees shall be renewed by not less than one-third at each regular election, and those of okrug, city, and raion committees, and the committees and bureaus of primary party organizations shall be renewed by one-half. Furthermore, members of these leading party bodies may be elected consecutively for not more than three terms, and secretaries of the primary party organizations for not more than two consecutive terms.

A party organization may, in consideration of the political and professional qualities of a person, elect him to its leading body for a longer period. In that case a candidate is considered elected if not less than three-quarters of the Communists attending vote for him.

Party members not re-elected to a leading party body on the expiration of their term may be re-elected at subsequent elections.

A decision on the removal of a member from the Central Committee of the CPSU and other leading organs shall be adopted solely by secret ballot, and is valid when not less than two-thirds of the members of the body concerned vote in favour of the decision.

b To extend the application of the elective principle and that of accountability in party organizations at all levels, including party organizations working under special conditions (Army, Navy).

c To enhance the role of party meetings, conferences, congresses, and plenary meetings of party committees and other collective bodies. To provide favourable conditions for a free and businesslike discussion within the party of questions concerning its policy and practical activities, for comradely discussions of controversial or insufficiently clear matters.

d To reduce steadily the salaried party staffs, enlisting Communists more extensively as non-salaried workers doing voluntary work.

e To develop criticism and self-criticism to the utmost as a tried and tested method of work and a means of disclosing and rectifying errors and short-comings and properly educating cadres.

In the period of full-scale communist construction the role and responsibility of every party member will steadily increase. It is the duty of a Communist, in production, in social and personal life, to be a model in the struggle for the development and consolidation of communist relations, and to observe the principles and norms of communist morality. The CPSU will reinforce its ranks with the most politically conscious and active working people, and keep pure and hold high the name of Communist.

The development of intra-party democracy must ensure greater activity among Communists and enhance their responsibility for the realization of the noble ideals of communism. It will promote the cultivation in them of an inner, organic need to act always and in all matters in full accordance with the principles of the party and its lofty aims.

The party will continue to strengthen the unity and solidarity of its ranks, and to maintain the purity of marxism-leninism. The party preserves such organizational guarantees as are provided by the Rules of the CPSU against all manifestations of factionalism and group activity incompatible with marxist-leninist party principles. *The unshakable ideological and organizational unity of the party is the most important source of its invincibility, a guarantee for the successful solution of the great tasks of communist construction.*

The people are the decisive force in the building of communism. *The party exists for the people, and it is in serving the people that it sees the purpose of its acitivity*. To further extend and deepen the ties between the party and the people is an imperative condition of success in the struggle for communism. The party considers it its duty always to consult the working people on the major questions of domestic and foreign policy, to make these questions an object of nation-wide discussion, and to attract the more extensive participation of non-members in all its work. The more socialist democracy develops, the broader and more versatile the work of the party among the working people must be, and the stronger will be its influence among the masses.

The party will in every way promote the extension and improvement of the work of the soviets, the trade unions, the Komsomol, and other mass organizations of working people, and the development of the creative energy and initiative of the masses, and will strengthen the unity and friendship of all the peoples of the USSR.

The CPSU is an integral part of the international communist and working-class movement. The tried and tested marxist-leninist principles of proletarian internationalism will continue to be inviolable principles which the party will follow undeviatingly.

The Communist Party of the Soviet Union will continue to strengthen the unity of the international communist movement, to develop fraternal ties with all the communist and workers' parties and to co-ordinate its actions with the efforts of all the contingents of the world communist movement in the joint struggle against the danger of a new world war, for the interests of the working people, for peace, democracy, and socialism.

Such is the programme of work for communist construction which the Communist Party of the Soviet Union has mapped out.

The achievement of communism in the USSR will be the greatest victory mankind has ever won throughout its long history. Every new step made towards the bright peaks of communism inspires the working masses in all countries, renders immense moral support to the struggle for the liberation of all peoples from social and national oppression, and brings closer the triumph of marxism-leninism on a world-wide scale.

When the Soviet people enjoy the blessings of communism, new hundreds of millions of people on earth will say: 'We are for communism!' It is not through war with other countries, but by the example of a more perfect organization of society, by rapid progress in developing the productive forces, the creation of all conditions for the happiness and well-being of man, that the ideas of communism win the minds and hearts of the masses.

The forces of social progress will inevitably grow in all countries, and this will assist the builders of communism in the Soviet Union.

The party proceeds from the marxist-leninist proposition: history is made by the people, and communism is a creation of the people, of its energy and intelligence. The victory of communism depends on people, and communism is built for people. Every Soviet man brings the triumph of communism nearer by his labour. The successes of communist construction spell abundance and a happy life to all, and enhance the might, prestige, and glory of the Soviet Union.

The party is confident that the Soviet people will accept the new Programme of the CPSU as their own vital cause, as the greatest purpose of their life and as a banner of nation-wide struggle for the building of communism. The party calls on all communists, on the entire Soviet people – all working men and women, kolkhozniks, and workers by brain – to apply their energies to the successful fulfilment of the historic tasks set forth in this Programme.

UNDER THE TRIED AND TESTED LEADERSHIP OF THE COMMUNIST PARTY, UNDER THE BANNER OF MARXISM-LENINISM, THE SOVIET PEOPLE HAVE BUILT SOCIALISM.

UNDER THE LEADERSHIP OF THE PARTY, UNDER THE BANNER OF MARXISM-LENINISM, THE SOVIET PEOPLE WILL BUILD COMMUNIST SOCIETY.

THE PARTY SOLEMNLY PROCLAIMS THE PRESENT GENERATION OF SOVIET PEOPLE SHALL LIVE IN COMMUNISM!

4.34
Rules of the CPSU 31 October 1961
[Replaces Rules adopted 1952; see 3.45]

[Revises preamble, 3.45]. The CPSU is the tried and tested militant vanguard of the Soviet people, unifying on a voluntary basis the progressive and most conscientious part of the working class, the kolkhoz peasantry, and the intelligentsia of the USSR.

Founded by V.I. Lenin as the leading detachment of the working class, the Communist Party travelled the glorious road of struggle, brought the working class and the toiling peasants to the victory of the great October Socialist Revolution, and established the dictatorship of the proletariat in the USSR. Under the leadership of the CPSU, the exploiting classes were abolished in the Soviet Union and the moral and political unity of Soviet society was given shape and strengthened. Socialism triumphed completely and irrevocably. The Communist Party, the party of the working class, is now the party of all the Soviet people.

The party exists for and serves the people. It is the highest form of social and political organization, the guiding force of Soviet society. The party directs the great constructive activity of the Soviet people and gives an organized, systematic, and scientifically valid character to its struggle for the attainment of the ultimate goal: the victory of communism.

The CPSU bases its work on a strict observance of leninist norms of party life – the principle of collective leadership, the comprehensive development of intra-party democracy, communist action and initiative, and criticism and self-criticism.

An inviolable law of party life is the ideological and organizational unity and the monolithic character of its ranks, together with the highly conscious discipline of all Communists. Any manifestation of factionalism or cliquishness is incompatible with marxist-leninist party spirit and party membership.

The CPSU is guided in all its activities by marxist-leninist knowledge and by the Programme based on it, which defines the main party tasks for the period of the construction of communist society.

Creatively developing marxism-leninism, the CPSU fights resolutely against any manifestation of revisionism and dogmatism, both of which are profoundly alien to revolutionary theory.

The CPSU is an integral part of the international communist and workers' movement. It adheres to the well-tried marxist-leninist principle of proletarian internationalism, participates actively in strengthening all international communist and workers' movements and fraternal ties with the great army of communists from all countries.

I PARTY MEMBERS, THEIR OBLIGATIONS AND RIGHTS

1   [Revises 3.45, art. 2]   A member of the CPSU may be any citizen of the Soviet Union who accepts the party Programme and Rules, actively participates in the construction of communism, works in one of the party organizations, fulfils party decisions, and pays membership dues.

2   [Revises 3.45, art. 3]   A party member must:

a fight for the creation of a material and technical basis for communism; exemplify the communist attitude toward work, increase labour productivity, and come forward as a leader of all that is new and progressive; support and propagate progressive methods, try to master technology, improve his own qualifications, and look after the increase of communal, socialist property which is the foundation of power and prosperity of the Soviet motherland;

b firmly and steadfastly implement party decisions; explain party policies to the masses; promote the strengthening and expansion of the party's bonds with people; display tact and attention to individuals and respond promptly to the problems and needs of the toilers;

c actively participate in his country's political life, in the managing of state affairs, in economic and cultural construction, and be an example of the fulfilment of social obligations; he must promote the development and strengthening of communist social attitudes;

d master marxist-leninist theory; raise his own ideological level, and promote the formation and education of man in communist society. He should lead the decisive struggle against any manifestation of bourgeois ideology, against vestiges of the private-ownership psychology, and against religious prejudices and other survivals of the past; he must observe the principles of communist ethics and place the interests of society above personal interests;

e be an active champion of the ideas of socialist internationalism and Soviet patriotism among the workers, lead the struggle against the survivals of nationalism and chauvinism, and contribute by word and deed to the friendship of the peoples of the USSR and to the brotherly ties of Soviet people with people of other countries from the socialist camp, and with the proletariat and workers of all countries;

f strengthen in every possible way the ideological and organizational unity of the party, defend the party from the penetration into her ranks of people unworthy of the noble name of Communist; he must be upright and honest before the party and people, show vigilance and protect party and state secrets;

g develop criticism and self-criticism, boldly expose short-comings and strive to eliminate them, struggle against ostentation, conceit, complacency and localism, rebuff any endeavours to suppress criticism, oppose any actions causing harm to the party and the state and report them to party organs and, if necessary, to the Central Committee of the CPSU;

h steadfastly implement the party line in the selection of cadres according to their political and professional qualifications. He must be implacable in all cases where leninist principles have been violated in the selection and training of cadres;

i maintain the party and state discipline demanded equally of all party members. The party has one discipline, and one law for all communists irrespective of their merit or position they occupy;

j promote in every possible way the strengthening of the defensive power of the USSR and wage a tireless battle for peace and friendship among nations.

3   [Revises 3.45, art. 4]   A party member has the right:

a to elect and be elected to party organs;

b to discuss freely questions of policy and practical party activities at party meetings, conferences, congresses, and sessions; to introduce motions, to openly discuss and maintain his opinion until the decision of the organization has been taken;

c to criticize any Communist, irrespective of the position he holds, at party meetings, conferences, congresses, and plenary meetings of committees. Individuals guilty of suppressing criticism and persecuting critics are responsible to and will be penalized by the party, to the point of expulsion from the CPSU;

d to participate personally in party meetings, conferences, and congresses at which the question of his activities or conduct is to be discussed.

e to address questions, statements, and suggestions to any party body, even to the Central Committee of the CPSU and to demand an answer to the point of his appeal.

4   [Revises 3.45, art. 5]   Admission to party membership is without exception on an individual basis. Those who are conscientious, active, and devoted to the work of communism, both peasants and representatives of the intelligentsia, are granted membership in the party. New members are accepted from among candidates who have passed the established term of probation.

Persons who have attained eighteen years of age may be admitted to the party. Young people up to the age of twenty (inclusive) may enter the party only through the Komsomol. The procedure of acceptance into party membership from candidate membership is as follows:

a Those entering into party membership must present the recommendations of three CPSU members who have been party members for at least three years and who have known the candidate through mutual work (in industry or community affairs) for not less than one year.

Note 1: In regard to the acceptance of Komsomol members into the party, the recommendation of the Komsomol raion or city committee is equal to the recommendation of one party member.

Note 2: Members and candidate members of the Central Committee of the CPSU must refrain from giving recommendations.

   b The question of admission to the party is considered and a decision is made at a meeting of the primary party organization; its decision takes effect upon confirmation by the raion committee, or in cities where there are no raions, by the city committee. During the deliberations on admission into the party, the presence of those recommended is not obligatory.

   c Citizens of the USSR who were previously members of the Communist Party in other countries are accepted into the Communist Party of the Soviet Union on the basis of regulations established by the Central Committee of the CPSU.

Individuals who previously belonged to other parties are accepted into the CPSU on the regular basis, but only with confirmation by the oblast committee, krai committee, or central committee of a union republic.

5   [Revises 3.45, art. 6]   Persons who give a recommendation assume before the party the responsibility for providing an objective evaluation of the political, professional, and moral qualities of the person being recommended.

6   [Revises 3.45, art. 7]   Seniority of party membership of those entering the party is counted from the day on which the primary party organization decides at its general meeting to admit the candidate in question to party membership.

7   [Revises 3.45, art. 8]   The method of registering party members and candidate members and their transfer from one organization to another is determined by the appropriate instructions of the CPSU Central Committee.

8   [Revises 3.45, art. 9]   The problem of the party member or candidate member who has not paid his dues for three months without valid reason is subject to discussion in the primary party organization. If it subsequently turns out that the party member or candidate member has in fact broken his connection with the party organization, he is considered to be a non-member of the party, which decision is taken by the primary party organization, submitting it for approval to the raion or city committee of the party.

9   [Revises 3.45, art. 14]   Party members or candidates are responsible for the non-fulfilment of their obligations under the Rules or for any other error they may commit; they may be penalized by a reproach, reprimand, or a severe reprimand, with a notation entered on the registration card. The party's highest disciplinary measure is expulsion from the party.

In unavoidable cases, the party organization may demote a party member to candidate membership for a period of one year as a party disciplinary measure. The decision of the primary party organization concerning the transfer of a party member to candidate membership is approved by the raion or city committee of the party. Upon expiration of the established period of demotion to candidate membership, he may be reaccepted into party membership on the usual basis and may retain the record of his former party membership.

For minor offences, it is necessary to adapt the party measures of instruction and influence in the form of comradely criticism, warning, or reprimand.

In considering expulsions from the party, maximum attention and thorough analysis of the validity of the accusation brought against the Communist must be guaranteed.

10 [Revises 3.45, art. 10] The question of the expulsion of a Communist from the party is decided at a general meeting of the primary party organization. The primary party organization's decision concerning expulsion from the party is accepted if no less than two-thirds of the party members present at the meeting vote for it, and if it is approved by the party's raion or city committee. The decision of the raion and city committee regarding expulsion from the party is enforced through ratification by the oblast committee, krai committee, or by the central committee of the communist party of a union republic.

Before the decision concerning expulsion from the CPSU is ratified by the oblast committee, krai committee, or central committee of the union republic, the party card or candidate member card remains in the hands of the Communist in question; he retains the right to attend closed party meetings.

Following expulsion from the party, he retains the right to make an appeal within two months to the above-mentioned party bodies, the Central Committee included.

11 [Revises 3.45, art. 11] The question of bringing members and candidate members of the central committee of the union republic as well as members of the krai, oblast, okrug, city, and raion committees (members of the revision commission included) to party responsibility is discussed in primary party organizations.

Decisions of party organizations concerning the imposition of penalties on members and candidate members of these party committees and on revision commission members are taken in the customary manner.

Proposals of party organizations concerning expulsion from the CPSU are presented to the respective party committee of which the Communist in question is a member. Decisions regarding expulsion from the party of members and candidate members of central committee, krai, oblast, okrug, city, and raion committees and revision commission members are taken at the plenary session of the corresponding committee by a majority of two-thirds of its members.

The question of the expulsion of a member or candidate member of the Central Committee or Central Revision Commission member is decided at the party Congress, and in the interim between congresses, at a Central Committee plenum by a majority of two-thirds of the Central Committee members.

12 [Revises 3.45, art. 13] If a party member commits an offence punishable under the Criminal Code he is expelled from the party and answerable for it according to the law.

13 [Revises 3.45, art. 15] The appeals of persons expelled from the party or persons who have been punished, and also decisions of party organizations to expel members from the party must be reviewed by the appropriate party organ not later than one month from the date of their receipt.

II CANDIDATES FOR PARTY MEMBERSHIP

14 [Revises 3.45, arts. 16 and 18. First sentence of art. 18, 3.45, is included] Those entering the party serve a period of candidacy necessary for their familiarization with the Programme and the Rules of the CPSU and as a preparation for admission into party membership. The party organization must help the candidate prepare for entering into CPSU membership and must verify his personal qualities. The term of candidacy is one year.

15 [Revises 3.45, art. 17] The procedure for admission to candidate membership (individual basis of admission, the submission of recommendations and their verification, the decision by the primary organization on admission and its confirmation) is identical with that for admission to party membership.

16 [Revises 3.45, art. 18] After the expiration of the period of candidacy, the primary party organization considers and decides the matter of the candidate's acceptance into party membership. If, after the period of candidacy, the candidate has not proved his worth and through his personal qualities is not acceptable for CPSU membership, the party organization decides on whether to deny him admission into party membership; following the ratification of the said decision by the party raion or city committee, he is considered excluded from membership in the CPSU.

17 [Revises 3.45, art. 19] Candidates for party membership take part in all activities of the party organization and exercise the right of consultative vote at party meetings. Candidates for party membership cannot be elected to leading positions of party organs or as delegates to party conferences and conventions.

18 [Revises 3.45, art. 20] Candidates for membership in the CPSU pay the same party dues as members of the party.

III ORGANIZATIONAL STRUCTURE OF THE PARTY
Intra-party democracy

19 [As in 3.45, art. 21] The guiding principle of the organizational structure of the party is democratic centralism, which signifies:

  a Election of all leading party organs from the highest to the lowest levels;

  b Periodic reports of party organs to their own party organization and to the higher organs;

  c Strict party discipline and subordination of the minority to the majority;

  d Unconditional adherence by lower party organs to the decisions of higher party organs.

20 [Revises 3.45, art. 22] The party is organized on territorial production lines: primary organizations are formed in accordance with the place of work of Communists and are amalgamated into raion, city, and other party organizations on a territorial basis. The organization serving a given territory is the highest in relation to all party organizations serving its sectors.

21 [As in 3.45, art. 23] All party organizations are autonomous in resolving local problems, as long as these decisions do not contradict party decisions.

22 [As in 3.45, art. 24] The highest leading organ of each party organization is the general meeting (for primary organizations), conference (for raion, city, okrug, oblast, krai organizations), congress (for communist parties of union republics, for the CPSU).

23 [As in 3.45, art. 25] The general meeting, conference, or congress elects a bureau or committee which is its executive organ and directs all current work of the party organization.

24 [New] Elections of party organs are carried out by closed (secret) ballot. During the elections all party members have the unrestricted right to challenge the candidates and to criticize the latter. Voting must take place with each candidacy considered separately. The candidates for whom more than half of the participants of the meeting, conference, or convention voted, are considered elected.

25 [New] During the elections of party organs, the principle of a systematic renewal of their membership and the succession of leadership is observed.

At each successive election, the membership of the Central Committee of the CPSU and its Presidium is renewed by at least one-fourth. Members of the Presidium are elected, as a rule, to no more than three successive terms. Some party leaders, by virtue of their acknowledged authority or high political, organizational, or other qualities, can be elected to the leading organs for an extended term. In such a case, the corresponding candidate is considered elected upon condition of receiving at least three-fourths of the vote in a closed (secret) ballot.

The membership of central committees of union republic communist parties, krai committees, and oblast committees is renewed by at least one-third at each successive election; membership of okrug, city, and raion committees and of party committees or of bureaus of primary party organizations, by one-half. In the process, members of these leading party organs can be elected for not more than three successive terms. Secretaries of primary party organizations can be elected at no more than two successive convocations.

26 [New] A member and candidate member of the CPSU Central Committee must, in all his activities, justify the high confidence placed in him by the party. If a member or candidate member forsakes his honesty and dignity, he cannot remain in the Central Committee. The question of a member or candidate member of the Central Committee withdrawing from membership in the CPSU Central Committee, is decided at a plenum of the Central Committee by a closed (secret) ballot. The decision is considered accepted if at least two-thirds of all the members of the CPSU Central Committee vote in its favour.

The question of the expulsion of a member or a candidate member of the central committee of a union republic communist party, of a krai, oblast, okrug, city, and raion committee of the party from membership in the party organ, is decided at a plenum of the respective committee. The decision is considered accepted if, as a result of a closed (secret) ballot, at least two-thirds of the votes cast by members of the given committee are in favour of it.

If a member of the Central Revision Commission does not justify the high confidence which the party has placed in him, he must be removed from membership in the Commission. The decision is considered accepted if, in a closed (secret) ballot at least two-thirds of the votes of Central Revision Commission members are cast for the removal from its membership of a Central Revision Commission member.

The question of the removal of revision commission members of republic, krai, oblast, okrug, city, and raion party organizations from membership in these commissions is decided at meetings of the corresponding commission in the way envisaged for members and candidate members of party committees.

27 [Revises 3.45, art. 28] The free and businesslike discussion of questions concerning party policy in individual party organizations or in the party as a whole is the inalienable right of a party member and an important principle of intra-party democracy. Only on the basis of intra-party democracy can criticism and self-criticism be fostered and party discipline, which should be conscious rather than mechanical, be strengthened.

Discussion of controversial or insufficiently clear issues is possible within the framework of individual organizations or within the party as a whole.

General party discussions are necessary:
  a if several party organizations at the oblast or republic level acknowledge that it is necessary;
  b if there is not a sufficiently strong majority in the Central Committee on the most important questions of party policy;
  c if the Central Committee acknowledges the necessity of taking counsel with the whole party on various political questions.

Widespread discussion, particularly discussion on an all-union scale, concerning questions of party policy must be pursued in a manner by which the free expression of party members' views is assured and by which possible attempts to form factional groups which would destroy the party's unity and split the party are out of the question.

28   [New]   The highest principle of party leadership is collective leadership, the indispensable condition for the normal activity of party organizations, the proper training of cadres and the development of communist activity and independent action. The cult of personality and, linked to it, violation of intra-party democracy, cannot be tolerated in the party; they are incompatible with the leninist principles of party life.

Collective leadership does not relieve workers of personal responsibility for matters entrusted to them.

29   [New]   The central committees of union republic communist parties, krai, oblast, okrug, city, and raion committees of the party systematically inform the party organizations of their work during the period between congresses and conferences.

30   [New]   Meetings of the most active members of raion, city, okrug, oblast, and krai party organizations and of communist parties of the union republics are convened to discuss the most important party decisions, to work out measures required for their implementation and also to examine questions of local life.

IV   THE HIGHER PARTY ORGANS

31   [Revises 3.45, art. 29]   The party congress is the highest organ of the CPSU. Regular congresses are convened at least once every four years. The convocation of the party congress and the agenda are announced not later than a month and a half prior to the congress. Special (extraordinary) congresses are convened by the Central Committee on its own initiative or on the demand of at least one-third of the party members present at the preceding party congress. Special (extraordinary) congresses are convened on two months' notice. A congress has a quorum if at least one-half of all the party members are represented.

Norms of representation at a party congress are established by the Central Committee.

32   [As in 3.45, art. 32]   If the Central Committee does not convene a

special (extraordinary) congress as set forth in article 31, the organizations demanding it have the right to form an organizational committee possessing the rights of the Central Committee with respect to the convening of a congress.

33   [Revises 3.45, art. 31]   A congress:

a hears and approves the reports of the Central Committee, the Central Revision Commission, and other central organizations;

b revises, changes, and confirms the Programme and Rules of the party;

c defines the party line on questions of internal and external policies (examines and resolves the most important questions of party construction);

d elects the Central Committee and the Central Revision Commission.

34   [As in 3.45, art. 32]   The congress elects the Central Committee and Central Revision Commission and determines their size. If the Central Committee loses members, they are replaced from among the candidate members of the Central Committee elected by the congress.

35   [New]   During the interval between congresses, the Central Committee of the CPSU directs all activity of the party and of local party organs, carries out the selection of and assignment of leading cadres, directs the work of central state and public workers' organizations through party groups within them, creates various party organs, institutions, and enterprises, and leads their activity, appoints editors of central newspapers and magazines who work under its control, and distributes the funds of the party budget and controls its implementation.

The Central Committee represents the CPSU in dealings with other parties.

36   [As in 3.45, art. 38]   The Central Committee of the CPSU regularly informs party organizations about its work.

37   [Revises 3.45, art. 39]   The Central Revision Commission of the CPSU reviews the speed and correctness with which business is conducted within the central organs of the party and the treasury and enterprises of the Central Committee of the CPSU.

38   [Revises 3.45, art. 33]   The Central Committee of the CPSU holds at least one plenum every six months. Candidate members of the Central Committee attend plenums of the Central Committee with a consultative vote.

39   [Revises 3.45, art. 34]   The CPSU Central Committee elects a Presidium to direct the work of the Central Committee between plenums, a Secretariat for the direction of current work – mainly the selection of cadres and organization of the verification of performance; it establishes a bureau of the Central Committee of the CPSU for the RSFSR.

40   [Revises 3.45, art. 35]   The Central Committee of the CPSU organizes

a Committee of Party Control which is attached to the Central Committee.

The Committee of Party Control of the Central Committee of the CPSU:

 a checks on the observance of party discipline by CPSU members and candidate members, makes Communists who are guilty of violating the party Programme and Rules and party and state discipline answerable for it, as well as violators of party ethics;

 b examines appeals against decisions of the central committees of communist parties of union republics and of krai and oblast committees concerning expulsion from the party and party penalties.

V REPUBLIC, KRAI, OBLAST, OKRUG, CITY, AND RAION ORGANIZATIONS

41 [New] Republic, krai, oblast, okrug, city, and raion party organizations are guided in their activities by the Programme and Rules of the CPSU, conduct all work within the republic, krai, oblast, okrug, city, and raion in line with party policy, and organize the implementation of directives of the CPSU Central Committee.

42 [New] The basic duties of the republic, krai, oblast, okrug, city, and raion party organizations and their leading organs are:

 a political and organizational work among the masses, mobilization of them for carrying out tasks of communist construction, all possible development of industrial and agricultural production for the fulfilment and overfulfilment of state plans; concern for a steady rise in the material welfare and cultural level of the toilers;

 b organization of ideological work and marxist-leninist propaganda, growth in the communist consciousness of the toilers, management of the local press, radio, and television, control over the activities of cultural-educational establishments;

 c direction of soviets, trade unions, Komsomol, co-operatives, and other public organizations through party groups within them, deeper involvement of the toilers in the work of these organizations, development of independent action and activity by the masses as a required condition for the gradual transition from a socialist state to communist self-government by the people.

Party organizations do not supplant soviet, trade union, co-operative and other public organizations of the toilers, and do not tolerate the confusion of party functions with functions of other organizations or unnecessary duplication in work.

 d selection and placing of leading cadres, their instruction in the spirit of communist ideology, honesty, and uprightness, and their great responsibility before the party and the people for the task entrusted to them;

 e the deep involvement of Communists in the execution of party work in the field of public affairs as non-staff workers [not as paid employees in a given field];

f The organization of various party establishments and enterprises within their republic, krai, oblast, okrug, city, or raion, and the direction of their activities; allocation within their organization of party funds; rendering systematic information to their superior party organ and accountability to it on their own work.

The leading organs of the republic, krai, and oblast organizations

43 [As in 3.45, art. 40] The highest organ of the oblast, krai, or republican party organization is the oblast and krai party conference or the congress of a communist party of a union republic, and in the intervals between their meetings the oblast committee, krai committee, central committee of a communist party of a union republic.

44 [Revises 3.45, art. 41] Regular oblast and krai conferences, and congresses of the communist party of a union republic are convened once every two years by the oblast or krai committee, or by the central committee of the communist party of a union republic, and special (extraordinary) conferences by order of the oblast or krai committee or the central committee of the communist party of a union republic on the demand of one-third of the total number of members belonging to the oblast, krai, or republic party organization.

Congresses of the communist party of union republics that are subdivided into oblasts (Ukraine, Belorussia, Kazakhstan, Uzbekistan) may be held once every four years.

Norms of representation at the oblast or krai conference or the congress of the communist party of a union republic are established by the corresponding party committee.

The oblast or krai conference or congress of the communist party of a union republic hears the reports of the oblast or krai committee, the central committee of the communist party of the union republic and the revision commission; it discusses at its discretion other questions of party, economic and cultural construction and elects the oblast or krai committee, the central committee of the communist party of the union republic, the revision commission, and the delegates to CPSU congress.

45 [Revises 3.45, art 42] The oblast and krai committee, and central committee of the communist party of a union republic elect the bureau, including the committee secretaries. Party membership of at least five years is required for a secretary. At the plenums of committees, the chairman of party commissions, the section heads of these committees, and the editors of party newspapers and magazines are also confirmed.

A secretariat may be created in oblast and krai committees and in the central committees of communist parties of union republics to deal with current problems and to verify the execution of decisions.

46 [Revises 3.45, art. 44] A plenum of the oblast and krai committee, and central committee of a union republic is convened at least once every four months.

47 [Revises 3.45, arts. 43 and 45] The oblast or krai committee, or central committee of the communist party of a union republic directs the okrug, city, and raion party organizations, checks on their activities, and systematically hears the reports of the okrug, city, and raion party committees.

The party organizations of autonomous republics and also of autonomous and other oblasts within krais and union republics work under the direction of the krai committees and the central committee of the communist party of the union republic. [Section VI, 1952 Rules, on the okrug, is deleted.]

The leading organs of the okrug, city, and raion (rural and urban) party organizations

48 [New] The highest organ of the okrug, city, or raion party organizations is the okrug, city, or raion party conference or the general meeting of communists convened by the okrug, city, or raion committee at least once every two years, and special meetings, at the committee's decision or upon the demand of one third of the total number of party members belonging to the corresponding party organization.

The okrug, city, or raion conference (meeting) hears the reports of the committee or revision commission, discusses at its discretion other questions of party, economic and cultural construction, elects the okrug, city, and raion committee, the revision commission and delegates to the oblast or krai conference or congress of the communist party of the union republic.

The norms of representation at the okrug, city, or raion conference are established by the corresponding party committee.

49 [Revises 3.45, art. 50] The okrug, city, or raion committee elects a bureau, including the committee secretaries, and also appoints the committee's section heads and newspaper editors. Party membership of at least three years is required for secretaries of the okrug, city, or raion committee. The committee secretaries are confirmed by the oblast and krai committees and central committee of the communist party of the union republic.

50 [New] The okrug, city, or raion committee organizes and sets up the primary party organizations, directs their activity, systematically hears reports on the work of the party organizations and keeps track of its Communists.

51 [Revises 3.45, art. 52] The plenum of the okrug, city, raion, committee is convened at least once every three months.

52 [New] The okrug, city, or raion committee has non-staff instructors [not paid employees], forms permanent or interim commissions on various questions of party work and uses other means of drawing communists into the activity of the party committee on a public participatory basis.

VI PRIMARY PARTY ORGANIZATIONS

53 [Revises 3.45, art. 54] The primary organizations are the basis of the party. Primary party organizations are formed at the places of work of party members – at plants, factories, in sovkhozes and other enterprises, in kolkhozes, in units of the Soviet Army, in establishments, educational institutions, etc. with at least three party members present. Territorial party organizations may also be formed according to Communists' place of domicile in villages and the house management to which they are attached.

54 [Revises 3.45, art. 55] In enterprises, kolkhozes, and institutions that have over fifty members or candidate members of the party in the entire organization, party organizations may be formed in shops, units, farms, brigades, sections, etc. with the approval of the raion, city, or okrug committee.

In shop, unit and analogous organizations, and also in primary party organizations that have less than fifty party members and candidates, party groups may be formed in brigades and other production subdivisions.

55 [Revises 3.45, arts. 54 and 56] The highest organ of the primary party organization is the party meeting which is held at least once a month.

In larger party organizations numbering more than three hundred Communists, a general party meeting is convened as often as necessary within the period established by the party committee or at the demand of several party shop (or office, section) organizations.

56 [Revises 3.45, art. 59] To conduct current work, the primary or shop party organization elects a bureau for a period of one year, whose size is established by the party meeting. In primary and shop party organizations numbering less than fifteen party members a secretary of the party organization and deputy are elected, not a bureau.

For secretaries of primary and shop party organizations party membership of at least one year is required.

In primary party organizations of less than one hundred and fifty party members, the position of party worker released from production is not, as a rule, instituted.

57 [Revises 3.45, art. 56] In large enterprises and establishments with more than 300 party members and candidates (and in necessary cases, taking into account industrial peculiarities or territorial isolation, in organizations with over one hundred members), with the permission of the oblast

or krai committee or central committee of the union republic, party committees may be formed, and the shop and departmental party organizations may be granted the rights of a primary party organization.

In kolkhoz party organizations, party committees may be formed when there are fifty communists present.

A party committee is elected for a term of one year, and its size is determined at a general party meeting or conference.

58 [Revises 3.45, art. 57] The primary party organization is guided in its activities by the Programme and Rules of the CPSU. It conducts work directly among the toilers, unites them around the CPSU, and organizes the masses for the implementation of party policies and for the struggle of the construction of communism.

The primary party organization:

a accepts new members into the CPSU;

b instructs Communists in the spirit of devotion to party tasks, ideological conviction, and communist ethics;

c organizes the study by Communists of marxist-leninist theories in close connection with practical communist construction, speaks out against any attempts at revisionist distortion of marxism-leninism and its dogmatic interpretation;

d concerns itself with heightening the vanguard role of Communists in labour and in the social-political and economic life of the enterprise, kolkhoz, establishment, educational institution, etc.

e comes forward as an organizer of the toilers in the solution of each successive task of communist construction, places itself at the head of socialist competition for the fulfilment of state plans and obligations of the toilers, mobilizes the masses for the discovery and best use of the internal reserves of enterprises and kolkhozes for the widespread introduction in production of the achievements of science, technology, and the experience of advanced workers, strives for the strengthening of labour discipline, a steady increase in labour productivity, and an improvement in the quality of products, is concerned with the preservation and increase of public wealth in enterprises, solkhozes, and sovkhozes;

f conducts mass agitation and propaganda work, educates the masses in the spirit of communism, helps the toilers in developing the habit of managing state and social affairs;

g on the basis of the widespread development of criticism and self-criticism, leads the battle against manifestations of bureaucratism, localism, violations of state discipline, suppresses attempts to defraud the state, and takes measures against slackness, mismanagement, and wastefulness in enterprises, kolkhozes, and establishments;

h renders assistance to the okrug, city, or raion committee in all its activities and reports to it on its work.

A party organization must strive that each communist himself, in all

aspects of his life, observes and imparts to the toilers those moral principles which are set forth in the CPSU Programme – the moral code of the builder of communism:
devotion to the work of communism, love for the socialist motherland and for the socialist countries; conscientious work for the good of society: he who does not work, does not eat;
concern by each person for the preservation and increase of public property;
a lofty consciousness of public duty, intolerance toward the violation of public interests;
collectivism and comradely mutual aid: one for all, all for one;
a humane attitude and mutual respect amongst people: man is a friend, comrade, and brother to man;
honesty and uprightness, moral purity, simplicity, and modesty in public and private life;
mutual respect within the family, concern for the education of children;
irreconciliability to injustice, idleness, dishonesty, self-seeking, and money-grabbing;
friendship and brotherhood of all peoples of the USSR, intolerance toward national and racial hostility;
irreconciliability to enemies of communism, of peace and freedom of nations;
brotherly solidarity with the toilers of all countries, with all peoples.

59 [Revises 3.45, art. 58] Primary party organizations of industrial and trade enterprises, sovkhozes, kolkhozes and also design organizations, construction bureaus, and scientific research institutes directly linked with production have the right to control the activities of the administration.

The party organizations of ministries, state committees, sovnarkhozes and other central and local soviet economic establishments and departments which do not exercise the functions of control over administrative activities, must actively influence the perfection of staff work, instruct employees in the spirit of lofty responsibility for work entrusted to them, take measures for the maintenance of state discipline and the improvement of public services, lead the decisive battle against bureaucratism and red tape and promptly inform the appropriate party organ of short-comings in the work of the establishment and also of individual workers, irrespective of their positions.

VII THE PARTY AND THE KOMSOMOL

60 [Revises 3.45, art. 62] The All-Union Leninist Communist League of Youth — an independent public organization of youth, is an active help and reserve of the party. The Komsomol helps the party educate youth in the spirit of communism, draws it into the practical construction of the

new society, prepares a generation of thoroughly well-rounded people who will live, work and manage public affairs under communism.

61 [Revises 3.45, arts. 52 and 63] Komsomol organizations exercise the right of broad initiative in discussing and raising questions concerning the work of enterprises, kolkhozes, and establishments before the appropriate party organizations. They must be in fact an active champion of party directives in all areas of communist construction, particularly in those where there are no primary party organizations.

62 [Revises 3.45, art. 60] The Komsomol works under the direction of the CPSU. The work of local organizations of the Komsomol is directed and controlled by the corresponding republic, krai, oblast, okrug, city, and raion party organizations.

Local party organs and primary party organizations rely upon the Komsomol organizations in work related to the communist education of youth, and support and publicize their useful undertakings.

63 [As in 3.45, art. 61] Members of the Komsomol who are accepted into the CPSU leave the Komsomol at the moment they enter the party if they do not occupy leading posts in Komsomol organizations.

VIII PARTY ORGANIZATION IN THE SOVIET ARMY

64 [New] Party organizations of the Soviet Army are guided and directed in their activity by the Programme and Rules of the CPSU and work on the basis of instructions of the Central Committee.

Party organizations of the Soviet Army assure that party policy is put into practice in the armed forces, unite their personnel around the Communist Party, educate soldiers in the spirit of the ideas of marxism-leninism and selfless devotion to the socialist motherland, actively promote the consolidation of unity among the army and the people, are concerned with the strengthening of military discipline, and mobilize personnel for execution of combat duties and political training, the mastering of new techniques and weapons, the irreproachable discharge of their military duties, commands or instructions of headquarters.

65 [Revises 3.45, arts. 64 and 65] The direction of party work in the armed forces is carried out by the CPSU Central Committee through the Main Political Administration of the Soviet Army and Fleet, which exercises the rights of a section of the CPSU Central Committee.

Heads of the political sections of military districts and fleets and heads of the political sections of the army must have five years' party membership, and the heads of political sections of units – three years.

66 [Revises 3.45, art. 66] Party organizations and political organs of the Soviet Army maintain a firm tie with local party committees, and systematically inform them of political work in military units. The secretaries of military party organizations and the leaders of political organs participate in the work of the local party committees.

IX PARTY GROUPS IN NON-PARTY ORGANIZATIONS

67 [As in 3.45, art. 67] In congresses, conferences, and meetings called by soviet, trade union, cooperative, and other mass organizations of workers, and also in the elected organs of these organizations, party groups are organized if there are at least three party members. Their task is the all-round strengthening of party influence and the projection of its policies in non-party circles, the struggle against bureaucratism, the verification of the fulfilment of party and soviet directives.

68 [As in 3.45, art. 68] Party groups are subordinate to the appropriate party organizations (Central Committee of the CPSU, central committee of the communist party of a union republic, krai committee, oblast committee, okrug committee, city committee, or raion committee).

Party groups are bound to strict and undeviating obedience to the decisions of the leading party organs in all questions.

X THE FINANCIAL MEANS OF THE PARTY

69 [As in 3.45, art. 69] The financial means of the party consist of members' dues, income from party enterprises and other revenue.

70 [Revises 3.45, art. 70] Monthly membership dues for party members and candidates are established at the following rate: those whose monthly earnings are:

up to 50 rubles pay	10 kopeks
from 51 to 100 rubles	0.5 per cent
from 101 to 150 rubles	1.0 per cent
from 151 to 200 rubles	1.5 per cent
from 201 to 250 rubles	2.0 per cent
from 251 to 300 rubles	2.5 per cent
above 300 rubles	3.0 per cent
	of their monthly earnings.

71 [As in 3.45, art. 71] Initiation dues are levied upon admission to candidate membership at the rate of 2 per cent of the monthly salary.

4.35
On the Mausoleum of Vladimir Ilyich Lenin 30 October 1961

The XXII Congress of the Communist Party of the Soviet Union resolves:
1 The mausoleum on Red Square next to the Kremlin wall which was created to perpetuate the memory of VLADIMIR ILYICH LENIN – the immortal founder of the Communist Party and the Soviet state, the leader and teacher of the toilers of the whole world, is henceforth to be named: THE MAUSOLEUM OF VLADIMIR ILYICH LENIN
2 The continued presence in the mausoleum of the sarcophagus with the coffin of I.V. Stalin is recognized as unsuitable, since Stalin's serious

violations of leninist precepts, his abuse of power, his mass repressions of honest Soviet people, and his other actions during the period of the cult of personality make it impossible for the coffin with his body to remain any longer in the mausoleum of V.I. Lenin.

Pravda, 31 October, 1 November, 1961

KPSS v rezoliutsiiakh VIII, 173-325

4.36
On the Creation in City and Raion Party Committees of Non-Staff Party Commissions for the Preliminary Examination of Questions of Admission to the Party and the Personal Affairs of Communists 11 January 1962

> This decision meant that rank-and-file members were to be drawn – on an unpaid, part-time ('non-staff') basis – into the investigation of charges laid against party members of violating the party Rules. Such a 'democratization' of intra-party life was easily justified in terms of efficiency. However, it did implicitly threaten the monopolistic control of the local party bureaucracy over discipline. The revelation that non-staff party commissions had been introduced experimentally in Moscow and Leningrad suggested the existence of serious doubts about the wisdom of this step, as did its de-emphasis after Khrushchev's fall.

1 On the basis of the experience of the Moscow, Leningrad, and Moscow oblast party organizations, to permit the central committees of communist parties of union republics, krai committees, and oblast committees of the party to create non-staff party commissions of city and raion committees for the preliminary examination of questions concerning admission to the party and the personal affairs [i.e., disciplinary problems] of Communists;
2 The newly created non-staff party commissions of central committees of union republics, krai and oblast committees, and city raion committees should be guided by the regulations that were excerpted in the Central Committee resolution of 13 December 1960 [4.31].

To establish that one of the secretaries of the city or raion party committee is to be present at sessions of the non-staff party commission when it is considering questions of admission to the party and the personal affairs of Communists.
3 To entrust the editors of the journal *Partiinaia zhizn'* with publishing an account of the present resolution, along with the Central Committee

resolution of 13 December 1960, and to publish materials on the experience of the work of non-staff part commissions of city and raion committees of the party in Miscow, Leningrad, and Moscow Oblast.

Paraphrased version in *Spravochnik partiinogo rabotnika* (1963), 470

KPSS v rezoliutsiiakh VIII, 330–1

Plenum of the Central Committee 5–9 March 1962

This plenum was one of a series which were in effect transformed into mass meetings by the invitation (from the party Presidium) of a large number of officials as guest participants. These included regional party officials who were not members of the Central Committee and also others who held specialized posts in the state apparatus which were relevant to the issue of the day. In the present case the problem was agriculture again, and Khrushchev made the major report, embodying proposals for a major management reform, which are reflected in the following resolution.

4.37
The Present Stage of Communist Construction and the
Party's Tasks with Respect to the
Improvement of Agricultural Leadership 9 March 1962

... The plenum of the Central Committee of the CPSU considers that the existing structure of the administration of agriculture fails to meet the increasing demands; it limits the possibility of making use of the potential of socialist agriculture; and it is in need of radical reconstruction. We do not really have an organ which is truly concerned with the administration of agriculture, which organizes production and procurements, is deeply involved in the needs of kolkhozes and sovkhozes, seeks to ensure the most effective use of land, equipment, and other instruments of production. The administration of agriculture must be radically restructured, brought in closer contact with production, made concrete and operational.

The Central Committee and the government have recently done a certain amount of work on restructuring agricultural organs. The Ministry of Agriculture has been reorganized and its attention concentrated on the development of agricultural science and education, on the general productive application of the achievements of science and advanced practice.

'Soiuzselkhoztekhnika' [All-Union Agency for Agricultural Machinery] has been taken out of the system of the Ministry of Agriculture. The procurement system has been reorganized.

However, the reorganization of agricultural organs has not reached the production sphere, has not touched directly upon the leadership of kolkhozes and sovkhozes. Yet this is the main thing. In their practical guidance of agriculture the party organizations must get down to each kolkhoz and sovkhoz, working actively to ensure the fullest possible exploitation of the potential of each.

Many party and soviet organs have not understood the new situation which arose in agricultural production after the reorganization of the MTSS and the sale of equipment to the kolkhozes. This revolutionary measure was put through in order to give greater scope to the development of productive forces in agriculture, to unify under a single management, that of the kolkhozes, both land and equipment, to unbind the initiative of the kolkhoz in the organization of production and heighten its responsibility for the better employment of land and equipment.

The reorganization of the MTSS did not reduce but, on the contrary, enhanced the responsibility of party and soviet organs for the organization of kolkhoz production. Whereas at one stage the MTSS fulfilled the function of organizing kolkhoz production, under present conditions – with the considerable growth of the kolkhozes and sovkhozes – new and more advanced forms are needed for administering and supervising the organization of kolkhoz production. Yet the forms of leadership of kolkhoz production employed by party and soviet organs have remained in many respects unchanged, have remained just as they were before the reorganization of the MTSS.

The necessity for a serious restructuring of the leadership of agriculture is also dictated by the considerably expanded role of the sovkhozes, in recent years, in the production of grain and animal products. More than three thousand large-scale sovkhozes have been created in the country, especially in connection with virgin lands development.

Questions of the guidance of the productive activities of kolkhozes and sovkhozes are now at the forefront of attention. In the view of the plenum of the Central Committee it is necessary to create organs of agricultural administration which would be concerned with planning, with supervising the production and the procurements of agricultural products, which would have a real and active influence on the organization of production in each kolkhoz and sovkhoz and would be responsible for providing the country with agricultural products. It is necessary to liquidate the shameful phenomenon of kolkhozes and sovkhozes in identical conditions of soil and climate obtaining completely different results per unit of labour input. This situation is to be explained primarily by the absence of proper leadership, by the absence of energetic and purposeful work in those kolkhozes and sovkhozes which lag behind the leading ones.

The plenum of the Central Committee resolves: ...

2   The Presidium of the Central Committee of the CPSU and the USSR Council of Ministers are charged with reorganizing the administration of agriculture in the country by setting up in the oblasts, krais, and republics agricultural committees and also territorial kolkhoz-sovkhoz or sovkhoz-kolkhoz (depending upon whether kolkhozes or sovkhozes predominate) production administrations for the guidance of agricultural production. In the republics, krais, and oblasts the agricultural committees are to be headed, respectively, by the first secretary of the central committee or of the krai or oblast party committee. It is suggested that a Union Agricultural Committee [for the whole USSR] be set up in the centre.

Production administrations must be structured democratically since they will be concerned with both kolkhozes and sovkhozes. It is suggested that inter-raion territorial kolkhoz-sovkhoz production administrations contain party organizers from the central committees of the union-republic parties or from the krai or oblast party committees.

The central committees of the union republic parties and the republic councils of ministers are to develop a regulation on Kolkhoz-Sovkhoz Production Administrations and on Agricultural Committees.

Pravda, 11 March 1962   *KPSS v rezoliutsiiakh* VIII, 332–46

4.38
Instruction on the Conduct of Elections of Leading Party Organs
29 March 1962

1   The CPSU Rules stipulate that elections of leading party organs are held:
once yearly in primary party organizations and in shop party organizations and party groups;
once every two years in raion, city, okrug, oblast, and krai party organizations and in the union republic parties.

In the parties of those union republics which are divided into oblasts (the Ukraine, Belorussia, Kazakhstan, Uzbekistan) elections of central party organs may be held once every four years.

2   Accounting and electoral meetings [i.e., meetings to hear the report of the leadership on its activities and to hold new elections] of primary party organizations and city and raion party conferences (raion meetings) are held, as a rule, outside working hours.

3   In primary party organizations the elections of party committees, of

bureaus, or where there is no bureau, of secretaries and their deputies, are held at general party meetings. In some primary party organizations with more than 500 members, if permission is received from the oblast or krai party committee or from the central committee of the union republic party, the elections of party committees may take place at party conferences. The norms for representation at conferences are established by the party committee with the concordance of the raion or city party committee.

The elections of raion, city, okrug, oblast, and krai party committees are held at their respective party conferences, and those of the central committees of union republic parties – at the union republic party congresses. Revision commissions are elected at the same time as party committees. Norms of representation at the conferences and congresses are established by the respective party committees.

4 Delegates to raion, city, and okrug party conferences are elected at general meetings (conferences) of primary party organizations.

In cities which are divided into raions the delegates to city party conferences may be elected at raion party conferences.

Delegates to oblast and krai party conferences and to the congresses of union republic parties are elected at raion, city, and okrug party conferences. Delegates to the congresses of the union republic parties may be elected at oblast party conferences.

In the party organizations of cities which are divided into raions, elections of delegates to oblast and krai party conferences, and to the congresses of union republic parties may be held directly at the raion party conferences, if the oblast or krai party committees or the central committees of the union republic parties so permit.

5 The reports of party organs are discussed and approved at the plenums of their respective committees, and in primary party organizations – at meetings of the party committees and the bureaus of party organizations; the reports of revision commissions are discussed and approved at meetings of the commissions.

The preliminary discussion of the reports does not deprive members of party organs of the right to criticize the leadership of a party organization openly at party meetings, conferences, and congresses.

6 Party members and candidate members temporarily attached to primary party organizations participate in the accounting and electoral meetings of these party organizations on the same basis as others.

7 The following persons are elected by show of hands to preside over party meetings, conferences, and congresses:
at accounting and electoral meetings of primary party organizations and shop party organizations – a presidium or a chairman and a secretary;
at conferences and congresses – a presidium and other leading organs.

The number of persons to be elected to these leading organs is determined by the particular meeting, conference, or congress.

Delegates with a consultative vote and representatives of higher party committees may be elected to the leading organs of conferences and congresses.

Procedure for renewing the membership of party organs

8   Elections of party organs are to follow the principle of systematic replacement of their membership and systematic change in their leadership. Article 25 of the CPSU Rules stipulates that in all regular elections to the central committees of union republic parties and to krai and oblast party committees not less than one-third of the members are to be replaced; in the same elections to okrug, city, and raion party committees, and to the party committees or bureaus of primary party organizations half of the members are to be replaced.

Furthermore, members of these leading party organs may not be elected for more than three successive terms.

Secretaries of primary party organizations may not be elected for more than two consecutive convocations.

The norms for replacement of the members of revision commissions are the same as for the corresponding party committees.

The norms for replacement of the membership of party committees must be applied separately for members and for candidate members of these organs.

9   Depending upon a person's political or professional qualities he may occasionally be elected to a leading organ for a longer period by the meeting, conference, or congress. In such cases election must be by three-fourths of the votes of Communists participating in the voting.

When a Communist is elected to an analogous organ of another party organization, the time spent as member of the previous committee is not taken into account.

10 Party members departing from a leading party organ due to the expiration of their statutory period of membership may be reelected at subsequent elections.

When a Communist is elected to a committee, his time as candidate member of the given committee or of the revision commission is not taken into account. Members of party committees cannot be elected candidate members of these committees or members of revision commissions immediately after expiration of their statutory period of membership in the committee (as defined in article 25 of the CPSU Rules).

Submission and discussion of candidacies to party organs

11 Elections to leading party organs take place after the assembly, conference, or congress has heard and discussed the report of the corresponding party organ, and that of the revision commission, and has taken decisions on them. Before holding the election the party meeting, confer-

ence, or congress decides by show of hands how many members the organ is to have.

12   At party meetings and at the sessions of party conferences and congresses, participants (in party meetings) or delegates (to conferences or congresses) may stand for election as new members of party organs; such candidacies are submitted separately for the position of member or candidate member of a party committee or member of a revision commission.

Conference or congress delegates with a deliberative vote and party members who are not delegates to the given party conference or congress may also stand for election to party organs.

The presidium of the meeting, conference, or congress puts any motion for closing the list of candidates to a vote by the meeting, conference, or congress; such motions are decided by show of hands.

13   At raion, city, okrug, oblast, and krai party conferences, and at congresses of the union republic parties, the presidium may call together the representatives of delegations for a preliminary discussion of new candidates to party organs. At meetings (conferences) of primary party organizations the representatives of shop organizations may come together for the same purpose if the meeting (conference) so decides.

The names of candidates agreed upon in discussions among the representatives of delegations are submitted to the party conference or congress in the name of this group of representatives.

The preliminary submission of the names of new candidates to a party organ during discussions among the representatives of delegations does not limit the right of delegates to submit and discuss candidates at the conference or congress itself.

14   Before the submission of candidacies the meeting, conference, or congress is told, for the information of those present, the names of members and candidate members of party organs whose terms of membership in these organs have expired.

15   Participants in meetings and delegates to conferences and congresses discuss all candidates personally in the order in which they have been placed on the list. Each participant in the meeting or delegate to the conference or congress has an unlimited right during elections to challenge or criticize candidates.

Motions to cut off discussion of a given candidate are decided, at the meeting, conference, or congress, by show of hands.

16   After the discussion of candidates who have been challenged, a show of hands vote must be taken in each case to decide whether or not to include such candidate on the list to be voted by secret ballot.

Candidates who have not been challenged are not submitted to show of hands vote and are placed on the list to be voted by secret ballot.

17   Party conference and congress delegates with a consultative vote

(and candidate members of the CPSU at meetings of primary party organizations) participate (with a consultative vote) in the discussion of candidates to party organs.

Voting procedure

18   The following persons are elected by secret ballot:

a   members of party committees and bureaus and also secretaries and their deputies (where there is no bureau) of primary and shop party organizations; members and candidate members of raion, city, okrug, oblast, and krai party committees, and of the central committees of the union republic parties; members of revision commissions.

Note: The elections of party-group organizers may be held by show of hands if the Communists in the party group do not insist on a secret ballot.

b   delegates to conferences of primary party organizations, to raion, city, okrug, oblast, and krai party conferences, and to congresses of union republic parties.

19   The following persons are elected by show of hands:

a   the secretaries of party committees and the secretaries of bureaus of primary and shop party organizations, as well as their deputies – at meetings of party committees and bureaus of primary and shop party organizations;

b   secretaries and members (candidate members) of the bureaus of raion, city, okrug, oblast, and krai party committees, and of the central committees of the union republic parties – at plenums of the corresponding committees;

c   chairmen of revision commissions – at meetings of the commissions.

20   For conducting the vote by secret ballot and counting the ballots the party meeting, conference, or congress elects by show of hands a voting commission with as many members as are determined by the meeting, conference, or congress. The voting commission elects a chairman and a secretary.

Before the ballot the chairman of the voting commission explains to the participants in the assembly, or to the conference or congress delegates, the procedure for voting by secret ballot.

Before the vote is held the voting commission prepares the ballots (lists) and seals the ballot boxes.

Voting commissions are not elected in primary party organizations with less than ten party members. The party meeting directs its presiding officer or a party member of the given organization to count the ballots. The results of the vote are entered in the records of the meeting.

21   In enterprises with multiple shifts the reports and elections of party committees and of the bureaus of primary party organizations take place at

The party meeting of each shift will discuss reports and submit and discuss new candidates to party organs. After there has been discussion of the proposed candidates at the meeting of each shift a single list is compiled for voting by secret ballot, this vote being taken at the party meeting of each shift.

The party meeting of each shift elects a voting commission, and the overall count of the ballots of the meetings of all shifts is taken at a combined meeting of all the voting commissions. The results of the balloting are communicated to the Communists at the party meetings of the shifts or the shops.

22   Elections of party organs by secret ballot are held at closed meetings or closed sessions of conferences or congresses at which only CPSU members or delegates with deciding votes may be present.

Representatives of higher party organs have the right to be present at both open and closed meetings.

23   Each participant in a meeting, and each conference or congress delegate with a deciding vote, receives a single ballot (list) with the names of those selected by the meeting, conference, or congress to stand for election as member of the particular party organ and, separately, the names of those standing for election as candidate members. When the ballots are distributed, a notation is made on the mandate of the conference or congress delegate, or on the list of the CPSU members present at the meeting, that such-and-such party member participated in the vote.

24   In a secret vote each participant in the meeting, each conference or congress delegate, has the right to strike out some of the names on the ballot or add other names, regardless of any preliminary agreement on the number of persons to be elected to the given party organ.

25   When the balloting is over the voting commission, without leaving the meeting, conference, or congress room, opens the ballot boxes and counts the ballots separately for members and candidate members of the party organ. When the counting is over the voting commission drafts a minute giving the results of the vote and recording the number of 'ayes' and 'nays' for each candidate. The minute is signed by all members of the voting commission.

No one other than the members of the voting commission has the right to be present in the room where the ballots are being counted.

26   The voting commission reports to the meeting, conference, or congress the results of the vote on each candidate separately. Candidates are elected if they obtain the votes of more than half of the CPSU members, or of the delegates with deciding votes, present at the meeting, conference, or congress.

Communists standing for election to party organs for a term in excess of that defined in paragraph 25 of the CPSU Rules are elected if they receive

the votes of not less than three-fourths of those participating in the voting.
27   The minutes of the voting commission on the results of the election are approved by the meeting, conference, or congress.

If the secret balloting leads to the election of somewhat more or fewer members (candidate members) to the party organ than was agreed upon beforehand, the meeting, conference, or congress may resolve by show of hands to approve the new size of the party organ, in accordance with the results of the vote by secret ballot. If a majority of the participants in the meeting, conference, or congress vote to leave the size of the party organ as agreed upon beforehand, the discussion of the candidates must be reopened and another vote taken by secret ballot.

28   All the materials of the vote by secret ballot are kept secret in the party organ until the next elections, at which time they are destroyed according to regulations.

Spravochnik partiinogo rabotnika IV (1963), 482–8

Plenum of the Central Committee   19–23 November 1962

The November 1962 Plenum of the Central Committee was called to approve a radical reorganization of party leadership in the economy. Once again a large number of non-members of the Central Committee were invited by the Presidium on the basis of their interest in the issue, and again Khrushchev delivered the principal report (*Current Digest of the Soviet Press* XIV, no. 46, 3–8; no. 47, 3–14; no. 48, 3–11).

A number of important personnel changes accompanied the reorganization. L.N. Efremov was elected as a candidate member of the Presidium. A.P. Rudakov was elected to the Secretariat of the Central Committee and Chairman of the new Bureau of the Central Committee for Industry and Construction; V.I. Poliakov was elected as a secretary of the Central Committee and Chairman of the new Bureau of the Central Committee for Agriculture; Iu.V. Andropov was elected as a secretary of the Central Committee; V.N. Titov was elected as a secretary of the Central Committee and Chairman of the new Commission for Organizational Party Questions of the Central Committee; P.N. Demichev was confirmed as Chairman of the new Bureau of the Central Committee for Chemical and Light Industry; L.F. Ilichev was confirmed as Chairman of the new Ideological Commission of the Central Committee; A.N. Shelepin was confirmed as Chairman of the new

Party-State Control Committee of the Central Committee and of the Council of Ministers of the USSR; and N.M. Shvernik and Z.T. Serdiuk were confirmed, respectively, as Chairman and First Deputy-Chairman of the Party Commission.

4.39
On the Development of the National Economy of the USSR and the Reorganization of Party Leadership of the Economy
23 November 1962

... The XXII Congress of the CPSU advanced as one of the party's high-priority and major tasks the continued improvement of the leadership of the economy. Now it is also necessary to bring party leadership of industry, construction, and agriculture into line with the demands of the times. In conditions of the full-scale building of communism when the party's role is growing immeasurably the organizational reconstruction of the leadership of the economy is of great political significance.

In our day the party is required not only to come up with the right slogan in time but also to give skilful daily concrete guidance to production, to the development of industry, agriculture, and all branches of the economy.

The rate of development of the country's economy depends primarily upon the efforts of millions of people, upon their ability to organize the implementation of the party's policies and the plans for economic construction.

However, the organizational forms of economic leadership which crystallized at an earlier stage, and which in their day played a positive role, now serve as a hindrance to a more planned and concrete approach in all branches of industry and agriculture, to the adoption of timely and effective measures for eliminating existing short-comings; they engender an unplanned and unsystematic, purely verbal, technique of economic leadership, prevent the party cadres from being properly assigned, and impede the better use of their knowledge and experience.

In order to eliminate these short-comings and improve the leadership of the economy, *the leading organs of the party must be structured from top to bottom according to the production principle*. [Article 20 of the party Rules adopted by the XXII Congress reads: 'The party is structured according to the *territorial-production principle*: primary organizations are created at the place of work of Communists and are united by territory into raion, city, etc. organizations. An organization serving a given territory is superior with respect to all party organizations serving parts of it.' (My italics – G.H.) This provision of the Rules was still in force in November 1962; and in the period after Khrushchev's fall, the bifurcation of the party according to the 'production principle' was specifically criticized as a violation of the Rules.]

Structuring the party organs according to the production principle will make possible a more concrete and planned leadership of industry, construction, and agriculture, concentrating attention primarily on production problems. Such a restructuring will vitalize all aspects of the party's activities and will bind organizational and ideological work even more tightly to the task of creating the material and technical basis of communism and of educating the new man.

The creation of the material and technical basis of communism demands an accelerated rate of technical progress. At present the leadership of most scientific research and design organizations is dispersed among the sovnarkhozes, ministries, and departments, which makes it difficult to conduct a unified technical policy in all branches of the economy and impedes the introduction of new technology.

The plenum of the Central Committee of the CPSU considers it essential to restructure the leadership of scientific research and design organizations, to liquidate parallelism, establish working relations among them, and implement measures aimed at centralizing the leadership of the country's technical policy.

The plenum of the Central Committee directs the attention of party, soviet, and economic organs to the considerable short-comings in the organization of industry, housing, and cultural affairs. Some sovnarkhozes, union-republic state planning organizations, and local party organizations frequently start on new construction without ensuring conformity with state interests, without checking on the availability of designs, materials, labour, and equipment, and scatter their funds among a variety of projects.

Design and construction are too costly, and modern standardized designs are being introduced extremely slowly. The efforts of construction-design organizations are not properly guided and coordinated. Many design offices work in isolation and have poor liaison with other design organizations and scientific research institutes. USSR Gosstroi does not take the initiative in organizing construction design.

To eliminate these short-comings the party organizations must introduce order into construction design and must improve the leadership of capital construction.

Five years' experience with the sovnarkhozes has shown that the large sovnarkhozes provide more skilful management of industrial branches, have greater capacities for manipulating material and technical resources, and are in a better position to ensure concentration, specialization, and co-operation in production. Now a new step must be taken to enlarge the sovnarkhozes and enable them to make even fuller use of the advantages and the potential of the socialist system.

The expanding scale of the economy and the rapid advance of science and technology demand an even greater elevation of the scientific level of planning. However, in many respects the functioning of Gosplan, Gosekonomsovet, and other planning organs is not up to the demands of the present stage of our country's economic development. Economic plans are not always based upon precise economic calculations and investigations, the rates of development of individual branches and economic regions are determined in accordance with the existing proportions, and no provision is made for accelerated growth of the most promising branches of industry such as, for example, chemistry and electronics.

In accordance with the requirements of the CPSU Programme, economic planning must be improved, and the reconstruction of the planning organs which has already commenced must be brought to a conclusion.

The plenum of the Central Committee directs the attention of all party organizations, of state and economic organs, of trade unions, the Komsomol, and of other social organizations, to the need for continued development of democratic principles of participation by the toilers in the guidance of production, for a correct balance between one-man leadership and broad involvement of the masses in the administration of enterprises and construction.

The role and significance of party, state, and social control grow immeasurably in the period of the full-scale building of a communist society. The measures taken by the party in recent years to liquidate the consequences of the cult of personality have made possible a certain improvement in the operation of supervisory organs. However the truly leninist organizational structure of party and state supervision has not yet been entirely restored.

The major short-comings in the organization of supervision reflect seriously on the course of our economic and cultural development. The organs of state supervision are still inadequate in checking on the fulfilment of major party and governmental directives, in struggling against deception, embezzlement, bribe taking, bureaucratism, red-tape, and other negative phenomena alien to the spirit of the socialist system.

The plenum of the Central Committee considers that implementation of new measures to improve party leadership of the economy, to perfect economic administration in industry and construction, to create a unified system of party and state supervision in the country, will play an important role in advancing the economy and in resolving the party's chief task – the continued advance of the public welfare and the satisfaction of the material and spiritual requirements of the toilers of the Soviet Union.

On the basis of the party's general policy of reducing the administrative apparatus and improving its operation, the plenum of the CPSU Central

Committee emphasizes that a radical restructuring of the operations of party, soviet, and economic organs will not lead to a rise in the numbers of administrators but, on the contrary, will reduce their number and also reduce the cost of their upkeep.

The Soviet people, to whom has fallen the honour of being the first to build a road to communism, have accumulated great experience in economic construction. In its restructuring of the economy the Communist Party proceeds from the leninist directives on the need for continuous improvement in the organizational forms of the new society and in the administration of the socialist economy.

The plenum of the Central Committee of the Communist Party of the Soviet Union resolves:

I

With respect to party leadership of the economy:

1   The measures for restructuring party leadership of the economy developed by the Presidium of the Central Committee of the CPSU and set forth in the report by Comrade N.S. Khrushchev during the present Central Committee plenum are approved.

2   It is recognized as essential that the leading organs of the party be reorganized from top to bottom on the production principle, thus ensuring more concrete management of industry and agriculture.

As a rule, two independent party organizations are to be formed within the existing krais and oblasts:

a krai or oblast party organization incorporating all Communists in industry, construction, transportation, educational institutions, and scientific research institutes, design organizations, and others serving industrial production and construction;

a krai or oblast party organization incorporating all Communists in kolkhozes and sovkhozes, experimental stations, agricultural educational institutions, and scientific research institutes, enterprises processing agricultural products, procurement organizations, and other organizations and institutions associated with agricultural production.

The krai or oblast party organization will thus include:

a krai or oblast party committee for the management of industrial production;

a krai or oblast party committee for the management of agricultural production.

3   In order to improve leadership of the economy, a central committee bureau for industrial leadership, and one for agricultural leadership, are to be formed in the Central Committee of the CPSU and in the central committees of the union republic parties.

To resolve matters of republic significance and to co-ordinate the activities of these two bureaus, the central committees of the union-republic parties are to elect presidiums.

4   It is advisable that kolkhoz-sovkhoz production administrations be formed by enlarging the existing rural raions; the party committees of rural raions are to be transformed into the party committees of these production administrations.

For party leadership of construction and enterprises on the territory of newly formed rural production administrations where no city party committees exist, zonal industrial production party committees are to be formed.

5   The newly formed party organs for the leadership of industrial and agricultural production are to be guided in all of their actions by the appropriate provisions of the CPSU Rules for krai and oblast party organizations; the party committees of kolkhoz-sovkhoz production administrations are to be guided by the provisions of the CPSU Rules on city and raion party organizations.

6   The election of new leading party organs is to take place in December 1962, and January 1963, at conferences of the party organizations of kolkhoz-sovkhoz production administrations and also at city, city-raion, oblast, and krai conferences of the party industrial and agricultural organizations.

II

With respect to the economic administration of industry, construction, and planning:

1   To ensure conduct of a unified technical policy in the economy, the management of scientific research and design organizations is to be restructured. To this end:

a the leading scientific and design institutes and the design offices of factories with test and experimental facilities are to be placed under the state committees of the USSR Council of Ministers for industrial branches;

b the state committees are to have responsibility for introducing new methods and technology into production, for the level of technical development of the given branch, and for specialization of industrial production;

c the state committees for industrial branches are to see to it that scientific research and design organizations specialize in particular types of machinery and equipment and ensure maximum interchangeability of parts and assemblies;

d in view of the magnitude of capital construction in the country and the need for a radical improvement in its management as well as for a more rapid introduction of standardized designs in production, USSR Gosstroi is to be reorganized into a union republic organ, and design and scientific research organizations concerned with construction are to be subordinated to it – with the exception of the design organizations of the Ministry of Power and Electrification and the Ministry of Transportation Construction; Gosstroi is to have responsibility for technical policy in capital construction and is to develop title lists.

2   Construction organizations are to be removed from the competence of the sovnarkhozes. Autonomous construction organizations or unions are to be formed in the republics and economic raions, with the sovnarkhozes acting as their customers.

3   The State Committee of the USSR Council of Ministers for Coordination of Scientific Research and the Presidium of the USSR Academy of Sciences are directed to develop, in collaboration with the union republic councils of ministers, proposals for improving the functioning of the USSR Academy of Sciences and the academies of sciences of the union republics, with the purpose of concentrating scientific efforts on the solution of basic problems directly associated with the development of production.

4   The measures set forth in the report by Comrade N.S. Khrushchev on the further enlargement of the sovnarkhozes, with due regard for the economic compatibility of the individual raions, are approved.

5   In connection with the enlargement of the sovnarkhozes and enterprises the USSR Council of Ministers is directed:

a   to review the legal position of the sovnarkhozes and ensure that they are endowed with extensive rights, are guarded against petty interference, and are able to display considerable independence in resolving economic problems and in making use of reserves to increase industrial production;

b   to develop, and submit to the USSR Supreme Soviet for approval, a draft regulation of the socialist enterprise, having in mind extension of rights of directors of enterprises and leaders of construction organizations and ensuring more active involvement of the toilers in the administration of production.

6   In the interests of improving the future planning of the country's economic development and of giving leadership to the implementation of the yearly plans, a more precise delimitation of the functions of the various central planning organs is required.

To this end, the functions of USSR Gosplan relating to the yearly implementation of future plans are transferred to a new organ – the USSR Sovnarkhoz, and this body to be endowed with the necessary executive functions. The Gosekonomsovet is transformed into USSR Gosplan and is to take charge of future planning.

III
With respect to party-state supervision:

1   The system of supervision in the country is to be reorganized on the basis of Lenin's directive that party and state supervision should be com-

bined, that a system of unified and permanent supervision with the participation of the broad masses of toilers should be created.

2   A single organ of party and state supervision is to be established – the Committee of Party-State Control of the CPSU Central Committee and the USSR Council of Ministers, and it is to have the necessary organs at the local level.

The major tasks of the organs of party-state in carrying out the CPSU Programme, are organizing systematic verification of the execution of party and governmental directives, further improving the leadership of communist construction, and ensuring observance of party and state discipline and of socialist legality.

3   The existing Committee for Party Control of the CPSU Central Committee is to be transformed into the Party Commission of the CPSU Central Committee and is to have the duty of examining appeals from decisions of the central committees of the union republic parties, and krai and oblast party committees, on expulsions from the CPSU and the imposition of party punishments.

4   It is no longer advisable to preserve the Commission for State Control of the USSR Council of Ministers, and its organs at the local level ...

Pravda, 24 November 1962   *KPSS v rezoliutsiiakh* VIII, 386–95

4.40
Regulation Establishing the Committee of Party-State Control of the Central Committee of the CPSU and the Council of Ministers of the USSR   18 January 1963

The Central Committee of the CPSU and the Council of Ministers of the USSR have approved the regulation establishing the Committee of Party-State Control of the Central Committee of the CPSU and the Council of Ministers of the USSR, and establishing the necessary organs at the local level.

The regulation states that establishing verification and supervision of execution on a proper basis is a very important leninist principle of the activity of the Communist Party and the Soviet government in building a new society as well as a mighty instrument for improving party and state leadership, strengthening the ties between the party and the people, and involving the masses in the administration of the affairs of society. As our country advances further toward communism, as the guidance of economic construction becomes more complex, and as productive forces undergo a gigantic development, the role of mass supervision will increase more and more.

In fulfilling the directive of the XXII Congress of the CPSU the November (1962) Plenum of the Central Committee resolved on a radical reorganization of the system of supervision in the country, basing it on the leninist idea that party and state control are to be unified and creating a system of unified, all-encompassing permanent control with participation by the broad masses of communists and by all the toilers. In the flexible union of the soviets and the party Lenin perceived the guarantee of success and the source of the extraordinary force of our policies.

The regulation states that the essential element in the functioning of the Committee of Party-State Control of the Central Committee of the CPSU and the USSR Council of Ministers, and of its organs at the local level, is its assistance to the party and state and carrying out the CPSU Programme, in organizing the systematic verification of the de facto execution of party and governmental directives, in further improving the guidance of communist construction, in struggling for the comprehensive advance of the socialist economy, in ensuring observance of party and state discipline and of socialist legality.

The organs of party-state control must look profoundly into our whole socialist economy, must be well informed of the situation, and must give a correct and objective evaluation of progress in fulfilling party and governmental decrees.

In their activities the supervisory organs must be guided unwaveringly by V.I. Lenin's instruction: *'They must check on the agents and review the de facto execution of tasks* – this, once again this, and only this is the crux of the whole matter today, the crux of our whole policy.'

The decisive conditions of success of the organs of party-state control are: the broadest and most active involvement of both the communist and the non-communist masses, of women and of youth, in the work of control; extensive publicity through meetings of toilers, through the press, the radio, television, the cinema; an attentive attitude to letters and complaints, signals and proposals by Soviet people.

The organs of party-state control must be the practical organizers of mass popular control, which is the most democratic kind and which is not found, and could not be found, in a single capitalist state.

Being organs of the party and the government, the committees of party-state control not only verify and punish but, what is of primary importance, prevent errors and the possibility of abuses of all kinds, help the CPSU Central Committee and the USSR Council of Ministers to train cadres and prevent them from short-comings and blunders in their work, head them toward the successful fulfilment of economic and political tasks.

The committees of party-state control and the whole gigantic army of their active members should structure their efforts so that bureaucrats and red-tape experts, parasites, bribe takers, thieves, speculators, and deceivers feel the inevitability of their punishment and tremble before the great power of Soviet public opinion.

The organs of party-state control are obliged to give active support and encouragement, and to develop, all that is new, advanced, and progressive in every facet of our life, resolutely and persistently to strive for the elimination of whatever short-comings are disclosed, to take effective measures to ensure that verification leads to an improvement in the situation and to the unconditional fulfilment of party and governmental directives.

Assumption of these duties by the organs of party-state control does not deprive party, soviet, and economic organizations of their responsibility for verifying the execution of decisions. On the contrary, as the regulation proclaims, it is necessary to heighten the responsibility of party, soviet, economic, planning, and other organs, and of the whole party and state apparatus from top to bottom, for organizing the irreproachable execution of party and governmental directives.

The Committee of Party-State Control carries out all its activity under the direct leadership of the Central Committee of the CPSU and the USSR Council of Ministers and is accountable to them.

Since the Committee of Party-State Control of the Central Committee and the USSR Council of Ministers is a union republic organ, it is made up of the leading persons of the Committee, representatives of trade unions, of the Komsomol, and of the press, of workers, kolkhozniks, and intellectuals – all persons in whom there is general confidence.

The republican, krai, and oblast committees of party-state control are organs of the party central committees and of the union republic councils of ministers, of the krai and oblast party committees, and of the krai and oblast soviets of workers' deputies, and are approved at plenary meetings of the appropriate party committees. They will include leading persons on these committees, representatives of lower-level supervisory organs, of trade-union and Komsomol organizations and of the press, and comrades of authority from among workers, kolkhozniks, and intellectuals.

In the krais and oblasts in which there are two independent krai and oblast party committees and two krai and oblast soviets of workers' deputies, two committees of party-state control will also be formed.

City and raion committees of party-state control and committees of party-state control in the kolkhoz-sovkhoz production administrations and in the industrial zones are organs of the republic, krai, and oblast committees of party-state control and are also approved at the meetings of the appropriate party committees. The committees will include representatives of trade union, Komsomol, and other social organizations, of the press, and comrades of authority from among workers, kolkhozniks, and intellectuals.

In enterprises, construction sites, kolkhozes, sovkhozes, institutions, and in the management offices of housing units groups are to be formed for collaborating with the committees of party-state control by delegating to these groups representatives of party, trade union, Komsomol, and other social organizations elected at meetings of these organizations and also at general meetings of kolkhozniks and of persons living in a particular building. These collaborating groups are to include the most active and prestigious comrades, both Communists and non-party workers, kolkhozniks, specialists, employees, scholars, persons engaged in literature or art, housewives. The presidents of these collaborating groups and their deputies are to be elected at general meetings of the group members and approved by the party committee or the bureau of the primary party organization. The largest collaborating groups may elect their own bureaus.

In shops, departments, sectors, and brigades of enterprises, construction sites, kolkhozes, and sovkhozes collaborating groups are formed, or individuals are appointed, from the delegates of party, trade union, Komsomol organizations, and kolkhoz meetings. Collaborating groups work under the guidance of the party organizations and the appropriate local organs of party-state control and act as organizational centres around which all activities of social control are grouped.

Collaborating groups are endowed with extensive rights with respect to the questioning of administrations, party, trade union, and Komsomol organizations, and party-state control committees about eliminating the short-comings which they have brought to light and bringing culprits to justice. Proposals by collaborating groups are to be examined by the directors of enterprises and construction sites, of kolkhozes, sovkhozes, and institutions, by primary party organizations, and by trade union and Komsomol organizations.

Collaborating groups will report periodically on their activities at party, trade union, and Komsomol meetings, and at meetings of the toilers.

The Committee of Party-State Control of the CPSU Central Committee and the USSR Council of Ministers, and its organs at the local level, will verify – directly and, when necessary, jointly with departments of the CPSU Central Committee, the staff of the USSR Council of Ministers, local party committees, party, and soviet organizations – the de facto execution of party and government directives by ministries, state committees, departments and other organizations, enterprises, construction sites, kolkhozes, sovkhozes, and institutions; they will supervise the fulfilment of economic plans, bring to light internal reserves and unused opportunities for expanding production in industry and agriculture, for improving the quality of production, lowering its unit cost, and raising labour productivity; they will struggle for the strictest economy, for the correct and most expedient expenditure of resources and material values.

The organs of party-state control must help the party improve the functioning of the state and the administrative apparatus and at the same time lower its cost; they must resolutely suppress violations of party and state discipline, manifestations of localism, of a departmental approach, of covering up, padding costs and estimates, lack of economy, and wastefulness; they must struggle mercilessly against bureaucratism and red tape, bribe taking, speculation, abuse of official positions, and against encroachments on socialist principle, 'he who does not work shall not eat'; they must come out against any other activities harmful to communist construction.

The Committee of Party-State Control of the CPSU Central Committee and the USSR Council of Ministers, and its organs at the local level, have the right to instruct the leaders of ministries, state committees, departments, and other organizations, enterprises, construction sites, kolkhozes and institutions to eliminate short-comings in the fulfilment of party and governmental decrees and violations of them; they have the right to listen to reports and demand explanations, as well as the necessary documents and materials, from persons in leading positions who are inadequately carrying out party and governmental decrees and instructions, whose work is bureaucratic and tangled in red tape; they have the right to penalize those guilty of submitting incorrect or false information or conclusion. The leaders of soviet and economic organizations, of enterprises, construction sites, kolkhozes, and institutions are obliged immediately to remedy any violations or short-comings disclosed by the collaborating groups and communicate the results to the organs of party-state control.

The Committee of Party-State Control of the Central Committee of the CPSU and the USSR Council of Ministers and corresponding organs at the local level have the right to recommend to the appropriate organs and organizations that they hear reports of leading persons at sessions and meetings of executive committees of soviets of workers' deputies, at meetings of ministerial boards, of state committees and departments, of party committees, at general meetings of workers, kolkhozniks, and employees devoted to ways of eliminating short-comings in carrying out party and governmental decrees; to countermand illegal orders and actions of organizations, institutions, and officials 'capable of damaging state interests; to set, for persons guilty of unsatisfactory fulfilment of party and governmental decisions, a time within which corrective action must be taken; when necessary, to forward matters to comradely courts for their examination; to make suitable deductions from the salaries of officials guilty of material damage to the state or to co-operative or social organizations; to call offenders to account, impose disciplinary penalties, demote officials or fire them; to forward materials on abuses and other criminal activities to the organs of the public procurator in order that guilty persons may be brought to trial.

The regulation emphasizes that the organs of party-state control are to make efficient use of their rights, neither overdoing things in imposing fines and penalties nor sparing persons whose actions have damaged the cause of communist construction.

In addition to their ordinary staffs the committees of party-state control at all levels are to establish auxiliary sections, permanent and temporary social commissions, non-staff inspectors and controllers who are recommended for work with the organs of party-state control by party, soviet, and social organizations. In their work of verifying, investigating, and reviewing, the organs of party-state control may enlist the aid of workers in party, soviet, and economic organs, in enterprises, construction sites, kolkhozes, sovkhozes, and institutions, members of revision committees, and the supervision-review personnel of ministries, state committees, and departments.

To ensure broad publicity for their work the organs of party-state control make active use of the press, the cinema, radio, and television; they publish systematically the results of their investigations and the measures adopted; in their work of control they enlist the aid of worker and rural correspondents, of journalists, writers, poets, and artists.

The regulation indicates that the organs of party-state control are to train their staff and non-staff workers, the members of collaborating groups and individual collaborators, in the spirit of true leninist qualities and traits of character, of a high sense of responsibility to the party and the state for the fulfilment of their duties.

Pravda, 18 January 1963

4.41
On Reorganizing the Work of the Higher Party Schools
in Accordance with the Resolution of the November
Plenum [4.39] of the Central Committee 19 March 1963

The Central Committee of the CPSU resolves:
1 Following the reconstruction of party and soviet organs on the production principle the Higher Party Schools are to have:
a section for training and retraining the cadres of party and soviet organs in industrial management;
a section for training and retraining the cadres of party and soviet organs in agricultural management;
a section for newspaper, radio, and television personnel.

2   The primary task of the Higher Party Schools is to train and retrain party and soviet cadres who are thoroughly familiar with marxist-leninist theory and economics, and with the organization of industrial enterprises, kolkhozes, and sovkhozes, and who are capable of finding creative and effective solutions for problems arising in economic, party organizational, and ideological work.

3   The curricula of the Higher Party School of the Central Committee and of the local Higher Party Schools are hereby approved (appendices 1, 2, 3, 4 and 5).

4   The Higher Party School of the Central Committee is directed to prepare by 15 August of this year lists of courses for the two-year and four-year higher party schools in the light of the new curriculum ...

Spravochnik partiinogo rabotnika (1964), 257–63

4.42
On the Implementation of the Decisions of the XXII Congress of the CPSU, and of the November Plenum of the Central Committee, with Respect to the Selection, Assignment, and Training of Leading Cadres in the Industrial Party Organization of Donets Oblast

14 May 1963

The Central Committee of the CPSU has discussed the fulfilment by the Donets oblast industrial party organization of the decisions of the XXII Party Congress and the November Plenum of the Central Committee with respect to the selection, assignment, and training of leading cadres. The ensuing resolution points out that in implementing the decisions of the XXII Party Congress and the November Plenum, the Donets oblast industrial party organization has made a considerable effort to improve the selection, assignment, and training of cadres. Knowledgeable organizers, capable of resolving successfully the tasks of communist construction, have been brought forward in party, soviet, and economic work. After the November Plenum of the Central Committee there was a qualitative improvement in the composition of leading cadres: more than 95 per cent of the secretaries of the city and raion committees, and of the industrial party committees, have higher education, and of them two-thirds have an engineering education. Work is being done to heighten the theoretical level and business qualifications of party cadres. There exists a broad network of schools and seminars where leading and engineering-technical personnel study concrete economic questions, the achievements of science and most advanced practices, and economic management, a majority of leading personnel participate in propaganda and mass political work ...

However, the work of the oblast industrial party organization with respect to cadres does not yet fully meet the demands of the XXII Congress and the November Plenum of the CPSU Central Committee. The selection, assignment, and training of cadres is not a central preoccupation of all party, soviet, and industrial organs, as a result of which there are serious short-comings and errors.

The oblast committee and many city and raion committees of the party countenance violations of the leninist principle that cadres are to be selected on the basis of political and professional qualifications; and give insufficient study to its implementation; often weak persons, lacking in initiative, have been advanced to leading positions. The supervision and organization of the execution of decisions have not become fundamental to the leadership style of many party committees. Party organs condone an irresponsible attitude on the part of some leading persons vis-à-vis the execution of party and governmental directives, make little effort to organize people to work better, do not set a good example, and are complacent toward backwardness in sectors of work entrusted to them.

Party and economic organs do not display the necessary concern to create a reserve, limit themselves as before to a narrow circle in the matter of promotions; persons who have failed and compromised themselves are still being shifted around from one leading position to another. The party directives on the need for a solicitous and attentive attitude toward cadres are being inadequately implemented. Instead of making a thorough study of the local situation and extending practical assistance, some leading persons resort to the bare issuing of orders, and reprimand and fire people without cause. As a result of the lack of supervision by the Donets city party committee, last year in the Donets' coal group of mines alone, thirty-six mine supervisors and half of the chief engineers were replaced in 102 coal pits. During the last two years a total of two-thirds of the supervisors and chief engineers of the coal pits and construction sites in the oblast have been replaced.

The sovnarkhoz, the leaders of enterprises and construction sites, and many party organizations have failed to take suitable measures to carry out party and governmental decisions calling for improved work with specialists; nor do they create the necessary conditions for getting them established in production and for ensuring their creative growth; they promote to leading positions too few capable young engineers and technicians who have proven themselves in action. Many specialists are being used as ordinary workers, while at the same time there are more than 25,000 persons doing the work of engineers and technicians in industry and construction who lack professional education and of whom only one-third are presently studying in institutes and technical schools.

The oblast party committee and many other party committees have failed to draw the requisite conclusions from the decisions of the XXII Congress and the November Plenum on intensified ideological and educational work with cadres, train them inadequately in the spirit of communist moral principles and of the strictest observance of party and state discipline. Some party organizations inadequately develop criticism and self-criticism, are not searching and principled in their evaluation of the conduct of those leading workers who abuse their official position, cover up errors and short-comings, behave immodestly, and display a private ownership mentality.

There is almost no heightening of the responsibility of party organizations and leading cadres for the ideological and political education of the toilers. The oblast party committee has failed to take effective measures to carry out the 11 March 1959 resolution of the CPSU Central Committee on the state of mass political work among the toilers of the oblast and ways of improving it. Some persons in party, soviet, trade union, and economic organs make few political speeches and associate little with the workers either in production or in everyday life. Many party committees fail to concern themselves with the content and effectiveness of ideological work, do not judge it by the production and moral political performance of the group, but only on the basis of the number of party measures taken. Thus the Gorlov city party committee feels that ideological work is proceeding well in the Kochegarka coal pit while at the same time there has been quite a lot of absenteeism, drunkenness, and hooliganism among the workers there. The party organs do not struggle actively to eradicate criminality, hooliganism, and other amoral manifestations.

The situation is particularly unfavourable with respect to the education of cadres in light industry, food processing, and trade where a public spirit implacably opposed to bribe taking and theft of public property has not been created. In Donets a group of swindlers and rogues, which even included the directors of a number of enterprises, stole more than 3 million rubles worth of goods.

There are serious short-comings in the work of the courts, with respect to cadres, the procuracy, and the police. Some persons in these organs have violated socialist legality and proper standards of conduct.

The oblast party committee is insufficiently self-critical in evaluating the situation in the oblast and does not carry out the necessary supervision of the fulfilment of party and government decisions on work with cadres. During the last two years the bureau of the oblast party committee has not discussed the reports of city and raion party committees and of primary party organizations on the selection, assignment, and training of cadres, nor has it submitted them to meetings of party members and the plenums of the oblast committee for discussion.

These major omissions in cadre work have had a negative effect on the economic activities of many enterprises and construction jobs, hinder the exploitation of the gigantic reserves and opportunities for a more successful fulfilment of the targets of the Seven-Year Plan ...

The Central Committee has drawn the attention of the bureau of the Donets industrial oblast party committee, and of its first secretary, Comrade Liashko, to the serious errors in the selection, training, and assignment of cadres in the oblast party organization and has ordered the oblast party committee to eliminate them as well as to develop and implement measures aimed at improving cadre work in the light of the requirements of the XXII Congress and the November Plenum. The oblast party organization must direct its efforts at the continued development of production and at the fuller satisfaction of the material and spiritual demands of the toilers, at the absolute fulfilment, by each enterprise and construction site, of state plans and socialist obligations with respect to all technical and economic indices.

The Central Committee has ordered the oblast party committee to ensure strict observance of the leninist principle that cadres are to be selected and posted on the basis of their political and professional qualities, to evaluate the activities of leaders on the basis of the concrete results of their work, resolutely to replace unprincipled leaders who have lost their feeling for the new, and no longer to condone the transfer from one leading position to another of weak persons who lack initiative and have not shown themselves worthy of trust. Young and energetic organizers who know their jobs must be advanced more boldly to leading positions, ensuring at the same time a correct balance between old and experienced cadres and young ones. The unjustifiably high turnover of cadres in coal mining and construction must cease.

The oblast party committee has been ordered to plan a cadre reserve for promotion, to be more active in locating skilful and capable workers, helping them to perfect their specialized knowledge and develop the skills needed for rational economic management, to reinforce their supervision of the use of specialists in production, and to create the conditions in which persons with practical talents can acquire a technical education and increase their business qualifications ...

The oblast party committee must increase the role and responsibility of party, soviet, trade union, and Komsomol organizations in the struggle against plunderers of public property, idlers, and bribe-takers. In each group it must create an atmosphere of intolerance toward anti-social manifestations, and it must in every way cooperate with the organs of party-state control and of defence of public order. In the struggle against violators of the law it is to make full use of Soviet laws and is to penetrate more deeply into the activities of the courts, the procuracy, and the police, reinforcing their authority. The oblast committee must improve the selection of persons for these organs and their ideological training, seeking to achieve a high level of moral stability, undeviating observance of legality, and the accurate and effective disclosure and suppression of criminal acts ...

Spravochnik partiinogo rabotnika (1964), 279–85

Plenum of the Central Committee 18–21 June 1963

The June 1963 Plenum of the Central Committee was the first all-union plenum devoted to ideological questions to be held since Stalin's death. The main report, 'Current Tasks of Ideological Work of the Party,' was delivered by the Secretary L.F. Ilichev (*Current Digest of the Soviet Press* xv, no. 23, 5–12; no. 14, 7–17). There was also a long speech by Khrushchev that dealt with foreign and domestic problems (*ibid.*, no. 24, 3–6; no. 25, 3–11). In addition to members and candidate members of the Central Committee and members of the Central Revision Committee a large number of invited officials attended the plenum.

The plenum gave official sanction to the trend toward ideological conformity in evidence since the Cuban missile crisis in late 1962. Much attention at the plenum was paid to the need to struggle against the influence of bourgeois propaganda. Nationalism among the non-Russian peoples of the USSR was also treated as a serious danger. In contrast with the similar post-1965 ideological crackdown, however, there was much stress at the June Plenum on 'overcoming the cult of personality.' The plenum, it should be noted, was held shortly before the crucial Sino-Soviet talks of July 1963, the failure of which confirmed the seriousness of the schism in the international communist movement. A resolution on the forthcoming talks with China was formally approved by the plenum – perhaps as an attempt to demonstrate to the Chinese that no basic differences of opinion on policy toward China existed among the Soviet leaders. At the plenum L.I. Brezhnev and N.V. Podgorny were elected secretaries of the Central Committee.

4.43
On the Current Tasks of Ideological Work of the Party 21 June 1963

... Now the ruling circles of the imperialist countries, while not rejecting other forms of struggle against socialism, are counting primarily on ideological diversion against the socialist states, shameless anti-communism. Under the anti-communist flag the imperialists discriminate economically and politically against the countries of the socialist system, feverishly spur on the arms race. They try, using every technique, to bring the 'war of ideas' into the socialist countries. Under the guise of the slogan, 'peaceful coexistence of ideologies,' they try to drag into our society false conceptions of a 'non-party' art, 'absolute creative freedom,' the absence of ideological conviction, disinterest in politics, 'conflict of generations,' and thus to corrupt ideologically unstable people.

The preaching of peaceful coexistence of ideologies is treachery to marxism-leninism and betrayal of the cause of the workers and peasants.

The greater the economic and political power of the socialist countries, the deeper the crisis of world capitalism and the more acute the class struggle on a world scale, and the greater the role of marxist-leninist ideas in rallying and mobilizing the masses to struggle for communism.

In the view of the CPSU, its primary duty to the Soviet people and its international duty to the toilers of the whole world compel it to conduct an implacable offensive against the inhuman imperialist ideology, to guard the toilers against its noxious influence, to impart the great ideas of communism to the masses even more actively, to be constantly concerned with the purity of marxist-leninist doctrine, its development, and its enrichment.

Together with the fraternal marxist-leninist parties the CPSU has elaborated the principal tasks of the world liberation movement, has launched a decisive struggle against bourgeois ideology as well as against revisionism, dogmatism, and sectarianism.

The elaboration of the great plan for building communism in the USSR and creating the conditions for its realization is the product of the whole prior development of Soviet society and especially of the major socio-economic measures put through by the party during the past decade. By dethroning, at its XX Congress, the cult of I.V. Stalin and casting it aside, the party put an end to violations of leninist norms of party and state life, to subjectivism and dogmatism in economics, politics, and ideology, and gave full scope to the initiative and activity of the popular masses ...

The immortal creations of K. Marx, F. Engels, V. I. Lenin, the CPSU Programme, and the documents of our party serve as the foundation for educating the masses in the spirit of communism. The goal is to ensure that every toiler, and every Communist in particular, has assimilated the aims set forth in the party Programme and fights actively for their realization.

Soviet society affords all necessary conditions for resolving the tasks of the communist education of the toilers. However, many party, state, and social organizations are far from making adequate use of these conditions.

The gap between ideological work and life, formalism, and the striving to evaluate the results of such work only in terms of the amount of ideological measures implemented, has not yet been overcome. Ideological and political work do not always take into account the level of preparation of the toilers and their breakdown by nationality and age-group; considerable numbers of workers, kolkhozniks, and employees are still outside any continuous ideological influence. In many rural raions, mass political work is still being conducted unsatisfactorily. There are serious short-comings in the education of youth. Work among women is lagging in many republics, krais, and oblasts, and the remnants of feudal attitudes toward women have not been overcome.

Many party, trade union, and Komsomol organizations do not fight day by day to ensure that the principles of the moral code of the builder of communism become the behaviour norm of each Soviet person; the masses are being poorly mobilized for a decisive advance against the remnants of the past in the consciousness and behaviour of people. Idlers, greedy and grasping self-seekers, thieves, speculators, bureaucrats – these are the last refuge of an ideology and morality which is alien to us. Against them a merciless struggle must be waged, using the whole power of social influence and the full force of the Soviet laws.

Some party committees poorly organize and verify the fulfilment of party and governmental directives on the communist education of the toilers, fail to analyse the content of the work of ideological institutions, creative unions, publishers, newspapers, magazines, the radio, television, coordinate their activities poorly, condone serious blunders and errors in ideological work, and have a frivolous attitude to questions of the marxist-leninist tempering of cadres.

In recent years the CPSU has put through a series of important measures for improving party and governmental leadership of agriculture, industry, and construction. Measures designed to improve the leadership of ideological activity are the logical extension of these profound transformations. The creation of a communist economy and culture and the education of the new man demand a continued improvement in the organizational forms of ideological work, the creative application of new methods and techniques for influencing the masses ideologically and politically, and the strengthening of party guidance of ideological processes.

The Central Committee plenum resolves:

The efforts of the party, of state organs, of the trade unions, of the Komsomol, and of all other social organizations are to be concentrated on the following *fundamental directions* of ideological work, which reflect the present stage of the construction of communism in the USSR and of the class struggle in the international arena:

shaping a communist world outlook on the part of the toilers; overcoming the remnants of the past in the consciousness and behaviour of Soviet people;

inculcating good working habits in active and conscious builders of communism;

raising the educational and cultural level of the people;

educating the people in the spirit of Soviet patriotism and socialist internationalism; struggling resolutely against anti-communism and against bourgeois ideology in all its forms.

In its essence *Soviet patriotism* is internationalist and incompatible with any tendencies toward national narrow-mindedness, in whatever form they may be manifested. The love of all the peoples of the USSR for their multinational motherland is organically combined with a feeling of respect and fraternal friendship for the peoples of other socialist countries, for the toilers of the whole world.

Education in Soviet patriotism, in love for our socialist motherland, for the great Communist Party of the Soviet Union – is the most important and fundamental task of ideological work. Soviet people feel a patriotic pride in their beautiful motherland, in their great leninist party. They realize profoundly that whatever is created in our country is created by their hands, by the selfless labour of the people, at the cost of intense effort and expenditure of energy.

Therefore they cannot but feel indignation at the various philistines, loafers, self-seekers, and parasites who so diligently help themselves from our national wealth without giving society anything in return. Soviet people cannot understand those who have lost the self-respect of a Soviet citizen, who do not notice the gigantic accomplishments of the people, the heroic in our life, who are ready to blacken everything which is dear to the toilers and has been won by their sweat and blood, which constitutes our power and glory.

The Soviet people and our party cannot agree with those who greet with a sour smile any depiction of the bright aspects of our life, who pin the label of 'varnishers' on writers and artists who reflect the lofty and noble truth of our life, the heroism and romanticism of the struggle for a new society.

There must be an improvement in the work of party organizations, and of society as a whole, in educating Soviet people, especially the youth, in the glorious revolutionary traditions of the Communist Party, the working class, and the toiling peasantry, in the spirit of pride in the great accomplishments of the Soviet people, of the honour and self-respect of a citizen of the Soviet Union, of constant readiness to spring to the defence of the socialist motherland.

The plenum orders party organizations to intensify their efforts at educating the toilers in the spirit of socialist *internationalism*, to reinforce fraternal friendship of the peoples of the Soviet Union – which is a major achievement of socialism, to promote actively the mutual enrichment of the cultures of the peoples of the USSR, to struggle implacably against all manifestations of nationalism, such as localism, the doctrine of national exclusiveness and uniqueness, idealization of the past, eulogies to reactionary traditions and customs. By its very nature nationalism is hostile to socialism, to the marxist-leninist world-view, to friendship among peoples; it is in contradiction with the objective process of the development and rapprochement of the socialist nations.

The consolidation of the economic might of the Soviet Union and the growth in its defence capacity and that of all the socialist countries, their economic successes, the advances of science and technology, the unprecedentedly powerful anticolonial national liberation movement of the oppressed peoples which has gained major victories, the successes of the international communist movement – have all changed the correlation of forces on the world scene to the benefit of peace and socialism and to the disadvantage of imperialism and war.

The CPSU and the Soviet government are steadfastly and consistently carrying out the leninist policy of the peaceful coexistence of states, regardless of their social orders, of political peace and friendship among peoples.

This policy is expressed, in particular, in the active struggle of the Soviet Union and the other socialist states for general and complete disarmament, for the prohibition of nuclear weapons and their destruction.

To the peace-loving line of the Soviet Union and the other socialist state the imperialist camp opposes an increasingly frenzied arms race, a policy of deceit of the peoples, of aggression, and of international provocation.

The CPSU and the Soviet government proceed from the premise that war is not inevitable under contemporary conditions, that by the united efforts of the socialist states and through a mighty surge in the struggle of the working class, the peasantry, the intelligentsia, and of all peace-loving forces, war may be prevented. However, the party and the whole Soviet people cannot help but take into account the fact that the soil for aggressive wars will remain as long as imperialism continues to exist. One must be aware that the policies of imperialism can lead to the unleashing, by its most aggressive and adventurist forces, of a world thermonuclear war; for this reason the peoples must be particularly vigilant.

So as not to be taken unawares the Soviet state is doing, and will do, all that is necessary for the further strengthening of the country's defensive might, to educate the entire people and its valorous Armed Forces in devotion to the socialist motherland and to the lofty ideals of communism. We must continue in every way to improve the technical equipment of the Army and Navy, to heighten the fighting skill, the military preparedness, and the ideological temper of Soviet fighting men, their readiness at all times to carry out their sacred duty of defending the motherland.

Party, Komsomol, trade union, and other social organizations should train all Soviet people in love and respect for the glorious Armed Forces of the Soviet Union, bestowing continued attention and care on the Soviet fighting men and recalling that consolidating the security of our motherland and the power of the Soviet Army and Navy is the vital concern of our entire people.

The plenum calls party, state, and social organizations to pay special attention to the need for increased political vigilance against the ideological diversions of imperialism, against attempts by the latter to disarm Soviet people ideologically and morally ...

The heart of the ideological work done by the party, the Soviets, the trade unions, and the Komsomol must be the inculcation, in each Soviet person, of love and respect for socially useful labour.

It is necessary to bring every toiler to a clear realization that ensuring high productivity is a nation-wide task and the principal condition of the building of communism; that socialist competition must be broadly developed, that most advanced practices must be applied generally, that heroes of labour must be surrounded with honour and respect, and that a struggle must be waged against bureaucratic attitudes toward the creative initiative of the toilers; that all the power of public opinion must be brought to bear against idlers, loafers, and drunkards.

The plenum attributes great importance to the continued development of the movement for communist labour, which combines organically the struggle for high labour productivity, for the mastering of new technology, the striving for knowledge, new inter-personal relations, and the living affirmation of the moral code of the builder of communism.

All the power of ideological persuasion must be used to instil a communist attitude toward *social wealth* and to eliminate the view, found in some people, that socialist public property is something alien and official; people must be taught to want to multiply the wealth of the motherland, to raise the quality of production and reduce its unit cost, to struggle implacably against mismanagement and wastefulness, against the covering up of failure, against disregard for obligations incurred; communist criticism and self-criticism must be developed.

Soviet people must be educated every day in the spirit of *collectivism* – one of the fundamental pillars of socialism and communism; the educational role of the collective must be heightened in every way.

The party committees and primary party organizations are ordered to see to it that an indissoluble tie exists between mass agitational work and the concrete tasks of the collectives of industrial enterprises and construction undertakings, of kolkhozes, sovkhozes, and institutions; they must drive out formalism, indifference, and the routine approach, conducting political work differently among different groups of the population, taking the best workers as examples for training the other members of the group, disseminating broadly the experience of leading workers and kolkhozniks, developing feelings of comradeliness and mutual aid.

Labour and everyday life are the indivisible components of the communist way of life. The plenum orders all party committees, local soviets of workers' deputies, trade unions, and the Komsomol to unleash a struggle to strengthen communist everyday life, to elevate its cultural level, to drive all relics of the past out of our everyday life and family relations.

A stubborn struggle must be waged against religious survivals, scientific atheism must be more broadly propagated. The movement for communist labour must be genuinely unified with the movement for communist relationships in everyday life.

The plenum orders party committees and organizations to be more attentive to the everyday problems of the toilers, to organizing their cultural leisure, to the activities of cultural and educational institutions – the strong points of the educational efforts of party organizations. Physical culture must be steadily inculcated in everyday life, and physical education, especially in the school, must be viewed as a major means of maintaining and improving the health and working capacity of Soviet people, their moral steadfastness and willpower, and for ensuring them a healthy and cultured leisure. The attention of party committees and soviet organs is to be directed to the need for putting an end to negligence in cultural educational work and in sport in many towns and villages, especially in the countryside and on construction sites.

The training of the whole Soviet people in the spirit of communist consciousness, the formation of a scientific-materialistic world-view in all Soviet people, demands a general expansion of the study of *marxist-leninist theory* by Communists and non-party people. Marxist-leninist theory must be studied in intimate connection with life so that the knowledge acquired will help the toilers to achieve better results in production, will promote the consolidation of communist social relations and communist morality in the life of the Soviet people.

The plenum considers it necessary to heighten the role of *science* in the formation of a communist world-view, in the ideological and scientific education of the people. Soviet science must occupy a pre-eminent position in all areas of world science; science must serve to acquaint the toilers with scientific and technical creations. Instilling knowledge in the masses is the honoured duty of Soviet scientists.

The major tasks of workers in the *social sciences* are to disseminate the living practice and the historical experience of the masses in their struggle to build communism, to develop revolutionary theory boldly and creatively and struggle for its ideological purity; to conduct creative discussions on fundamental philosophical, economic, historical, legal, and other problems of science.

Particular attention should be devoted to a combined study of problems of the development of socialism into communism and increasing labour productivity, and efforts must be intensified in the scientific administration and planning of the economy.

Our scholars should analyse more profoundly the processes occurring in the struggle between the two opposed world systems, the collapse of the capitalist order and the rise of the revolutionary workers' and national liberation movement; they should study the ways and forms of further strengthening the unity of the countries of the socialist commonwealth, the general laws of their development.

The mastery of revolutionary theory – of marxism-leninism – by the working class enables them to understand the laws of social development, the policies of the party, the paths taken by the movement to communism, and to be active and conscious creators of the new life.

Therefore a successful solution of the party's ideological tasks demands an improved organization of *propaganda* of marxism-leninism, this being the decisive link in all ideological work; its ideological level must be raised, and the forms of political enlightenment of the masses must be perfected.

The party feels that particular attention should be devoted to the further development among communists and non-party people of a vital interest in the thorough mastery of marxist-leninist doctrine. In this the party is resolutely opposed to a formal or administrative approach to the organization of political enlightenment or to a declarative or dogmatic style in party propaganda. The plenum notes that the underestimation of self-education in political study, which prevails at the local levels, reduces its effectiveness and is harmful to a rise in the ideological level of Communists and non-party people. Genuine reliance must be placed on the independent study of theory, completely overcoming the gap between propaganda and life, between propaganda and the concrete tasks of communist construction. Political studies must take into account the level of training, the nature of the occupation, and the occupation, and the interests of Communists and non-party people, as well as the voluntary principle in selecting forms of instruction.

The plenum considers that the continued and thorough study of economic theory by leading cadres, workers, and kolkhozniks is of special importance for increasing their activity in the struggle to make use of the potential increase in labour productivity, for reducing the cost of production and improving its quality, and is an important instrument for perfecting the organization of labour and for a continued broadening of the participation of toilers in the administration of production ...

The plenum emphasizes that the continued development of *literature and art* is of gigantic significance for educating the new man and for forming a communist culture.

The plenum warmly supports the ideas and propositions formulated in the addresses by Comrade N.S. Khrushchev at his meetings with creative workers; these set forth the leninist course of our party in literature and art and voice the concern of the party for their continued flourishing.

While supporting all that is truly valuable and reflects the artist's striving to disclose and capture in striking images the grandiose achievements of the epoch of the building of communism, the grandeur of the exploits of the Soviet man, the party will in the future continue its uncompromising struggle against all ideological wavering, against any preaching of the peaceful coexistence of ideologies, against formalistic stuntsmanship, drabness, and hack-work in artistic creation, in favour of a party and people's approach to Soviet art – the art of socialist realism.

The plenum orders the central committees of the union republic parties, the krai, oblast, and city party committees to activate ideological and educational work in creative organizations, to train every artist to be a staunch ideological fighter for communism who is aware of his responsibility to the people, to promote stronger ties between persons active in art and in the daily life of the people, in the practice of communist construction ...

Pravda, 22 June 1963   *KPSS v rezoliutsiiakh* VIII, 430–47

Plenum of the Central Committee   14 October 1964

The October Plenum was called on short notice to confirm the removal from office of Nikita Khrushchev. On the afternoon of Tuesday, 13 October 1964, Khrushchev had been invited to resign at a meeting of members of the party Presidium. Khrushchev was uncooperative, demanding – as he had done once before in June 1957 – that the issue be placed before the full membership of the Central Committee. At the plenary session of the Central Committee held the following day a five-hour long report dealing with Khrushchev's policies and behaviour is said to have been delivered by Mikhail Suslov. Suslov accused Khrushchev of weakening the party (especially through the 1962 reorganizations), infringing the rights of the Central Committee and the party Presidium as collective decision-making organs, creating chaos in agriculture and industry, and behaving capriciously in foreign as well as domestic affairs. Khrushchev was permitted to give a reportedly long, rambling, and abusive reply to Suslov. A vote was later taken approving the proposal to remove Khrushchev, although the decision was apparently not unanimous. The plenum, it seems, also passed a resolution that henceforth the posts of party First Secretary and Chairman of the Council of Ministers should not be held simultaneously by a single individual. As a party scholar later wrote: 'The plenum released N.S. Khrushchev from the duties of First Secretary and member of the Presidium of the CPSU and of Chairman of the Council of Ministers of the USSR, and recognized [priznal] the inexpediency henceforth of assigning to a single person the duties of First Secretary of the Central Committee and Chairman of the Council of Ministers of the USSR.' (P.A. Rodionov, *Vysshii printsip partiinogo rukovodstva*, Moscow, 1967, 219.) In keeping with this concept of division of power, Kosygin was formally appointed Chairman of the Council of Ministers by the Presidium of the Supreme Soviet on 15 October.

4.44
Communiqué [On the retirement of Khrushchev]   14 October 1964

A plenum of the Central Committee of the Communist Party of the Soviet Union was held on 14 October of this year. The plenum approved the request of Comrade Khrushchev, N.S., concerning his release from the responsibilities as First Secretary of the Central Committee of the CPSU, member of the Presidium of the CPSU and Chairman of the Council of Ministers of the USSR in connection with advancing old age and his declining health.

The plenum of the Central Committee of the CPSU elected as First Secretary of the Central Committee of the CPSU Comrade Brezhnev, L.I.

Pravda, 16 October 1964   *KPSS v rezoliutsiiakh* VII, 494

Appendix

Members of the Secretariat, 1952-1964

General Secretary, 1922-March 1953: I.V. Stalin
First Secretary, September 1953-October 1964: N.S. Khrushchev
First Secretary, October 1964-April 1966: L.I. Brezhnev
General Secretary, April 1966-Present: L.I. Brezhnev

Elected member at a party congress ═══

Congress	XIX 1952	XX 1956	XXI 1959[1]	XXII 1961
Stalin, I.V.	died 4 III 53			
Aristov, A.B.	to 14 III 53	from VII 55	to 4 V 60	
Ignatov, N.G.	to 7 III 53	from 16 XII 57	to 4 V 60	
Brezhnev, L.I.	to 7 III 53	───────────	to 14 VII 60	from 21 VI 63
Malenkov, G.M.	to 14 III 53			
Mikhailov, N.A.	to III 53			
Pegov, N.M.	to III 53			
Ponomarenko, P.K.	to 7 III 53			
Suslov, M.A.	───────────	───────────	───────────	───────────
Khrushchev, N.S.	───────────	───────────	───────────	to 14 X 64
Beliaev, N.I.		from VII 55 to 12 XI 58		
Pospelov, P.N.	from 7 III 53	───────────	to 4 V 60	
Furtseva, E.A.		───────────	to 4 V 60	

Congress	XIX 1952	XX 1956	XXI 1959[1]	XXII 1961
Shepilov, D.T.		from VII 55 to XII 56	from 15 II 57 to VII 57	
Ignatev, S.D.	from 7 III 53 to 7 IV 53			
Shatalin, N.N.	from 7 III 53 to II(?) 55			
Kuusinen, O.V.			from VI 57	died 7 V 64
Kirichenko, A.I.			from 16 XII 57 to 4 V 60	
Mukhitdinov, N.A.			from XII 57 to X 61	
Kozlov, F.R.				from 4 V 60 to 16 XI 64
Demichev, P.N.				
Ilyichev, L.F.				to 26 III 65
Ponomarev, B.N.				
Spiridonov, I.V.				to IV 62
Shelepin, A.N.				
Andropov, Iu.V.				from 23 XI 62
Poliakov, V.I.				from 23 XI 62 to 16 XI 64
Rudakov, A.D.				from 23 XI 62; died 11 VII 66
Titov, V.N.				from 23 XI 62 to 19 IX 65
Podgorny, N.V.				from 21 VI 63 to XII 65
Ustinov, D.F.				from 26 III 65
Kulakov, F.D.				from 19 IX 65
Kapitonov, I.V.				from 6 XII 65

[1] The XXI Party Congress was an 'extraordinary' congress at which elections were not held.

APPENDIX

Members of the Presidium,[1] 1952–1964

Full member ═══ Candidate member ───

Congress	XIX 1952	XX 1956	XXI 1959[2]	XXII 1961
Stalin, I.V.	died 4 III 53			
Andrianov, V.M.	to III 53			
Aristov, A.B.	to III 53	from VII 57		
Beria, L.P.	to VII 53			
Bulganin, N.A.		to IX 58		
Voroshilov, K.E.		to 19 VII 60		
Ignatev, S.D.	to III 53			
Kaganovich, L.M.		to VII 57		
Korotchenko, D.S.	to III 53	from VII 57		
Kuznetsov, V.V.	to III 53			
Kuusinen, O.V.	to III 53	from VII 57		died 17 V 64
Malenkov, G.M.		to VII 57		
Malyshev, V.A.	to III 53			
Melnikov, L.G.	to VII 53			
Mikoyan, A.I.				
Mikhailov, N.A.	to III 53			
Molotov, V.M.		to VII 57		
Pervukhin, M.G.				
Ponomarenko, P.K.	from III 53			
Saburov, M.Z.		to VII 57		

RESOLUTIONS AND DECISIONS

Congress	XIX 1952	XX 1956	XXI 1959[2]	XXII 1961
Suslov, M.A.	to III 53	from VII 55		
Khrushchev, N.S.				to 14 x 64
Chesnokov, D.I.	to III 53			
Shvernik, N.M.	from III 53		from VII 57	
Shkiriatov, M.F.	to III 53			
Brezhnev, L.I.	to III 53		from VII 57	
Vyshinsky, A.Ia.	to III 53			
Zverev, A.G.	to III 53			
Ignatov, N.G.	to III 53		from VII 57	
Kabanov, I.G.	to III 53			
Kosygin, A.N.	to III 53	from VII 57	from V 60	
Patolichev, N.S.	to III 53			
Pegov, N.M.	to III 53			
Puzanov, A.M.	to III 53			
Tevosian, I.F.	to III 53			
Iudin, P.F.	to III 53			
Bagirov, M.D.	to VII 53			
Kirichenko, A.I.	from VII 53	from VII 55	to V 60	
Mukhitdinov, N.A.			from XII 57	
Shepilov, D.T.		to VII 57		
Furtseva, E.A.			from VII 57	
Kozlov, F.R.		from II 57	from VII 57	to XI 64
Zhukov, G.E.		to VII 57	to XII 57	

APPENDIX 323

Congress	XIX 1952	XX 1956	XXI 1959[2]	XXII 1961
Beliaev, N.I.			from VII 57 to V 60	
Pospelov, P.N.			from VII 57	
Kalnberzin, Ia.E.			from VII 57	
Kirilenko, A.P.			from VII 57	from IV 62
Mazurov, K.T.			from VII 57	from III 65
Mzhavanadze, V.P.			from VII 57	
Podgorny, N.V.			from V 58 from V 60	
Poliansky, D.S.			from V 58 from V 60	
Voronov, G.I.				from I 61
Grishin, V.V.				from I 61
Shcherbitsky, V.V.				to XII 63 from XII 65
Rashidov, Sh.R.				
Efremov, L.N.				from XI 62
Shelest, P.E.				from XII 63; from XI 64
Shelepin, A.N.				from XI 64
Demichev, R.N.				from XI 64
Ustinov, D.F.				from III 65

1 The title of 'Politburo' was changed to 'Presidium' at the XIX Party Congress in October 1952, and changed back to 'Politburo' at the XXIII Party Congress in March 1966.
2 The XXI Party Congress was an 'extraordinary' congress at which elections were not held.

Index

Academy of Sciences, 90, 144, 297
Academy of Social Sciences, 144
agitator, 14, 138
admission to party, 11–12, 44, 153–4, 164, 266–7, 269, 282–3
agitation and propaganda, 13, 14, 45–6, 81–2, 133–8, 140, 166–7, 245–50, 308–16
agriculture, 15, 24–33, 39–40, 47–9, 94–5, 110–15, 119–20, 122, 125–7, 129–30, 136, 157–9, 161–2, 218–24, 283–5
Albania, 7
All-Union Society for the Dissemination of Political and Scientific Knowledge, 150
Andropov, Iu. V., 291
anti-party group, 3, 6, 92–8, 154, 164
appointments policy, 12, 118–14, 132, 165, 304–8
Aristov, A.B., 21, 37, 53, 93
armed forces, 42, 100–2, 131, 156, 162, 241–2, 280, 312–13
atheism, 33–6, 249, 314 (*see also* religion)
Austria, 5, 96
Azerbaidzhan, 137

Beliaev, N.I., 37, 93
Belorussia, 141
Beria, L.P., 21–2, 43, 116
'Bogdan Khmelnitsky,' 115–16
Brezhnev, L.I., 3, 93, 308, 317
Bulganin, N.A., 5, 21, 36, 92–3, 164
Burdzhalov, E.N., 88–90

China, 70, 155, 179, 308
Central Union of Consumer Co-operatives, 32–3
Central Committee, 3–4, 21
Chou En-lai, 7
Churaev, V.M., 53
city, 117–18
classes, 175, 209, 224
Cominform (Communist Information Bureau), 70
Comintern (Communist International), 70
collective leadership, 4–5, 8, 38, 43, 69, 131, 163–4, 260, 264
communism, 155, 163, 168, 208–11, 240, 263–4
Communist Party of China, 67–8
Communist Party of France, 68
Communist Party of the USA, 68
co-operatives, 32, 166, 239–40
cult of personality, 6, 13, 36, 37, 43, 52, 58–72, 93, 95, 116, 163–4, 272, 308–9
culture, 40, 162, 255–6, 315–16

Dankevich, K., 116
Demichev, P.N., 155, 291
democratic centralism, 94
Dennis, E., 68
dictatorship of the proletariat, 163, 172, 177, 194, 234–5
dogmatism and sectarianism, 167, 195
Donets Oblast, 304–8 (*see also* Stalino Oblast)

Efremov, L.N., 291

education 40–1, 159–60, 250–2
elections
  party, 261, 270, 285–91
  soviet, 235
Eliutin, V.P., 55
expulsion from party, 97, 153–4, 267–9, 282–3

Five-Year Plan: 1951–55, 38, 40; 1956–60, 46–51
France, 69, 187, 208
Furtseva, G.A., 93

Georgia, 141
Germany, 60–1, 178, 187, 189, 203
Gil, S., 81
Glavlit (Glavnoe upravlenie po literatury i izdatel'stv – Main Administration of Literature and Publishing), 82
Gosplan (Gosudarstvennaia plannovyi komitet – State Planning Committee), 87, 294, 297
Gosekonomsovet (Gosudarstvennyi nauchno-ekonomicheskil sovet – State Scientific-Economic Council), 294, 297
Gosstroi (Gosudarstvennyi komitet po delam stroiel'stva – State Committee for Construction Affairs), 293, 296–7
Great Britain, 187, 208
Great Patriotic War (World War II), 147
Grishin, V.V., 103

Higher Party School, 54, 57, 144, 304
history, party 13, 141, 151–2
History of the All-Union Communist Party (Bolsheviks). Short Course, 13, 141
History of the Communist Party of the Soviet Union, 152
Hungary, 5, 7, 13, 89

Iasnov, M.A., 53

Ignatiev, S.D., 21
Ignatov, N.G., 53, 93, 103
Ilichev, L.F., 155, 291, 308
imperialism, 172–3, 182–9, 196–201
industry, 38–9, 46–8, 82–8, 124–30, 160–1, 212–16
incentives, 130, 159, 162, 175–6, 228–29
Italy, 69, 208

Japan, 178, 187–8, 189
Jen Min Ji Pao, 67

KGB (Komitet gosudarstvennoi bezopasnosti – State Security Committee), 11, 17
Kaganovich, L.M., 6, 21, 92, 94, 96–8, 164
Kalnberzin, Ia E., 93
Kapitonov, I.V., 53
Kazakhstan 15, 30–1, 141, 216
Khachaturian, A., 115
Khrushchev, N.S., 3–7, 9–17, 21, 24, 36–7, 53, 82, 88, 92–3, 110, 114, 118, 124, 154, 155, 283, 291–2, 297, 308, 316–17
  'secret speech,' 6, 13, 36
Kirgiziia, 118–23
Kirichenko, A.I., 37, 92–3, 103
Kirilenko, A.P., 53, 93
kolkhoz-sovkhoz territorial production administration, 10, 283–5, 296
Komsomol (Communist Youth League), 45, 239, 279–80
Korneichuk, A., 116
Korotchenko, D.S., 93
Kosygin, A.I., 3, 93, 317
Kozlov, F.R., 53, 82, 93, 154
krai (territory, administrative level under union republic), 275–6, 295
Kuusinen, O.V., 93

labour productivity, 161
law, 42–3, 63–5, 95, 238
Leningrad, 137, 140, 153–4

INDEX

MTS (mashino-traktornaia stantsiia – machine tractor station), 9, 25–33, 39, 44–5, 91, 110–15, 158, 218
Malenkov, G.M., 6, 21, 92, 94, 96–8, 116, 164
Malinovsky, R. Ia., 100
Matiushkin, N.I., 90
Mausoleum of Vladimir Ilyich Lenin, 281–2
Mazurov, K.T., 93
Miaskovsky, N., 115
Mikhailov, N.A., 21
Mikoyan, A.I., 13, 88, 92–3
Milarshchikov, V.P., 53
Ministry of Agriculture, 26, 30, 283–4
Ministry of Culture, 26, 116
Ministry of Health, 32
Ministry of Higher Education, 55
Ministry of Internal Affairs (MVD), 21–2
Ministry of Power and Electrification, 297
Ministry of State Security (MGB), 21
Ministry of Sovkhozes, 30, 32
Ministry of Trade, 32
Ministry of Transportation Construction, 297
Molotov, V.M., 6–7, 21, 92, 94, 96–8, 116, 164
Moscow, 140, 153–4
Mukhitdinov, N.A., 93, 103
Muradeli, V., 115–16
Mzhavanadze, V.P., 93

national democracies, 199
national liberation movement, 196–201
nationality policy, 16, 41–2, 50–1, 93–4, 97, 116, 121, 123, 127, 136, 142–3, 160, 176–7, 242–5, 308, 311–12
non-staff party workers, 9, 282–3

oblast (region, administrative level under union republic), 98–9, 117–18, 275–6, 295

organizational work, party, 98–100, 117–23

Pankratova, Anna, 88
Partiinaia zhizn' (Party Life), 138, 282
party organizers, 72
party schools, 12, 54–8, 303–4
party-state control committee, 11, 165–6, 237, 298–303
party work in the military, 100–2
peaceful coexistence, 6, 140, 178, 204–8, 312
peaceful transition to socialism, 193–4
people's democracies, 179
Pervukhin, M.G., 92–3, 164
Podgorny, N.V., 308
Poland, 7, 13, 71
Poliakov, V.I., 291
Ponomarev, B.N., 155
Popov, G., 115
Pospelov, P.N., 21, 53, 93
Presidium, party, 3–4, 93, 100
primary party organization, 90–2, 117, 138–40, 277–9
Pravda, 116, 138
production principle, 10, 12, 17, 292–3
Programme, party, 7, 17, 52–3, 154, 163, 165, 166–264
Prokofiev, S., 115
propaganda (*see* agitation and propaganda)
property, 160, 162
Puzanov, A.M. 53

RSFSR Bureau, 53–4
raion (district, administrative level under oblast or city), 44, 98–9, 117–18, 276–7, 296
Rashidov, Sh. R., 155
revisionism, 7, 167, 194–5
Rudakov, A.P., 291
Rules, party, 9, 10, 12, 51–2, 79, 97, 139, 154, 163, 165, 262, 264–81, 292, 295

Saburov, M.Z., 92, 164
Saratov, 141
Satiukov, P., 116
sciences, 159, 162, 176, 216–17, 252–5
sections, Central Committee, 53, 90, 133, 138
secretariat, party, 3–4, 21, 81, 93
Serdiuk, Z.T., 291
Seven-Year Plan, 8, 15, 17, 124–32, 135, 139, 155, 156, 158–60
Shaginian, M., 81
Shatalin, N.N., 21
Shcherbitsky, V.V., 155
Shebalin, V., 115
Shelepin, A.N., 291
Shepilov, D.T., 37, 82, 92, 97, 164
Shostakovich, D., 115
Shvernik, N.S., 93, 291
Siberia, 216
social democracy, 204
socialism, 61
social sciences, 314–15
soviets, 73–81, 130–2, 176, 235–7
sovnarkhoz (sovet narodnogo khoziaistva – Council of the national economy), 15–17, 82–8, 94, 157, 226, 293, 297
Spiridonov, I.V., 155
Stalin, I.V., 3, 8, 11, 21–4, 36, 58–60, 62–8, 89, 115–16, 155, 163, 281, 309
Stalino Oblast, 133–8
State Committee for Co-ordination of Scientifiic Research, 297
State Committee on Labour and Wages, 105

State Economic Commission, 87
Suslov, M.A., 13, 21, 37, 92–3, 103, 316
Sverdlovsk, 137, 141

territorial-production principle, 292
'The Great Friendship,' 115
Titov, V.N., 291
Togliatti, P., 68
trade unions, 103–10, 226–7, 239

union republics, 41, 74, 94, 98, 117–23
Ukraine, 14, 216
Ulianovsk, 141
United States, 71, 208
Uzbekistan, 141

Vasilevskaia, V., 116
virgin lands, 15, 30–3, 39, 95, 158
Voprosy Istorii (Problems of History), 13, 88–90
Voronov, G.I., 155
Voroshilov, K.E., 21, 92–93, 164

welfare, 49–50, 159, 162, 228–34
'With the Whole Heart,' 116
world socialist system, 179–82, 189–96, 256–9
World War II (*see* Great Patriotic War)

Yugoslavia, 66, 89, 92, 94, 100, 179

Zhukov, G.R., 93, 100–2
Zhukovsky, G., 116
Zinoviev, G., 89

www.ingramcontent.com/pod-product-compliance
Lightning Source LLC
Chambersburg PA
CBHW020353080526
44584CB00014B/1002